Oman
Guide

there's more to life...
ask**explorer**.com

THE WORLD'S FINEST WATCHES, JEWELLERY, ACCESSORIES, SUNGLASSES, HANDBAGS, SCARVES, TIES, WRITING INSTRUMENTS AND MUCH MORE.

ROLEX   Cartier   Chopard   PIAGET   MIKIMOTO   GP GIRARD-PERREGAUX

TUDOR   ORIS   FREDERIQUE CONSTANT GENEVE   Bell & Ross   CA CARAN d'ACHE

Khimji's
·WATCHES·

3DZ LASIK
We make your dreams come true
المركز الفنلندي للعيون
Finland Eye Center
See the difference..
MUSCAT Tel : +968 24564488 I Fax : +968 24561132
SOHAR +968 26846662 I SALALAH Tel : +968 23298515
E-mail : info@finlandeyecenter.com
www.finlandeyecenter.com

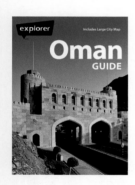

Oman Guide 2014/2nd Edition
First Published 2012
2nd Edition 2014   ISBN 978-9948-20-509-8

Front Cover Photograph – Muscat Gate – Pete Maloney

Explorer Publishing & Distribution
PO Box 34275, Dubai
United Arab Emirates
Phone   +971 (0)4 340 8805
Fax   +971 (0)4 340 8806
Email   info@askexplorer.com
Web   askexplorer.com

Welcome...

...e Oman Guide, your complete resource for visiting or living in ...f the world's most intriguing and varied countries. Backed by a ...e of insider knowledge, travel and off-the-beaten-path ...ing, this guide is packed with everything you need to know ...Muscat and beyond.

...pe to restaurants, housing to hobbies, entertainment to ...ing, and shopping to socialising... it doesn't matter whether ...staying days, weeks, months or years, this guide will help you ...the most of your time in the Sultanate of Oman.

...an only fit so much exhaustive information on to these pages, so make askexplorer.com your companion to life in the Middle East. And don't forget that Explorer publishes hundreds of maps and activity guides that help to make the good life in Oman, and in the neighbouring UAE, even better. Head to askexplorer.com/shop to get your hands on these.

In your hands, in the glove box, in your rucksack; on your laptop, iPad or iPhone... wherever you're going and whatever you're doing, be sure to take us with you.

There's more to life...
The Explorer Team

We'd love to hear from you, whether you make a great insider discovery or want to share your views about this or any of our products. Fill in our reader survey at askexplorer.com/feedback – and get 20% off your next online purchase.

   ask**explorer**.com

CONTENTS

CONTENTS

DISCOVER OMAN 139

OUT OF THE CITY 171

RELAX & REFRESH 209

CONTENTS

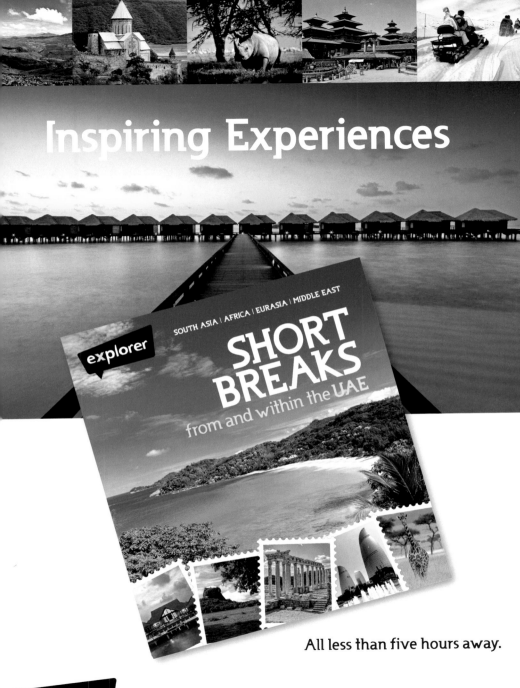

Inspiring Experiences

SOUTH ASIA | AFRICA | EURASIA | MIDDLE EAST

explorer

SHORT BREAKS
from and within the UAE

All less than five hours away.

explorer

there's more to life...

ask explorer.com

   askexplorer

Ancient settlement in Oman

OMAN HIGHLIGHTS

OMAN HIGHLIGHTS

Experience all the amazing sides of life in this fascinating country with Explorer's Oman checklist.

Traditional dhow in the harbour

Whether you're visiting Oman on a long weekend break from the UAE, or are about to make the sultanate your new home, you'll have plenty to look forward to when exploring this diverse destination. The varied natural landscape makes for the perfect outdoor playground, and during the cooler months, you can simply pack up your camping gear, hop in your 4WD and set off exploring.

There are a number of hiking trails, mountain biking tracks and climbing paths to suit everyone from absolute beginners to the more advanced adventurer (although if you're new to exploring the great outdoors, you'd be best off contacting one of the recommended tour companies to guide you through). When the temperature heats up, take to the water – Oman is home to some spectacular ocean scenery,

from pristine beaches to the famous Musandam fjords that have earned the area its nickname, the 'Norway of Arabia'. You might even be lucky enough to spot dolphins, sea turtles and whales, and that's even before heading under the waves for some of the region's best diving.

Of course, there's more to Oman than its spectacular scenery. The capital, Muscat, makes for a brilliant city break, with its stunning traditional architecture, growing arts and culture scene, and luxury five-star hotels that are destinations in their own right.

Alternatively, head for tropical Salalah, a city so lush and green with coconut groves, banana trees and frankincense plantations that it'll make you feel a million miles from the desert.

01
GO UNDERGROUND
Oman's caves provide a mystical underground world containing glittering stalagmites and stalactites, white gypsum crystal and subterranean lakes. These underground treasures are just begging to be explored.

02
VISIT THE GRAND MOSQUE

The grandeur of the Sultan Qaboos Grand Mosque strikes you as soon as you see it, and inside it is just as magnificent. One of the largest in the Arab world, its highest minaret reaches almost 100m. The mosque is open to visitors between 8.30am and 11am, Saturday to Thursday.

03

BE AMAZED BY THE MUSEUMS

The Natural History Museum in Muscat is a fascinating tour of Oman's wildlife, while a trip to the Bait Al Zubair Museum offers a glimpse into the past.

04

FOLLOW THE FRANKINCENSE TRAIL

In ancient times, frankincense was more valuable than gold because of its aromatic fragrance and relative scarcity. Oman was a producer and you can follow the historical tracks of this heritage in Dhofar, or sample the product in one of the souks.

05
STROLL THROUGH THE CITY OF GOLD

Muscat is full of examples of gilt-inspired architecture; as you wander the city streets you'll find many buildings with a golden glow. The Oman International Bank in Al Khuwair, for example, has huge front doors that are plated in 24 carat gold.

06
DRIVE THE WADIS

Oman's wadis (dry gullies carved through rock by rushing water) offer spectacular driving opportunities for off-road enthusiasts. It can be hard navigating the narrow tracks, but if you need a break you can have a swim in one of the freshwater pools.

07

CARRY ON CAMPING

You can pitch your tent just about anywhere in Oman for a night out under the stars. Choose from the white beaches, the rocky mountains or the desert dunes, set up camp, and then just relax and enjoy your surroundings.

08
BASK ON THE BEACH

Oman has a long coastline and many beautiful beaches. Qurum Beach, stretching from the Crowne Plaza to Al Azaiba and beyond, is particularly popular. Most beaches are public, although many of the five-star hotels have their own private beaches for visitors and guests.

09
TAKE TO THE WATER

The beautiful Gulf of Oman has some amazing diving and snorkelling spots, best pointed out by one of the dive centres, although many hotels and major tour operators run activities including surfing, sailing and fishing.

10

DISCOVER THE PAST

Oman is one of the region's most ancient and longest inhabited countries. Step out of the towns and cities, and you'll find all manner of beautiful monuments to the country's culture, religion and heritage.

11

HIKE THE PEAKS

The spectacular mountain scenery of Oman, with its miraculous staircases crisscrossing the peaks, is paradise for those who like exploring the country by foot. The cooler climate in these higher areas is a relief after the heat of the plains and coast.

12

SET SAIL ON A DHOW

Watch these traditional boats being hand-built in the yard in Sur. Each dhow takes as long as 12 months to build but can last for more than 100 years. To enjoy a trip, several tour operators offer cruises on traditional dhows.

OMAN PROFILE

OMAN PROFILE

One of the Middle East's oldest nations, today Oman is a fascinating mix of old and new, of ancient traditions and modern culture.

Mirani Fort

Oman's huge, varied geographical landscape of rugged mountains, desert dunes, wild coastline and lush oases, coupled with its prime position between eastern and western powers on the Indian Ocean has resulted in a country that welcomes foreigners and modern development while remaining laid-back and Islamic to its core.

Oman Today

With a history dating back to 7,000BC, modern Oman's heritage remains palpable – from the Bedouin tribes that remain in the mountains to the illustrious maritime history that saw Oman's influence reach the east coast of Africa – and vice versa. It was one of the first countries to embrace Islam and this is easy to believe considering the Omani values of tolerance, peace, humility and hospitality.

While modern Oman is blessed with that highly coveted of resources, oil, modern development is more considered and slower-paced than in neighbouring countries such as the UAE and Saudi Arabia. Visitors to Oman will enjoy a relatively rustic experience throughout the country – donkeys and camels are a regular sight along the roads, traders in the souks haggle with warm enthusiasm, and fishermen haul their nets. But there are plenty of luxury hotels, smart shopping malls and modern pursuits worthy of a 21st century destination.

It's a fascinating place to visit, and a safe, family-friendly place to live. From the fjords of Arabia in Musandam, to the spectacular rocky mountains and beautiful beaches of Muscat, Oman awaits.

OMAN OVERVIEW

Situated in the south-eastern quarter of the Arabian Peninsula, the Sultanate of Oman is bordered by the Kingdom of Saudi Arabia to the west, Yemen to the south-west and the United Arab Emirates (UAE) to the north-west. Its official total land area is 309,500 square kilometres, making it the third largest country in the peninsula. Mountain ranges and a narrow strip of coastal plains break up a topography that is predominantly made up of valleys and deserts. Oman's spectacular coastline, some 2,000km long, extends to the Gulf of Oman and the Arabian Sea as well as the Indian Ocean.

The country is divided into eight administrative regions: three governorates (Muscat, Dhofar and Musandam) and five regions (Al Dakhliyah, Al Dhahirah, Al Batinah, Al Wusta and Al Sharqiyah). Each region is further divided into smaller 'wilayats' (districts) headed by a 'wali' (district governor). The capital of the country is Muscat.

Musandam, known as the 'Norway of Arabia' because of its majestic fjords, lies at the furthest east point of the Arabian Peninsula and is separated from the rest of the country by the UAE. It is an area of great strategic importance, lying south of Iran and controlling the main navigable stretch of the Strait of Hormuz, through which 90% of the world's crude oil passes. An Omani enclave also lies in the small village of Al Madha in the UAE.

Off the coast, there are several islands, the largest of which is Masirah Island in the south-east. It is a strategic entry point from the Arabian Sea to the Gulf of Oman, and houses military facilities used by the United States, although nowadays it is perhaps more notable as a hotspot for watersports enthusiasts.

Oman's countryside is among the most stunning and varied in the Gulf region. It features 'sabka' (salt flats), 'khwars' (lagoons), oases, and stretches of sand and gravel plains dominated by stark mountains of rock and brownish-green ranges of ophiolites. The Hajar Mountains are the largest range, stretching from Musandam through the UAE to northern Oman, and rising to 3,000m at Jebal Shams, the country's highest peak. This countryside is crossed by 'wadis' (riverbeds), which are formed by the force of torrential water during the rainy season.

Oman is home to a large part of the seemingly endless Rub Al Khali (Empty Quarter) desert, which continues into Saudi Arabia and the UAE. The other main desert is the Ramlat Al Wahaybah (Wahiba Sands), home to nomadic Bedouin tribes. In contrast, the Dhofar region in the south is renowned for its green, tropical appearance and monsoon season with relatively high rainfall. It is one of the few places in the world where the frankincense tree grows; ancient trade in this resin features prominently in Oman's history.

Most of the population lives along the coast, on the Al Batinah plains and in the Muscat metropolitan area, but Oman's city centres are virtually devoid of skyscrapers, unlike many other cities in the region. Stout, pretty, whitewashed buildings sit alongside ornate mosques, low-rise hotels and luxury villas.

Oman is proud of its ancestry and traditions, and rightly so. The country has a long list of cultural attractions to be explored. From crumbling forts and ancient cities, to lively souks and fascinating museums, Oman has the history that many other GCC nations lack.

Population

A national census is taken roughly every 10 years, the most recent being in 2010. However, the National Centre for Statistics and Information (NCSI) regularly issues bulletins and as of 2013, Oman's population is 3.83 million. Of this, 2.15 million Omanis account for 56%, with 1.68 million expatriates making up the remaining 44%. In comparison, Oman's population according to the 2010 census was 2.77 million of which 1.96 million were Omanis and 816,000 were expatriates. The expatriate population in the country has increased by 106.4%, catapulting growth of the total population by 38% since the census in 2010. The Omani population has grown by 9.7% in the same period.

Flag It Up

The flag of Oman comprises three equal horizontal bands of white (top), red (middle) and green (bottom) with a thicker vertical red band on the hoist side. White stands for peace and prosperity, red for the battles fought against foreign invaders, and green for the fertility and greenery of the land. Centred at the top of the vertical band (in white) is the nation's emblem, an Omani 'khanjar' (dagger) and belt, superimposed on two crossed swords.

Of the 1.68 million expatriates, 1.35 million were employed by the private sector of which 44% were employed in the construction sector alone. The next two biggest sectors in terms of expatriate employees, at about 12% each, are manufacturing followed by wholesale, retail trade and repair of motor vehicles.

A total of 50.7% of the Omani population is male and 49.3% is female. As for the expatriates, the number of males is five times that of females. When it comes to the total population, males account for 65%.

Of the total number of Omanis, 76% are below 30 years of age, while in the case of the expats, the 20-59 year age group accounts for 91% of the population. Most expats in the Sultanate are employed (87.2%).

The governorate of Muscat is the most populated with over 1.15 million people, an increase of 48% (775,878) over 2010. Al Batinah is second with 966,734 people, an increase of 25%. Some 42% of expatriates (703,793) live in Muscat, followed by Al Batinah with 285,642 people, and Dhofar with 184,186 people.

On an interesting note, Omanis are the fourth most emotional people in the world according to a Gallup poll on the emotional state of the world, conducted between 2009 and 2011 across 150 nations. A Gallup report of the poll says that behavioural indicators such as positive and negative emotions are a vital measure of a society's well-being are now being used to evaluate countries because traditional indicators such as GDP and 40 hour worksheets alone do not quantify the human condition.

In 1970, the life expectancy was 40 years. Today Omani males have a life expectancy of 72.2 years and females 75.4, compared to the global life expectancy of 68 years for males and 72 years for females.

Oman has seen great progress in education over the last 10 years. Illiteracy among Omanis is now 12.2% compared to 17.7% in 2003 and 31.8% in 1993.

The average size of an Omani household in Muscat is 7.8 members.

Oman Fact Box

Coordinates – 21°00′ North 57°00′ East.
Borders – 410km with UAE, 676km with Saudi Arabia and 288km with Yemen
Total land area – approx. 212,460 sq km
Total coastline – 2,092km
Highest point – 2,980m (Jebel Shams)

HISTORY

Archaeological evidence suggests that an early form of civilisation existed in Oman at least 5,000 years ago. The name 'Oman' is said to come from the Arab tribes that migrated to the area from a place in Yemen called Uman. Omanis were among the first Arabs to embrace Islam, in 630AD, and the country became an Ibadhi state (following the Ibadhi sect of the Muslim religion) ruled by an elected religious leader, the Imam.

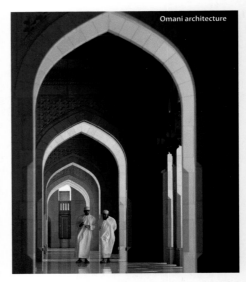
Omani architecture

From the first to the third centuries, Oman was a prosperous seafaring nation, but tribal warfare over the election of a new Imam halted this expansion and Persian forces invaded the coastal areas. The Portuguese followed in 1507, with a view to protecting supply lines to the east and constraining Oman's trading power. They were driven out of their main bases, first from Hormuz in 1622, and eventually from Muscat in 1650, by Sultan bin Saif Al-Ya'arubi. This marked the start of Omani independence, making it the oldest independent state in Arabia.

From the 1600s to the 1800s Oman vied with Portugal and Britain for trade in the Gulf and the Indian Ocean. During the Ya'aruba Dynasty (1624-1744), it entered an era of prosperity and many of its great buildings and forts were built.

Oman's history has been a struggle for power between the interior (ruled by an Imam), and the coastal areas and Muscat (ruled by a Sultan). In 1744, Omani tribes elected Imam Ahmed bin Said, founder of the present Al Busaidi Dynasty. He expelled Persian invaders, united the country, and moved the capital from the interior to Muscat. He also adopted the title of Sultan, which remains to this day.

The Omani empire reached the height of its power in the 19th century under Sayyid Said bin Sultan. He extended control all the way to Zanzibar, Mombasa and parts of Persia, Pakistan and India, and established links with France, Britain and the United States, making Oman the first Arab state to establish relations with the USA. When he died the empire was split between his two sons. One became Sultan of Zanzibar and the other the Sultan of Muscat and Oman.

OMAN TIMELINE

Oman's history can be dated back millenia, and it was an important stop on the trade routes between the east and west. More recently, the discovery of oil and a strong Islamic heritage keeps Oman on the global map for trade, economy and tourism.

Stone Age	Modern human settlement in the region dates back to ca. 7,000BC
1508	Oman falls under Portuguese control
1659	The Ottoman Empire takes control of Oman
1744	Ottoman Turks are overthrown by Ahmed bin Said of Yemen, who becomes Imam and starts the leadership of the Al Busaidis, which remains to this day
1890	Areas of Oman come under British Protectorate (as part of the Trucial States)
1962	Oil is discovered in Oman
1970	Sultan Qaboos comes to power as the Sultan of Oman
1971	Oman becomes a member of the United Nations and the Arab League
1975	Sultan Qaboos defeats Dhofar rebellion
1981	Oman joins with other Gulf countries to form the Gulf Cooperation Council (GCC)
1984	The first branch of Oman International Bank opens its doors
1986	Sultan Qaboos University opens
1996	Sultan Qaboos issues a decree clarifying the laws of royal succession and granting basic human rights for all citizens of Oman
1997	Two women are elected to the Consultative Council
1999	Oman and the United Arab Emirates settle their border disputes
2000	Oman joins the World Trade Organisation (WTO)
2003	All Omani citizens over the age of 21 are given the power to vote
2004	The first female government minister is appointed; a royal decree grants foreigners the right to purchase freehold property in certain developments in Oman
2006	Oman signs a free trade agreement with the USA
2007	Cyclone Gonu hits Oman causing the death of more than 50 people and creating damage costing approximately $4 billion
2009	Gulf Cup of Nations (football) is won by Oman for first time
2009	First residents move into The Wave
2010	Muscat holds the Asian Beach Games
2011	The Royal Opera House Muscat opens
2012	Wadi Daygah Dam, the biggest dam in Oman, is officially opened
2013	The Laser Masters' World Championships are held at Al Mussanah
2014	The commercial activities of container ships and cargo vessels move from Port Sultan Qaboos to Sohar Industrial Port

Sultan Said bin Taimur came to power in 1932. He was able to enforce his rule over the interior, partly with the backing and encouragement of the British who needed stability in order to search the interior for oil. However, after establishing his rule, the Sultan became progressively more isolated, closing the nation's borders and shielding his country from the influences of the outside world. Eventually the only contacts were through the Sultan's mainly British advisors and certain well established trading links.

Trading On Its Location

Oman's geographical position on some of the world's most important trade routes between Africa and Asia has given it a unique dimension. From the first to third centuries, the southern part of the country was one of the wealthiest regions in the world due to the ancient trade in Arabian horses and the world's purest frankincense. Oman became a prosperous seafaring nation, sending dhows to Africa, India and the Far East.

In the 1960s, a serious new threat arose from Dhofar. By 1965, the Dhofar rebellion was underway, led by the communist Dhofar Liberation Front and aided by South Yemen through the Chinese. On 23 July 1970, a day henceforth celebrated as Renaissance Day, Sultan Qaboos bin Said overthrew his father, Sultan Said bin Taimur, to assume power. He was only 30 years old at the time but already had a strong vision for his country. Born in Salalah on 18 November 1940, he is the only son of the late Sultan Said bin

Taimur and is eighth in the direct line of the Al Busaidi Dynasty. He spent his youth in Salalah, where he was educated until he was sent, at the age of 16, to a private school in England. In 1960, Sultan Qaboos entered the Royal Military Academy at Sandhurst as an officer cadet, where he reportedly discovered a love for classical music. After military service in Germany he studied local government administration in England and went on a world tour, before returning to Salalah for six years. He devoted this time to studying Islam and Omani history. The Sultan married in 1976 but later divorced. He has no children.

Using the new oil wealth, Sultan Qaboos immediately set about transforming Oman and modernising the infrastructure. In 1970, Oman had only three primary schools, 10 kilometres of paved roads, two health centres, no infrastructure to speak of, and a per capita income of less than $50 a year.

Today, it is a peaceful, stable and relatively prosperous nation. The Sultan is a strong yet benign leader, drawing his people into the modern world but at the same time preserving much of the character and heritage of his country, making Oman a unique place to visit.

ROYAL FAMILY

Oman's system of government is an absolute monarchy, and hereditary through the male line of Sayyid Turki bin Said bin Sultan of the Al Busaidi Dynasty, the great-great-grandfather of the present ruler, Sultan Qaboos bin Said. Sultan Qaboos bin Said is the Head of State and Supreme Commander of the Armed Forces. He is also Prime Minister, Defence Minister and Foreign Minister, although the day-to-day running of these and other ministries is performed by a Council of Ministers. The political and economic capital, and seat of government, is Muscat.

Given Oman's history of warring factions, it would have been difficult to put in place any kind of long-lasting economic, social and political reforms without some form of constitution. In November 1996, Sultan Qaboos passed the Basic Laws of the State. It is not actually a constitution in the official sense, but it does outline a series of basic human rights for Omani citizens. More importantly, it defines the rules of succession, as the Sultan has no children.

The Basic Law provides for a bicameral legislature presided over by the 'Majlis Oman' (Council of Oman). It consists of the 'Majlis A'Shura' (Consultative Council) whose members are elected by Omani citizens to

Inside Sultan Qaboos Grand Mosque

represent the various wilayats, and the 'Majlis Al Dawla' (State Council) whose members are appointed by the Sultan.

Oman's legal system is based on Islamic Shariah law and English common law, with ultimate appeal to the Sultan. Capital punishment is rare and subject to review by judicial and religious authorities. The Sultan has reportedly said that his country is not yet ready for full parliamentary democracy, implying that he considers this as the way forward. Nothing has been publicly finalised, although in November 2002 every Omani citizen over 21 years was granted the right to vote.

In his 39 years of rule, the Sultan has been an extremely capable, far-sighted and benign leader, held in high regard by his people. This is most apparent in their reactions when he travels around the various wilayats on his annual 'Meet the People' tour.

CULTURE & LIFESTYLE

As you explore the many sides of Oman, you'll find that the local people are warm and welcoming. Oman's historical position on an important trade route means that the Omani population has been exposed to many different cultures over the centuries, and locals are generally tolerant, welcoming and friendly. Because of the active efforts of the government to increase local participation in the workforce, a large percentage of jobs are held by Omanis, so you have more opportunities to interact with the locals than you might elsewhere in the region.

Visitors are generally able to roam freely in the souks and villages, and may be pleasantly surprised by genuine offers of coffee. Perhaps the only exceptions are mosques and the Lewara quarter, adjacent to the Mutrah Souk in Muscat, where many Shi'a Muslims live.

As you travel deeper into the interior the people become more conservative but no less hospitable. The forbidding mountains and formidable deserts have kept them isolated from external influences so a foreign face becomes a welcome diversion. To get a quick overview of Oman, its traditions and its people, spend some time in one of the many excellent museums in the Muscat area.

Oman's distinctive culture is influenced by Islamic traditions and regional heritage. Islam is more than just a religion: it is a way of life that governs everyday events, from what to wear to what to eat. Unfortunately, Islamic fundamentalism and its recent links to terrorism has caused some misunderstanding of this hugely popular religion and of Muslim countries and culture in general. In reality, Islam is a peaceful and gentle religion that is followed by millions of faithful Muslims around the world.

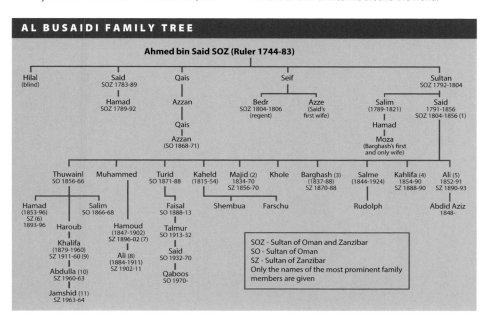

AL BUSAIDI FAMILY TREE

Most Omanis follow the Ibadhi sect, named after its founder Abdullah bin Abadha. Ibadhism is regarded as 'moderately conservative' and a distinguishing feature is the choice of a ruler by communal consensus and consent. Some Omanis are Sunni Muslims and live primarily in Sur and the surrounding areas, and in Dhofar. The Shi'a minority live in the Muscat-Mutrah area.

The basis of Islam is the belief that there is only one God and that the Prophet Mohammed is his messenger. There are five pillars of the faith (the 'hadith'), which all Muslims must follow ; the Profession of Faith (a statement of the belief, as above), Prayer, Charity (giving of alms), Fasting (during the holy month of Ramadan) and Pilgrimage. Every Muslim, if possible, is required at least once in their lifetime to make the pilgrimage or 'Hajj' to the holy city of Mecca (or Makkah) in Saudi Arabia.

Additionally, a Muslim is required to pray five times a day, facing Mecca. The times vary according to the position of the sun. Most people pray at a mosque, although it is not unusual to see them kneeling by the side of the road if one is not near. It is not considered polite to stare at people praying or to walk over prayer mats. The modern call to prayer, broadcast through loudspeakers on the minarets of each mosque, ensures that everyone knows it's time to pray. Prayer timings are also published in local newspapers. Friday is the holy day. Other religions are recognised and respected, and followers are free to practise their faith.

The official language is Arabic, but English is widely spoken, and most of the road signs and menus are bilingual.

Ramadan

Ramadan is the holy month in which Muslims commemorate the revelation of the Holy Quran. For 30 days, Muslims fast during daylight hours, abstaining from eating, drinking and smoking. In the evening, the fast is broken with an Iftar, or feast. The start is determined by the sighting of the moon and usually falls 11 days earlier than the previous year.

Non-Muslims are requested to respect this tradition by not eating, drinking and smoking in public places between sunrise and sunset. Most hotels provide screened rooms for those not fasting. Bars are closed all month and the sale of alcohol is prohibited. Ramadan ends with a three-day celebration and holiday – Eid Al Fitr, or 'Feast of the Breaking of the Fast'.

Other Places Of Worship

Good Shepherd Protestant Church Ghala, 968 24 692 464

Holy Spirit Catholic Church Ghala, 968 24 590 373, *holyspiritchurchoman.com*

Krishna Temple 968 24 798 546

Protestant Church In Oman Ruwi, 968 24 799 475, *churchinoman.com*

Salalah Christian Centre Ad Dahariz Ash Shamaliyyah, 968 23 235 727, *pasalalah.org*

Shiva & Bajrangbali Temple Muscat, 968 24 737 311

St Anthony's Church 968 26 841 396, *soharchurch.org*

St Francis Xavier's Church 968 23 235 727

St George Orthodox Church 968 26 843 892

Sts Peter & Paul Catholic Church Ruwi, 968 24 701 893, *ruwichurch.org*

Muscat Gate

COMMERCE

Forty years ago, Oman was an economically poor nation but it is now a middle-income developing country with a vibrant economy, free universal welfare services and impressive infrastructure. Real GDP growth has been averaging 5% annually over the past 20 years. In recent years, Oman has experienced deflation thanks to government subsidies securing essential consumer items such as fuel and grain and lower import prices in local currency terms.

Endowed with modest oil reserves, Oman aims to create a viable non-oil economy by shifting economic emphasis to tourism, agriculture, fisheries, mining and light industry, while continuing aggressive development of natural gas to offset depleting oil production. Oman's main export partners are Japan, South Korea, China, Thailand, Taiwan, Singapore and the USA. The main import partners are the UAE, Japan, India, the UK, the USA and Germany.

Workers' Rights

In 2006, Oman made some changes to its labour laws, making it something of a leader within the region. Workers are now permitted to form labour unions and to carry out peaceful strikes. Oman will also punish employers who are found guilty of labour law violations or employing forced labour.

In its foreign relations Oman maintains a stance of non-alignment and non-interference in the affairs of other countries, but is committed to Arab unity. Since taking power in1970, Sultan Qaboos has managed the extremely tricky task of maintaining friendly relations with just about everyone.

In recent years Oman has developed into a backroom mediator in solving the more politically volatile issues of the region. It was testimony to the Sultan's unique position on the world's stage when, in October 1998, he was presented with the International Peace Award by former US president Jimmy Carter, and in 2001, the Peace Prize from the Jewish-American Committee.

Oman belongs to the World Trade Organisation (WTO), the International Monetary Fund (IMF) and various pan-Arab economic groups, like the Arab Gulf Cooperation Council (AGCC) and the Indian Ocean Rim Association (IORARC) – Oman is in fact a founding member of both. It is not a member of the Organisation of Petroleum Exporting Countries (OPEC), although its pricing policy tends to follow that of OPEC fairly closely. At around 40%, oil remains the largest contributor to GDP. Most of Oman's estimated recoverable oil reserves (5.5 billion barrels) are located in the northern and central regions.

Most of the major embassies or consulates are located in the Shatti Al Qurum area and the Al Khuwair diplomatic area. A few are in the Ruwi commercial business district (CBD).

Omanisation

Efforts to diversify the economy also include 'Omanisation', or a gradual replacement of the expat workforce with Omani nationals. This means that all companies must employ a certain percentage of Omanis. Around 40,000 young Omanis enter the job market each year, some with skills and some without. Government training schemes are in place to give nationals the necessary skills. By 2020, the government aims to have at least 95% of public sector jobs filled by Omanis, and at least 75% of private sector jobs.

TOURISM DEVELOPMENTS

Oman is the essence of Arabia: stunning landscapes, rich marine life and a culture honed by the desert sands. A Ministry of Tourism was established in 2004, underscoring tourism's importance to the new economy; and the gradual growth in the sector is considered a good thing, since it has allowed for more time to expand services and hotels to meet the demands of the modern traveller. The country is a successful model of how modernisation can be achieved without giving up the local cultural identity. Oman's heritage of more than 500 forts, castles and towers are awesome tourist attractions, as are the international dune rallies, yacht races and annual festivals like the Muscat Festival and the Salalah Tourism Festival in Salalah.

Fast-paced developments are a Middle East phenomenon, and Oman is no exception. Key projects include the upgrade of both Seeb and Salalah airports (omanairports.com). The Wave (thewavemuscat. com) has become an exclusive residential beachfront community and is part of a huge development that includes a marina, luxury hotels, a golf course, retail outlets and recreational areas. Almost all the best-known hotel chains are present. There are currently around 100,000 beds, with hotels continually upgrading their offerings to better attract travellers.

Duqm

In a bid to attract tourists and citizens, the industrial oil town of Duqm is undergoing massive development. The designated tourist area occupies 24sqkm and includes an 18km stretch of beach. Welcome additions so far include the Crowne Plaza Duqm, a stunning hotel near the Port of Duqm, and Oman's first floating hotel, Veronica Duqm. The newly completed port and dry dock is one of the largest in the Middle East and North Africa and Duqm International Airport is scheduled to open in 2014.

Jebel Sifah (ITC)

Jebel Sifah is an integrated tourism complex (ITC) and is one of Muriya's key developments. The goal is to create a tranquil, haven-like resort town 45 minutes from downtown Muscat. Jebel Sifah is a scenic destination, flanked by white beaches and turquoise waters on one side, and the Hajar Mountains on the other. The appeal of Jebel Sifah lies in its close proximity to the capital. The drive from Muscat is a lovely one, offering views of the mountains and the sea all the way along. There are also a number of ferries and tours that make the trip by sea. The 6.2 million square metre Jebel Sifah resort is home to apartments and villas. There are due to be four five-star hotels (a Four Seasons Hotel & Resort, Banyan Tree Hotel & Resort and a Missoni Hotel are planned), while Sifawy Boutique Hotel has already opened its doors to guests. One of the most ambitious elements is the 100 berth 'inland marina' and marina town, which will become a social hub, with shops, restaurants and cafes. Real estate here is freehold.

Muscat Hills Golf & Country Club

Muscat's first green golf course opened in early 2009, with 18 holes and a state-of-the-art clubhouse. The RO.20 million development also incorporates luxury villas, available for freehold purchase, some of which are already occupied. muscathills.com

Muscat International Airport and Salalah International Airport

Phase 1 of work on both of these projects is scheduled for completion in 2014. This initial phase will expand passenger capacity to 12 million passengers a year at Muscat International Airport and to 1 million passengers a year at Salalah International Airport. Passenger traffic to Muscat is growing at 6.5% and aircraft traffic at 4.5% annually. Oman Airports Management Company is also seeking to attract airlines from various regions such as Asia, Middle East, Africa, Europe and the US.

Oman Botanic Garden

Oman Botanic Garden, an impressive 420 hectare project run by the Diwan of Royal Court, will be an education and conservation attraction showcasing over a thousand species of Oman's plants. Divided into huge plots which reflect the climate and landscape of various areas in Oman, visitors will experience everything from arid desert to cool forests. There will also be a mini village that demonstrates local skills, plus exhibitions, displays and education facilities. Currently a building site, the garden welcomes booked groups only to view its progress; the project will only open to visitors in the future. oman-botanic-garden.org

Muriya Development

Salalah Beach

Salalah Beach is located in the sole tropical destination on the Arabian Peninsula adjacent to the southern Omani town of Salalah. When complete, this development will feature an array of retail and restaurant facilities, 2 PGA golf courses, a marina and two hotels. At present, only a fraction of the site is being developed though the Juweira Boutique Hotel is operational. salalahbeach.com

The Wave

This development comprises of a mixture of luxury residential properties, retail and dining facilities, a marina and Oman's first PGA Standard 18 hole links golf course designed by Greg Norman. The development involves significant land reclamation and will eventually spread out over seven kilometres along Oman's coastline.The next phase of development will see four luxury hotels and a 50 unit retail area. thewavemuscat.com

Developing A Nation

Muriya is the developer that is shaping a lot of Oman's future leisure and tourism offerings. The company is a joint venture between the government-owned Omran and Orascom Hotels & Developments. Most of Muriya's projects include lifestyle elements, such as marinas, golf courses and retail, and if you're looking to buy a home in Oman, it is one of the few developers offering 'freehold' properties, which can be owned 100% by foreigners.

THE FUTURE

In 2010, the Omani government unveiled a five-year strategic plan for the development of travel and tourism with the aim 'to develop tourism as an important socio-economic sector in the sultanate in a manner that reflects the sultanate's historical, cultural and environmental heritage, and sense of traditional hospitality and value'. A lot has been achieved since then and by late 2013, the Ministry of Tourism stated that 'the tourism sector's contribution to Oman's GDP is currently at 2.4% and we want to increase it to 3% by 2015'.

Oman is on the road to major development in tourism with a slew of projects underway or in the pipeline in Muscat. Phase 1 of the Qurum District Development Project in Muscat is complete and the next phase to build a public plaza is underway.

According to Muscat Municipality, this project is aimed at converting the area into a landmark that will attract tourists and businesses. A similar facelift is in the pipeline for Mutrah, a major tourist destination. There it is hoped that the infrastructure can be modernised while the heritage and culture of the area is protected. The Ministry of Transport and Communications has also approved the masterplan for the development of Port Sultan Qaboos for tourism use. The new plan includes building new terminals for cruise ships (third generation), terminals for passengers, and shops and multipurpose buildings that will be designed to reflect marine heritage and history. Time and again, it can be seen that the government wishes to modernise facilities while preserving Oman's heritage and culture.

It is not only in Muscat that there are major developments. An ambitious plan underway is the Sah Al Ahmar Project near Fanja. This will be the country's biggest sports infrastructure development project and is expected to be completed in 2015. At a cost of $300 million, the project aims to put in place world-class sports infrastructure and state-of-the-art sports facilities as well as a shopping mall, a five-star hotel, an aqua park, a nine-hole golf course, a cinema and 60 villas. Furthermore the long-anticipated Oman Railway Project is finally due to begin with construction of the railway in late 2014 and it is hoped that a section of the railway will become operational by 2018. The 2,244km rail network,the country's first, will link Buraimi (bordering the United Arab Emirates) to six major settlements in Oman. It will eventually connect to a planned rail network across the six-nation Gulf Cooperation Council (GCC) and then to neighbouring Yemen.

A testament to the healthy tourism sector in Oman is the number of proposed hotels, including the Kempinski Wave Hotel, which is due to open at the end of 2015. However, according to Colliers International, a leading advisory services provider in the MENA region, there is huge scope for international economy hotels to set up properties in Oman as not one economy class hotel in the category is slated for launch in 2013-17. Over 6,600 hotel rooms and service apartments are currently in the pipeline for Muscat in the next five years, with all in the four and five-star segment, and no internationally branded economy hotels have been announced to open in the coming years. One unique project in the pipeline is an eco-resort in the remote coastal town of Shuwaimiya, located approximately 320km northeast of Salalah. Known as Junoot Eco-resort, the vision is to offer visitors and residents an eco-friendly, sustainable and socially conscious development that preserves Omani culture. The project plans to use local earth as building materials, simple earth architecture techniques, and introduce solar panel technology to create eco-friendly structures.

The Environment

With its extremely diverse terrains and rich marine life, Oman plays an important environmental role in the region. Since the 1970s, it has paved the way for conservation measures in the Arab world.

Oman has been named one of the world's top 10 most environmentally committed countries. The country is party to international agreements on biodiversity, climate change, desertification, endangered species, hazardous wastes, marine dumping, Law of the Sea, whaling and ozone layer protection.

Setting an example

In fact, in 1984, Oman became the first Arab state to create a ministry dedicated to environmental issues. Environmental protection laws have been in place since 1974.

At the Earth Summit in 1989, Sultan Qaboos established the biannual Award for Environmental Conservation, the first Arab prize to be awarded in this area. Various organisations have been formed to protect the environment, as well as to educate people on the importance of environmental issues and the protection of human health; 2001 and 2002 were declared Years of the Environment.

The Sultan has always been committed to an extensive 'greening' programme of his cities. Highways are lined with colourful bougainvillea, grassed areas, palm trees and flowers, all maintained by an army of workers who also pick up the litter on the roadside. It's no surprise then that Muscat Municipality received the UN Public Services Award for cleanliness in June 2003.

Wildlife protection

The Sultanate aims to protect endangered wildlife species by establishing nature reserves, while working together with local communities to ensure their success. The turtle breeding beaches at Ras Al Hadd and Ras Al Jinz are protected sites, as are the Daymaniyat Islands, which form a bird sanctuary to which entry is restricted during the breeding season.

Also, the beaches of Masirah Island are internationally recognised as a breeding site for turtles, among which the most prominent species include the Loggerhead, Olive Ridley, Green and Hawksbill. The Environment Society of Oman has since 2006 carried out a series of tracking projects with the involvement of local communities to monitor the movements of turtle populations across the Sultanate.

Wadi Al Sarin, one of Oman's oldest reserves, is home to the Arabian tahr, while Jebel Samhan in Dhofar is a refuge for the Arabian leopard. Saleel Park is a nature reserve inhabited by gazelles and rare trees. Hunting and killing of any wildlife is strictly prohibited and carries stiff penalties.

Environmental challenges

Despite these significant efforts, there are still some serious environmental threats facing the Sultanate, such as groundwater pollution, rising soil and water salinity, desertification and beach pollution from oil spills. In 2007, the Arabian Oryx Sanctuary on the Jiddat Al Harasis became the first ever nature reserve to be delisted as a UNESCO Heritage Site, following widespread poaching and, according to UNESCO, the decision by Oman to reduce the size of the area by 90%. For more information, contact the Environment Society of Oman (environment.org.om).

Qurum developments

The construction of the Environmental Information Centre in Qurum, one of the ambitious projects of the Ministry of Environment and Climate Affairs (MECA), began at the end of 2013. Being built at a cost of RO.3.5 million and spread over an area of 4,000 square metres, the centre will be the hub of marine and environmental research in the sultanate and will also be a tourist attraction as it will boast a 300 seat multipurpose auditorium, an environmental museum and decks for bird watching. According to Ahmed Mubarak Al Saidi, Director of Marine Environment Conservation, MECA, one of the major focuses of the centre will be on mangrove research, although it will encompass other marine research. The centre will be the first of its kind in the region as, not only will it be a centre for scientific research (with facilities such as an environmental museum, a laboratory and a centre for environmental observation), it will also provide recreational avenues such as a cafe, library, exhibition halls and lecture rooms. As it will be close to Qurum Natural Reserve and its mangroves, artificial lagoons and pathways will be constructed to give access to tourists so that they can feel nature around them.

Sultan Qaboos Grand Mosque

OMAN ESSENTIALS

Mutrah

OMAN ESSENTIALS

One of the Middle East's oldest nations, today's Oman is a fascinating mix of ancient traditions and modern culture.

Nestled in the south-eastern quarter of the Arabian Peninsula, the Sultanate of Oman is a phenomenally diverse destination and a favourite holiday spot for many GCC residents. For those times when you just want to escape the bright lights and city life of Dubai or Abu Dhabi, a visit to Oman is like stepping into a different world.

Outdoor enthusiasts will find plenty to rave about; the natural landscape is a mix of mountains, desert, wadis and beaches. Whether you camp or climb, dive or snorkel, mountain bike or hike, Oman is like one big outdoor playground. For some striking scenery, check out tropical Salalah, known for its lush greenery and cool weather, which makes a welcome escape from the rest of the region during the hot summer months. There's also Musandam, home to stunning fjords that are best explored from the deck of a traditional dhow.

In contrast, the capital city Muscat makes for a fab city break. It's a fascinating mix of old and new, where pretty, white washed buildings sit alongside ornate mosques, low-rise hotels and luxury villas. What Muscat may lack in the mega malls and skyscraper jungles of Dubai and Abu Dhabi, it more than makes up for with its ever-expanding cultural scene, world-class dining and opulent hotels.

Oman's strong connections to its history and culture, as well as some of the friendliest locals in the region, make it a destination that you'll want to visit again and again. Fortunately, it is also relatively easy to visit. In the following chapter, you'll find all the information you need on travelling to Oman, visit and residency visas, regulations and getting around – whether you're planning a short break or getting ready to settle in

VISITOR ESSENTIALS

Getting Here

The capital of Oman, Muscat, is located at the crossroads of Europe, Asia and Africa, so it is an easily accessible city; most European cities are only seven hours away. However, Muscat's proximity to larger Middle East hubs, such as Dubai, Abu Dhabi and Doha, means that you might need to connect via another Gulf city.

Muscat International Airport is located approximately 20 minutes from the main part of the capital. It is a comfortable, modern airport that also offers domestic flights to Salalah and Khasab (Musandam). Salalah and Khasab airports handle limited international flights. The country's national carrier is Oman Air (omanair.com), which operates direct flights to various regional destinations.

Flying to either Salalah or Khasab (Musandam) cuts down a full day's journey from Muscat to 90 minutes and is the quickest option if you don't plan to camp or visit the many attractions along the way. Oman Air offers three daily flights from Muscat to Salalah, and flights to Khasab four times a week.

Driving from the UAE to Oman requires a border crossing. Coming from Dubai, the border most frequently used is Hatta while coming from Abu Dhabi, the border crossing most frequently used is Buraimi. On the UAE side, travellers must have their passports stamped with an exit stamp before proceeding to the Omani border post where they can obtain an entry visa for Oman. There is now a very high volume of traffic between the two countries so be prepared for long delays at either or both of the border stations. If you are taking a car into Oman, you will need to produce evidence at the border that the car is insured in Oman.

Visas & Customs

Visas

Getting into Oman is not difficult but the process of acquiring a visa varies from person to person. Travellers from different countries are grouped into one of two lists.

Nationals set out in List 1 can obtain a Visa on Arrival at all land, sea and air terminals whether individually or part of a group, regardless of their sex or age, or they can obtain their visa at Oman diplomatic missions in their own countries.

Chinese, Russian and Ukrainian nationals may obtain visit visas following the same procedure as for other nationals in List 1 provided they are part of a tourist group arriving in the Sultanate through a local tourist agent or a hotel. In the case of groups, the number of females must not exceed the number of males.

List 1

Andorra, Argentina, Australia Austria, Belgium Bolivia, Brazil, Brunei, Bulgaria, Canada, Chile, Colombia, Croatia, Cyprus, Czech Republic, Dar al-Salam, Denmark, Ecuador, Estonia, Finland, France, French Guiana, Germany, Greece, Hong Kong, Hungary, Iceland, Indonesia, Italy, Ireland, Japan, Latvia, Lebanon, Liechtenstein, Lithuania, Luxembourg, Macedonia, Malaysia, Malta, Moldova, Monaco, Netherlands, New Zealand, Norway, Paraguay, Poland, Portugal, Romania, San Marino, Slovakia, Seychelles, Singapore, Slovenia, South Africa, South Korea, Spain, Suriname, Sweden, Switzerland, Taiwan, Thailand, Turkey, United Kingdom, Uruguay, USA, Vatican, Venezuela

List 2

Egypt, India, Iran, Jordan, Morocco, Syria, Tunisia

Nationals set out in List 2 can obtain a Visa on Arrival through air entry points only, either individually or as part of a group. They should have purchased a complete tourist package from specific tourist companies in their countries which are approved by the Omani Ministry of Commerce and Industry. The package must include accommodation and air tickets using a national airline. These visas are granted regardless of sex or age. Visas which have been organised through sponsors will be deposited at the airport and visitors should collect them from the Oman Air Visa Collection Counter.

Duty Free Allowances

- Tobacco: 400 cigarettes
- Perfume: 100ml
- DVDs: five
- Cigarettes: 400 (max)
- Wine or liquor: two bottles (up to two litres) or 24 cans per non-Muslim adult aged 21 or older. Note that you are not allowed to bring alcohol into the country in private cars at land border crossings, and that the above figures can alter according to your nationality.

For passengers arriving at Muscat International Airport, those who are eligible for Visa on Arrival are able to make visa payments at the Travel Foreign Exchange bureau located in the Immigration Hall.

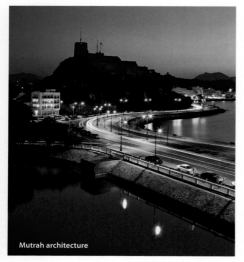
Mutrah architecture

Payments can be accepted in most currencies or by credit card and a receipt will be issued to the traveler. This receipt is then presented at the Immigration Desk where the visa will be issued. Passengers will be returned to their point of origin on the same carrier at their own expense and a fine of RO.200 will be imposed if they arrive with improper or missing documentation. Passengers who are not eligible for Visa on Arrival must organise their visas before they leave their country. This can be done through a sponsor which is usually one of the tourist companies or hotels licensed for tourism. Israeli stamps on a passport are not a problem but Israeli passport holders are not permitted into Oman.

Nationals set out in List 1 arriving from the Emirate of Dubai or from Qatar to Oman bearing a tourist entrance visa or stamp from either country are not required to obtain a separate visa for Oman provided they travel directly from Dubai or from Doha to Oman. This is known as the Joint Tourist Facility with the Emirate of Dubai and Qatar.

People living in Gulf Cooperation Countries (GCC) can avail of the Visa for Foreigners residing in GCC countries when entering Oman. Restrictions apply to non-degree related professional (e.g. labourers, carpenters). It is also granted to members of their families as long as they enter Oman together.

Visa extension is available from the Royal Oman Police (ROP) Visa Information Counter at Muscat International Airport from 7.30am to 1pm, Sunday to Thursday, excluding public holidays.

Requirements for entry visas change from time to time so before traveling to Oman, check out the relevant data at omanairports.com and rop.gov.om.

Types of Visa on Arrival

Depending on your nationality (see List 1) you may be able to get a Visa on Arrival. These vary in terms of cost and validity, depending on how long you intend to stay. A 10 day visa costs RO.5. This can be extended for a further 10 days for the same price; if you overstay your visa, you will be charged RO.10 per day.

For a longer stay, you can get a one-month visa for RO.20. This can be extended for a further month for the same cost; if you overstay your visa, you will be charged RO.10 per day.

If you're planning multiple trips to Oman, a Multiple Entry visa will cost RO.50 and will be valid for one year. The overstay fine is RO.10 per day, and you will not be able to extend the validity.

In the case of a 10 day or one-month visa, your passport must be valid for at least six months. In the case of the multiple entry visa, it must be valid for at least a year.

Joint Tourist Visa Facility with the Emirate of Dubai and Qatar

If you're visiting Dubai or Qatar on a tourist visa, (and are from one of the countries specified in List 1) you may be able to get a joint tourist visa in order to visit Oman. Passengers on a Dubai visa must arrive and depart from Dubai, and their Dubai visit visa must be valid for at least 21 days. Passengers on a Qatar tourist visa must also be from List 1 to quality, and must arrive and depart from Doha. Their Qatar visa must state 'Allowed to visit Oman'.

Visa for Foreigners Residing in GCC Countries

GCC residents can get an Oman Visa valid for 28 days for a fee of RO.5, as long as their Resident Visa is valid for at least six months from the expiry date. This can be extended for one week, for a further RO.5.

Customs

Items which are banned from entering Oman include weapons, arms and ammunition; fireworks; drugs; and pornographic materials.

Travellers on medication which comes under 'Banned Narcotic Drugs' must have a medical prescription that has been certified by the Ministry of Health in their respective countries and further attested by their Omani embassy or consulate before bringing it into Oman.

All individuals, establishments and companies which carry, import or export RO.6,000 or more, or its equivalent from any currency or bearer negotiable instruments (such as cheques, bills of exchange, stocks and shares, etc.) precious metals or precious stones, must declare them to the customs authority. Use the declaration form in compliance with the law of money laundering and its executive regulation.

Health Requirements

No health certificates are required for visitors coming into Oman, except for those who have recently been in a yellow fever-infected area. If this is the case, you will need a certified vaccination at least 10 days before arriving.

Travellers from Africa may be spot-tested for malaria upon their arrival. Vaccinations for Hepatitis A and B, and typhoid are recommended. Check out the World Health Organisation's list of recommended vaccinations on who.int. It is also highly advisable to take out comprehensive travel and medical insurance.

Pets

It is not advisable to bring your pets on holiday with you, as there are strict quarantine rules – various vaccinations and health certificates from the Department of Health, as well as from your own vet, may be required. Your pet may also be subject to a six-month quarantine period although, strictly speaking, this is not required when coming in from a rabies-free country.

Getting Around in Oman

The most popular way to get around Muscat and to the interior cities of Nizwa, Sur and Sohar is by car. If you don't own a car, you can hire one or make use of the many taxis available.

Oman's highways are of an excellent standard and international traffic symbols are in use. Major roads usually have two to four lanes, with intermittent roundabouts (traffic circles) at busy intersections. If

you are new to the roads, be aware that drivers on the inside lane have priority over those entering the roundabout, so don't be surprised if someone jumps from the inside lane to the exit, cutting you off in the process. Further into the interior, the quality of roads is reduced to graded tracks that often seem to branch out in every direction. These tracks are often bumpy, hence the popularity of 4WDs.

Road signs are almost always in both English and Arabic, as are street and house numbers. However, people tend to rely on landmarks rather than road names to give directions. Landmarks are usually shops, hotels, petrol stations or distinctive buildings. To confuse matters further, places are sometimes referred to by a nearby landmark, rather than their real name.

Driving

Car Rental

You'll find all the main rental companies, plus many local firms, in Muscat and Salalah. The larger, more reputable firms generally have more reliable vehicles and a greater capacity to help in an emergency. Make sure that you get comprehensive insurance and that it includes personal accident coverage. Most international and foreign licences are accepted.

If you are using a rental car and you're caught speeding or commit some other driving offence, don't think you'll get away with it because you're a tourist. Tickets for speeding and parking offences can be charged to your credit card, sometimes weeks after your departure.

Avis Oman As Seeb, 968 24 510 342, *avisoman.com*
Al Maha Rent A Car Various locations, 968 24 603 359
Budget Rent A Car Al Khuwair Al Janubiyyah, 968 24 683 999, *budgetoman.com*
Dollar Rent A Car Al Khuwair Al Janubiyyah, 968 24 562 877, *dollaroman.com*
Europcar Al Khuwair Al Janubiyyah, 968 22 004 466, *europcaroman.com*
Global Car Rental Shatti Al Qurum, 968 24 697 140
Hertz 968 24 521 187, *nttomanhertz.com*
Mark Rent A Car Ruwi, 968 24 782 727, *marktoursoman.com*
Sixt Al Khuwair Al Janubiyyah, 968 24 482 793, *sixt-oman.com*
Thrifty Car Rental Al Khuwair Al Janubiyyah, 968 23 211 493, *thrifty.com*
Value Plus Rent A Car Wadi Kabir, 968 24 817 964, *valueoman.com*
Xpress Rent A Car 968 24 490 055, *sunnydayoman.com*
Zubair Leasing Various locations, 968 24 500 000, *zubairautomotive.com*

Mutrah Mosque

Parking

In most towns and cities in Oman, parking is increasingly becoming a problem and in tourist hotspots such as Mutrah in Muscat, it can be extremely difficult to secure a parking spot. Thankfully, plans are afoot for the construction of some multistorey car parks but it may be years yet before the problem is alleviated.

Increasing numbers of pay-and-display parking meters are appearing around the country. Parking meters operate from 8am to 12pm and 5pm to 9pm, Sunday to Thursday. The cost is very reasonable at 100 baisas per hour and is free on Fridays, Saturdays and all public and declared holidays. If you do not purchase a parking ticket, do not display the ticket properly or do not renew an expired ticket, you may be unlucky enough to be fined by a traffic warden. The cost of a parking fine is RO.3.

Petrol/Gas Stations

Petrol stations in Oman are numerous and are run by Shell, Oman Oil and Al Maha. Most offer extra services such as a car wash or a shop selling the usual necessities such as bread and milk, cigarettes and newspapers. Most visitors will find petrol far cheaper than in their home countries – prices range from 120 baisas per litre for Super (98 octane), 114 baisas per litre for Regular (95 octane) and 146 baisas per litre for diesel.

Speed Limits

Speed limits are clearly marked and are usually 60, 80 or 100 kmph within the Muscat area, and can be 120 kmph on roads to other parts of the Sultanate. When entering a built-up area the speed limit can drop suddenly from 120 kmph to 80 kmph, so keep your eyes peeled for signs and speed traps. The roads have both fixed and moveable speed traps which are activated by travelling over nine kilometres above the speed limit.

Accidents

Road safety is serious issue in Oman, which has the highest death rate from road accidents in the GCC and third highest in the Eastern Mediterranean region, according to the Global Status Report on Road Safety 2013 issued by the World Health Organisation. More than 1,000 deaths a year are caused by road accidents; an average of three deaths per day. Statistically, nearly 60% of lives lost in road mishaps are due to speeding. Road traffic accidents are the third biggest killer of people in Oman.

Accident awareness efforts have been made by the Royal Oman Police in the past three to four years and the National Strategy on Road Safety 2011-2013 aimed to drastically improve road safety. Furthermore, the Oman Road Safety Association aims to make the roads of the Sultanate safer for all users with its mission to lead the nation's efforts in reducing road accidents and minimising fatalities, injuries, disabilities and post-crash suffering.

If you are involved in a traffic accident, call 24 560 099 (or 9999 for emergencies or for the Fire Department) to report the incident to the ROP, and wait for them to arrive. If the accident is minor (nobody has been injured) and the vehicles are blocking the road, move them to a safe spot nearby; in more serious incidents, leave the vehicles where they are and wait for the police to arrive. Unfortunately, when you have an accident in Oman you become the star attraction as the passing traffic slows to a crawl with rubberneckers. In the event of a road accident where medical assistance is required, the police will arrange an ambulance to the nearest hospital.

Blood Money

If you are driving and cause someone injury or death, you may be liable to pay 'blood money' which is essentially compensation. According to ancient law, the payment of blood money for injury – arush – and death – diya – can be requested by the victim's family. The amount of blood money varies according to the circumstances of the injury/death and the extent of the hardship that the injury/death will cause. It is, therefore, absolutely imperative to have motor insurance as it will cover you for blood money assuming that you are driving with a valid driving licence, have not consumed alcohol or drugs and your car is legally registered. If you are unable to pay the blood money, you may face a prison term.

Taxis

Taxis are very common and a popular way to explore the city. They are always driven by an Omani national; these are unmetered. At Muscat International Airport, you can easily recognise the airport taxis; they're white with blue stripes. Oman Airports Management Company (OAMC) regulates these taxis and has fixed the fares to destinations in and outside of Muscat.

Away from the airport, the taxis are white with distinctive orange stripes and there are no fixed prices so it is a good idea to negotiate the price before departure. Do not be afraid to haggle over the cost, and do some research ahead of time so you have an idea of what it. It may also be a good idea to ask someone to write down the address for you in Arabic just in case your driver speaks little English. There are also mini-buses (Baiza buses) along the main highways. The principle is that you share the bus with others and you pay a lower price as a result. Two of the most popular taxi companies in Muscat are Muscat Taxi (99 143 222) and Hello Taxi (24 607 011).

Discover
O m a n

with the right wheels

Oman is full of delightful surprises. The best way to discover them is with Budget Rent A Car.

With six branches across the country, we offer you a 1800-strong fleet of European, American and Japanese cars, from 4WDs to luxury vehicles and practical cars. And an equally diverse range of services, to fulfil all your needs on the road.

For the right car at the right price, call us.
Explore Oman in top gear!

| *Short-term rental* | *Long-term lease* | *Transfers* |
| *Guided tours* | *Trips to the interior areas* |
| *International car hire reservations at special prices* |

Buses

There is a reasonable bus service in Oman operated by the Oman National Transport Company. This company provides coach transport between the main towns and cities in Oman and also provides a bus service to Dubai. The main places it serves are Sohar, Sur, Buraimi, Salalah and Dubai. Timetables can be accessed on ontcoman.com or by calling the head office in Muscat on 24 490 046. Comfort Line (24 702 191) also provides a coach service from Dubai to Muscat, while Gulf Transport Company (93 212 665) serves Muscat, Dubai, Salalah and Yemen.

Cycling

Since the introduction of the Tour of Oman into the country in 2010, cycling has become an increasingly popular way to navigate the cities. There are no designated bike lanes in the country but in the quieter areas there are good riding spots, and you can rent bikes on Mutrah Corniche in the evenings through the O'Bike Project. There are also great opportunities for mountain biking, with many clubs and groups as well as some high profile races, including the Wadi Bih Mountain Bike Challenge. Check out bikeoman.com for more local information on this exciting activity.

Walking

Muscat is spread out over a long, thin area between the mountains and the coast, and therefore is not the easiest place to explore on foot. However, if you limit your exploring to specific 'pocket' areas, you can cover quite a lot of ground on foot.

A walk around Qurm Park or along Qurm Beach is highly recommended for some beautiful sights in this tranquil and picturesque suburb. During low tide hordes of people walk or jog along the stretch of beach between the Crowne Plaza and the Grand Hyatt.

You can also explore the Mutrah area on foot, taking in the corniche, the famous Mutrah Souk and the port. A wander around the old town of Muscat is fascinating for its insight into life in simpler times – the ramshackle houses and narrow streets are a huge contrast to the turquoise and gold splendour of the Sultan's palace. The roads in this area follow a confusing and convoluted one-way system, so exploring on foot is actually easier than by car.

If you don't mind doing some walking of a more serious nature you could always tackle the trekking paths through Oman's mountains. Check out Explorer's Oman Off-road guide, which features some spectacular trekking routes of varying degrees of difficulty, and with a little bit of effort (and a good pair

of boots), you'll be rewarded with amazing views of the country. Most of the routes follow trails through the Hajar Mountains, but there is a route from Riyam to Mutrah that is easy to follow.

Obviously the heat in summer, with daytime temperatures of over 40°C, makes walking a sweaty experience. After sunset it does cool down and a walk can be pleasant, but still a bit on the warm side. From October to March the temperatures are perfect for being outdoors. For those interested in walking and/or running, check out the Jebel Hash Harriers (jebelhashoman.com) and the Muscat Road Runners (muscatroadrunners.com).

Boats

With approximately 2,000km of stunning coastline, there are plentiful opportunities for boat excursions in Oman. The National Ferries Company (NFC) provides transport services between various destinations along the Omani coast, most importantly between Muscat and Khasab in the Musandam peninsula. The ferry leaves Muscat on Mondays and Thursdays, and the return trips take place on Wednesdays and Saturdays. The journey takes approximately three hours each way.

The NFC also runs ferries between Khasab and Shinas, in the North Al Batinah region, and between Khasab and Liwa. Passenger rates start at RO.35 per adult (one-way) to travel from Muscat to Khasab, with VIP passes costing RO.140.

It is important to note that journey schedules and ticket prices are estimates and are subject to change, so always check before you travel.

O'Bike Project, Mutrah Corniche

الشـركة الوطنية للعبارات
NATIONAL FERRIES COMPANY

For Booking and more information

Toll Free : 800 72 000
Email : reservation@nfc.com
Web : www.nfc.com

Cruising with Nature

Cruises depart from many beaches and cities and there are specialist centres such as Marina Bandar Al Rowdha in Muscat. Popular tour companies include Jassa Beach Sea Tourism (jassabeach.com) and Sea Tours (seatoursoman.com). These tours are not limited to Muscat as both Musandam and Sur are famous for their marine trips.

Almouj Marina

If you have a boat to berth, your best bet is Almouj Marina. Oman's premier eco-friendly marina facility accommodates yachts from 10 to 40 metres. Located in The Wave, the marina is home to Oman Sail, which functions as a social hub and sporting venue, and also runs diving trips and a sailing school. If you're an experienced, qualified sailor, you can even charter a boat yourself.

Female Visitors

Women should face few, if any, problems while travelling in Oman. It is generally safe to walk unescorted in Muscat and Salalah. Out of respect for the culture, it's a good idea to dress modestly, covering shoulders and knees. Pack a long-sleeved shirt, long skirt and scarf as you will find these invaluable, especially when visiting the mosques and souks.

Travelling With Children

Oman is a very family-friendly place and children of all ages will have a wonderful time. There are endless activities, particularly in the winter, for those who love nature and adventure. Many families go out at weekends to camp and explore Oman's many wadis, beaches and mountains. Hotels and malls are generally well geared up for children, offering everything from babysitting services to activities and small play centres. Restaurants, on the other hand, have children's menus but tend not to have many high chairs; it's best to ask when making reservations. Meanwhile, the Muscat Festival (muscat-festival.com) also offers all sorts of fun-filled activities for the whole family.

People With Disabilities

Most of Oman's hotels have wheelchair access and toilet facilities for people with special requirements. There are also reserved parking spaces in most car parks. Some places do have wheelchair ramps, but often with incredibly steep angles. Always ask beforehand if somewhere has wheelchair access and make sure to

get specific explanations – an escalator is considered wheelchair access by some. The airports cater fairly well for disabled passengers. Request a wheelchair facility with your respective airline at the time of booking your flight and you'll be met off the plane by a porter with a wheelchair who will assist you right through the wheelchair-friendly terminal building. When departing, request a porter and a wheelchair at the check-in counter – the service is free of charge and the porter will escort you to the aircraft if required.

Unfortunately, disabled visitors may find the rest of Oman more challenging. Pavements are not always in good condition and Oman is still a country where the car is king, making it fairly pedestrian unfriendly. There are pedestrian walkways that are wheelchair friendly, but getting to those walkways is often far from easy.

The country's malls, by contrast, are almost all well equipped for disabled visitors with ramps, elevators and disabled toilets. There are parking spaces available for disabled drivers at most malls (although they are often occupied by other drivers).

Dress

Most Omanis wear traditional dress during work and social hours. Men wear an ankle-length, collarless gown with long sleeves (dishdasha) that is usually white, with a cap (kumar) or turban (masar). Women wear a full-length, black cloak-dress (abaya) in public. Modern women often wear trousers or a long skirt underneath. You can still see women, usually in the interior but also in Muscat, wearing the 'burkha' (mask) that covers the brow, cheekbones and nose.

Omani caps

Dress Code

Although Oman is a Muslim country, there is no need for women to wear head scarves or veils or dress in floor-length, long-sleeved garments. However, respect for local customs is recommended, and it is better to dress a little bit more conservatively than you might in your home country. Lightweight summer clothing is suitable for most of the year, but something slightly warmer may be needed in the evening for the winter months. In winter and summer, be sure to take some sort of jacket or sweater when visiting hotels, as the air conditioning can reach arctic temperatures.

Short, revealing or tight clothing can be worn, but it may attract unwelcome attention. It is always best to keep shoulders and knees covered in public, but you can show some more skin in hotel bars, clubs and restaurants. On the beach, topless sunbathing is a definite no-no.

Attitudes in rural areas are usually a lot more conservative than in the cities. You will also have to dress appropriately if you visit the Sultan Qaboos Grand Mosque – long skirts or trousers and long-sleeved shirts for ladies, with neck, chest and head covered, and long trousers for men.

Food & Drink

Traditional Omani cuisine is fairly simple; typically, rice is cooked with beef, mutton, chicken or fish, which has been marinated in a blend of herbs and spices. The country's restaurants serve up a range of excellent cuisine, particularly locally caught seafood. Both meat lovers and vegetarians will find plenty of choice on local menus.

Omani meals are eaten with the right hand. The main meal is usually eaten at midday, while the evening meal is lighter. Salads are quite simple – lettuce, cucumber and tomatoes served with a slice of lime for dressing. Maqbous is a saffron coloured rice dish cooked over spicy meat. Skewered meats (kebabs) are often served with flat bread (khoubz). Harees is a staple wheat-based dish with chicken, tomato, seasoning and onion. Fish and shellfish are used widely in dishes such as mashuai – whole spit-roasted kingfish served with lemon rice.

Omani 'halwa' is a popular dessert made of eggs, palm honey sugars, water, ghee and almonds, flavoured with cardamom and rose water. These ingredients are blended and cooked to form a sweet, dense block with a delicious flavour and consistency. Traditionally, the making of halwa is very much a male preserve, with recipes being handed down from generation to generation.

During Ramadan you can sample Omani food at its best. Dishes such as shuwa, arsia (lamb with rice) and mishkak (similar to kebabs) are mainly served during Eid celebrations. Shuwa is elaborately prepared by seasoning a large piece of meat (often lamb) and wrapping it in banana leaves, sacking and then burying it in a pit on top of red-hot coals. The meat is left to cook slowly over a couple of days in the embers and when unwrapped, is tender and succulent. Many hotels set up a Bedouin-style tent outdoors in the winter months – this is an ideal opportunity to sample authentic Omani cooking. However, the Bedouins themselves enjoy a far more limited diet, depending on where they are travelling. Their standard fare is usually camel meat (dried or boiled), served with rice.

The serving of traditional coffee (kahwa) is an important social ritual in the Middle East. Local coffee is mild with a taste of cardamom and saffron, and is served black without sugar. It is served with dates, to sweeten the palate between sips. It is considered polite to drink about three cups of the coffee when offered (it is served in tiny cups, about the size of an egg cup).

Other favourite local drinks are laban (heavy, salty buttermilk) and yoghurt, which is often flavoured with cardamom and ground pistachios. Fresh juices, made on the spot from fresh fruits (mango, banana, pineapple, pomegranate), are delicious and very cheap. In particular, the mixed fruit cocktail should not be missed.

Shawarmas (lamb or chicken carved from a rotating spit, then rolled in flat bread with salad) are sold in small shops throughout Oman. If you don't eat meat, you can try a vegetarian version of this delicious, inexpensive snack made with foul (a paste made from fava beans) or falafel (deep-fried balls of mashed chickpeas). Salads like fattoush and tabbouleh are cheap and healthy. Don't miss out on trying the ultimate Arabic dessert – umm ali (similar to British bread and butter pudding) is made with milk, bread, nuts and raisins and it's delicious.

However, you can eat your way around the world in Oman – there is a huge choice of international cuisines thanks to the cosmopolitan mix of nationalities living here. Not only can you feast on exotic foods in the numerous five-star hotels, but you can also find cheaper options (like shawarmas and falafel) at the many street cafes and independent restaurants. You'll also find all the obligatory fast food outlets such as McDonald's, KFC and Pizza Hut.

Tipping

Many hotels and restaurants automatically include a service charge of at least 8% (check your bill). This is in addition to the government tax of 9%. However, none of this is likely to end up with your waiter, so a tip of a few hundred baisas is greatly appreciated. The same applies for petrol pump attendants, taxi drivers and generally anyone providing a service.

Language & Customs

Arabic is the official language in Oman, although English is widely spoken, particularly in the main towns and cities. Other commonly heard languages include Urdu, Baluchi, Swahili, Hindi and a number of other Indian dialects. In cities like Muscat and Salalah, most road signs and restaurant menus appear in both English and Arabic; however, in remoter areas, you may see considerably less English.

Learning a few words of Arabic will be useful, especially outside the cities. Arabic isn't the easiest language to pick up (or to pronounce), but if you learn the usual greetings you're more likely to receive a warmer welcome. Most Omanis appreciate the effort and will help you with your pronunciation. Just give it a try – it certainly won't hurt and it definitely helps when dealing with officials of any sort. See the table opposite to get you started, and there are plenty of Arabic courses on offer in Muscat or even online if you want to develop it further.

Face To Face

Omanis greet profusely on meeting and parting, and it would be polite to return the gesture with a friendly remark (master those greetings) or a handshake. Unlike the firm western handshake (a sign of aggressiveness), the handclasp is light and may be followed by placing the hand over the heart to show sincerity.

Some Muslims prefer not to shake hands with the opposite sex, so when meeting an Omani man or woman, wait until they offer their hand before you go in for the handshake. Light cheek-to-cheek kissing between men is also common, but reserved for family and close friends.

Avoid bad and forceful language and discussing local politics with casual acquaintances. It is also considered impolite to ask someone about their origin or birthplace.

Arabic Family Names

Arabic names have a formal structure that traditionally indicates the family and tribe of a person. Names usually start with that of an important person from the Quran or someone from the tribe. This is followed by the word 'bin' (son of) for a boy and 'bint' (daughter of) for a girl, and then the name of the child's father. The last name indicates the person's tribe or family. For prominent families Al, the Arabic word for 'the', comes immediately before it. For instance, the ruler of Oman is Sultan Qaboos bin Said (Al) Said.

When women get married, they do not change their name. Family names are very important here and extremely helpful when it comes to differentiating between the thousands of Mohammeds, Ibrahims and Fatimas.

Dos & Don'ts

Although Oman is a fairly liberal Arab country, there are a few things to watch out for. When taking your holiday snaps, adhere to signs banning photography and always ask permission when taking photos of local citizens. If the answer is 'no', respect that and don't push it. It's illegal to drink alcohol in public places and the penalties are harsh. The same goes for drink driving and for drunk and disorderly behaviour. Be warned that it is illegal to bring alcohol into Oman by road.

If you don't want unwelcome attention, dress conservatively. This is even more important in rural areas where its considered as offensive if you dress showing too much skin, so cover up shoulders and knees as a rule.

Pork

Pork is taboo in Islam. Muslims should not eat, prepare or serve pork. For a restaurant to serve pork, it should have a separate fridge, preparation equipment and cooking areas. Supermarkets also require pork to be sold in a completely separate area. You can buy pork in most Al Fair supermarkets and in MacKenzies Deli (mackenziesdeli.com) in MSQ but you have to find the walled-off pork section first. All meat products for Muslim consumption have to be halal – this refers to the method of slaughter. As pork is not locally farmed you will find that it is more expensive than many other meats. However, after a few Friday brunches with chicken sausages and beef bacon, you will be surprised how easy it is to have a fry up without pork.

Alcohol

The attitude to alcohol in Oman is far more relaxed than in some other parts of the Middle East. The government grants alcohol licences to hotel outlets and independent restaurants, plus a few clubs, but alcohol cannot be purchased in local supermarkets. Permanent residents who are non-Muslims can easily get liquor supplies under a permit system from the Royal Oman Police. However, it is illegal to carry alcohol around, the only exception being when you are taking your purchases home directly from the liquor shop or airport duty free. Keep your receipt as this gives you the right to transport alcohol. It is also illegal to resell alcohol to others. If you have an accident while driving under the influence of alcohol, the penalties are high and, in addition, your vehicle insurance will be invalid. Alcohol is not served during Ramadan, even in hotels.

Drinking & Driving

The Royal Oman Police exercises a strict zero-tolerance policy on drinking and driving. It is illegal even to transport alcohol around Oman, except from the

BASIC ARABIC

General

Yes	na'am
No	la
Please	min fadlak (m) min fadlik (f)
Thank you	shukran
Please (in offering)	tafaddal (m) tafaddali (f)
Praise be to God	al-hamdu l-illah
God willing	in shaa'a l-laah

Greetings

Greeting (peace be upon you)	as-salaamu alaykom
Greeting (in reply)	wa alaykom is salaam
Good morning	sabah il-khayr
Good morning (in reply)	sabah in-nuwr
Good evening	masa il-khayr
Good evening (in reply)	masa in-nuwr
Hello	marhaba
Hello (in reply)	marhabtayn
How are you?	kayf haalak (m)/kayf haalik (f)
Fine, thank you	zayn, shukran (m) zayna, shukran (f)
Welcome	ahlan wa sahlan
Welcome (in reply)	ahlan fiyk (m)/ahlan fiyki (f)
Goodbye	ma is-salaama

Introductions

My name is...	ismiy...
What is your name?	shuw ismak (m)/shuw ismik (f)
Where are you from?	min wayn inta (m)/min wayn inti (f)
I am from...	anaa min...
America	ameriki
Britain	britani
Europe	oropi
India	hindi

Questions

How many/much?	kam?
Where?	wayn?
When?	mataa?
Which?	ayy?
How?	kayf?
What?	shuw?
Why?	laysh?
Who?	miyn?
To/for	ila
In/at	fee
From	min
And	wa
Also	kamaan
There isn't	maa fee

Driving

Is this the road to...?	hadaa al tariyq ila...
Stop	kuf
Right	yamiyn
Left	yassar
Straight ahead	siydaa
North	shamaal
South	januwb
East	sharq
West	garb
Turning	mafraq
First	awwal
Second	thaaniy
Road	tariyq
Street	shaaria
Roundabout	duwwaar
Traffic light signal	ishaara
Close to	qarib min
Petrol station	mahattat betrol
Sea/beach	il bahar
Mountain/s	jabal/jibaal
Desert	al sahraa
Airport	mataar
Hotel	funduq
Restaurant	mata'am
Slow down	schway schway

Accidents & Emergencies

Police	al shurtaa
Permit/licence	rukhsaa
Accident	haadith
Papers	waraq
Insurance	ta'miyn
Sorry	aasif (m)/aasifa (f)

Numbers

Zero	sifr
One	waahad
Two	ithnayn
Three	thalatha
Four	arba'a
Five	khamsa
Six	sitta
Seven	saba'a
Eight	thamaanya
Nine	tiss'a
Ten	ashara
Hundred	miya
Thousand	alf
Million	million

airport (or liquor store if you're a licence holder) directly to your hotel or home.

There is a minimum 48 hours in jail for any traffic offence in which the driver tests positive for alcohol. According to the Traffic Law, the minimum fine for driving under the influence of alcohol/drugs and causing an accident is RO.500 and not less that a year imprisonment. In severe cases, further preventative measures can include bigger fines, black points on the licence and suspension or forfeiture of the licence for up to five years. Driving under the influence (DUI) accounts for around 15 deaths each year in Oman.

Being drunk and disorderly in public can carry similar charges to drink driving. Taxi drivers are unlikely to report your inebriated state to the police as long as you do not cause trouble.

Shisha
Smoking the traditional shisha (water pipe) is a popular and relaxing pastime that is enjoyed throughout the Middle East. It is usually savoured in a local cafe while chatting with friends. They are also known as hookah pipes or hubbly bubbly, but the proper name is nargile.

Shisha pipes can be smoked with a variety of aromatic flavours, such as strawberry, grape or apple, and the experience is unlike normal cigarette or cigar smoking. The smoke is 'smoothed' by the water, creating a much more soothing effect. Smoking shisha is one of those things that should be tried at least once while you're in Oman, especially during the evenings of Ramadan, when festive tents are erected throughout the city and filled with people of all nationalities. You can buy your own shisha pipe from the souks, and once you get to grips with putting it all together you can enjoy the unique flavour anytime you want.

Photography
Normal tourist photography is allowed and in some parts of the country, actively encouraged. However, taking photographs near government buildings, religious institutions, military installations, ports and airports is not allowed, and you will see signs prohibiting photography in certain areas. Always ask permission when taking photos of local citizens – the Arabic phrase 'mumkin sura, min fadlak?' meaning 'may I take your picture please?' Children and men will usually oblige but local women may not, especially if the photographer is male.

PDAs
Not a reference to the handheld gadget but to public displays of affection: these are not looked on favourably in the region, and anything more than an innocent peck on the cheek will at best earn you disapproving looks from passersby.

Appropriate Attire
While beachwear is fine on the beach, you should dress more conservatively when out and about in public places. If in doubt, ensuring that your shoulders and knees are covered is a safe bet. A pashmina is always useful for the journey home or in case the air conditioning is set to 'deep freeze'.

Meeting People
Long handshakes, kisses and warm greetings are common when meeting people in the Middle East. It's normal to shake hands with people when you are introduced to them, although if you are meeting someone of the opposite sex, be aware that a handshake may not always be welcome. It's best to take your cue from the other person and not offer your hand unless they first offer theirs. It's polite to send greetings to a person's family, but can be considered rude to enquire directly about someone's wife, sister or daughter. You may see men greeting each other with a nose kiss; this is a customary greeting in Oman but is only used between close friends and associates and you should not attempt to greet someone in this way.

Climate
Oman's climate varies considerably with the different regions, but sunny blue skies and warm temperatures can be expected most of the year. The best time to visit Oman is in winter, between October and April, when temperatures average between 25°C and 35°C during the day and about 18°C at night.

The north is hot and humid during the summer, with temperatures passing 50°C during the day in June and July, and averaging about 32°C at night. Humidity can rise to an uncomfortable 90%. The 'gharbi' (western) wind from the Rub Al Khali desert can raise coastal town temperatures by another 6°C to 10°C.

The interior is usually hotter than the coastal area, often reaching 50°C in the shade. In the mountains, night temperatures can occasionally fall to -1°C with a light dusting of snow. Rainfall is infrequent and irregular, falling mainly between November and March. Average annual rainfall in the Muscat area is 75mm, while rainfall in the mountains can be as high as 700mm.

The southern Dhofar region usually has high humidity, even in winter. Between June and September the area receives light monsoon rains, from the Indian Ocean, called the 'khareef'. The area around Salalah is lush and green and at certain times of the year is swathed in a cooling mist – it's hard for visitors to reconcile this image with the usual Arabian landscapes of forbidding deserts and rocky, inhospitable mountains.

ANNUAL EVENTS

ANNUAL EVENTS

From running to camel races and bullfighting to biking, there's a lot to look forward to when you're planning your time in Oman.

Camel racing

Oman hosts a number of exciting annual events throughout the year. Many of these are long-running events organised by the vibrant expat community, and attract visitors from all over the world.

It's a great destination if you're planning a 'racecation', with a number of running and biking events that attract participants from the GCC region and beyond. These events make full use of the Sultanate's naturally challenging landscape, with highlights including the popular Wadi Bih Run (an ultramarathon that you can partake in as an individual or as part of a team of five) and the Tour of Oman, a world-class cycling competition.

Oman's other natural wonders – its animals – get to take centre stage throughout the year too. Camel racing is a hugely popular sport, where you get to see the 'ships of the desert' compete against each other.

This usually takes place during public holidays and is spread out over several days. Throughout the cooler months there are also opportunities to see horse racing and show jumping; Oman is known for its pure bred Arabian horses. Alternatively, for something completely different and unexpected, check out the traditional bullfighting, where trainers pit huge Brahmin bulls against each other for the promise of a hefty cash prize.

It's not just the great outdoors that feature prominently in the Oman calendar, as there are a number of annual cultural events to choose from too. The Muscat Festival, for example, is held at the beginning of each year and showcases Oman's vibrant history with everything from traditional food, drink and dancing to arts and crafts. Events are held at various locations throughout the capital.

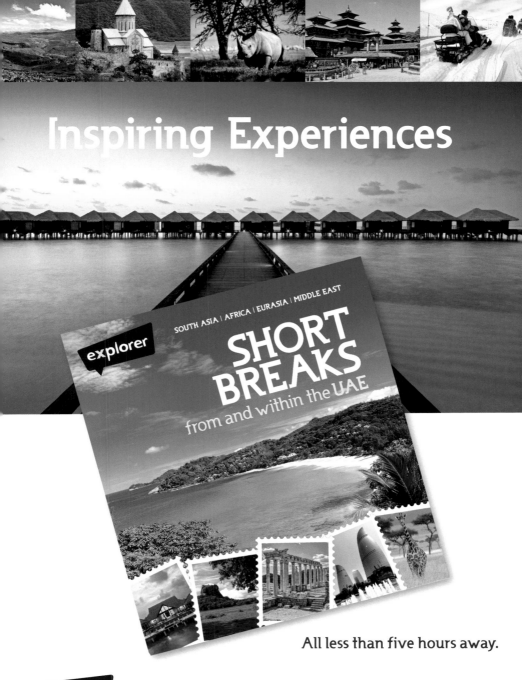

Inspiring Experiences

SOUTH ASIA | AFRICA | EURASIA | MIDDLE EAST

explorer

SHORT
BREAKS
from and within the UAE

All less than five hours away.

Grand Hyatt hotel

PLACES TO STAY

PLACES TO STAY

From luxury five-star hotels to modern apartments for city centre living, you're sure to find a home away from home in Oman.

The Chedi, Muscat

As a result of Oman's expanding tourism sector, the sheer range of hotels and resorts to choose from has never been better. From recently opened gems like the Salalah Rotana to long-established favourites like the Shangri-La, and secluded showstoppers like Six Senses Zighy Bay, many of these world-class hotels are worthy destinations in their own right.

The area that you pick will depend entirely on what type of holiday you're looking for: is it a romantic break? An adventure with the kids during the school holiday? Or are you heading out with friends to soak up some culture and search for adventure? Unsurprisingly, many visitors opt for a stay in Muscat; the capital city boasts some of Oman's most stunning hotels and resorts, as well as its most popular dining and nightlife spots, not to mention a wealth of cultural attractions, such as malls and mosques.

On the other hand, much of Oman's appeal lies in the opportunities to leave city living behind. For a taste of the tropics, there are a number of hotels in Salalah, whose emerald green scenery and cooler temperatures are a true escape from the rest of the GCC. In fact, Salalah is a great choice of destination if you're visiting during the summer months, as the mercury doesn't rise nearly as high here as it does in other part of the region.

And of course, if you're feeling adventurous there's always the option to skip the hotel altogether and pack up your tent instead. During the cooler months, there's nothing better than camping out under the stars – just pick your favourite stretch of beach, desert or wadi, and spend a night in the great outdoors. Plenty of Oman's tour operators will even organise desert camping as part of their excursions.

HOTELS

Oman has no shortage of places to stay, from luxury hotels to hotel apartments, rest houses, officially approved campsites and even desert camps for tourists. However, the cheap and cheerful market is limited, so try some of the smaller hotels or rest houses for more competitive rates. Visitors can expect attractive promotions during the summer months when occupancy rates are lower. However, during peak times, such as the khareef in Salalah or festival time in Muscat, it can be difficult to find a room, and advance booking is a must.

Al Awabi

Alila Jabal Akhdar
Al Roose Jebel Akhdar **968 25 344 200**
alilahotels.com/jabalakhdar
Map **1 F4**
This hotel may be more than two hours' drive from Muscat, but it's more than worth the journey. Dramatically perched on the edge of the mountainside overlooking a stunning gorge, this is a true destination hotel, where traditional Omani design elements are combined with modern luxury. There are 78 suites and two villas, as well as a cliff-side restaurant, swimming pool and luxury spa, set against the stunning backdrop of the Hajar Mountains

Jabal Akhdar Hotel
Saiq Plateau Jebel Akhdar **968 25 429 009**
Map **1 G4**
Perched 2,400m up on Jebel Akhdar ('the green mountain'), this sleepy hotel offers a friendly welcome to weary travellers and, although not luxurious by any means, it has everything a tired and hungry explorer could need for a night. Plus, the breakfast is hearty enough to set you on your way for another day of hiking, biking or off-roading.

Sahab Hotel
Jebel Akhdar Nizwa **968 25 429 288**
sahab-hotel.com
Map **1 G4**
This tranquil luxury boutique hotel is situated on the Saiq Plateau which is located 2,004m above sea level in Jebel Akhdar. Over 5,000sqm of native plants and 270 million year old fossils are located in the gardens surrounding the 27 luxurious hotel rooms and suites. Facilities include an infinity pool and Jacuzzi and gardens with panoramic views of the mountains.

Al Mussanah

Millennium Resort Mussanah
Wudam Al Sahil Al Musanah **968 26 871 555**
millenniumhotels.com
Map **1 G3**
The sprawling beachfront Millennium Resort offers 74 furnished apartments and 234 spacious rooms with large windows that let in the natural light and allow for great panoramic views of the 54 berth private marina. The resort also has two restaurants, one of which overlooks the delightful marina. There are many places of interest between 25km and 100km from Barka; for diving fanatics, the amazing Daymaniyat Islands offer coral gardens and numerous tropical fish, and are just a 10km boat ride away.

Barka

Al Nahda Resort & Spa
Nakhal St, Off Muscat Sohar Highway Barka
968 26 883 710
alnahdaresort.com
Map **1 G4**
This resort in Barka offers the chance for tranquillity and relaxation for all the family. Nestled in an oasis of 30 acres of gardens, there are rooms, apartments and villas. The Eram Spa offers an array of wellness treatments while children will enjoy cycling around the resort and swimming in the pool.

Al Sawadi Beach Resort & Spa
Al Sawadi Barka **968 26 795 545**
alsawadibeach.info
Map **1 G3**
Visitors have the option of staying in one of the chalet-style rooms, or bringing a tent and camping on the private stretch of beach that enjoys access to the resort's ample facilities. Those facilities include a swimming pool and gym, mini golf, and tennis and squash courts. Watersports like windsurfing, waterskiing, jetskiing and kayaking are all available. The dive centre offers PADI courses, and organises regular dive trips.

Khasab

Khasab Hotel
Nr Khasab Airport, Musandam Khasab
968 26 730 271
khasabhotel.net
Map **1 E1**
A small, friendly place located in the centre of town, the hotel has a swimming pool and an international restaurant, with rooms split between the older poolside wing and a newer building. It's quite basic but clean and perfectly fine for a night or two.

Musandam

Six Senses Zighy Bay

Zighy Bay, Musandam Daba **968 26 735 555**
sixsenses.com
Map **1 E1**
Located in one of Musandam's most secluded coves, this uber-luxurious resort may have been designed in a rustic style but it offers nothing but relaxed extravagance. Made up of individual pool villas, like all Six Senses resorts the focus here is on pampering. Expertly prepared dinners can be enjoyed from the comfort of your own villa (each villa also has its own splash pool) or from the mountainside restaurant with its breathtaking views of the bay. The spa treatments available are, of course, also of the highest quality. This is a hideaway like no other.

Muscat

Al Bandar

Shangri-La's Barr Al Jissah Resort & Spa Muscat **968 24 776 666**
shangri-la.com
Map **1 G4**
Apart from the 198 rooms (all with balcony or terrace), the stunning Al Bandar also has eight food and beverage outlets, making it just as popular with residents as it is with tourists. In the heart of the Barr Al Jissah Resort, it has a souk area selling upmarket brands, art and crafts. A large swimming pool snakes around the hotel, with sunbeds immersed in water so that you can relax in cool comfort. There is also a Jacuzzi and a kids' pool.

Al Bustan Palace, A Ritz-Carlton Hotel

Al Bustan St Muscat **968 24 799 666**
ritzcarlton.com
Map **2 L4**
This award-winning hotel nestles in a coastal oasis of 200 acres, fronting rugged mountains and with its own private beach. The elegant Arab theme of the lobby carries over to its 250 room and suites, all with private balconies. There are four international restaurants, including one of the best Chinese restaurants in Oman, China Mood.

Al Husn

Shangri-La's Barr Al Jissah Resort & Spa Muscat **968 24 776 666**
shangri-la.com
Map **1 G4**
Built with luxury in mind, Al Husn is a couples-only escape from everyday life, perfect for a romantic getaway. Each of the 180 bedrooms has a balcony or terrace and bathrooms are designed to ensure you can see the sea from your bath (which your butler will run for you, should you so wish!). Al Husn has a private gym, a beach, an infinity pool and a library, as well as some excellent restaurants and bars.

Al Maha International Hotel

Nr Sultan Qaboos Grand Mosque, Al Azaiba Muscat **968 24 494 949**
almahahotel.com
Map **2 E3**
This mid-range hotel is only 10 minutes from the commercial business district. Facilities include a banqueting room, gym and rooftop swimming pool.

Al Bustan Palace, a Ritz-Carlton hotel

Al Manaf Hotel Suites

Muscat **968 24 505 566**
almanafhotel.com
Map **2 E3**

This hotel is in Ghala, close to the Grand Mosque. It has 36 suites each comprising of a furnished sitting room, kitchen, bedroom and bathroom. The handy location, less than 10 minutes' drive from Muscat International Airport, makes it popular for short stays and business travel.

Al Reef Hotel

Safa St Muscat **968 24 124 813**
alreefhotel.com
Map **2 E3**

Designed for both business and leisure travellers, Al Reef Hotel is situated in Al Ghubrah. This budget hotel provides a restaurant, a health club, a cafe and a pastry shop.

Al Waha

Shangri-La's Barr Al Jissah Resort & Spa Muscat **968 24 776 666**
shangri-la.com
Map **1 G4**

This is the largest of the hotels within Shangri-La's Barr Al Jissah Resort, with 262 bedrooms. Designed for families, kids will love the Little Turtles club, where they can play in air-conditioned comfort or outdoors when temperatures allow. The hotel has numerous swimming pools, including a rubber-cushioned toddlers' pool and a kids' pool in the shape of a mushroom. Baby sitting services are available and adults are equally well served by the resort's eclectic mix of restaurants and bars.

Beach Hotel Muscat

Muscat **968 24 696 601**
beachhotelmuscat.com
Map **2 G2**

The Beach Hotel is located in the heart of Shatti Al Qurum, very close to the beach and the Royal Opera House, and within walking distance of various shopping, dining and nightlife options. The decor could perhaps do with a revamp but the rooms are clean and spacious, and the service is friendly.

Best Western Premier Muscat

Dawhat Al Adab St Muscat **968 22 033 333**
bestwesternoman.com
Map **2 F3**

This non-licensed four-star business hotel is situated in Al Khuwair, one of the commercial districts of Muscat, and is next door to the government ministries and embassies. It offers free wi-fi and features include a fitness centre, a restaurant and a cafe. Free private parking is available.

Bowshar Hotel

Sultan Qaboos St, Nr Sultan Qaboos Sports Complex, Ghubra-Wilayat Bowsher Muscat **968 24 501 105**
bowsharhotel.com
Map **2 F3**

This budget hotel is in need of updating, but on the plus side it is in a very convenient location in Bowshar and it offers quite reasonable rates, making it a good low-key option for travellers on a budget. Features provided include free wi-fi and a restaurant. Definitely one for a no frills break.

The Chedi Muscat

18th November St Muscat **968 24 524 400**
chedimuscat.com
Map **2 E3**

This elegant hotel, regularly voted as among the world's very best, is designed for relaxation and pampering. Guests have the choice of 158 rooms and villas from which to contemplate Muscat's Hajar Mountains. There are spa facilities, two infinity pools, poolside cabanas and a private beach.

City Seasons

Al Sultan Qaboos St Muscat **968 24 394 800**
cityseasonsgroup.com
Map **2 F3**

City Seasons Hotel Muscat is a four-star business hotel in Al Khuwair, the heart of the city's diplomatic area and commercial business district. Facilities in this luxurious hotel include meeting rooms and banquet halls, a business centre, a gym and a roof-top swimming pool. It is not licensed to see alcohol.

Crowne Plaza Muscat

Off Al Qurm St Muscat **968 24 660 660**
crowneplaza.com
Map **2 H2**

Located on a cliff overlooking Al Qurm town and beach, this hotel has one of the best views in Muscat. The pool seems to spill on to the beachfront below, which can be accessed by steps from the hotel gardens. It has three restaurants, including the excellent Iranian eatery Shiraz.

Golden Tulip Seeb

Nr Oman Intl Exhibition Centre, Al Maarid St Muscat **968 24 514 444**
goldentulipseeb.com
Map **2 C3**

The Golden Tulip Seeb is just 2km from Muscat International Airport and is adjacent to Oman International Exhibition Centre so it is very suitable for business visitors. It is in need of some renovation and updating but the breakfast is good with an extensive choice of continental and Arabic cuisine.

Grand Hyatt Muscat

3033 Way Muscat **968 24 641 234**
muscat.grand.hyatt.com
Map **2 G2**
The decor is often described as 'Disneyland meets Arabia', but most of the Hyatt's 280 rooms have amazing sea views, while the hotel has a delectable range of dining options: Tuscany for Italian fare; Mokha Cafe for casual all-day dining; Marjan Beachfront Restaurant and Bar for food and drinks with a view, and the lively Copacabana nightclub (Muscat's most happening night spot).

Green Oasis Hotel

24 Sohar St Muscat **968 26 846 077**
greenoasishotel.com
Map **1 E3**
This hotel comprises of 48 rooms and suites, an outdoor swimming pool, a gym and a sauna, as well as banqueting facilities.

Haffa House Hotel Muscat

Jibroo Muscat **968 24 707 207**
shanfarihotels.com
Map **2 J3**
Located in Ruwi, Haffa House Hotel Muscat offers budget accommodation. Facilities include a health club and a business centre. Monthly rates for suites are available.

Holiday Inn Muscat

Muscat **968 22 080 555**
ihg.com
Map **2 A2**
Muscat's latest edition to the hotel scene, Holiday Inn Muscat is located in As Seeb, 10 minutes away from Muscat International Airport and close to Muscat As Seeb City Centre. This modern and comfortable four-star hotel provides a business centre, a restaurant, an outdoor pool and a fitness centre.

Hotel Golden Oasis

Muscat **968 24 811 655**
hotelgoasis.com
Map **2 K3**
This budget hotel is located in Wadi Kabir and is in close proximity to Ruwi and Al Bustan. Facilities include a banquet hall, a restaurant and a cafe.

Hotel Ibis Muscat

Azaiba Dohat Aladab Rd Muscat **968 24 489 890**
ibishotel.com
Map **2 F3**
This three-star hotel is a 10 minute drive from the airport, just off the main Sultan Qaboos Highway in the Al Khuwair district. The hotel offers a restaurant, laundry, business centre and fitness facilities.

Hotel Muscat Holiday

As Seeb Muscat **968 24 487 123**
muscat-holiday.com
Map **2 F3**
This mid-range hotel is located in Al Khuwair, midway between Muscat International Airport and the central business district. Facilities include a health club with a swimming pool, a spa and internet cafe.

InterContinental Muscat

Al Kharjiya St Muscat **968 24 680 000**
intercontinental.com
Map **2 G2**
The InterCon, as it's known, is popular with expat locals for its outdoor facilities, international restaurants, and Al Ghazal pub. Alfresco restaurant Tomato is a must-try, as is Trader Vic's with its legendary cocktails. Some of the 258 guest rooms and 10 suites have views of Qurum Beach.

Majan Continental Hotel

Nr Royal Hospital, Al Ghubrah St Muscat
968 24 592 900
majanhotel.com
Map **2 E4**
Majan Continental is a four-star hotel located in Bowshar and is 1km from the Sultan Qaboos Grand Mosque. Its features include a large swimming pool, a tennis court and a health club. The hotel's spa offers a variety of therapies and treatments including yoga and meditation. It is licensed to see alcohol.

Muscat Dunes Hotel

Muscat **968 24 397 500**
muscatdunes.com
Map **2 F4**
This newly opened four-star hotel is located in Al Khuwair amidst the sand dunes and mountain scenery. Facilities include a business centre, gym and outdoor swimming pool.

Oman Dive Center

Nr Qantab R/A, Al Jissah St Muscat **968 24 824 240**
extradivers-worldwide.com
Map **1 G4**
Nestled in a sheltered cove, this popular collection of barasti huts offers charming (if a little rustic) accommodation. Perfect for water babies, boat and diving trips can be arranged and the alfresco restaurant will keep your energy levels up.

Park Inn By Radisson Muscat

Sultan Qaboos St Muscat **968 24 507 888**
parkinn.com
Map **2 F3**
In the main business district of Al Khuwair, the Park Inn is conveniently located just 15 minutes from

YOUR OMAN VACATION BEGINS HERE.

The beautiful scenery and legendary hospitality of Oman has made it the preferred destination for discerning travellers. Browse the ancient souks, wade the deep wadis, climb the towering peaks, explore the rich reefs and soak in the sun drenched beaches. Or, if you so prefer, you could just sit back and relax.

Starting just from RO 69 excluding taxes, enjoy a king-size bed, room overlooking the beautiful Hajjar mountains, breakfast for two and internet access all inclusive in the rates.

Do you live an InterContinental life?

For further information and bookings visit
www.intercontinental.com, call +968 24680000, e-mail
reservation@icmuscat.com or contact your travel agent.

In over 170 locations across the globe including HONG KONG • LONDON • NEW YORK • PARIS

Seeb International Airport and five minutes from the diplomatic area and beach. An appealing option, the biggest draws are the rooftop swimming pool and the fitness centre, although guests in the 175 bright rooms and seven suites will also enjoy the mountain views, and snacks and drinks in the RBG bar and grill.

The Platinum
Nr Oman Oil Petrol Pump Muscat **968 24 392 500**
theplatinumoman.com
Map **2 F3**
The Platinum is aimed predominantly at Gulf and Arab visitors (both in terms of architecture and its being unlicensed) and has 85 rooms and suites, a fine dining restaurant and Arab cafe, as well as a swimming pool, gym and steam room.

Ramada Muscat
Ruwi Sarooj St Muscat **968 24 603 555**
ramadamuscat.com
Map **2 G2**
This four-star hotel is located in Shatti Al Qurum, just a couple of minutes away from the beautiful Qurum beach. Facilities include free wi-fi and a small swimming pool. Alcohol is not served in this hotel.

Safeer Hotels
Muscat **968 24 473 900**
safeerhotels.com
Map **2 F3**
Safeer Hotels and Tourism offers many choices of three-star accommodation throughout Muscat. These include Safeer International Hotel, Safeer Continental Hotel, Safeer Hotel Suites, Safeer Plaza Hotel and Nuzha Hotel.

Sifawy Boutique Hotel
45km from Muscat Jebel Sifah
968 24 749 111
sifawyhotel.com
Map **2 F3**
Sifawy Boutique is a luxurious four-star resort offering 55 air-conditioned rooms, including 30 suites, all opening onto private balconies with amazing coastal views. It's 45 minutes from Muscat in a remote marine village, and the drive down the capital along the winding mountain roads is an incredibly scenic one.

If you're worried about being based that far away from the capital, rest assured that you won't need to go far for your dining and entertainment. The resort boasts two top quality restaurants, an outdoor pool area, a newly opened spa and a fitness centre as well as organising small shopping and nightlife events. The staff will also arrange diving, snorkelling and driving tours for guests, if you're feeling adventurous. Try the early morning dolphin watching tour for an unforgettable experience.

Samara Hotel
Muscat **968 24 481 666**
samarahotel.com
Map **2 F3**
Samara Hotel is located in Al Khuwair, which is convenient for travel within the city. This budget hotel offers a restaurant, coffee shop and gymnasium, all at low prices.

Tulip Inn Muscat
Way 3504 Muscat **968 24 471 500**
tulipinnmuscat.com
Map **2 F3**
Tulip Inn Muscat is in an excellent location for business and leisure travellers as it is located in the heart of Al Khuwair and is only a few minutes away from Muscat Grand Mall and the Royal Opera House. There are 153 rooms and suites to choose from, as well as a gym, sauna and steam room. Other features include a business centre, executive lounge and gift shop.

Nizwa

Al Diyar Hotel
Nizwa **968 25 412 402**
aldiyarhotel.com
Map **1 G4**
Located just outside Nizwa city centre, this hotel offers a relatively comfortable but uncomplicated stay, with basic facilities that include a swimming pool, a gym, a Lebanese restaurant and an internet cafe. Single, double and triple rooms and suites are available.

Falaj Daris Hotel
Nr Nizwa Souk Nizwa **968 25 410 500**
falajdarishotel.com
Map **1 G4**
Set amidst nicely landscaped gardens, with two outdoor pools, a play area and a gym, Falaj Daris Hotel is decently appointed if basic, with 55 rooms, two suites, and a few creature comforts like a restaurant, bar, aircon and satellite TV. It's also just a couple of minutes' drive from the town centre.

Golden Tulip Nizwa Hotel
150 kms from Muscat, Nr Hajar Mountains Nizwa
968 25 431 616
goldentulipnizwa.com
Map **1 F5**
The Golden Tulip Nizwa benefits from a picturesque setting with landscaped gardens and the Hajar Mountains in the distance. There are 120 guest rooms, many of which benefit from private access to the (temperature controlled) outdoor swimming pool. The Birkat Al Mawz restaurant serves international cuisine and the hotel has two comfortable bars, as well as a gym and sauna.

"An oasis of peace and serenity at the feet of Hajjar Mountains"

☎ +968 2543 1616   🖳 +968 2543 1619

Email : rsvn@goldentulipnizwa.com

Website : www.goldentulipnizwa.com

Airport : Muscat International Airport (140 km)

Transports : Private Taxis available from Hotel to Airport

Location : Golden Tulip Nizwa Hotel is a 4 star deluxe property built in the charming traditional Omani style architecture. Recently renovated, the hotel is strategically located for adventure tours through Oman's exciting interiors.

Dining facilities : Multicuisine restaurant, Bar, Coffee Shop, Pool Bar, Sports Bar and 24 hrs Room Service.

Hotel facilities : 120 rooms

Meeting facilities : Jabal Al Akdhar, Nizwa's Premier venue for spectacular social and corporate events equipped with mordern facilities.

Number of meeting rooms : 2

Max. persons : 400

Smallest - Largest room : From 25m² to 450m²

P.O. Box 1000, 611 Nizwa

Qurum

Ramee Guestline Hotel Qurum
Mutrah Al Buraymi **968 24 564 443**
ramee-group.com
Map **2 H2**
This hotel is located in Qurum in close proximity to Qurum Beach and to the Royal Opera House. Facilities include an outdoor pool and fitness centre. The hotel could do with updating and rooms tend to be basic. The hotel is licensed to sell alcohol and is home to Rock Bottom Cafe, a popular night spot.

Salalah

City Hotel Salalah
Salalah **968 23 295 252**
cityhotelsalalah.com
Map **4 G7**
This three-star hotel is located in the city centre of Salalah and can be reached in five minutes from the airport. It has 90 rooms and there is free wi-fi. Twin deluxe rooms feature four single beds and two bathrooms so it is very suitable for families.

Crowne Plaza Resort Salalah
Al Khandaque St Salalah **968 23 238 000**
crowneplaza.com
Map **4 K8**
Set in a private garden beside the sea, this hotel features 119 rooms and nine suites. There are three pools, kids' facilities and entertainment, health and fitness facilities and a miniature golf course. Guests have three restaurants to choose from, including the excellent Dolphin Beach Restaurant that offers alfresco dining with stunning views of the white sands and Indian Ocean.

Hamdan Plaza Hotel
Al Wadi St Salalah **968 23 211 025**
hamdanplazahotel.com
Map **4 F7**
Although not a luxury resort, this three-star hotel certainly fits into the 'comfortable' category, with a variety of rooms and suites, gym and pool, and wi-fi throughout. There's an international and an Oriental restaurant, with drinks available in rooms.

Hilton Salalah Resort
Sultan Qaboos St Salalah **968 23 211 234**
salalah.hilton.com
Map **4 D9**
This five-star beachfront hotel offers style and comfort. Its simple Omani-style exterior hides a luxurious domed lobby and mirror-like marble floors. Its beachfront location, 12km from Salalah centre, allows guests to truly get away from it all and enjoy the hotel's facilities. There are three international restaurants, two entertainment outlets, a health spa and a doctor on call.

Juweira Boutique Hotel
Salalah Beach Marina, Taqa Rd Salalah
968 23 239 600
juweirahotel.com
Map **1 D2**
This five-star hotel is located on the marina promenade of Salalah Beach. It offers a wide variety of activities and facilities ranging from board games and swimming to snorkeling and scuba diving trips. There are two swimming pools and an outdoor Jacuzzi. As Sammah seafood restaurant offers a selection of locally-sourced seafood specialities with stunning views of the marina town and the sea.

Samharam Tourist Village
Salalah **968 23 211 420**
shanfarihotels.com
Map **4 E9**
Situated on a sandy beach in Salalah, this five-star resort offers villas and open-plan chalets. Hotel facilities include a restaurant, a swimming pool and a tennis court.

Salalah Marriott Resort
Salalah Beach Mirbat **968 23 275 500**
marriott.com
Map **1 C10**
This five-star resort is located an hour from Salalah. It has 170 rooms and 67 suites with balconies overlooking the pool, beach and Indian Ocean. There is a wide range of facilities and activities including a wellness centre and spa. The resort is just 25km from the UNESCO site of Khor Rori.

Salalah Plaza Hotel
Muscat **968 23 210 794**
salalahplazahotel.com
Map **4 E8**
Opened in 2012, Salalah Plaza Hotel is a three-star hotel just 10 minutes' drive from Salalah Airport. The decor is modern, and the family rooms include a living room, a dining area and kitchen.

Salalah Rotana Resort
Taqah Road, Salalah **968 23 275 700**
rotana.com
Map **1 C11**
This stunning five-star hotel near Salalah Beach is perfect for escaping the summer heat. There are over 400 rooms and suites built around sparkling lagoons and other water features, and the five-star facilities include two swimming pools, a state of the art gym and the luxurious Zen the spa.

Sifawt hotel

Radisson Blu hotel

Safari Rooftop Grillhouse, Grand Hyatt

Sohar

Al Wadi Hotel

Sohar **968 26 840 058**
omanhotels.com
Map **3 A7**
This three-star hotel is suitable for both business and leisure travellers. It has 78 rooms, a bar, a restaurant, a conference room and a gym.

Crowne Plaza Sohar

Falaj Al Qabail R/A Sohar **968 26 850 850**
ichotelsgroup.com
Map **1 E3**
Crowne Plaza Sohar is a five-star hotel located 9km from Sohar's Special Economic Zone in the Port of Sohar. There are two floodlit tennis courts and a four-lane bowling alley. Other facilities include a gym, a swimming pool and four restaurants.

Home Away From Home

If you're looking to stay somewhere a little more homely than a hotel, try a hotel apartment. Delmon Hotel Apartments (delmonhotelapartments.com) is a cosy spot with comfortable rooms that's close to a range of attractions including the Grand Mosque and Muscat Diving Centre.

Sohar Beach Hotel

Sallan Beach, Al Tareef Sohar **968 26 841 111**
soharbeach.com
Map **3 B6**
Occupying a beachside location, the Sohar Beach Hotel is designed in the style of a traditional Omani fort. This four-star hotel features 45 guestrooms, suites and chalets. Most of the rooms enjoy views over the swimming pool and garden.

Sur

Sur Beach Hotel

Sur **968 25 542 031**
sigoh.com.om
Map **1 H5**
Sur Beach Hotel is a three-star hotel. Facilities include a banqueting hall, a swimming pool and a tennis court. The decor is dated but the rooms are spacious.

Sur Plaza Hotel

Sur Main Rd Sur **968 25 543 777**
omanhotels.com
Map **1 H5**
A few kilometres from Sur, this hotel is a perfect base from which to explore the surrounding area, including the turtle nesting sites at Ras Al Hadd and Ras Al Jinz.

Other Places To Stay

Al Falaj Hotel Nr Ministry of Education, Ruwi, 968 24 702 311, *omanhotels.com*
Al Khuwair Hotel Apartments Way 3923, Al Kulliyah St, 968 24 784 144, *safeerhotel.net*
Al Manaf Hotel Nr Petrol Station, 968 95 617 808, *almanafhotel.com*
Al Qabil Rest House Sur Rd, Nr Wahiba Sands, 968 25 581 243
Alila Jabal Akhdar Resort Jebel Akhdar, Nizwa, 968 25 344 200, *alilahotels.com*
Beach Hotel Apartments Nr InterContinental, 968 24 696 601, *omanbeachhotel.com*
City Seasons Al Sultan Qaboos St, 968 24 394 800, *cityseasonsgroup.com*
Delmon Hotel Apartments 968 24 818 181, *delmonhotelapartments.com*
Dhofar Park Inn International Nr LuLu Centre, 968 23 292 272
Esra Hotel Apartments 968 26 730 562, *khasabtours.com*
Extra Divers Musandam Nr Golden Tulip Hotel, 968 26 730 501
Ghaba Rest House Muscat-Salalah Highway, 968 99 358 639
Golden Tulip Nizwa Hotel 150 km from Muscat, Nr Hajar Mountains, 968 25 431 616 *goldentulipnizwa.com*
Golden Tulip Resort Dibba Mina Rd, 968 26 836 654, *goldentulipdibba.com*
Hala Hotel Apartments 968 24 810 442
Khuwair Hotel Apartments 968 24 789 199
Majan Guest House Firq R/A, 968 25 431 910
Manam Hotel Apartments Nr Honda Showroom, 968 24 571 555, *manamhotel.com*
Midan Hotel Suites Way 3205, Al Marefah St, 968 24 499 565, *midanoman.com*
Nomad Guest House 968 95 495 240, *nomadtours.com*
Nuzha Hotel Apartments Al Mujamma St, Darsait, 968 24 602 355, *safeerhospitality.com.om*
Radisson Blu Hotel Way 209 , 968 24 487 777, *radissonblu.com*
Safeer Hotel Al Muthaf Rd, 974 44 353 999
Safeer Hotel Suites Madinat Sultan Qaboos St, 968 24 691 200, *safeerintll.com*
Salalah Rotana Resort 968 23 275 701, *rotana.com*
Samharam Tourist Resort 968 23 211 420, *shanfarihotels.com*
Seeb International Hotel 968 24 543 800, *seebinternational.com*
Sifawy Boutique Hotel 45km from Muscat, 968 24 749 111, *sifawyhotel.com*
Sohar Beach Hotel Sallan Beach, Al Tareef, 968 26 841 111, *soharbeach.com*

CAMPING

Camping is an extremely popular pastime among both the Omani people and the expat community, thanks mainly to it being extremely easy, with few rules about where you can and can't camp. Should you be tired and need a place to catch 40 winks after a long day of driving or hiking, it really is as easy as pulling off the road, finding a suitably flat place and pitching your tent.

Beach and wadi camping are best in winter, because their low altitudes mean the summer months are just too hot (never camp in the wadi bed itself as flash floods can occur even when you least expect them). The mountains, however, can be lovely during the summer months, because at altitude the temperatures remain lower for longer. Also, it is advisable to shy away from the mountains during the coldest months (November to February) as temperatures can drop to below zero; believe it or not, it has even been known to snow on Jebel Akhdar and Jebel Shams.

The most popular beach areas to camp in are Tiwi, Fins, Ras Al Jinz and Bandar Khayran. Tiwi and Fins are easily accessed by car, but both can be quite busy, especially during holiday weekends, so it is best to leave early to secure your space on the beach. You can't simply arrive and erect your tent in Ras Al Jinz, as much of the beach is a protected nature conservation area, so you'll need to head for the allocated camp site which is a fair distance from the actual beach.

The easiest way to get to Bandar Khayran, meanwhile, is by boat. You should find a boat at Qantab and it will cost about RO.5, but it is always best to negotiate the price with the boatman first. The boatman will take you and your luggage to a small secluded beach, where you will be able to stay for as long as you want. Arrange a time for the boatman to collect you; be sure to pay him on the return journey.

Camping near wadis is as easy as driving down the wadi in your 4WD, stopping, and then finding a comfortable but raised place on the banks well above the wadi where you can pitch your tents and spend the night. In Explorer's *Oman Off-road* guide, you'll find several routes dedicated to some of the more picturesque wadis in Oman. Although they are all worth a visit, some of the best to visit and camp at are Snake Gorge, Wadi Al Abyadh and Wadi Dhaiqah.

Jebel Akhdar and Jebel Shams also have places for camping and, again, as with any mountain camping, try to do it during the spring to autumn months. The main problem with mountain camping is pegging your tent down, so remember to take a hammer with you for knocking pegs into the dirt or, alternatively, rocks or bags and buckets of sand can help you weigh down and secure your tent.

Finding good camping equipment in Oman is just as straightforward as finding a campsite. There are numerous outlets that sell camping gear, with the best place arguably the Sultan Center which has everything you could ever need for one night of roughing it through to a full week of luxury camping. Carrefour and LuLu's also stock good ranges of camping equipment.

The dome style tent, in various sizes, is the most readily available, although you will find some small, mountain style hiking tents here and there if you look carefully. Gas bottles and all the accessories that go with them can also be purchased in all of the stores mentioned.

If you prefer traditional barbecuing when out camping, you can either build a small fire using whatever you can find in the area along with some kind of grill or, easier, take a small barbecue and the necessary charcoal or wood with you. Again, Carrefour and LuLu's will have everything you need for the BBQ to lighter fluid and utensils.

In conclusion, camping is one of the great Omani experiences, as you are not hampered by the rules and regulations that you would face in most other countries. It is a taste of something more real and basic, in that you won't readily find a camping spot with electricity and you're unlikely to see anyone towing a caravan or trailer. All that is necessary for a great, and cheap, weekend is a full cooler box, a tent, a barbecue and a sense of adventure.

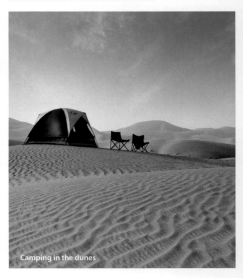
Camping in the dunes

THERE'S MORE TO LIFE THAN BRUNCH

UAE & OMAN
ULTIMATE EXPLORER

OFF-ROADING, DIVING, CAMPING, HIKING, WEEKEND BREAKS AND MUCH MO

ask**explorer**.com/shop

1000 Nights Camp
Bidiyyah **968 99 448 158**
1000nightscamp.com
Map **1 G5**
Located in the heart of the Wahiba Sands, 1000 Nights is camping with more than a touch of luxury thrown in. Tents, although based on traditional Bedouin tents, are semi-permanent with shared bathroom services. There's even an onsite pool, restaurant with terrace and a conference centre. All the nearby desert activities make it as popular for team building as for adventurous family holidays.

Al Areesh Desert Camp
Wahiba/Sharqiyah Sands Al Qabil **968 24 493 232**
desertdiscovery.com
Map **1 G5**
Al Areesh Desert Camp offers Bedouin-style accommodation in Wahiba Sands. It's basic, but every tent is fitted with electricity and there are some ensuite rooms. In the evenings, the campfire becomes the scene for the Bedouin musicians and singers.

Al Naseem Camp
Wahiba Sands Bidiyyah **968 24 493 232**
desertdiscovery.com
Map **1 G5**
This is a great base camp for turtle watching, because it's very near the Ras Al Jinz nature reserve. And it's even greater if you're the type of camper who needs running water, flushing toilets and hot showers – Al Naseem has all of these, as well as electric lighting, soft mattresses (singles only), and continental breakfasts! What makes it really special is the entertainment area, covered in palm fronds, where you can dine and lounge on carpets and cushions in true Omani style.

Al Raha Tourism Camp
Wahiba Sands Bidiyyah **968 99 343 851**
alrahaoman.com
Map **1 G5**
This desert camp offers visitors a chance to sample a tourist-friendly version of Bedouin life – as well as dabble in some dune buggy driving, dune bashing in 4WDs, sandboarding and, of course, camel rides. Accommodation is in clean but basic; concrete rooms with an attached toilet, or Bedouin-style tents with communal bathrooms. Expect buffet meals as well as live music and entertainment.

Desert Nights Camp
Nr Sand Coloured Mosque, 11km from Al Wasil
Bidiyyah **968 92 818 388**
desertnightscamp.com
Map **1 G5**
The ultimate chic camping experience, this camp is around two hours from Muscat in the Wahiba Sands

and gives visitors a taste of Bedouin life and a slice of luxury. The 30 tents boast en-suite bathrooms, aircon and mini bars, while there's an onsite restaurant and bar, as well as traditional camp fire entertainment. Ideal for the adventurous, visitors can enjoy everything from henna tattoos and star gazing to camel safaris, dune bashing, quad biking and excursions to Wadi Bani Khalid.

Jabal Shems Heights Resort
Nizwa Jabel Shams **968 92 721 999**
jabalshems.com
Map **1 G4**
Perched on the mountainside of Jebel Shams (the Gulf's highest peak at around 3,000m) this camp is ideal for adventurers looking to scale the summit or explore the amazing hiking trails that wind across the range. There are 15 Bedouin-style tents with shower and toilet facilities, six family rooms, a 'wild' camping area and even a restaurant and BBQ terrace. The views are, understandably, among the best you'll find anywhere in the Middle East.

Jebel Shams Resort
Muscat 968 99 382 639
jebelshamsresort.com
Map **1 G4**
Jebel Shams Resort is located atop the highest mountain in Oman and is close to the edge of Oman's grand canyon. The resort has 20 chalets, 15 Arabic tents, a restaurant and a coffee shop. A heated swimming pool is under construction. The drive up the mountain takes about 30 minutes and guests are advised to use 4WD vehicles.

Safari Desert Camp
25km from Al Ghabbi, Wahiba Sands Bidiyyah
968 92 000 592
safaridesert.com
Map **1 G5**
Another permanent camp that uses Bedouin-style tents, each with its own attached toilet facilities. Located in the Wahiba Sands, there are several activities on offer here, such as henna by the camp fire and dinner in the majlis BBQ restaurant, while several excursions can also be arranged.

The View
Muscat 968 24 400 873
theviewoman.com
Map **1 G4**
Although just a two-hour drive from Muscat, this stunning property feels like a world away. This is Oman's first eco-luxe resort, with tent-styled accommodation and en-suite facilities. It is located in the beautiful mountainous region of Jebel Shams and its restaurant has stunning views of the canyon.

ON THE DESERT TRAIL

You can't live in, or even holiday in, Oman without experiencing the vast, dramatic majesty of the desert; waking up to a fierce red sunrise between a set of dramatic dunes is a unique Arabian experience. But, if adventure is something you think is best served up, well, by others, then there are plenty of 'luxury camping' venues (such as the Desert Nights Camp, pictured) scattered throughout the Wahiba Sands, offering everything from proper toilet facilities to restaurants and bars.

Oman retains its traditional architecture

LIVING IN OMAN

LIVING IN OMAN

Everything you need to consider, do, and apply for if you've decided to start a new life in the Sultanate of Oman.

The natural and rugged coastline

Oman is for most people a wonderful place to live, with excellent career opportunities, a network of social contacts, unique activities and, apart from a few sweaty months in summer, brilliant weather. Most expats tell you their standard of living is better than it was back home, they travel more, spend more time with family, enjoy outdoor living and make more friends.

Having said that, any big move can be a challenge, particularly if it's a culture that you're unfamiliar with. Familiarising yourself with the social and cultural dos and don'ts can go a long way to making your feel more relaxed and helping the move go smoother. When it comes to all the paperwork, it is definitely worth planning ahead; do as much as you can in terms of obtaining and attesting documents before your arrival. This will make the transition much smoother.

Once you've got your residency visa, and you and your family have settled in, it's time to get to know your new home. This chapter will outline everything you need to know, from practical considerations such as getting around, buying a car and seeking out healthcare, to fun stuff like social groups and community meet-ups.

The neighbourhood profiles contain all the information you need to know when choosing your base in Oman, with the pros and cons for the most popular expat areas including schools, location and local amenities. And if you decide to make the move more permanent, there's even information on how to buy property in Oman. Elsewhere in the section, you'll also find all the advice you need to further your career in this part of the Gulf, including finding work and changing jobs.

BECOMING A RESIDENT

Considering Oman

While some expats come to live in Oman for a fixed term, there are many thousands of foreigners who stay for much longer periods and are in no hurry to move on. And it's not hard to see why: sunshine almost every day of the year, great leisure facilities, a beautiful mix of scenery (ocean, mountain, desert, greenery), luxurious hotels and their top-notch in-house restaurants, and a pace of life that is neither too hectic nor too boring. And to top it all, the salaries are tax-free.

That said, moving to a new country nearly always involves an element of stress. However, once you get over the initial culture shock, most expats discover that Oman is a relaxed and friendly country; it is modern (and developing all the time), and yet it still retains a certain charm from the past that is unique to the region.

One of Oman's greatest assets is its people, who are warm and welcoming, and who have a long history of fascinating traditions. You'll also find a large group of friendly expats, and before you know it you'll meet loads of people. Remember that rules and regulations change frequently in this part of the world, so keep your eye on the local press and be prepared for the unexpected.

Before You Arrive

Some people love expat life and take to it like a duck to water, but there are equally a few who never manage to adjust. Therefore, it is not always a good decision to cut all ties with your home country (like selling your property and closing your bank accounts) before you've tested the waters for a year or so. However, you will need to get your financial affairs in order, particularly if you have to continue paying tax in your home country.

If you have accepted a job offer in Oman, most of the administrative tasks will be taken care of by your employer, but you might still want to visit the country before you take up your post to look at houses and schools. If you have children of school-going age, you will need to start investigating schools straight away. There are not many schools to choose from and with Muscat expanding all the time, some schools are running out of places in certain age groups.

If you negotiated your contract well, you will have made provision for shipping costs – both for when you arrive and when you leave. If you are staying for more than a year, it is probably well worth it to ship out some of your belongings, as this can make you feel at home and settled in sooner.

There's a lot of paperwork to be taken care of but your employer will almost always do this on your behalf – leaving you to worry about more important things like whether you've got enough summer clothes in your wardrobe!

It's a good idea to get a big batch of passport photos taken before you arrive. You will need countless passport photos over the coming months, as just about every procedure requires at least one. You'll also need plenty of passport copies.

It is unusual for people to arrive in Oman on a visit visa to look for work – most people already have jobs lined up before they arrive. However, if you are coming to Oman to look for work, do your research before you arrive. Contact recruitment agencies and sign up with online job sites as far in advance as possible. There may also be agencies in your home country that specialise in overseas recruitment.

Not The Best, Not The Worst

The sixth Expat Explorer survey was conducted using interviews from over 7,000 expatriates in more than 100 countries in 2013 and covered a range of areas including financial incentives, quality of life, ease of raising children and the cost of living. The ranking of the Sultanate in the overall Expat Economics League Table was eight, with the top three slots going to Switzerland, China and Qatar while the country's ranking in the overall expat experience was 35th. Oman was ranked number one on expat satisfaction with the local economy while the survey also revealed that expatriate spending on schooling in Oman is higher than the global average. Political stability has been a strong factor for expatriates to consider when moving to the Middle East and according to the survey, Oman is considered to be the most politically stable country in the region.

When You Arrive

The list of things you'll have to deal with in the first few weeks can be a little daunting, and you may well be in for a lot of form filling, queuing, and coming and going. Try not to let it spoil your first impressions of the country though, because hopefully you'll soon be a fully fledged resident enjoying your new life, and all that boring bureaucracy will be a distant memory.

For many procedures you'll have to produce your 'essential documents' shortly after your arrival.

At the very least, these will include:

- Original passport
- Passport copies (including photo page and visa page)
- Passport photos
- Copy of labour card (if you are working)
- Copy of sponsorship certificate for non-working residents

Some nationalities also need to get a health certificate from their home country, stating that they are free from illness and communicable diseases.

Residency Visas

For foreigners to live and work in Oman, they must usually be sponsored by an employer or family member. To obtain a residency visa as an employee, you need a local sponsor and a labour permit from the Ministry of Manpower. The requirements vary by nationality and are subject to change at short notice, so it's always best to check with the visa section of the Omani Embassy in the country where you currently live.

Once your employer sponsors you, you can then arrange sponsorship for your family members. Two family sponsorship options are available: a family joining visa or a family residence visa. Children can be sponsored provided they are younger than 21 years old.

Expats may also be eligible to apply for a Contractor Visa or an Investor Resident Visa – refer to Royal Oman Police (rop.gov.om) to get the latest information on visitor visas, residence permits and employment, investor or student visas.

Residence Visa

Before getting a visa you must get a No objection certificate (NOC). This is an official document stating that neither your Omani sponsor nor the government has any objection to your entering the country. There are two types of residence visas – one for employment (when you are sponsored by your employer) and one for residence only (when you are sponsored by a family member).

It is common for the employer to apply for a residency visa for an employee before the employee travels to Oman and it is usual that the paperwork will be sorted out before the employee arrives in the country. The employer will also incur any expenses in relation to the visa. When the employee arrives in Oman, the employer or designated representative will meet him/her at the airport and take him/her to the Royal Oman Police station to have fingerprints taken. Those working must have labour clearance and an employment residence visa; spouses and family members are each issued with a 'joining family' residence visa.

It is illegal to work on a joining family residence visa, even part time. If you wish to work you must get an employment visa. If you are working for the same sponsor as your spouse, exchanging the visa is usually a simple process. If you obtain a job elsewhere, you must transfer sponsorship to your new employer and go through the whole process from the beginning. Your new sponsor will do what's necessary.

Most expats seeking employment or applying for residency in Oman do not have to provide a Medical Fitness Certificate from their home country, stating

Mariya waterfront development

that they are free from illness and not carrying any communicable diseases. However, citizens from the following countries must provide one – India, Pakistan, Philippines, Bangladesh, Indonesia, Sri Lanka, Egypt, Syria, Sudan and Ethiopia. This list of countries can often change so it is a good item to check the Ministry of Health website (moh.gov.om) before you travel. Some nationalities or categories of workers also need special permits, e.g. Filipino housemaids need labour permits from the Filipino Embassy in Oman and these must be attested by Oman's Ministry of Foreign Affairs.

Stricter Laws

As of 1 June 2014, expats working in Oman will be subject to stricter visa laws if they wish to change jobs. Any expat who has completed less than two years of service in their current role should have to then leave Oman for two years before returning to take on a new role. The only way to avoid having to do so will be to obtain an NOC (No objection certificate) from the current employer.

Sponsorship By Employer

Your employer should handle all the paperwork, and will usually have a staff member (who is thoroughly familiar with the procedure) dedicated to this task alone. This staff member is usually called the PRO, which stands for Public Relations Officer. After your residency is approved, they should then apply directly for your labour clearance. You will need to supply the essential documents and your education certificates. You must have all your certificates attested by a solicitor or public notary in your home country and then by your foreign office to verify the solicitor as bona fide. The Oman embassy in your country of residence must also sign the documents. While this sounds like a run around, it is much easier if you get this done before you arrive in Oman.

In September 2013, in a move to regulate the expatriate workforce, the Directorate-General of Passport and Residences at the ROP introduced guidelines which do not allow family status to those drawing a monthly salary of less than RO.600. This decision has proved to be very controversial with many employees on the lower salary scale, unhappy that they will be unable to have their families join them in Oman.

New Visa Laws

Effective from 1 July 2014, employment visas will not be issued for foreigners who previously worked in the Sultanate and have not completed two years from the date of their last departure from the country. The only way that an expat worker seeking to move employers can avoid being forced to leave the country

for two years, even if they have completed their initial contract, is to obtain a No objection certificate (NOC) from their current employer. However, an expat worker with an NOC can transfer to another employer inside Oman even before the initial contract is complete.

Driving Licence

The driving licence that you use in Oman will depend on the duration of your stay, and whether you're on holiday or living in the Sultanate. Visitors may drive a hired or borrowed car on a valid international or home country licence for up to three months but, if you're staying for longer, you'll need to transfer your driving licence to an Omani one. You must be a resident to apply for a driving licence. Residents from many countries, including the UK and US, may simply exchange their national licence for an Omani one at the Directorate of Licensing and Vehicle Registration in Qurum and As Seeb in Muscat, or at one of the other centres located throughout the country.

To do this, you will have to have an eye test, and pay the fee of RO.20.

The following documents are required for a licence exchange:

- A completed licence exchange form bearing your sponsor's signature and the company stamp
- A copy of your passport and residence visa
- Your original (home) driving licence along with a copy. The foreign licence must have been issued at least a year ago
- Blood group certificate

If you're not from an 'exchange' country, you'll need to apply for an Omani licence. To do this, you should be at least 18 years old, free of any handicap that could hamper your ability to drive, and you'll need to pass the eyesight test.

The following documents are required to apply for an Omani licence:

- Two passport photos
- A completed application form
- A copy of your ID card or passport
- An NOC from your sponsor
- A blood group certificate
- A copy of your residence permit

Your company PRO should take you to the police station and help you through the process of applying for a licence exchange or booking a driving test. Remember to always carry your driving licence when driving; there's a chance that you will be fined if you fail to produce it during a spot check.

Driving licences in Oman are valid for 10 years and can be renewed at the traffic police HQ on Death Valley Road.

Liquor Licence

If you want to buy alcohol you'll need a liquor licence; only non-Muslim residents in possession of a labour card are allowed to apply. Equally, for married couples, only the husband can apply, and his wife cannot use the licence to buy alcohol unless he works in the interior. Licences are valid for two years, but can't be used outside of the city in which they were issued.

Your liquor licence permits you to buy a limited amount of alcohol each month; this allowance is calculated based on your salary, and is usually not more than 10% of it. You can apply for a larger allowance if you feel you have certain extraordinary circumstances (for example, if your job entails corporate entertaining).

To acquire a liquor licence bring the following documents to Ruwi Police Station (usually the PRO from your company will go with you):

- Copy of passport and Labour Card
- An NOC from your employer
- Two passport-size photographs
- Labour card original application form (this is to confirm your basic salary as registered by the Ministry of Manpower)
- Employment contract attested by the Ministry of Manpower to confirm employment and eligibility to apply for a permit
- Completed permit application (this can be done at the police station)
- If you are renewing your permit, bring your old permit with you.

The permit lasts for 24 months and the cost of it is calculated on 0.04% of the value of the licence on a monthly basis. For example, a RO.100 monthly permit will cost you RO.96 and it will last you for two years. Payment for the liquor licence is with a bank card only as no cash is accepted.

The main alcohol retailers in Oman are:

- African + Eastern (A&E)
- Oman United Agencies (OUA)
- Desert Trading Company (DTC)
- Marketing and Services Company (MASE)
- Gulf Supply Services (GSS)

When You Leave

Before jetting off, there are certain things that have to be wound up before you leave Oman for good. You will have to disconnect your electricity and water supply and get your security deposit back from your landlord (minus any damages).

You will also have to sell your car – not always an easy task, and used car dealers have learned to smell a departing expat a mile away, so be prepared for some very low offers.

You will probably then need to ship your household contents back home, and sell whatever you are not taking with you. The more notice you can give the shipping company, the better.

If you are selling loads of stuff, you can put a notice up on the community noticeboards (they can be found near Al Fair supermarkets in MSQ centre and Sarooj Centre). Alternatively, arrange and advertise a garage sale or list your items on sites such as omanbay.com or muscatads.com.

HOUSING

If you are arriving in Oman on a full expat package then accommodation is usually included in your employment contract. Some companies provide a rent allowance, others let you choose a property and then liaise with the landlord and make payment on your behalf, and some provide staff accommodation. Most expats live in the capital, Muscat; the main areas are Muscat, Mutrah, Ruwi, Wattayah, Qurum, Shatti Al Qurum, Madinat Al Sultan Qaboos (MSQ), Al Khuwair, Al Ghubrah, Al Azaiba and As Seeb. Muscat's hilly terrain means that people living on the top floors usually have a great view, while expat families more commonly prefer one of the many villas. The cost of accommodation is relatively high and, as the city is spread out over a large area, it pays to consider commuting distances when choosing where to live.

Residential Areas

Once you have received confirmation that you are relocating to Oman, it can be difficult to choose which residential area you would prefer to live in. Of course, your budget may affect your decision, and you may decide to live in an area that is a little further out of town and therefore a bit cheaper. You should also consider closeness to schools (if you have children) – the traffic situation in Muscat is gradually worsening with the rising population and you don't want to get stuck in a jam every morning on your school run. Also important is the proximity of entertainment venues – if you've got an exorbitant taxi fare to pay every time you go out anywhere it might deter even the most social of butterflies.

That said, every area of Muscat has its advantages and disadvantages, and with Muscat being a relatively small city you should be able to get to most places in less than half an hour. The following pages will give you some insight into the various residential areas.

Property at The Wave development

Muriya is a development with traditional design

Mutrah

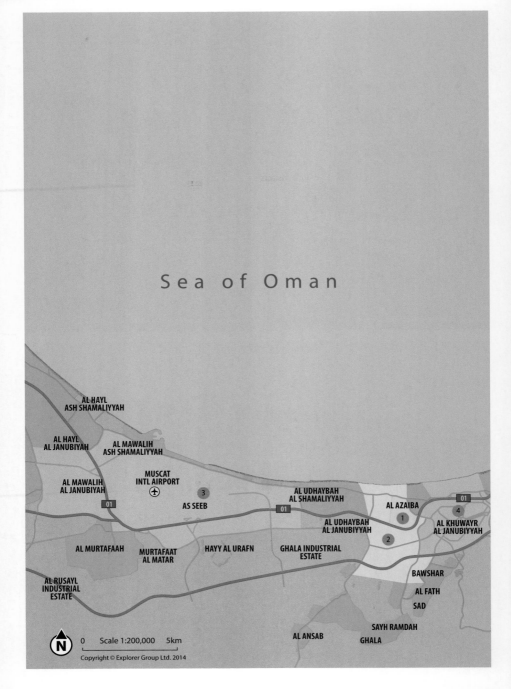

Sea of Oman

AL HAYL
ASH SHAMALIYYAH

AL HAYL
AL JANUBIYAH

AL MAWALIH
ASH SHAMALIYYAH

AL MAWALIH
AL JANUBIYAH

MUSCAT
INTL AIRPORT

01

AS SEEB

AL UDHAYBAH
AL SHAMALIYYAH

01

AL AZAIBA

AL UDHAYBAH
AL JANUBIYYAH

AL KHUWAYR
AL JANUBIYYAH

01

AL MURTAFAAH

MURTAFAAT
AL MATAR

HAYY AL URAFN

GHALA INDUSTRIAL
ESTATE

BAWSHAR

AL RUSAYL
INDUSTRIAL
ESTATE

AL FATH

SAD

SAYH RAMDAH

AL ANSAB

GHALA

N

0   Scale 1:200,000   5km

Copyright © Explorer Group Ltd. 2014

S e a   o f   O m a n

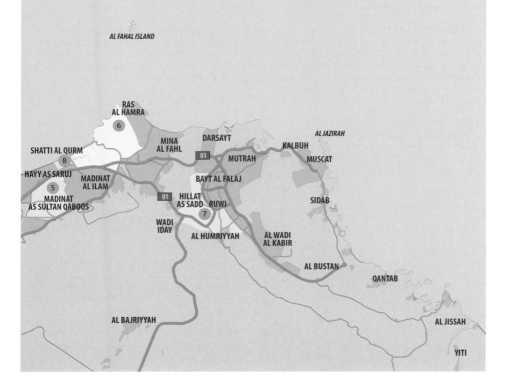

Al Azaiba

Al Azaiba merges with Al Ghubrah to the east and As Seeb to the west and is mostly a residential area but is fast becoming a business district.

You should note that this is a very popular location with expats, plus it can be very expensive if your tastes stretch to one of the premium beachfront villas on Street 37.

Best Points
The beautiful long stretch of beach is a big plus.

Worst Points
While there are currently not that many shops or amenities, this is slowly improving as the neighbourhood grows in popularity.

Accommodation
Large villas on the beach are sought after and prices are very steep. Old and new villas are available with gardens or paved areas and maid's accommodation. Some landlords can smell a naive expat a mile away and may quote you an inflated price if they think you don't know better, so do some price comparisons before you agree to anything.

Shopping & Amenities
There are plenty of shops in neighbouring areas to keep you in stock of everything but there is nothing of note locally apart from a few large dealerships and service centres which line the road parallel to the highway. The Sultan Centre supermarket and Al Fair supermarket are conveniently located in the centre of Al Azaiba.

Entertainment & Leisure
The endless sandy beaches will keep you busy outdoors. Although Al Azaiba is primarily a residential area, health clubs such as Euforie Muscat and cafes such as Costa Coffee are appearing.

Healthcare
There are no hospitals in the area but a number of medical clinics (including the Newlife Fertility Clinic) and dental clinics have opened in the last few years.

Education
The number of nurseries and schools has increased and popular ones include Modern International School, United Private School and Teaching and Learning Communities (TLC) International School.

Traffic & Parking
Al Azaiba is mostly a residential area, so you won't face too much frustration on the roads and parking is easy to find. However, there is some ongoing construction which might lead to diversions and occasional delays.

Safety & Annoyances
Lurking youths 'hanging out' and stray dogs roaming around are the two main annoyances, but as long as you pick your neighbourhood carefully you should be fine. Stray dogs are usually dealt with by the ROP.

Al Ghubrah Ash Shamaliyyah & Bowshar

This area covers a large expanse from the beach to the mountains and is in easy reach of many businesses and the main Sultan Qaboos highway.

Best Points
The scenery in Bowshar is fantastic.

Worst Points
Peak hour traffic congestion and ongoing road works make this a hotspot for traffic jams.

Accommodation
Accommodation is mainly two-storey villas, with a few apartment blocks above the shops and businesses in Ghubrar. Rents are lower in Bowshar and you have the advantage of a spectacular view of the sand dunes and mountains. Oasis Residence has some options for shopping, eating out plus a bakery and health club. The Dolphin Complex is also popular with families because of the leisure club facilities (including pool, tennis court and gym), the safe outdoor play area for kids and licensed restaurant.

Shopping & Amenities
The biggest and best supermarket in Muscat – LuLu Center – is located just off the Bowshar Roundabout, between Bowshar and Ghubrar. There is also a variety of small shops in Ghubrar selling everything from fabrics to fertiliser. While this means you can usually buy essential items at all hours, it also results in a certain amount of traffic congestion, particularly at peak times. Muscat Grand Mall is also in close proximity.

Entertainment & Leisure
There are three hotels in the area: the Bowshar Hotel, Park Inn and the Chedi. The Bowshar is basic and not a particularly great haunt for western expats, while The Chedi is spectacular in its understated, Zen-like architecture and superbly decadent restaurant. The Chedi also has one of Oman's most popular and luxurious spas. Park Inn is a great business hotel with a rooftop pool and several restaurants.

Healthcare
Muscat Private Hospital – the main healthcare choice for expats – is located here. It offers a complete range of in-patient and out-patient facilities, and has

a 24 hour emergency room (24 583 600). Al Raffah Hospital also offers surgical, inpatient, outpatient and diagnostic care (24 618 900/1/2/3/4).

Education
There are various Arabic and Indian schools in the area, but no education facilities for western expat children.

Traffic & Parking
The Ghubrar Roundabout has undergone construction to ease the flow of heavy traffic, which usually congests the area. The smaller 'Sail' roundabout is now a junction for the same reason. At peak times (mornings, lunch times and evenings) you might find a few traffic backups that could delay you for five minutes or so.

Safety & Annoyances
Construction in Ghubrar can really slow down traffic, so keep this in mind when planning your commute.

As Seeb

This is not usually the first choice for expats when looking for a home, mainly due to the distance from the city centre and all the facilities they will probably desire (such as schools and medical services). However, many are now moving to the area due to low prices (and a lack of accommodation in other parts of town). The areas of Al Hail and Al Mawaleh are now very popular and they are in close proximity to the residential and commercial complex, The Wave.

Best Points
Lower rents and larger houses, and some of Muscat's best shopping right on your doorstep.

Worst Points
Out of town location means lots of time in the car and expensive taxi fares.

Accommodation
Rents are a little lower this side of the airport, and villas are spacious and more likely to have a small garden or paved area outside. If you don't mind travelling a few extra minutes, this is a great opportunity to live in a much bigger villa at a lower price.

Shopping & Amenities
It doesn't get much better than having Muscat's two largest shopping malls right on your doorstep. Markaz Al Bahja and Muscat City Centre have all the large shops you will need, and you will find plenty of smaller local shops in As Seeb town and Seeb souk itself.

Entertainment & Leisure
There is a cinema in Markaz Al Bahja, as well as a super play area that will keep your kids busy round the year. This is particularly useful during summer, but during the cooler months there is plenty of white sandy beach to have fun on, as well as a beach park. The Golden Tulip Seeb is predominantly a business hotel, although it does have a few restaurants, including one on the roof which is excellent in winter, and some good leisure facilities. The Seeb International Exhibition Centre is nearby.

Waterfront living at The Wave

Healthcare

The area is home to various small clinics offering private outpatient treatment to all nationalities. It is also the location of the Sultan Qaboos University Hospital, which is not usually available to expats unless you require treatment that is not available at one of the city's private hospitals. Starcare Hospital is conveniently located beside Muscat City Centre.

Education

Sultan Qaboos University is in the area, and although this is a reputable institution it is only for Omanis. It is, however, an establishment that hires quite a few international lecturers. The Caledonian College of engineering is open to all nationalities and offers a variety of under and postgraduate courses. Two recent additions to the primary and secondary school sector are Azzan Bin Qais International School and Al Rowad International School (which follows the Canadian curriculum).

Traffic & Parking

Traffic can be busy around the airport area but a new flyover has helped and it is much calmer in As Seeb town and in Al Hail. The highway can become a bit of a racetrack beyond the airport, so keep your wits about you. On the whole, roads in the area are good.

Safety & Annoyances

The crime rate is reportedly rising here, but is still very low. Be sensible with protecting yourself and your property as you would anywhere else. While you may be able to hear the odd plane taking off at the nearby airport, this should not be too much bother.

Al Khuwair Al Janubiyyah

Al Khuwair is fast becoming one of Muscat's most desirable places to live due to its central location, and good range of amenities and services. There are many schools and hospitals nearby and Muscat Grand Mall is convenient for shopping.

Best Points

The beautiful mountain backdrop with Taimur mosque, the nearby shopping malls and schools, and the reasonable rents.

Worst Points

Traffic congestion, particularly during peak times near the roundabout.

Accommodation

Al Khuwair offers mainly two-storey villas, but also many apartments in the business district which runs along the road parallel to the highway.

Shopping & Amenities

There are some big-name electrical shops, local home furnishing stores, clothing stores and art supply stores located along the slip road and off the Al Khuwair Roundabout towards Madinat Al Sultan Qaboos. There is also a Mars hypermarket and a Rawasco supermarket in central Al Khuwair. Muscat Grand Mall, Oman's newest addition to the shopping centre scene, is home to an array of shops and restaurants.

Entertainment & Leisure

The Radisson Blu is superbly located although its famed view of White Mountain and Taimur mosque is now hidden behind a raised highway. It houses bars and restaurants and a swimming pool to keep you entertained. Opposite the hotel are a number of shisha cafes (try Kebab King) with their plastic tables and chairs spilling out onto the pavement, and selling food and fresh juices. These are very popular with locals and expats alike, and a great place to spend a cool evening with friends, watching football or politics on the big-screen TV.

Other notable hotels include the Park Inn which is licensed, while the City Seasons, Hotel Ibis and Platinum have a variety of restaurants. The service road running parallel to Sultan Qaboos Highway also has a wide selection of restaurants and diners to choose from.

Healthcare

There are many small clinics offering a variety of medical treatments. Badr al Samaa Polyclinic offers general healthcare.

Education

Al Khuwair is home to the College of Technology, which seems to be expanding at an alarming rate judging by the number of cars parked within a 1km radius. It is not open to expat students. The American British Academy offers the international baccalaureate syllabus as part of its primary and secondary education courses.

Traffic & Parking

Flagrant disregard for parking regulations around the mosque during prayer time can certainly make for an interesting time on the roads! The roundabout becomes a car park and roads leading from it are lined with double-parked vehicles.

Safety & Annoyances

Some of the younger residents and students like to practise 'doughnuts' and other noisy tricks in their cars and beach buggies when most people are trying to sleep. Be mindful of occasional random acts of vandalism that include spray painting on cars and vehicle damage.

Madinat Al Sultan Qaboos

Fondly known as 'Little Britain', this area is extremely popular with western expats, the diplomatic corps and young families.

Best Points
MSQ is a tranquil, leafy suburb that comes with a great range of amenities.

Worst Points
Traffic in the mornings and around the Home Centre junction, plus escalating rents.

Accommodation
MSQ has a mixture of older villas with established gardens, swanky new apartment blocks with swimming pools, and garden courts. It is one of the number one areas sought after by expats, due to its proximity to the British School and the American British Academy, and it has soaring rental prices to reflect the fact.

Shopping & Amenities
It's all here – there is a large Al Fair supermarket (with a pork room), a liquor store, a travel agent, a vet, a medical centre, and much more.

Entertainment & Leisure
There are many restaurants and cafes in the area including Pizza Hut, Starbucks and Costa Coffee. Kargeen is famous among both locals and expats for its great food and excellent ambiance while the licensed restaurant Pavo Real offers authentic Mexican cuisine. Family favourites include MacKenzies Deli and D'Arcy's Kitchen.

Healthcare
The Medident Centre offers general medical care, as well as dentistry and prenatal care. It is staffed by expats.

Education
One of the reasons that this neighbourhood is so popular amongst expat families is its proximity to the renowned British School Muscat, arguably Muscat's best school. The British School provides high-quality education for children from the age of 3 right up to A-levels, and follows the English National Curriculum. It is also a community meeting point for all kinds of activities from Scottish dancing to karate. MSQ is home to a few embassies and the British Council, which holds a range of English language courses for non-English speakers. The British Council also offers CELTA courses for people wishing to teach English as a second language. Nurseries such as Bright Beginnings and Abu Adnan offer activities and daycare.

Traffic & Parking
Parking can get a little busy around Al Fair, but there are other parking areas dotted about so you will never have to walk far. Traffic at the junction near Home Centre can hold you back, so avoid lunch times if possible. Drop-off time in the mornings around the schools and nurseries can also be tricky.

Safety & Annoyances
Due to the popularity of this area, traffic can be heavy and there are a lot of children around so make sure to drive carefully.

Al Qurum (including Qurum Heights)

Residential Al Qurum is home to a mixture of residential and commercial buildings, and it is safe to say that this is one of the most desirable areas in which to live (and the most expensive).

Best Points
Due to its hilly setting, Qurum has amazing views.

Worst Points
The traffic around Qurum junction can get quite congested at peak times.

Accommodation
Mainly large villas set amid a range of undulating slopes; therefore your chances of landing a villa with a view are high. This is also the location of the Petroleum Development Oman housing compound (complete with private leisure facilities). Shatti Al Qurum is the epitome of luxury living, with huge white villas spaced out along quiet suburban streets. However, unless you are a foreign diplomat, a wealthy local or an well paid CEO, it may be out of your budget.

Shopping & Amenities
Qurum is home to four large shopping centres, including Qurum City Centre. In the area, you'll find big name brands, fabric shops, a fancy dress shop, a petshop, a selection of banks and supermarkets, including Carrefour in Qurum City Centre.

Entertainment & Leisure
There is no shortage of leisure options in the area. You'll find a selection of restaurants and bars, some of which are in the Crowne Plaza hotel (which also boasts a health club and a great swimming pool). Kids will be able to spend hours in Marah Land, and you could spend many a cool evening strolling around the adjacent Qurum Natural Park. In terms of beaches, you've got Al Marjan beach and the long stretch of beach running from Qurum to Al Azaiba and beyond.

Healthcare

Qurum is home to the Al Hayat Polyclinic, Al Masaraat Clinic and various smaller clinics.

Education

Muscat International School, offering an international curriculum to both local and expat children from kindergarten to A-Level, is in Qurum, making it a popular spot with families.

Traffic & Parking

There is a healthy amount of free parking around the shopping centres, which is a huge plus for the neighbourhood. However in some areas a 50 baisa ticket is required. Traffic can get congested around the Qurum junction, especially during peak times.

Safety & Annoyances

The 'PDO Pong' is sometimes noticeable if the wind blows in a certain direction. This is just an odour from the PDO petrochemical plant, and it is harmless.

Ruwi

Ruwi is home to the Central Business District areas of Muscat. Ruwi High Street comes alive in the evenings as people throng the streets, window shopping and people watching at the roadside cafes.

Best Points

Shopaholics with an eye for a bargain can pick up a good range of fake designer items here.

Worst Points

There is a lot of traffic throughout the area.

Accommodation

As Ruwi is predominantly a business area, accommodation is mainly in the form of low-cost apartments.

Shopping & Amenities

Ruwi is fantastic for little fabric shops and pirated DVDs. There is a KM Trading Centre, popular amongst locals and expats with many shops selling sunglasses, jewellery and cheap clothing.

Entertainment & Leisure

Star Cinema shows Arabic and Indian film releases. The City Cinema Ruwi is also a good option for subcontinent releases, and if you feel like sampling some authentic Pakistani kebabs and flat bread shop across to the restaurant opposite. There are also plenty of roadside Indian and Arabic restaurants in the area where you can get a decent curry or a tasty shawarma for pocket change. The Golden Oryx is an excellent dining venue, serving up Chinese and Thai food in an authentic setting. The Al Falaj Hotel houses the very well-known Japanese restaurant Tokyo Tara.

Healthcare

The Badr Al Samaa and Kims Oman Hospital are located near Ruwi Christian church, and there are also several homeopathic clinics, a Chinese herbal medicine clinic and various smaller clinics dotted around the area.

Ruwi is a thriving commercial centre

Education

Ruwi is home to the Pakistan School, but there are no educational establishments offering English or American curriculae.

Traffic & Parking

Traffic is very busy and parking can be a problem. You may find a spot on one of the roads behind Ruwi High Street, or near LuLu Centre (Darsayt).

Safety & Annoyances

With all the comings and goings of the local businesses in the area, and the resulting traffic, Ruwi can be noisy. Do remember to dress conservatively when walking around, especially near the High Street. This applies to both men and women.

Shatti Al Qurum

Shatti is home to the embassies and their staff, and is a highly desirable area near the beach and official offices.

Best Points

The area is close to a beautiful beach and a wide range of leisure options.

Worst Points

The beach gets busy, especially during low tide. Lifeguards are not always on hand and retreating tides can be strong.

Accommodation

Unfortunately living in Shatti Al Qurum is out of most people's reach. The area is characterised by huge villas with stained glass windows and mature trees, as well as rows of private parking spaces for numerous cars outside. There is an apartment block above Bareeq Al Shatti mall but it's on the pricey side.

Shopping & Amenities

There is plenty here – the Al Sarooj Plaza houses a big Al Fair and a selection of smaller shops. Next to the centre there is a Shell petrol station with a large 24 hour convenience store. Bareeq Al Shatti mall is a great spot for a coffee while Jawharat A'Shati is a handy shopping complex with restaurants, a post office, some souvenir shops, a WH Smith store, a party balloon outlet, a card shop and a nail bar for that all-important manicure.

Entertainment & Leisure

City Cinema, Shatti Al Qurum is popular at weekends – it shows all the current Hollywood releases although censors remove scenes that contravene Islamic sensibilities. The Al Deyar restaurant has a collection of outside tables and offers shisha and snacks late into the night. Another place to visit is Cafe Barberra next to the cinema for a quick tasty bite. Future Gym is next door and is well equipped for both men and women. There is also bowling in nearby Al Masa Mall and Ayana Spa for massages and beauty therapies.

The beach is a stone's throw away and popular for football, walking and jogging. Starbucks, Costa Coffee and D'Arcy's Kitchen all have outdoor seating areas that are great for watching the world go by; at Costa, there are tables practically on the sand.

The InterContinental Muscat has an excellent choice of restaurants and bars, as well as one of the best health clubs in the city.

Healthcare

Muscat Eye Laser Center is nearby and also Precision Dental Clinic, and The American Dental Centre. VLCC (24 695 157) offers dietary and skincare consultancy and treatments. If it's cosmetic surgery you're after, Emirates Medical Center is located in Al Sarooj Plaza.

Education

There are few educational facilities in the immediate area but there are many close by, including the Little Fingers nursery in Madinat Al Alam.

Traffic & Parking

There are many places for parking near the shops and cinema and also near the hospital. Traffic is not a problem but you may wait a while at roundabouts during rush hour.

Safety & Annoyances

This is a very popular area, especially near the beach area, so traffic and parking can be a problem.

Main Accommodation Options

Your employer may provide a house or apartment for you as part of your contract. However, if they provide you with an allowance instead, you will be able to choose what type of accommodation is suitable. The following options are available:

Apartment/Villa Sharing

You can cut your accommodation costs in half by sharing an apartment or villa with colleagues or friends. It's also a great way to avoid those long, lonely nights of feeling homesick and wondering what all your mates back home are up to. Some villas are so big that even if you've got numerous house mates, you should still be able to find a quiet corner. To look for shared accommodation or find a suitable housemate, check the notice boards outside supermarkets.

Standard Apartment

Apartments are found all over the Muscat area and vary from tiny studio apartments to vast penthouses. Muscat's hilly terrain means that people living on the top floors usually have a great view. Rents are usually between RO.350 and RO.1,350 per month.

Villas

Whether your budget stretches to a luxurious four-bedroom palace overlooking the beach in Qurum, or a more modest villa in outlying areas such as Al Azaiba or As Seeb, you should find something to fit your budget. If your villa has a swimming pool, central air conditioning, covered parking, electric gates, a big garden or outside maid's quarters, the price will be higher. A garden court is a group of small, semi-detached villas built around a communal garden (often with a swimming pool). There are quite a few of these found in the Madinat Al Sultan Qaboos area. Villas currently from RO.600 to RO.6,000 depending on size and location.

Serviced Apartments

Serviced apartments are fairly expensive and therefore more suited to shorter stays. Some people live in serviced apartments for a month or two until they find the house they want, or while they await the arrival of their family members or furniture shipment. Apartments can be rented on a daily, weekly, monthly or yearly basis and are fully furnished right down to the last detail, with a cleaning and laundry service included. The main contacts for serviced apartments are ASAS Oman (24 568 555), Al Noorah Gardens Guest House (24 697 203), and Safeer Hotel Suites.

Housing Abbreviations

BR Bedroom
C A/C Central air conditioning (usually included in the rent)
D/S Double storey villa
En suite Bedroom has a private bathroom
Ext S/Q Servant quarters located outside the villa
Fully fitted Includes major appliances (oven, refrigerator, washing machine)
Hall flat Apartment has an entrance hall (entrance doesn't open directly onto living room)
L/D Living/dining room area
Pvt garden Private garden
S/Q Servant quarters
S/S Single storey villa
Shared pool Pool is shared with other villas in compound
W A/C Window air conditioning (often indicates older building)
W/robes Built-in wardrobes

Finding A Home

If you drive around Muscat, you'll see several 'To Let' signs outside available properties, so if you have a preferred area in mind this is a good way to look for a house. You may also be able to rent directly from the landlord and therefore avoid paying agents' commission. However, a reliable estate agent can save you a lot of time and effort by arranging viewings. Look out also for properties nearing completion; try and find the watchman who will give you the landlord's number. Browse the classified ads in the local newspapers, or keep an eye on supermarket noticeboards.

If you use an agent, you have the choice of local agencies or internationally recognised ones. You can organise an agent through your company PRO but it's always wise to check that the recommended agent is a registered real estate broker, authorised to conduct leasing in Muscat. Hamptons International is a highly reputable real estate agent, which comes highly recommended by the expat community. Reputable agencies will show you a selection of suitable properties, assist with the paperwork and ensure that the required municipality procedures are followed. Landlords should pay the agent's commission and you should bear no cost or 'finder's fee'.

Real Estate Agents

Al Habib & Co Block 133, Ruwi Street, Bldg 560, 968 24 700 247, *alhabibonline.com*
Al Qandeel Real Estate Services Nr Bareeq Al Shatti, 968 24 643 800, *alqandeel.com*
Better Homes Way 2710, Building 1212, 968 24 699 855, *bhomes.com/oman*
Cluttons & Partners Hatat House, Ground Flr, Hatat Complex, 968 24 564 250, *oman.cluttons.com*
Eamaar Real Estate Nr Emirates Airline Office, 968 24 647 666, *eamaar.com*
Gulf Property World 968 24 697 588, *gpw-oman.com*
Hamptons International Al Manahil Bldg, 968 24 699 773, *hamptons-int.com*
Hay Al Rahbah Property Management Services, 968 24 604 811, *assarain.com*
Hilal Properties Al Husoon Bldg, Nr Shatti Plaza & City Cinema, 968 24 600 688, *hilalprp.com.om*
OmanHomes.com Arzat Bld, Office 102, 968 24 488 087, *omanhomes.com*
The Wave Muscat Rentals 968 24 534 400, *thewavemuscat.com*

Buying Property

Being able to buy a property in Oman if you are an expat is a new phenomenon – until the relevant change in the law was announced by royal decree in

2006, non-nationals could only rent accommodation. Expats can only buy property within areas designated as 'integrated tourist complexes' or ITCs. ITC licences are granted by the Ministry of Tourism, and have so far been approved for The Wave, Muscat Golf and Country Club, and the Muriya Jebel Sifah project. Properties within these complexes can be bought for investment purposes, meaning that you can buy one to let out to a third party. You are also permitted to sell your property at any time after the construction is completed.

It is important to note that in the event of the death of a property owner, the laws regarding transfer of ownership are governed by the laws of that person's home country. It is essential to have a valid will in place if you are considering purchasing property in Oman. If no heir applies to inherit the property within one year, the Ministry of Tourism will manage the property for 15 years, after which time ownership reverts to the Government of Oman.

Property Developers

Eamaar Real Estate Nr Emirates Airline Office, 968 24 647 666, *eamaar.com*
Muscat Hills Golf & Country Club Nr Muscat International Airport, 968 24 514 080, *muscathills.com*
Oman Tourism Development Company SAOC (OMRAN) Way 3341, Al Azaiba, 968 24 391 111, *omran.om*
The Wave Muscat 968 24 534 400, *thewavemuscat.com*

Mortgages

Since the government announced that expatriates would be entitled to purchase freehold property in certain developments, some of the banks have started offering mortgage options to expats. Mortgage conditions are different for expats as opposed to locals, especially in terms of how many years you can repay your loan for and how much deposit you have to put down. The mortgage industry is still in its infancy, and as more freehold residential developments near completion, there will be more on offer.

Renting

Although foreigners have been given the legal right to purchase property on certain developments in Oman, renting remains the main option for accommodation. In Oman, rent is usually paid annually and not monthly. This is good news for the landlord, but bad news for tenants who often have to come up with a sizeable lump sum to cover their rent for the whole year. If your company provides you with an annual accommodation allowance, then they will usually cover your rent upfront. If not, it's worth negotiating for your employer to pay the upfront sum, which you can then pay back on a monthly basis through salary deductions.

There remains a steady demand in the rental market (especially for better quality properties). The golden rule is that if you see a house you love, sign on the dotted line as soon as possible or someone else will snap it up. Rents vary considerably depending on the size of the accommodation and location. The average rent for a two-bedroom apartment in Muscat ranges between RO.350 and RO.700 while rent for a three-bedroom villa ranges from RO.600 to RO.1,500. Sharing accommodation provides a cost-effective way of living if you don't mind giving up some of your privacy, but be aware that mixed cohabitation is illegal unless you are related to your housemates.

Apart from your rent (paid annually), you will face additional costs when moving into a new house. These might include:
- A 3% municipality tax
- A security deposit (refundable when you vacate the premises, minus any damages)
- A deposit for your water and electricity accounts
  If you are renting a villa with a garden, your water costs will be higher since the grass and plants will need watering every day in Oman's hot climate.

The Lease

Your lease is an important document and will state, in addition to the financial terms, what you are liable for in terms of maintenance and what your landlord's responsibilities are. It is important that you (or your company PRO, who may have more knowledge about the pitfalls of rental contracts) read through the lease and discuss any points of contention before you sign it. You may be able to negotiate on certain clauses in your contract, such as how many cheques you can use to pay your annual rent, who is responsible for maintenance, and how much security deposit you should pay.

The entire leasing process in Muscat is governed by well-drafted legislation and the lease is prepared on a standard Municipality form. The standard lease, which can have minor changes made to it, is normally for one year (which is automatically renewable unless three months notice is given before expiry by either the landlord or the tenant). Annual rent for villas is often requested in advance in one cheque, although it is sometimes possible to agree with the landlord that six-month's rent is paid upon signing of the lease and the remainder of the amount by post-dated cheque.

To take out a personal lease (in your name, not your employer's name), you need to be a resident. The landlord will need a copy of your passport (with visa page), a no objection letter (NOC) from your employer, a copy of your salary certificate, a signed rent cheque and up to three post-dated cheques covering the remainder of the annual rent (the number of cheques depends on your landlord). If the rented property will be in your employer's name, then the landlord needs a copy of the company's trade licence, a passport copy of the person signing the rent cheque, and the rent cheque itself.

It is the landlord's responsibility to register the lease with the relevant municipality. The registering of leases showing rental at less than the real amount is against the law, and it is also a big risk for tenants, who will have no protection in the event of a dispute.

The landlord must ensure that the house is in good condition before you move in, so don't sign the lease until he has made the improvements you think need to be done (like painting, filling in wall holes, regrouting bathrooms and servicing the air-conditioning units).

Rent Disputes

It goes without saying that there are distinct advantages to keeping friendly relations with your landlord. There are no hard-and-fast laws protecting the tenant and therefore it pays to stay on your landlord's good side. If you have a disagreement with him that reaches a stalemate, the Ministry of Justice (24 697 699 800 77 777) will assist.

Moving

Moving house can be stressful, especially if you are moving to a new country. You can reduce the stress by planning the move well, and enlisting the help of a professional moving service. When moving your furniture to or from Oman, you can ship it by air or by sea. Airfreight is quick, and is good for small consignments and the essential things you can't live without. But to move a whole houseful of furniture you need to arrange a container by sea, and this will take several weeks. You can get a 20 or 40 foot container, depending on how much stuff you are moving. If you're really lucky and you know someone moving at the same time as you, you could share a container.

Customs

Customs officers may retain certain items such as CDs, DVDs, books and even photo albums, for further investigation. You will get these items back once they have been checked, although it may take several weeks.

Either way, ensure that you use a reputable company to pack your goods and make all the arrangements. If you are unlucky enough to move to Oman in the height of the summer (July or August), your belongings will travel at sustained high temperatures in the container ship, so some of your plastic items may warp and your china might have little surface cracks from the heat. A reputable moving company should be able to offer you advice on how to minimise damage by using proper packaging. A company with a wide international network is usually the best option.

When your shipment arrives in Muscat you may be called to the customs department so that you can be present when your crates are opened. This is done to ensure that you are not bringing anything illegal or inappropriate into the country. Someone from your company (such as the PRO) may be able to stand in for you, and you will only have to go if something suspect is found. The process can be exhausting, because the search can take a few hours, often out in the heat, and you will have to watch your carefully packed boxes being unceremoniously rummaged through.

Removal Companies

Gulf Agency Company (GAC) GAC Building, Dohat Al Adab St, 968 24 477 800, *gac.com/oman*
Inchcape Shipping Services Al Noor St, Way 3109 Bldg 483, Ground floor, 968 24 701 291, *iss-shipping.com*
Khimji Ramdas Shipping 968 24 795 901, *khimji.com*
Middle East Shipping & Transport Co Getco Towers, SBGH, CBD Area, 968 24 793 741, *suhailbahwangroup.com*
Yusuf Bin Ahmed Kanoo & Co Jibroo, 968 24 712 252, *kanooshipping.com*

Smooth Moves

- Get more than one quote – some companies will match lower quotes to get the job
- Make sure that all items are covered by insurance
- Make sure that you have a copy of the inventory and that each item is listed
- Don't be shy about requesting packers to repack items if you are not satisfied
- Take photos of the packing process, to use for evidence if you need to claim
- Carry customs-restricted goods (DVDs, videos or books) with you: it's easier to open a suitcase in an air-conditioned airport than empty a box out in the sun

Relocation Experts

Relocation experts offer a range of services to help you settle into your new life in Oman as quickly as possible. Practical help ranges from finding accommodation or schools for your children to connecting a telephone or information on medical care. In addition, they will often offer advice on the way of life in the city, putting people in touch with social networks to help them get established in their new lives. Sununu Muscat (sununumuscat.com) is a relocation specialist that can help to ease your move to Oman.

Furniture Shopping

If you are a new arrival in Oman and moving into a new home, chances are that you will need to buy some furniture. Most properties are unfurnished, and that means not only will you have no furniture, but in most cases you will have no electrical items or white goods either (not even a cooker) and not all villas have fitted wardrobes.

Oman is home to several big furniture shops so no matter what your tastes are, you'll find something you like. A lot of furniture is locally or regionally made, and is often extremely ornate. Simpler styles can be found in IDdesign (Markaz Al Bahja) and Home Centre (City Plaza). IKEA is just a few hours down the road in Dubai, so you can load your car up with flat-pack furniture.

Second-hand Furniture

Like any country that attracts a lot of expats, the population of Muscat is fairly transient, with people coming and going all the time. As a result there is quite a busy second-hand furniture market and you should have no trouble furnishing your new home cheaply. Keep your eyes on the supermarket noticeboards. Look out for adverts for garage sales, where families will sell the stuff they are not taking home at rock-bottom prices. Check out muscatads.com and oman.dubizzle.com for some bargains.

Utilities & Services

Water and electricity services are supplied by the government and are generally efficient and reliable. There is no mains gas service but bottled gas (LPG) is available for cooking. Power cuts – lasting from a few minutes to several hours – occur every now and then but rarely pose a major inconvenience. It helps to have a stock of candles and torches handy, just in case. Utility bills are paid at Oman Investment & Finance Company (OIFC) or through your bank or ATM. To use the ATM service, you have to register your details by phone (the bank will have the number).

Once you are registered, it means you can pay your bills outside banking hours, without having to stand in queues. The bank transfer system is slower than paying directly to OIFC so allow a few extra days so that you don't get disconnected. Wherever you pay, make sure your bill is stamped and that you keep it for reference – you may need it for proof of payment at a later date.

Electricity

The electricity supply in Oman is 220/240 volts and 50 cycles. Sockets correspond to the British three-pin plug but many appliances are sold with two-pin plugs, so you will need lots of adaptors (available in any supermarket or corner shop) – better still, change all the plugs.

Water

Though some water comes from natural wells, there is not enough to service the country's needs so most of the supply is from the sea, processed at the desalination plant at Al Ghubrah. The main supply of water is very reliable but not all of Muscat's residential areas are connected to it. If your house is not, you will have to rely on a water bowser to fill up your tank every two or three days. Water trucks for domestic use are blue (the green ones carry non-potable water, for municipal garden watering and industrial use) and they are everywhere – just flag one down or ask your neighbours which 'water-man' they use. You will often see several trucks filling up at one of the water wells dotted around the city. Expect to pay around RO.25 a month for truck water. Oman Oasis will deliver (800 71222).

Hot Water

The water in your cold taps gets so hot in summer that you can turn off your water heaters – in fact this is the only way to get cooler water, since your hot water unit is usually inside the house, away from the sun's glare. You know winter's coming when you have to turn the water heater on again!

If you are connected to the main supply, keep an eye on your bills and water meter; if you have an underground leak within your property boundary you could be held responsible for a hefty bill, even if you weren't aware of the leak. In the heat of summer, it's unlikely you'll have the chance to take a refreshing cold shower. Water tanks are usually located on the roof, where they are heated to near boiling point by the sun, and you can't even stand under the shower because it's so hot. Between April and October, the only way to get a cool shower is to turn off your water heater, and use the hot water tap.

Oman's water is safe to drink as it is purified eight times. However, it is heavily chlorinated (which affects the taste) so most people prefer to drink one of the many locally bottled mineral waters. Apart from the coffee shops, all restaurants will supply bottled water. If in doubt, ask for a sealed bottle to be brought to your table. You can get 20 litre bottles of purified water for use at home, either with a hand pump or a water cooler. These are available from shops and

APARTMENTS ARE COOL...

You can expect a higher A/C bill in a villa – not only is it probably bigger than your average apartment, but many apartment buildings include air-conditioning costs in the rent. Oman doesn't have mains gas but there are many suppliers of bottled gas. Gas canisters are available in various sizes, and you pay RO.15–20 as a deposit, and RO.3 per refill. Gas is delivered to houses by orange trucks that drive around residential areas. If you need gas, just flag one of the trucks down; popular times for the gas run are late mornings, early evenings and on Fridays. Once you've found a supplier, get his mobile number and you'll be able to call him whenever you need more gas. Most will deliver any time up to 9pm.

supermarkets, and you pay a RO.6 deposit per bottle, and refills cost RO.1. Alternatively, get a company to deliver the water to your house.

Rubbish Disposal & Recycling

The rubbish disposal system in Oman is efficient – it has to be, because the health hazards of mounds of domestic waste festering in the sweltering heat would be too great. Large metal containers (skips) are placed at regular intervals along residential streets and you just chuck your daily rubbish bags into them. Skips are emptied regularly by rubbish trucks (although not before the local 'bin cats' have had a good rummage). Since the beginning of 2013, Muscat Municipality has carried out a pilot scheme in certain areas (Al Azaiba, Mawaleh, Al Khoud) in which it has replaced the large trash containers at the side of the road with small ones which have been allocated to each individual household. At part of this scheme, municipality workers collect garbage from the houses every morning and residents are asked to leave the bins outside their homes before 5am each day. If the scheme is a success, it will be extended to cover other areas in Muscat and other parts of the country.

Waste management is a challenging issue for Oman as the per capita waste generation is more than 1.5kg per day, among the highest worldwide. The country is yet to realise the recycling potential of its municipal waste and most of the solid waste including paper, plastics, metals and glass is sent to authorised and unauthorised dumpsites for disposal and this is causing environmental and health issues. The government is working on this issue and hopes to establish 16 engineered landfills, 65 waste transfer stations and four waste treatment plants in different parts of the country by 2015.

The government does not provide recycling facilities as yet but there are still ways in which you can recycle some household products. For example, the *Muscat Daily* newspaper will collect any waste paper that you have (call them on 800 76000) and water bottles can be placed in recycling bins throughout Muscat (Royal Flight School, American British Academy).

Sewerage

All properties in Oman have septic tanks, which must be emptied on a regular basis by one of the yellow sewerage trucks.

The cost for having a septic tank emptied is between RO.20 and RO.25 each time, and you'll probably have to get it done about once a year (you'll know when it's time from the smell). If you need to order a sewerage truck, the easiest way is to call the number on the back of one of the yellow tankers, or ask a neighbour. Alternatively, call Haya Water (800 77111). Haya Water (haya.com.om) is currently

undertaking a RO.350 million sewerage recycling project which hopes to connect 80% of all properties in Muscat by 2018. This means that the existing septic tanks will be replaced with a modern piped waste water system connected to the main treatment plants.

Telephone

It is unlikely that your accommodation will have an active phone line when you move in. To apply for a landline connection you should submit the following documents to Omantel: a completed application form (in English), your passport (and a copy), your visa, and a copy of your tenancy agreement. Once you have submitted your application it will be one to two weeks before you are connected. Be warned that is has been known to take much longer. If you need additional phone sockets, be sure to ask at the time of application. You pay a deposit of RO.200, and RO.10 per line installation. Quarterly rental is RO.3 and calls are charged according to distance and time, ranging from 3 to 75 baisas per minute (emergency calls are free). Off-peak rates apply on long distance calls all day Friday and on national commercial holidays. Omantel offers many additional services such as call waiting, call forwarding and conference calling.

Thuraya

Omantel offers the Thuraya system – a satellite-based GSM (mobile phone) service that is valuable for emergency communication when travelling outside standard GSM range. Although Oman's populated areas have GSM network coverage there are still empty spaces with no reception.

If you're a regular camper and wadi basher, you may consider it worth buying a Thuraya phone – especially if you travel with small children or need to be accessible at all times for some reason. Thuraya currently provides access to 99 countries in Europe, the Middle East, Africa and Asia. The handset costs around RO.300 and doubles as a GPS receiver.

Broadband packages are also available through Omantel, Nawras and Friendi, through either a dongle or wireless router. Packages vary from around RO.20 per month.

You can also use the Jibreen service – a prepaid phone card that can be used to make local or international calls from any landline or payphone. The card is available in denominations of RO.1.5, RO.3 and RO.5, is valid for 90 days from first call, and is charged at the payphone tariff. For more information and details visit the Omantel website (omantel.net.om), which lists services and charges.

Omantel remains the sole provider of landline and internet services. The organisation was recently privatised and has invested in the latest technology to enable it to offer an efficient service. The main complaint is the slow speed of internet access, but as the country moves increasingly towards broadband and wireless connection, this is less of an issue. The government's 'access for all' policy keeps prices low, and rates often decrease but hardly ever increase.

Mobile Phones

In 2005, Nawras began operating as an alternative mobile phone service provider in Oman, ending the monopoly held by the government-owned Oman Telecommunications Company (Omantel). Friendi Mobile and Renna mobile services came to the market in 2009, offering great coverage and flexible packages including pre-paid recharge cards for amounts as low as 500 baisas. SIM cards start at RO. 2 and users can call fellow Friendi customers for 39 baisas 24 hours a day. Customer service is offered in a number of languages including Arabic, English, Malayalam, Hindi, Urdu and Bengali. For help with your GSM, voicemail, SMS or other mobile services, call 1234 (toll free).

Friendi, Omantel, Nawras and Renna offer a huge range of services and it might be difficult to choose the provider you like best. The companies usually have information desks in various malls, so go along for a chat with one of their representatives.

Bill Payment

Telephone bills are sent monthly and include rental charges and call costs. Only international calls are itemised on the bill, although the number of local and mobile calls and text messages is listed. You can pay your landline bill at the Omantel office in Al Khuwair (behind Al Zawawi mosque, next to the ice rink) which is easy and efficient, and the best way to ensure continuity of service. You can also pay through some banks (such as Bank Muscat or HSBC) or through the ATM, but these services have a processing time of up to 10 days. You can check your GSM and internet bills on Omantel's website. Apply online for a PIN and just log in to find out how much you owe (for more information on paying your landline and mobile bills for Omantel, see omantel.net.om). If you do not pay when you receive your bill, Omantel will helpfully send an email reminder. If you ignore that, they will cut you off without further warning.

Landlines continue to receive calls for several days but outgoing calls will be barred. If you do get cut off, take your bill to the Al Khuwair office, pay all outstanding debts and a reconnection fee of RO.1, and your service will be reconnected immediately. Always keep your bills and receipts for proof of payment. If you are a Nawras post-paid GSM subscriber, you can pay your bills at certain banks, online, through your ATM, over the phone, or at a Nawras store. See their website (nawras.om) for more information.

Missing Mobile

Lost your mobile? Call 1234 to temporarily or permanently disconnect your number. If you use the Omantel network you will have to provide the number of the document that you presented when you applied for your SIM card (probably your passport or labour card). To replace the SIM, you'll need to go to a branch of Oman Mobile with your essential documents in hand and a fee of RO.7. As soon as you have the new SIM card, your old one will be permanently disconnected. You can keep the same telephone number. There is a similar procedure to be followed with the other network providers.

No Mobile When Mobile

It is against the law to use a mobile phone handset while driving, so if you like to talk behind the wheel, use a hands-free kit. Failure to do so can result in you being pulled over and given a spot fine of RO.10.

Internet

Mobile and internet connections in Oman are growing tremendously and a report in 2012 by the International Telecommunication Union (ITU), a United Nations agency, praised the Sultanate for its success in the telecom sector. The number of internet users increased from 20% of the population in 2008 to 80% of the population in 2011. Extensive use of internet cafes and the younger generation participating in social media activities and blogging has contributed to the increase in the number of internet users, according to the report *Measuring the Information Society*. There are now many internet service providers in Oman including Omantel (omantel.om), Nawras (nawras.om), Friendi (friendimobile.com) and Renna (rennamobile.com).

No Naughty Sites

While using the internet in Oman you will have to do so under the watchful eye of a proxy. Sites that are considered harmful to the political, religious, moral or cultural sensitivities of the country are inaccessible.

The Telecommunication Regulatory Authority (TRA) in Oman aims to protect society values and this is regularly done through censorship of the internet, with the actual censorship done through automation software operated by ISPs. There is no publicly available criteria on the grounds on which websites are blocked but in general it is not a major problem for internet users in Oman as no major websites such as Google, Wikipedia, YouTube or Facebook have been blocked. Skype has been blocked with the reason given by the TRA that it believes that Skype should come to Oman and apply for a license before offering its services. However, it is widely believed that the reason Skype and other VoIP services are blocked is because the TRA wishes to protect the financial interests of local telecommunication companies.

Log & Surf

This facility allows you to surf the internet without a contract or subscription to Omantel. All you need is a computer with a modem, and a phone line. The charge will be billed to the line you are connecting from. To connect, just double click on 'My Computer', then on 'Dial-up Networking' and then on 'Make a New Connection'. Type in 'Omantel' for both your username and password, dial 1312 and click connect. Charges are a little higher – 25 baisas per minute from a landline and 50 baisas per minute from a mobile (to access the internet using your mobile you need to subscribe to the data service, for an extra RO.3 per month).

Satellite TV

Satellite offers an enormous choice of programmes and channels, and most expats have at least one satellite provider. You will need to pay for any equipment you need (dish and decoder) as well as installation. You can usually choose from a number of packages depending on what kind of programmes you like to see (for example, if you are not interested in watching sport, you can subscribe to a package that does not include any sports channels). There are quite a few 'free-to-air' satellite channels, and to view these you need to get the dish and decoder but then you pay no subscription fees. However, most are not in English. Equipment can be bought from main dealers or any of the small electrical shops. Second-hand dishes and decoders are often advertised on supermarket noticeboards and in the classifieds. Many apartment blocks have satellite systems already fitted. If not, ask your landlord about a cost-share system.

Telephone, Internet & Satellite TV Providers

Firstnet 968 26 844 076, *firstnettv.net*
Friendi Mobile Madinat Al Sultan Qaboos Centre, Al Balushi Building, Ground floor, 968 98 400 000, *friendimobile.om*
Nawras Airport Road, 968 95 022 509, *nawras.om*
Omantel 968 24 241 999, *omantel.om*
Orbit Showtime Network (OSN) 968 24 489 277, *osn.com*
Renna Villa 373 18th November St, 968 24 618 300, *rennamobile.com*

Household Insurance

As you probably won't own your house in Oman, it's easy to take a more relaxed attitude to household insurance. The Sultanate is very safe and the crime rate extremely low, but burglaries do occur and, if they do, it's predominantly expat residential areas that are targeted. Therefore, it's imperative that you have home insurance. Many national and international insurance companies have offices in Muscat – check the Yellow Pages for details. To take out a policy you will need confirmation of your address, your passport, a list of household contents and valuation, and invoices for any items over RO.250.

Domestic Services

Having maintenance done in your villa or apartment is usually just a case of making a quick call to the landlord. Remember that he is responsible for any plumbing or electrical work that needs to be done (unless otherwise stated in your lease), and will probably use a specific maintenance company every time. This is good if they know what they are doing, but bear in mind that landlords will often go for 'cheaper' rather than 'better'.

If you need some work done that your landlord won't pay for, you can use the services of a plumber, electrician or handyman. The table lists companies specialising in carpet cleaning, carpentry, plumbing, painting and electrical services, although these companies may also offer other services too. Often word of mouth is the best way to find a trustworthy company that shows up on time, does the job that needs doing, and doesn't charge you an arm and a leg.

Domestic Services Providers

Al Ahid Trading & Contracting 968 24 817 509
Al Wadi Al Kabir Carpentry Way 4223, Block 142, 968 24 812 856
Bahwan Engineering Co 968 24 597 510, *bahwanengineering.com*
Cape East & Partners 968 24 537 514, *capeplc.com*
International Sanitation Co Way 5222, 968 24 592 351, *albahja.com*
London Cleaning & Maintenance 968 24 478 341, *alyafeigroup.com*
National Electrical Contractors 968 24 571 363, *necoman.com*
Ocean Centre 968 24 707 833
Ruwi Furnishing Risail Commercial Complex, Clock Tower R/A, 968 24 521 118
Shafan Trading Old Road, 968 24 692 058
Specialised Technical Contractors 968 24 788 640
West Coast Trading J & P Azaiba Bldg, Qaboos St, 968 24 490 477

Domestic Help

One of the perks of expat life is how easy and common it is for people to have domestic help. Most expat families have some sort of home help, whether it's a full-time, live-in housemaid, or a part-time ironing lady. Most domestic helpers come from India, Sri Lanka, Bangladesh, Indonesia, Pakistan or the Philippines. A report by the National Centre for Statistics (NCSI) revealed that the number of domestic female and male workers in Oman reached 225,000 in 2013 – an increase of 25% since 2010. Some 91% of domestic workers are women, mostly coming from India and Indonesia.

Azooz Manpower (24 831 448) and Friends Manpower Services (24 489 268) are two domestic help agencies in Oman. When you employ a domestic helper, you must sponsor them and provide accommodation. Most villas have servant quarters (an independent room, usually fairly small, with a private bathroom). You have a duty of care to your domestic helper, and you must make all the arrangements (and payments) for their residence visa, medical test, and labour card. You are also obliged to pay for their medical bills and provide them with a return flight to their home country every two years.

If you go through an agency, it will cost you approximately RO.1,000 to hire a housemaid from abroad. This fee will include the price of the flight, the price of the employment visa and agency fee. To protect against the abuse of housemaids, many countries have now laid down certain stipulations which must be adhered to before housemaids from these countries will be allowed to work in Oman. For example, India's Ministry of Overseas Indian Affairs had introduced several conditions in the service agreements of housemaids being brought into Oman and other parts of the region. One condition is that employers will be required to produce a salary certificate of at least RO.1,000 per month and employers must also provide a bank guarantee of RO.1,100 when recruiting a housemaid. This security will be used for the repatriation of the housemaid in case her employer fails to honour the agreement. The amount is reimbursable to the employer at the end of the agreement. Housemaids from India should be between the ages of 30 and 50 years and the minimum wage per month is RO.75. Similarly, the government of the Philippines has stipulated that the minimum wage for a housemaid from its country must be RO.154. It is illegal for a housemaid to work for anyone other than her sponsor but, nonetheless, there are many maids willing to work at cleaning and babysitting on a part-time basis. Usually you can find these ladies by word of mouth or on the Muscat Maids Facebook page. Charges are usually RO.2–RO.2.500 per hour plus the price of the taxi.

Sponsoring a maid is a substantial financial commitment so make sure you have the right person. The best way to find a good helper is by word of mouth, so keep your ear to the ground in case a 'friend of a friend' is going back home and leaving behind their loyal, trustworthy maid who is good with pets and kids. You could also look on supermarket notice boards and in newspaper classifieds, but remember to check references if you are taking on someone unknown. There are several reliable maid agencies who can recommend a good maid and in some cases, help you with the paperwork.

Laundry Services

Although there are no self-service laundrettes, there are numerous laundries in Muscat. As well as dry cleaning and laundry, they all offer an ironing service. If you have specific cleaning or ironing instructions, make sure these are noted when you drop off your laundry – creases in trousers, for instance, are standard, so speak up if you don't want them pressed into your jeans.

Compensation policies for lost or damaged items vary. But even though some laundries may seem disorganised from the piles and piles of stuff behind the counter waiting to be ironed or collected, losses are rare. Some of the more upmarket laundry chains may offer a pick-up and drop-off service.

Laundry Companies

Al Tayyibat Services Nr American British Academy, 968 24 695 599
Grand Sultanate Laundry Hamriya Roundabout, 968 24 833 097
Ibn Iqbal Trading Est Nr O I B, 968 24 540 082
Kwik-Kleen Al Beit Al Akdhar Compound, 968 24 816 749, *ashaoman.net*
Snowhite Dry Cleaners Jibroo, 968 24 597 085, *snowhite-oman.com*
Wadi Al Khuwair Laundry Nr Zawawi Mosque, 968 24 695 825

Postal Services

There is no postal delivery service to home addresses, so everyone gets their mail delivered to a post office box. All mail is routed through the Central Post Office and then distributed to post office boxes in central locations. Most people use their company address, but it is also possible to get an individual PO Box number – just apply through your local post office. The postal system is fairly reliable and efficient but on occasion parcels will be returned, deemed 'undeliverable' and you'll have to pay to get them back. There is a regular airmail service and an express mail service. Most leading courier services also have branches in Oman.

Postal services are provided solely by the government-operated General Post Office (GPO). The GPO is reasonably efficient, with standard airmail letters taking 10-14 days to reach the USA, Europe or Australia. The GPO offers an express mail service (called EMS), and letters posted using the EMS get delivered in half the normal time. Letters cost from 50 baisas internally (15g maximum) and from 250 baisas internationally (10g maximum). Opening times vary but most branches open from 7.30am and close at 2pm, Sunday to Thursday and some have a short evening session. They are closed on Fridays but some open on Saturdays until 11am. For details, check out omanpost.om

Post Office Locator
Al Harthy Complex: (24 563 534)
7.30am to 2.30pm and 7pm to 9pm
Madinat Al Sultan Qaboos: (24 697 083)
8am to 2pm
Al Hamriya: (24 789 311)
8am to 2pm and 4pm to 8pm
Muscat: (24 738 547)
7.30am to 2pm and Thursday 8am to 11am
Mina Al Fahal: (24 565 465)
8am tp 2pm
Ruwi: (24 701 651)
7.30am to 2.30pm and 4pm to 6pm
As Seeb: (24 519 922)
8am to 3pm and 5pm to midnight
SQU campus: (24 413 333 ext 3161)
8am to 2pm
Jawaharat A'Shati Complex: (24 692 181)
9am to 1.30pm

Courier Services
The major international courier companies operate in Oman, although some limit their deliveries to Muscat only. Aramex (aramex. com) provides a 'Shop & Ship' service, which sets up a mailbox for you in both the UK and the US. You pay a small fee to set up the mailbox, and then you can get online purchases delivered there. Aramex will then deliver the contents of your mailbox to you in Oman. The rate is $15 for the first half-kilogramme, and $9 for every additional half-kilogramme. It's a great solution if the company you are buying from doesn't ship to the Middle East.

Courier Companies
Aramex Al Khuwair, Nr Nizwa University Office, Service road, Way 3533,114 Mutrah, 968 24 473 000 *aramex.com*
DHL Way 7777, Street 62, Exhibition St, 968 24 520 100, *dhl.com.om*
Federal Express (FedEx) 968 24 833 311, *fedex.com*
TNT 968 24 477 870, *tnt.com*
UPS Dohat Al Adab St, 968 24 683 943, *ups.com*

DRIVING IN OMAN

Compared to some other countries in the region, the driving on Oman's roads is fairly calm. However, there are still a lot of motorists who drive recklessly and with scant regard for the safety of pedestrians and other road users. The government promotes road safety with a number of high-profile campaigns such as the Salim & Salimah – Safe & Sound campaign (see salimandsalimah.org for more information).

If you are a new arrival in Oman and find the road conditions scary, the best advice is to get behind the wheel as quickly as possible. Your first few drives will be stressful but it won't take long to get the hang of defensive driving. The roads are monitored closely by the Royal Oman Police (ROP).

Drinking and driving is illegal – there is a zero-tolerance policy, so even if you've only had half a shandy or a bowl of trifle laced with sherry, don't get behind the wheel. Road blocks (where police pull drivers off the road and make them do a breathalyser test) are infrequent, but if you have an accident and you have any alcohol in your bloodstream, you are in very hot water. Not only will your insurance be invalidated, but you could face a hefty fine or even jail time.

Using your mobile phone while driving is prohibited, unless you are connected to a hands-free device. If caught, your fine could be as much as RO.70 (that's one expensive phone call). Always carry your driving licence with you. Failure to produce it in a spot check will result in a fine. If you have any queries on driving licences or traffic regulations, contact the ROP Directorate of Traffic on 24 510 227/228 or visit the website (rop.gov.om).

Driving Licence

Visitors do not need a temporary Oman licence to drive in Oman. All they need is a valid international licence or a licence from their home country (GCC and European nationalities only). The traffic law permits expatriates on a visit visa to drive rental cars for up to three months. Expats on employment visas, however, should have Oman driving licences.

The following driving licences are transferable without taking a driving test: GCC countries, Australia, Belgium, Brunei, Canada, Denmark, Finland, France, the Netherlands, Ireland, Italy, Japan (after translation), Jordan, Lebanon, Luxembourg, Monaco, Morocco, New Zealand, Norway, Spain, Sweden, Tunisia, Turkey, United States of America, United Kingdom, Germany.

Permanent Licence

To drive a light vehicle in Oman, you must be over 17 years of age (you have to be over 21 to drive heavy vehicles or trucks). Residents from many countries, including the UK and the US, can simply exchange their driving licence from their home country for an Oman licence. The only condition is that they have had the licence for one year or more. It costs RO.20 to transfer the licence, which can be done at the Directorate General of Traffic at various locations around the country (in Muscat, one is located close to Muscat International School in Qurum and another is close to the Oman International Exhibition Centre in As Seeb). Take along essential documents and you will need to have an eye test done before you go.

Strangely, married women have to take their marriage certificate and a letter of no-objection from their husband. Your company's PRO will usually go with you to help you through the process. If you do not have a driving licence from one of the 'automatic exchange' countries, you will need to take a driving test. The first step is to obtain a learning permit – start by picking up an application form from the traffic police headquarters. To do this you'll need to take your essential documents and RO.5. You will be given an eye test at the Traffic Police. Your next step is to find a good driving school. There are a few schools, but many instructors work individually and you will find them by word of mouth. Many operate from the main entrance of Qurum Natural Park.

They drive white cars with easily recognisable red diagonal stripes. There are female driving instructors for women, although no female test inspectors.

When your instructor feels you are ready to take the test, you will have to sit a three-part driving test, consisting of a reversing test, a road test and a Highway Code test. The first involves reversing between oil drums placed in two parallel rows barely wider than your car; you have to get it right first time and you can't take the road or theoretical tests until you've passed this test (known, with fear and loathing, as 'the barrels'). Once you've passed all three tests, you have to apply for your licence through the authorized driving school. The police are known to be strict in issuing new licences and this process can take several months. You'll need perseverance.

Oman driving licences are valid for 10 years and can be renewed at the traffic police headquarters. To renew your licence you will need a driving licence renewal form (stamped by your sponsor), your expired licence, a copy of your labour card and a passport copy.

Driving Licence Documents

- Licence Exchange form with signature and stamp of sponsor
- An NOC from your sponsor/company (in Arabic)
- Two photographs
- Passport and resident visa copy
- Original driving licence along with a photocopy (and translation, if requested by the Traffic Police)
- Blood Group Certificate

Additional Requirements For Female Applicants:

- NOC letter addressed to the Director of Licensing brought in person by the guardian or substitute

Oman has a modern road infrastructure

- If married, marriage certificate or birth certificate of a child
- If unemployed, a copy of husband's labour card and a letter from his sponsor/company

Driving Schools
Al Farsan Driving School Nr Al Qurum Natural Park, 968 24 565 779
Morning Star Driving School 968 24 478 506
Muscat Driving School Al Khoudh, 968 24 546 283
Oman Driving Institute 968 24 596 921

Buying A Vehicle

To own a car in Oman you must have a labour or resident card. If you decide to buy a car, you'll find that it is considerably cheaper to buy, maintain and run a car in Oman compared with most other countries. Every expat resident is allowed to own up to three vehicles. Whether you are buying a brand new car or a second-hand one, when it's time to close the deal you'll need to present certain documents.

You'll need to provide your essential documents, a vehicle purchase form (available from the police station or the showroom), plus your valid driving licence and a copy. The vehicle purchase form should be signed by your sponsor or company, and then taken to your insurance provider. In the case of a private sale, the seller should be with you, as the car must be insured in your name before the registration can be finalised.

Once the car is registered, you will get a vehicle registration card (a 'mulkia'). You should always have the mulkia with you in the car, although many people keep a copy in the car and leave the original mulkia at home.

registration and arranging finance. They will also usually offer good warranties and free servicing for the first few years. Unless you are paying cash for the car, you will need to get a bank loan or leave a post-dated cheque for every month of the finance period (typically 12, 24 or 36 months). When you collect your car you will drive with green licence plates until the vehicle registration is complete.

New Car Dealers
Al Jenaibi International Automobiles Way 533, 968 24 567 108, *bmw-oman.com*
Auto Plus International Commercial House, 968 24 478 080, *autoplusoman.net*
Bahwan Automotive Centre 968 24 578 000, *saudbahwangroup.com*
Daihatsu 968 24 578 000, *daihatsu.com*
Ford Oman 134 A Romelah St Wattayah, 968 24 578 000, *fordoman.com*
Honda Motor Company 968 24 560 391, *honda.com*
KIA Al Hamriya, 968 24 579 800, *kiaoman.com*
Lexus 968 24 578 913, *lexusoman.com*
Mohsin Haider Darwish Way 3113, 968 24 732 500, *mhdoman.com*
Porsche Centre Oman Sultan Qaboos St, 968 24 492 544, *porsche.com*
Proton Oman 968 23 210 143, *protonoman.com*
Shanfari Automotive Co 968 24 483 500, *shanfari.com*
Suhail Bahwan Automobiles 968 24 560 111, *suhailbahwanautogroup.com*
Towell Auto Centre 968 24 526 650, *towellauto.com*
Toyota Oman 968 80 073 444, *toyotaoman.com*
Wattayah Motors 968 24 584 510, *vw-oman.com*
Zawawi Trading Company 968 24 659 200, *omzest.com*
Zubair Automotive 968 24 500 000, *zubairautomotive.com*

New Vehicles

Most new car models are available through the main dealers. Many car dealerships have showrooms between the Al Wattayah and Wadi Adai Roundabouts, although there are others located all along the highway. Some dealers sell several makes of car.

Don't forget to haggle – most dealers will offer a discount on the advertised price of a new car. The best time of year to get a good deal is during Ramadan, when all the dealers have promotions. Some dealers even offer a 'buy one, win one' raffle ticket that gives you the chance to win a second car. You'll also get a good deal if a new batch of cars arrives, as last year's models immediately drop in price.

The dealer will take care of all the paperwork involved in the car purchase on your behalf, including

Used Vehicles

With cars being relatively cheap, and expats coming and going all the time, the second-hand car market is thriving. The main areas for used car dealers are Al Wattayah, Al Khuwair and Wadi Kabir, although you'll find dealers in other locations too.

The advantage of buying through a dealer is that they'll arrange the registration and insurance for you. In general, dealers do not offer warranties, unless you are buying a car that is still protected under its 'new car' warranty.

Newspaper classifieds offer little in terms of second-hand vehicles for sale, except for Sunday's *Times of Oman* supplement and the classified section of *The Week*. Supermarket noticeboards are a good source of cars for sale, and there is the car souk at the Friday

Market. If you do buy a second-hand car privately, it's a good idea to have it checked for major faults and damage before you buy. Reputable car dealers will perform a thorough check-up of a vehicle for about RO.15 in Wadi Kabir. You can also check the internet for deals on omancars.net, driveoman.com, omandubizzle.com and muscatads.com.

Used Car Dealers

Al Fajer Cars Nr Zain Factory, 968 24 491 111
Al Ittihad Cars Showroom 968 24 542 990
Al Jazeera Motors Nr City Plaza, 968 24 600 127
Al Siyabi Used Cars 968 24 698 195
Al Wathbah Trading 968 24 421 828
Auto Plus International Commercial House, 968 24 478 080, *autoplusoman.net*
Best Cars 968 24 578 322, *bestcarsoman.com*
General Automotive Company Sultan Qaboos St, Nr Mitsubishi Showroom, 968 24 584 500, *generalautomotive-oman.com*
Modern Cars Exhibition Bait Al Falaj St Darsait, 968 24 786 011
Mohsin Haider Darwish 968 23 212 891, *mhdoman.com*
New Zahra Trading Nr Hamriya R/A, 968 24 833 953
Nissan 968 23 214 784, *nissanoman.com*
Popular Pre-Owned Cars 968 24 560 111, *popularcarsoman.com*
Real Value Autos OTE Showroom Complex, 968 24 561 788, *realvalueautos.com*
Wattayah Motors 968 24 584 510, *vw-oman.com*

Ownership Transfer

To transfer a private vehicle into your name you need to fill in a form, which details the buyer's personal information and bears the signatures of both buyer and seller. The seller must appear in person before the Directorate of Licencing at the traffic police department. If the seller still has a loan outstanding on the vehicle the bank must give its approval, and if the loan has been paid the bank will issue a letter of discharge. All transactions related to buying or selling second-hand vehicles should go through the Royal Oman Police.

Vehicle Import

If you are importing a vehicle, you need to go with your shipping agent to the port to get the import papers from the port authorities (if you're lucky your shipping agent will do this without you). They'll give you a form with some details of the car on it, such as engine number, chassis number and date of production. Depending on the age of the vehicle, and

the mood of the person helping you, you might have to pay tax. The next thing you need is insurance. Even though the car is not registered, you can insure on the basis of the engine number or chassis number to identify the car.

The insurance company will give you a form, all in Arabic, which you'll need for the registration. The insurance company will fill in the form for you. You'll also need a letter from your sponsor to say they approve of you importing the vehicle.

The next step is to go to the Ministry of Commerce in Ruwi, behind the LuLu shopping centre. Take the vehicle export papers from the country of origin, the import papers from the shipping agent, the registration form in Arabic from the insurance company, the insurance papers, the sponsor letter, passport copies, your Oman driving licence, a copy of your labour card, and the original ownership papers. To be on the safe side, just take any document remotely connected with the vehicle, plus a few spare copies. After paying a fee of RO.1 you'll be given an approval form.

Armed with all your papers, your next stop should be the Directorate General of Traffic to have your car checked in the Annual Inspections section. Once your vehicle has been inspected, collect the inspector's report (from the small office in the inspection area) and proceed to the main office of the police station. Here you'll have to present your documents before being directed to the customs counter (in the same room).

After customs, you'll be sent back to the inspector's office and this is when you'll have to pay a fee of RO.20 – remember to keep the receipt. You will then get your licence plates, which you'll take home to affix to your car. The following day you should go back (to the same counter) and hand over the receipt (take all the other papers too, just in case). They will give you the final registration card, which is the same size as a credit card. Finally, go back to the insurance company and give them the registration number and show them the card.

Vehicle Finance

Many new and second-hand car dealers will be able to arrange the finance for you, often through a deal with their preferred banking partner. Strangely, it is unusual to set up a direct debit to cover your monthly car payment, and instead you will have to write out a post-dated cheque for every month of the life of your loan, and submit them all at the very beginning. So if you take a four-year car loan, you will have to write out 48 cheques before you can take ownership of your car. Always ask about the rates and terms of the loan, and then consider going to a different bank to see if they will offer you a better deal.

Vehicle Insurance

You must have adequate insurance before you can register your car in your name. The minimum requirement is third party insurance, but fully comprehensive insurance is advisable. To insure your car you need copies of your driving licence, your labour or residence card, and the 'mulkia' for your car. In some cases the insurance company will want to inspect the car first.

It is simple and inexpensive to insure your car for the UAE, should you wish to drive across the border. Remember, your insurance will not be valid if your licence is not valid, or if you have an accident while under the influence of alcohol.

Registering A Vehicle

All cars must be registered and the registration must be renewed annually. The registration document is called the mulkia, and should be carried with you in the car whenever you drive. Along with your essential documents, the following documents are also required:

- New registration form filled in by the applicant or their representative and stamped by the sponsor
- Insurance certificate
- Proof of purchase certificate
- Copy of a valid driving licence

There is a detailed list on the ROP website (rop. gov.om) of all required documents when registering your vehicle. Regulations can change overnight, so it is always a good idea to check what the requirements are before you go. Additional documents are needed if you have imported your car or bought it at an auction.

If your car is 10 years old or more, it will need to pass a roadworthy test. This involves an inspection to check that the chassis and engine numbers match those on the mulkia, that the lights and brakes work, that there are no smoke emissions and the paintwork is not damaged or fading. Once the car has passed the test, you can proceed with registration. If your car fails the test, you must first fix any problems and start the process again.

Traffic Fines & Offences

If you are caught driving or parking illegally, you will be fined (unless the offence is more serious, in which case you may have to appear in court). Around Muscat, there are a number of police-controlled speed traps, fixed cameras and mobile radar traps, which are activated by cars exceeding the speed limit by nine kilometres or more. Fines start at RO.10 and go up in increments of RO.5. All traffic fines should be paid at the traffic fines section of the Directorate General of Traffic. Your fines are 'banked' and you only have to pay them once a year when you renew your car registration, but you can check whether you've received any fines online at rop.gov.om/trafficfine.

Breakdowns

In the event of a breakdown, you will usually find that passing police cars stop to help you, or at least to check your documents. It is important to keep water in your car at all times – the last thing you need is to be stuck on the side of the road with no air conditioning and no water while you wait for assistance. If you can, pull your car over to a safe spot. If you are on the hard shoulder of a busy road, pull your car as far away from the yellow line as possible, display your red warning triangle and step away from the road until help arrives.

You can call the Arabian Automobile Association (AAA), a 24 hour breakdown service (similar to the AA in the UK). If you break down for any reason (even a flat tyre or if you run out of petrol), they will send a mechanic out to you as soon as possible. The number is 24 605 555; often the operator on duty won't speak great English, so be patient.

Traffic Accidents

Oman has a relatively high rate of road accidents, and the figures of death and injury on the roads increases every year. The government started a big road safety campaign to educate drivers about safe driving standards and how to reduce accidents. The name of the campaign is 'Salim and Salimah, Safe and Sound' (www.salimandsalimah.org), and the website contains a great deal of excellent information on accidents and road safety.

If you have an accident, don't move your car until the police arrive, even if you are causing a major road blockage. The police will usually arrive pretty quickly. In case of an accident, call 24 560 099 (note that 9999 is reserved for the Fire Department and emergency cases only). Expect a crowd of rubberneckers to gather around the accident – at least you'll have someone there who can translate from Arabic to English when the police arrive. The police will decide (on the spot) which party is responsible for the accident, and then all involved parties should go to the nearest police station.

In the case of minor accidents where there is no injury, you must move your car out of the way so that you don't cause a road blockage, and both parties can go to the police station together and report the incident and a decision is made about who was responsible, and who has to pay.

If your car can't be driven, the police will arrange for it to be towed away. When you get to the police station you might have to wait around for quite some time, so be patient. You'll need to present your driving licence and mulkia (registration card). If any of your documents are invalid you will immediately be blamed for the accident. If your company has a PRO, it's a good idea to get him to come down to the station to help you translate and fill in the many forms. If there is a fine to be paid, the police will hold your licence until you've paid it.

The police will fill in an accident report and you will be given a reference number. The car must be sent to a garage that is approved by your insurance company. The garage is not allowed to carry out repairs to any vehicle without the police report. If you are in an accident where someone is hurt or killed, and the case goes to court, you will not be allowed to leave the country until the case is settled.

Vehicle Repairs

By law, no vehicle can be accepted for repair after an accident without an accident report from the Traffic Police. Usually, your insurance company will have an agreement with a particular garage to which they will refer you. The garage will carry out the repair work and the insurance company will settle the claim. Generally, there is an RO.100 deductible for all claims, but confirm the details of your policy with your insurance company.

Besides accidents and bumps, you may also have to deal with the usual running repairs associated with any car. Common problems in this part of the world can include the air conditioning malfunctioning and batteries suddenly giving up the ghost. If your air conditioning is not working well it is usually a case of having the gas topped up, which is a fairly straightforward procedure.

However, if something more serious goes wrong it can be very costly to fix, mainly due to labour charges as the mechanic has to remove your dashboard to get access to the aircon. Car batteries don't seem to last too well in the heat, and it is not uncommon to comeback from your holidays to find your car won't start.

Also all the dealers do servicing of cars and repairs, but it does usually cost more if you do the repairs through a motor dealer service centre. Most cars are sold with a two to four year service plan that can be renewed every two years.

Vehicle Repairs
Al Khuwair Auto Maintenance Nr American British Academy, 968 24 602 393
East Arabian Establishment 968 24 815 161
Four Wheel Drive Centre 968 24 810 962

WORKING IN OMAN

A good expat package in Oman remains a golden opportunity to experience a different culture, a relaxed lifestyle and eternal sunshine. But if you're thinking about working here, be aware that it's unusual for people to arrive in Oman on a visit visa to look for work – most people already have jobs lined up before they arrive.

Expat workers come to Oman for a number of reasons – to advance their careers, for higher standards of living, to take advantage of new career opportunities, or just for the experience of living in a new culture. Some people are seconded to Oman by companies based in their home countries, and some actively seek out opportunities for a new job that includes a place in the sun. Few arrive on the spot hoping to find a job when they arrive.

Although expat positions are still available, the main setback to finding a good posting is the highly successful Omanisation programme. Some organisations have achieved over 90% Omanisation, so less than 10% of their workforce is comprised of foreigners. But while Omanisation has closed off certain sectors of industry to expat jobseekers, you should still be able to find a job in sectors like oil, medicine and education.

If you're considering coming to Oman to look for work, do your research before you arrive. Sign up with online job sites as far in advance as possible and visit the websites of some of Oman's larger organisations to see if they have any vacancies.

It's also a good idea to pick up a copy of the Apex Business Directory of Oman (businessdirectoryoman. com), which contains information, addresses and phone numbers of most companies operating here. There may also be agencies in your home country that specialise in overseas employment, or you could try your luck in the neighbouring UAE, where some international recruitment firms have set up their Middle Eastern offices. Oman-based recruitment agencies for expat positions are virtually non-existent.

Sponsorship
As in most parts of the GCC, for foreigners to live and work in Oman, they must usually be sponsored by an employer or family member. To obtain a residency visa as an employee, you need a local sponsor and a labour permit from the Ministry of Manpower. Your sponsor will typically take care of all practical arrangements related to the application process. However, you may need to get a health certificate

from your home country, stating that you are free from illness and not carrying any communicable diseases. The requirements vary by nationality and are subject to change at short notice, so it's always best to check with your embassy.

Once your employer sponsors you, you can then arrange sponsorship for your family members. Two family sponsorship options are available: a family joining visa or a family residence visa. Children under the age of 21 years can be sponsored. Expats may also be eligible to apply for a Contractor Visa or an Investor Resident Visa – refer to the website of the Royal Oman Police (rop.gov.om) to get the latest information on visitor visas, residence permits and employment, investor or student visas.

Working Hours & Benefits

If you're new to the GCC, you'll quickly become aware of the split-shift phenomenon. Traditionally, companies start work a little early, break for a long lunch (usually three hours), and return to work for a late-afternoon session. Split-shift timings are usually 8am to 1pm and 4pm to 7pm.

Not all companies follow these hours however, and many work a 'straight shift' with a short lunch break. Indeed, most private sector companies now work straight shifts from 7am to 4pm, as do several government organisations, which tend to operate from 7am to 2pm.

Since 1 May 2013, the official weekend is Friday and Saturday. Public holidays are declared by the government. Most are religious holidays and therefore are governed by the Hijri (lunar) calendar. Holiday can't be declared until the new moon has been seen by the Moon Sighting Committee so you won't know the exact day or duration of the holiday until the moon is sighted the night before.

During Ramadan, all Muslims and people working in government organisations have reduced working hours. Some private sector companies also reduce the hours, at times also for non-Muslim employees.

Omani labour law grants mothers their basic salary for 50 days, provided the employee has completed one year of continuous service with the employer.

Business Culture & Etiquette

Although it is an up-and-coming modern city, Muscat is still an Arab city in a Muslim country, and this affects every aspect of daily life, including how business is done. Even if your counterpart in another company is an expat, the head decision maker is often an Omani who could possibly have a different approach to business matters. Your best bet when doing business in Muscat for the first time is to watch closely, have loads of patience, and make a concerted effort to understand the culture and respect the customs. Don't underestimate your business contacts or assume that

you have a better way of doing things than them – Omanis can smell an arrogant expat a mile away and you'll soon find many business opportunities passing you by.

Finding Work

Expat workers come to Oman for various reasons, primarily because the salaries are great and there is no personal income tax. As an added bonus, the weather is sublime, it is a relatively safe country, and the lifestyle is easy. When weighing up the pros and cons of accepting an offer on Oman, remember that the Omani rial is pegged to the dollar. That said, despite the fluctuations of the US dollar against a number of major currencies, including the Japanese yen, the euro and the pound sterling, the US dollar remains the primary reserve cash currency in the world and is expected to remain so for many years to come. Time has shown that pegging the Omani rial to the US dollar has stabilised its currency exchange.

You might find that currency fluctuations decrease the actual value of your salary package when you compare it to what you would earn in dollars, sterling or euros back home. Nevertheless, there is no question that a good expat package in a good company in Oman is a golden opportunity to experience a different culture in a country where the sun always shines.

Finding Work Before You Arrive

It is better to have a job lined up before you come to Oman, as with a sponsor lined up all your paperwork will be taken care of on your behalf. If you fancy living in Oman for a few years and are on the lookout for a good opportunity, contact some reputable recruitment agencies in your home country who may have jobs available in this region.

If you want to do the legwork yourself, you have a number of options. You can 'cold-call' companies by sending out unsolicited CVs to targeted industries, although this is rarely the path to success. If you have friends or acquaintances in Oman, you can send them some copies of your CV (resume) and ask them to put out feelers for you. Or you can do some research on the internet to find out more about job vacancies in Oman.

Try visiting the following websites: gulfjobsites. com, careermideast.com, overseasjobs.com, ociped. com, and monster.com. Alternatively you could visit the websites of some of Oman's larger organisations to see if they have any vacancies. Try Petroleum Development Oman (pdo.co.om), British School Muscat (britishschoolmuscat.com), Muscat Private Hospital (muscatprivatehospital.com), Omantel (omantel.net.om), Nawras (nawras.om), or American British Academy (abaoman.edu.om).

If you are in the hospitality industry, try contacting the individual hotels directly. If you get a job offer, you will need to negotiate your employment package carefully to cover all bases. A good package covers housing, medical insurance, transport (either in the form of a company car or a car allowance), shipping or relocation costs, and education for your children.

Finding Work While You Are In Oman

Unless you have excellent contacts lined up before coming to Oman, don't expect to find work while you are on a visit visa. The slow pace of life means that decisions are not always made quickly.

There are no newspaper supplements for appointments, and any classified ads in the papers are usually targeted at Omanis or at labourers. When you arrive, pick up a copy of the Apex Business Directory of Oman, which contains information, addresses and phone numbers of most companies. You can find a copy at the Apex office in Ruwi (24 799 388).

If you have come to Oman with your spouse who is working and you wish to find a job for yourself, the options are limited unless you are in the teaching or medical professions. To find a job in these sectors, it's best to ask directly at schools, hospitals and clinics. The rigorous Omanisation programme does not permit an expat to hold a job that an Omani is qualified to do, which cuts out most administrative jobs and many others. If you are a well-qualified English teacher, then you should be able to find work as a teacher of English as a second language. There are several institutes offering English courses to non-native speakers, so call them to see if they have any vacancies. Try the Polyglot Institute, ELS Language Centers, Modern Gulf Institute, British Council and Salalah Language International.

Recruitment Agencies

Virtually non-existent, recruitment agencies in Oman generally cater for manual labourers from Asian countries. Your best bet is to contact a recruitment company in your own country or one of the many in Dubai. Check out gulftalent.com and aljazeerajobs.com as your starting point.

Employment Contracts

Accepting an expat posting can have its pitfalls, so before you sign your contract pay special attention to things like probation periods, accommodation, annual leave, travel entitlements, medical and dental cover, notice periods and repatriation entitlements. Once you accept your offer, you will be asked to sign both an English and an Arabic copy of your contract. The Arabic copy is the one that will be referred to in any legal dispute between you and your employer, so if you have any doubts about the integrity of the company, ask a lawyer or Arabic-speaking friend to look through it. However, if there was ever a legal dispute, the court would want to know why there was any discrepancy between the English and Arabic versions in the first place.

It is worth reading through a copy of the Oman labour law before you sign your contract. Labour law takes precedence over your contract, so if your contract reads differently from the labour law it's worth noting.

Plan sufficient time for finding a job in Oman

If you are sponsored by your spouse and want to work, you will need to get an NOC from his employer before you can sign a contract with your new employer. Your new employer will then apply for your labour card.

Labour Card

The old labour card, issued by the Labour Department, is a legal document certifying the employment status of an individual. If your employer is arranging your residency, your labour clearance should be processed directly after your residency has been approved. If you are on family residency and decide to work, your employer (not your visa sponsor) will need to apply for your labour clearance. Your sponsor should supply an NOC. Women on their husband's or father's sponsorship are not allowed to work unless they have a work visa.

In 2005 the government began replacing labour cards with resident cards. The resident card uses biometric recognition and is multifunctional, holding personal details, driving licence, and emergency medical information. It can be used for electronic validation at immigration checkpoints, and can even serve as an electronic cash card for transactions at government organisations. Cards are issued by the Directorate General of Civil Status. You will need a completed application form, passport, medical certificate, labour clearance from the Ministry of Manpower (private sector workers) and two photographs. Non-working residents (family members) need a completed application form, passport, birth certificate, medical certificate and two photographs. Further information can be requested from the Directorate General of Civil Status, located on the Seeb Airport Roundabout.

Health Card

There is no health card as such in Oman, however, you will need to undergo a medical test as part of your residency application process. This involves a blood test, taken at the Ministry of Health clinic in Ruwi, where they will test for infectious diseases (such as HIV and hepatitis) and your blood type. Your sponsor will advise you on the procedure and perhaps even accompany you to the clinic to assist. When you get to the clinic you will find a very long queue, so to avoid waiting all morning you should get there as early as possible.

Some nationalities are required to produce a health certificate from their home country if they are entering Oman on an employment visa. This test will be a comprehensive report including x-rays and blood tests. Your sponsor should be able to advise you, or you can check rop.gov.om (Royal Oman Police) for more information, as the procedure and documents may vary according to your nationality.

Labour Law

The current version of the Oman labour law was promulgated in 2003. The law outlines everything from employee entitlements (end of service gratuity, workers' compensation, holidays and other benefits) to employment contracts and disciplinary rules.

The Labour Law is considered fair and clearly outlines the rights of both employees and employers. Employees have the right to hold peaceful strikes in order to demand betterment of working conditions but it is prohibited to strike or instigate strikes at establishments that provide essential public services or at oil facilities or oil refineries, ports and airports. Copies of the labour law can be obtained from the Ministry of Manpower, manpower.gov.om.

Al Ahlam Higher Education Services
968 24 562 623, *ahlameducation.com*
CFBT Education Services & Partners Ar Rumaylah St, Blk 203, Bldg 458, Nr VW showroom, 968 24 560 259, *cfbtoman.com*
Ministry Of Commerce & Industry 968 24 813 500, *mocioman.gov.om*
Ministry Of Manpower Way 3501, 968 80 077 000, *manpower.gov.om*
Ministry Of Social Development Nr Ministry of Justice, As Sultan Qaboos St, 968 24 645 000, *mosd.gov.om*
The Public Authority For Investment Promotion & Export Development (PAIPED) 968 24 623 300, *paiped.com*

Changing Jobs & Bans

In relation to the contract of work, article 46 of the Omani Labour Law states that 'the employer shall give to the worker, upon his request, at the end of the contract, an end-of-service certificate free of charge, wherein he shall state the date of the worker's joining the service, date of leaving it, the type of work he was performing, the wage and other remuneration and privileges, if any'.

Previously, the employee would have to settle all bills, loans, etc. before he moves to a new job as it is usually the sponsor who would be liable for these in the case of non-payment. This would form the basis of the letter of release. Once this was done, the employee could freely move to a new company.

However, as of 1 June 2014, an employee must have completed at least two years of service with his employer before he can change jobs. If not, he will have to leave the country for two years before he can return to take on a new role, or provide an NOC from the employer he wants to leave . There have recently been reforms on such sponsorship schemes in Qatar, so it's an issue that might well come to the fore.

Free Zones

Free zones are not as prevalent in Oman as they are in other Gulf states, but there are a few developments. A technology park called Knowledge Oasis Muscat (kom. om) is situated in Rusayl Industrial Estate (near Sultan Qaboos University) and offers 100% foreign ownership of businesses. You pay no personal income tax, you are exempt from foreign exchange controls, and you pay no tax on your company profits for the first five years.

There are three Free Zones and one special economic zone in Oman:

Al Mazunah Free Zone – strategically located in the south west of Oman on the Oman-Yemen border. *almazunah.com*

Knowledge Oasis Muscat – a public-private sector led technology park located 32km from Muscat. *kom.com*

Salalah Free Zone – in the south of the country. *sfzco.com*

Port of Sohar – a special economic zone. *portofsohar.com*

Setting Up A Business In Oman

Setting up a business in Oman can be a lengthy and arduous task. Firstly, you will need to find a suitable Omani sponsor, which is easier said than done. Obtain professional legal advice throughout and ensure all agreements are written down, not just verbal. It may be easier to set up in Knowledge Oasis Muscat (kom.om) or in Salalah Free Zone (sfzco.com).

Networking

While Muscat is still a relatively small city, networking is critical, even across industries. Everyone seems to know everyone and getting in with the corporate 'in-crowd' certainly has its benefits. Business acumen can, at times, be more important than specific industry knowledge and therefore it pays to attend business events and meetings. Make friends in government departments and this will often land you in the front line for opportunities. Because bad news is rarely made public in the newspapers here, staying tuned in to the business grapevine helps prevent wrong decisions. For in-depth information about business in Oman, refer to your local business group or the commercial attache at your embassy or consulate.

British Business Forum Oman *bbfoman.org*
British Council Nr Petrol Station, As Sultan Qaboos St, 968 24 681 000, *britishcouncil.org*
Business Information Centre 968 24 494 500
Muscat American Business Council 6th Floor Bank Beirut Bldg Al Ghubrah, 968 24 566 140, *mabcoman.com*
Oman Chamber Of Commerce & Industry CBD Area, 968 24 707 674, *chamberoman.com*

The Public Authority For Investment Promotion & Export Development (PAIPED) 968 24 623 300, *paiped.com*
United Media Services SAOC 968 24 700 896, *oeronline.com*

Voluntary & Charity Work

Voluntary work is widely available throughout Oman and those who dedicate their time to worthy causes are held in high esteem.

Association Of Early Intervention For Children With Disability

18th November Rd, Villa 3215, Al Azaiba, Muscat
968 24 496 960
aei.org.om

This association has been established since 2000. It serves kids from birth to 6 years, who are at risk or disabled, with a comprehensive early intervention programme that covers social, medical, physical, academic and therapeutic services. The aim is to ensure a better quality of life for them and their families.

Centre For Special Education – Indian School Muscat

Darsayt **24 707 567**
indianschoolmuscat.com

This centre supervises and teaches children with special needs self-help skills, arts and crafts, music and pre-vocational skills. The teaching of the children is need-based in small groups and an individual education programme (IEP) is carefully designed for each child. Volunteers are given on-the-job training.

Dar Al Atta Society

Al Bashaer Road, Villa 119 Nr Pakistani Embassy, Muscat **968 24 692 996**
daralatta.org

This is a voluntary non-governmental organisation that seeks to provide the less privileged members of society with basics that secure them a decent living. Its work includes monthly food aids to needy families, reconstruction of houses that are not fit for habitation and providing emergency relief aid at times of natural crises.

Environment Society Of Oman

Way 2519, Suite 22, First Floor, Bldg 1197, Ajit Khimji Building Muscat **968 24 790 945**
eso.org.om

This is a non-governmental organisation that aims to help conserve Oman's natural heritage and raise awareness of environmental issues. Activities for members include participating in hands-on projects and awareness-raising activities.

LEGAL & FINANCIAL ISSUES

Oman is an Absolute Monarchy with a bicameral system. The Head of State and Supreme Commander of the Armed Forces is His Majesty Sultan Qaboos Bin Said. Laws in Oman are issued by Royal Decree as primary legislation, or by Ministerial Decisions as secondary legislation. Oman has the following court system – Supreme Court, Appellate Courts, Courts of first instance and Courts of Summary Jurisdiction. Each court is able to deal with matters relating to civil, commercial, labour, tax and personal (Shariah) law.

Although judges can practise either secular law or Shariah law, Shariah is the basis for all legislation as set out in the basic law (Royal Decree 101/96), which is in effect the constitution of Oman. Court proceedings are conducted only in Arabic. All official documents issued by the courts and used in proceedings must also be in Arabic.

The main legal issue likely to affect expats is property ownership. As a foreigner, this is limited to purchasing property within integrated tourist complexes only, such as The Wave and Muscat Golf and Country Club. Other issues where you might land on the wrong side of the law are linked to the rules of Islam: gambling is forbidden, and although you can drink under certain conditions you are inviting trouble if you get drunk and disorderly in public places. Living with a member of the opposite sex who is not a family member is illegal.

There is one prison near Mabella and one in Nizwa. Oman's prisons are best described as basic. Facilities are poor and hygiene is questionable. Your personal items (including shoes and belt) will be taken off you when you enter the prison and only returned when you leave. You may be allowed to make a phone call, or the prison may inform your sponsor or company PRO officer that you are in custody. For a first offence, bail can be paid after 48 hours – the bail amount is usually somewhere between RO.50 and RO.75. If you can't afford the bail then you have to remain in custody. Your embassy will not be able to offer financial or legal assistance.

Alcohol & Drugs

Attitudes to drinking in this region are a bit stiffer than you might experience back home (popping into your corner shop for a six-pack is a definite no-no). However, compared to some of the other GCC countries, Oman has a fairly relaxed view of alcohol. Non-Muslims can drink in licensed bars and restaurants, at private clubs, and at various social

Oman Association For The Disabled
Muscat **968 24 605 566**
donate.om
This is an NGO established to provide support, education and recreational activities for people with disabilities. The association also works at achieving a better understanding of the needs of people with disabilities in the community.

Oman Charity Club
Muscat **968 96 655 800**
This organisation is for expats living in Oman who want to help the less privileged in the country, giving them a chance to connect and organise charity drives. Activities include organising donations of clothes, toys and games, and visiting poor villagers.

The Art Of Living Oman Chapter
Mosaic Tower – B, Al Khuwair, Muscat **968 24 789 859**
artofliving.org
The Art of Living is a multifaceted, educational and humanitarian NGO. Almost a decade in existence, the Oman Chapter's voluntary work includes organising blood donations and fund raising programmes. See the website for more information.

The National Association For Cancer Awareness
Muscat **968 24 498 716**
ocanceROrg.om
The objectives of the organisation include creating public awareness of all types of cancer through community-based programmes.

events that are generously sponsored by major alcohol retailers. Muscat is not famous for its buzzing nightlife, but some hotel bars have extended their opening hours to 3am (thus brightening up the social scene a bit).

However, drunk and disorderly behaviour in public is frowned upon and fortunately most expats seem to respect this. If you want to buy alcohol for consumption at home, you need to apply for a liquor licence. Only non-Muslim residents with a labour card are allowed to apply. If you are married, only the husband can apply, and his wife cannot use the licence to buy alcohol unless he works in the interior. Licences are valid for two years, but can't be used outside of the city in which they were issued.

Your liquor licence permits you to buy a limited amount of alcohol each month. Your allowance is calculated based on your salary, and is usually not more than 10% of it. You can apply for a larger allowance on certain conditions (for example, if your job entails corporate entertaining). You can't 'bank' your allowance – you must either use it or lose it. Many expats have learned the benefits of stockpiling alcohol, particularly in the lead-up to Ramadan when liquor stores are closed for a whole month and bars do not serve any booze. It is illegal to drive around with liquor in your car, with the exception of transporting it from the liquor store to your home.

Drug offences usually result in serious sentences, and your time in prison can be anywhere from one month to 25 years, depending on the amount you were caught with, the type of drugs and the circumstances surrounding the arrest. In addition, your fine could be up to RO.20,000 and the court can even sentence you to death in severe cases. If you are caught with forbidden prescription medicines, it is important that you can produce the actual doctor's prescription for them. It will depend upon the judge's decision for what sentence you will receive, but it will again be severe.

Traffic Offences

It is absolutely necessary to have motor insurance in Oman. If you cause an accident resulting in a fatality, you may be liable to pay 'diya' (blood money) to the family. Essentially this is compensation. There is also 'arush' which is compensation for injuries. Your motor insurance will cover this provided you are driving with a valid driving licence, have not consumed alcohol or drugs and your car is legally registered. The court could take up to six months to finalise the sentence so you may be allowed to continue working until your sentence is given. You will not, however, be allowed to leave the country while your court case is pending. If you caused the accident while under the influence of alcohol, you can expect to be imprisoned immediately and the fines and/or prison sentence can be hefty.

Myths & Truths

- If you write a cheque that bounces, you will be given around a week to pay the amount (if it is your first offence). If you can't pay, you will be taken into custody.
- Be careful what stickers you place on your car – car stickers featuring donkeys (even if it is a national mascot of a particular region in your home country) are apparently illegal because the position of the sticker on the car indicates that anyone passing the sticker is a donkey themselves. You will receive a fine.
- Flogging does not happen in Oman.
- Pregnancy outside wedlock will result in deportation if you are caught.
- Smoking, eating or drinking in public places during Ramadan is considered highly offensive and can carry a jail term of up to three months.
- Unmarried men and women are not permitted to live together unless they are related (brother and sister, for example). However, before you rush down the aisle, rest assured that this law is rarely enforced. Just be discreet, and you should be fine.

Law Firms

Al Busaidy Mansoor Jamal & Co Muscat International Centre, CBD, Bait Al Falaj St, 968 24 814 466, *amjoman.com*

Curtis Mallet Prevost Colt & Mosle Qurum Plaza, 108 Al Wallaj St, 968 24 564 495, *curtis.com*

Hafedh Al Mahrouqi & Co Oman Commercial Centre, Hay Al Mina, 968 24 799 755, *omanilaw.com*

Hamad Al Sharji Peter Mansour & Co Standard Chartered Bank Bldg, MBD, 968 24 780 333, *sharjimansour.com*

Jihad Al Taie & Associates Majan House, 968 24 478 282

Said Al Shahry Law Office 968 23 289 833, *saslo.com*

SNR Denton & Co Al Fannar Bldg, 968 24 573 000, *snrdenton.com*

Trowers & Hamlins Al Jawhara Building Al Muntazah Street, 968 24 682 900, *trowers.com*

Insurance Companies

Arab Orient Insurance Company Office 401, 4th Floor, City Seasons Bldg, 968 24 475 410, *insuranceuae.com*

Arabia Insurance Company 968 24 793 299, *arabiainsurance.com*

AXA Insurance Gulf Safeway Building, Way 3303, Nr Assarain Complex, 968 24 400 100, *axa.com*

Dhofar Insurance Company (SAOG) 968 23 294 368, *dhofarinsurance.com*

Falcon Insurance SAOC Sultan Center, 968 24 660 900, *falconinsurancesaoc.com*

MetLife Alico Haffa House Hotel Muscat, 968 24 787 531, *metlifealico.com.om*

Nextcare Oman Al Sibakh House, Building 783, Way 4508, 968 24 475 571, *nextcare.ae*
Oman Insurance Company Sheraton Rd, Nr Star Cinema, CBD Area, 968 24 789 232, *tameen.ae*
Oman Qatar Insurance Company (SAOG) Villa 4, Way 2101, Hai Al Falaj, 968 24 700 798, *qatarinsurance.com*
Oman United Insurance Co (SAOG) 968 23 295 040, *omanutd.com*
Risk Management Services 968 24 704 004, *rmsllc.com*

Money

Cash is the preferred method of payment in Oman, although credit cards are accepted in larger department stores, restaurants and hotels. Cash and traveller's cheques can be exchanged in licensed exchange offices, banks and international hotels – a passport is required for exchanging traveller's cheques. To avoid additional exchange rate charges, take traveller's cheques in US dollars if possible. Local cheques are generally accepted in business but not for personal purchases. If you are taking a lease for accommodation, it is likely that you will pay by cheque and supply post-dated cheques for the remaining period of the rent. There are no restrictions on the import or export of any currency. Israeli currency is prohibited.

Exchange Rates

Foreign Currency (FC)	1 Unit FC = RO.	RO.1 = x FC
Australia	0.36	2.76
Bahrain	1.02	0.97
Bangladesh	0.004	211.63
Canada	0.35	2.80
Denmark	0.06	14.41
Euro	0.51	1.93
Hong Kong	0.04	20.12
India	0.06	156
Japan	0.003	264.5
Jordan	0.54	1.83
Kuwait	1.36	0.73
New Zealand	0.32	3.03
Pakistan	0.003	256.2
Philippines	0.008	112.46
Qatar	0.10	9.45
Saudi Arabia	0.10	9.74
Singapore	0.30	3.22
South Africa	0.03	27.31
Sri Lanka	0.002	338.24
Sweden	0.56	17.72
Switzerland	0.42	2.34
Thailand	0.01	82.71
UAE	0.10	9.54
UK	0.65	1.52
USA	0.38	2.59
Source: xe.com 27 July 2014		

Exchange Centres

Money exchanges are found all over Oman, offering good service and exchange rates (often better than the banks). Exchange houses are usually open from 8am to 1pm and 4pm to 10pm, and often operate in the evenings and at weekends. Alternatively, hotels will usually exchange money and traveller's cheques at the standard (non-competitive) hotel rate. At Seeb International Airport, there is a Travelex counter before immigration to facilitate visa payments.

Bargaining

Bargaining is a traditional part of doing trade in Oman and it is still widely used today, especially in the souks. You can sometimes end up paying half of the original asking price. A discount of 10% is usual, even in appliance stores, but not in supermarkets or department stores. It can also be a fun way to do business; vendors will square up to 'do battle', courteously offering their customers some kahwa (coffee), and in return customers should bargain hard. Start your negotiations by asking for the 'best price' and go from there.

Exchange Centres

Abu Mehad Money Exchange SABCO Commercial Center, 968 24 566 123
Al Barzah Money Exchange Nr Rawasco Supermarket, 968 24 487 444
Gulf Overseas Exchange Company 968 24 834 182
Hamdan Exchange 968 23 296 903
Laxmidas Tharia Ved (Exchange) Company Seaplus Jewelry Building, Hamyria Rd, 968 24 700 044
Modern Exchange Al Hashar Building, 968 24 832 133
Oman & UAE Exchange Centre LuLu Hypermarket, O. C. Centre, First Floor, Ruwi, 968 24 796 533, *omanuaeexchange.com*
Oman International Exchange Al Hamriya, Opp Muscat Pharmacy, 968 24 832 197
Oman United Exchange Company 968 24 794 305, *ohigroup.com*
Purshottam Kanji Exchange Company 968 24 793 468

Local Currency

The monetary unit is the Oman rial (RO or OR). It is divided into 1,000 baisas (also spelt 'baiza') making it a 3 decimal currency, not like most countries where it is a 2 decimal currency. Notes come in denominations of rials 50, 20, 10, 5, 1, 1/2 (500 baisas) and 100 baisas. Coin denominations are 50, 25, 10 and 5 baisas. Denominations are written in Arabic and English. It is best to take a few minutes to familiarise yourself with the currency, although shopkeepers are generally honest when giving you your change. The rial is tied to the US dollar at a mid-rate of approximately US$1 ~ RO.0.385, which has basically remained unchanged for a number of years.

The way prices are written can lead to some confusion. An item may be marked 'RO/OR.1,500'– the price could be one thousand five hundred rials or one rial and five hundred baisas. The value of the item will usually be obvious. For clarity in this book, prices are shown in a standard way: one rial and 500 hundred baisas will be shown as RO.1.500 and one thousand five hundred rials as RO.1,500, while 15 rials will be RO.15.

For an idea on what basic items cost in Oman, compared to your home country, see the cost of living table on p.110.

Banks

The well-structured and ever-growing network of local and international banks, strictly controlled by the Central Bank of Oman, offers the full range of commercial and personal banking services. Transfers can be made without difficulty as there is no exchange control and the Oman rial is freely convertible to other currencies. There is a good range of international banks in Oman, all of which offer standard facilities such as current, deposit and savings accounts, ATM facilities, cheque books, credit cards and loans. In addition, you could consider setting up an offshore account.

Many banks are represented in Oman

Many bank headquarters can be found clustered in Ruwi, Muscat's central business district.

There are also branches all over Muscat and Salalah, and in major towns such as Nizwa, Sur and Sohar. Banking hours are usually 8am to 1pm or 2pm, Sunday to Thursday.

Main Banks

Bank Dhofar 968 24 790 466, *bankdhofar.com*
Bank Sohar SAOG 968 24 730 000, *banksohar.net*
BankMuscat (SAOG) 968 24 795 555, *bankmuscat.com*
Banque Banorabe Central Bank St, 968 24 704 274
Central Bank Of Oman Central Business District, 968 24 777 777, *cbo-oman.org*
Habib Bank AG Zurich 968 24 817 142, *habibbank.com*
HSBC Bank Middle East Limited Nr Omantel Tower, Bank Sohar and the Central Bank of Oman, 968 80 074 722, *hsbc.co.om*
National Bank Of Abu Dhabi Commercial Business District (CBD) Building 320, Way 4010, Block 140, 968 24 761 000, *nbad.com*
National Bank Of Oman (NBO) Central Business District, 968 24 811 711, *nbo.co.om*
Oman Arab Bank CBD area, 968 24 706 265, *oman-arabbank.com*
Oman International Bank 968 24 682 500, *oiboman.com*
Standard Chartered Bank 968 24 773 535, *sc.com/om*

ATMs

Most banks operate automatic teller machines (ATMs) that accept a wide range of cards. Common systems accepted around Muscat include MasterCard, Visa, American Express, Global Access, Plus System and Cirrus. You should of course be able to use your bank card from your home country to withdraw cash, but bear in mind that your bank will most likely charge for each transaction.

ATMs can be found in shopping malls, at the airport, and various street locations in Muscat. Exchange rates used in the transaction are normally competitive and the process is often faster and easier than travellers' cheques.

Credit Cards

Larger shops, hotels and restaurants in Muscat and Salalah accept major credit cards (American Express, Diners Club, MasterCard and Visa) and they will often have the card logos displayed at the entrance. However, if you are travelling in the interior, or are shopping at souks and smaller shops, cash is usually the only form of payment accepted.

Taxation

Oman levies no personal taxes and withholds no income tax of any sort. However, the IMF is advising many Middle Eastern countries to introduce tax reforms to diversify their resources, so it could be on the cards in Oman.

The lack of direct income taxation makes Oman a great place to save money. Currently, the only taxes expatriates are obliged to pay are the 8% service tax at food and beverage outlets in hotels, a 4% tourism tax, a 5% municipality tax, and a 3% tax on rental accommodation. There is also a tax on alcohol bought at retail shops, and on pork.

Before leaving your home country to take up an expat posting, you should contact the tax authorities to ensure that you are complying with the financial laws there. Most countries will consider you not liable for income tax once you prove that you are not resident in that country. But you might still have to pay tax on any income you are getting from your home country (for example if you are renting out a property you own there, or if you are earning interest on a bank account).

Check with the revenue service of your country – the following websites may be helpful: UK (hmrc.gov.uk), USA (irs.gov), South Africa (sars.gov.za), Australia (ato.gov.au), Canada (cra-arc.gc.ca), New Zealand (ird.govt.nz).

Cost Of Living

Burger (takeaway)	RO.0.400
Bus (10km journey)	RO.0.500
Cappuccino	RO.1.500
Car rental (per day)	RO.20
Cigarettes (per pack of 20)	RO.0.750
Cinema ticket	RO.3.200
Golf (18 holes)	RO.55
Loaf of bread	RO.0.800
Milk (1 litre)	RO.0.530
Mobile to mobile call	RO.0.055
Petrol (gallon)	RO.0.120/Ltr
Pint of beer	RO.3
Potatoes (1kg)	RO.0.500
Rice (1kg)	RO.0.700
Salon haircut (female)	RO.20.000
Salon haircut (male)	RO.7
Shawarma	RO.0.250
Six-pack of beer (off licence)	RO.3
Strawberries (per punnet)	RO.1.800
Taxi (10km journey)	RO.3.500
Text message (local)	RO.0.010
Tube of toothpaste	RO.1
Water 1.5 litres (supermarket)	RO.0.300
Watermelon (per kg)	RO.0.600

FAMILY AND EDUCATION

Many expats describe Muscat and Oman as ideal for family life. The general pace of life is relaxed and affordable home help is at hand. You should bear in mind, however, that arranging a spot in a good school can be a difficult task. If you have children of school-going age, you will need to start investigating schools as early as possible. There aren't many schools to choose from and with Muscat expanding all the time, some schools are running out of places for certain age groups.

Maternity

Many expats choose to give birth in Oman and do so without any problems. The main difference is that you will not have the same choices regarding your birth plan as you would probably have in your home country. You don't have the option of a home birth or a water birth, but straightforward births are expertly handled. If you do decide to travel home to give birth, you will need to check with your doctor regarding whether it is safe to travel at an advanced stage of pregnancy. Your doctor will usually give you permission to fly up to 34 weeks, but you should check with your airline about their restrictions and requirements for pregnant passengers.

If you wish to have your child in Oman, your only choice to give birth is in one of the private hospitals, unless you develop complications that can only be dealt with in a government hospital. In addition, if you or your husband work for a government agency, you will be allowed to use the government hospitals.

In such cases you will be referred to the government hospital by the private hospital or clinic where you have had your prenatal care. Standards of care are excellent at both government and private hospitals, so don't worry if you are referred to a government hospital for your labour.

It is possible to get private health insurance to cover maternity costs, although there is usually a specific time period which must have lapsed before conception – in other words, you usually have to have been on the insurance plan for a year or so before you fall pregnant. Prices for private maternity packages start from around RO.900 for a standard antenatal, delivery and postnatal package – this should include all your ultrasound scans, blood tests, and any extra tests or procedures you require, but do factor in additional costs; for example, a longer stay.

Don't listen to any urban myths about having to go through labour without pain relief – the normal pain solutions such as gas and air, Pethidine and epidurals are common. You will pay extra for Pethidine or an epidural, and if you end up having a caesarean section, that will cost extra too. Your husband is allowed to be in the delivery room with you, and so is an independent doula if you have one.

Once your baby is born you need to have the birth registered within two weeks and then set about getting a passport for him or her from your embassy. There may be extra paperwork if the mother was also born outside of her country of origin or if her embassy is not represented in Oman.

Muscat Mums

Having a baby in a strange town can be taxing, since you've probably left your support network (mum, sister, friends) behind. Muscat Mums is an amazing group that was set up to help new mums find their feet, and they welcome all new members. To find out more visit muscatmums.com. Another excellent resource is pregnantinoman.com.

It is important to get all paperwork relevant to your new baby in order, particularly if you are planning to travel in the near future. You'll get an official birth certificate from the hospital where your child was born (it costs RO.6), and you then need to have this certificate stamped at the Ministry of Foreign Affairs Attestation Office (24 699 500) in Qurum. Then you need to go to your embassy, where your baby will be issued with a passport, before applying for your baby's residence visa through the usual channels. If you are British you can register your child's birth with the British Consulate – this is not compulsory but it means your child will have a British birth certificate and will be registered at the General Registry Office in the UK. You do not have to do this immediately after the birth, but you should try to do it before you leave Oman for good. If you don't, and you subsequently lose your child's birth certificate, you can only get a replacement from the British Consulate in Oman. But if you do complete this procedure, you will be able to get a replacement birth certificate from the UK. Before the birth, it is worth checking the regulations of your country of origin for citizens born overseas.

To register your child with the Oman authorities, you will need a completed application form, birth notification from the Ministry of Health (birth certificate), resident cards or passports of both parents, and the parents' marriage certificate. Legal responsibility for registering the child's birth rests with the father, although in his absence it may also be done in the order of their listing by any adult relative

present at the birth, any adult residing with the mother, the doctor or any midwife who attended the event. Even if your baby is born in Oman, it does not get Oman citizenship. It will take the citizenship of the mother or the father (or both). Speak to your embassy regarding citizenship rules for your baby.

Pregnant & Single?

While it is possible for single parents to sponsor their children here, having a baby out of wedlock in Oman is against the law. If you find yourself in this situation, you will need to make arrangements to have the baby outside of the country, or get married as soon as possible.

Sole Custody/Single Parents

There are no problems for a single parent wanting to bring their child into Oman as long as their passport and documentation is in order. If you have sole custody of your child and wish to sponsor him or her, you may need a letter from the other parent stating the child's name, passport number and nationality, and that they have no objection to the child living with you in Oman. The letter must be endorsed by the legal authority that issued the sole custody, and attested. If you have no way of contacting the other parent (or if they are deceased), then the attested divorce or sole custody paperwork (or death certificate) should suffice.

Antenatal Care

If you have your antenatal care in a private clinic, they will refer you to a hospital for delivery. Your gynaecologist will possibly be present at the birth. A doctor must deliver the baby – unlike in some countries where a midwife can perform a delivery in the absence of any complications. If you are over 35 or you are seen has having a greater chance of having a baby with spinal or neurological birth defects, you will be offered a variety of tests to check for certain problems.

Postnatal Depression

A relatively high number of women suffer from postnatal depression to varying degrees. In serious cases it can be debilitating and can even result in you or your baby being in danger of injury.

If you are having your baby in Oman, you will probably be far away from the important emotional support of your family and friends back home, and this can increase your chances of suffering from PND.

Al Harub Medical Centre Way 2830, House 2258, Sarooj, 968 24 600 750, *alharubmedical.com*
Healthy Minds Clinic Near Catholic Church, Al Farahidi St Way 3318, 968 99 350 547
Jane Jaffer 968 99 314 230

Getting Married In Oman

Since Oman law is governed largely by Islam, it is actually illegal for an unmarried couple to live together. It is even illegal to share a house with flatmates of the opposite sex who are not related to you. However, many couples do end up living together without getting into trouble – as long as you are discreet and stay out of trouble, you should be left alone to co-habit in peace.

Brit of Bother

Due to administrative restrictions, the British Embassy in Muscat is currently not able to conduct weddings. Contact the embassy directly for the latest updates.

The singles scene is not exactly swinging in Muscat and if you are single you may find yourself doing the rounds at endless family barbecues where everyone is married with children. But you never know – true love may be round the corner. It is not common for expats to stay in Oman to get married – the expense of flying all your family and friends out for a posh party in one of the many five-star hotels puts most people off. However, if you choose to have an Oman wedding, there are numerous options at your disposal.

The wedding packages at the Al Bustan Palace range from RO.25 per person to RO.50 per person (based on a minimum of 300 guests but the hotel can arrange different packages for smaller weddings). Packages include a buffet with soft drinks, a wedding cake, a red carpet and a dance floor. The happy couple can enjoy a complimentary dinner on the night of the wedding as well as a two-night stay in the executive suite with breakfast. However, there is no Bentley – or any car in fact – to transport the couple in style!

Local Weddings

If you get the opportunity to attend a local wedding, grab it! Local weddings in Oman are traditionally grand affairs, especially in terms of size – it is not uncommon for the guest list to reach figures of 200 or more. The ceremony takes place over two days, and includes traditional singing and dancing, as well as vast quantities of favourite local dishes.

If you'd rather save your money for the honeymoon, you can have a civil service at your embassy or consulate and a more modest reception in a hotel ballroom or restaurant (depending on number of guests).

There are Catholic and Protestant churches in Muscat (Ghala and Ruwi) and Protestant churches

Adoption

There are some orphanages in Oman but it is not clear whether expats are permitted to apply to adopt any of these children or not – it depends on who you speak to. Many couples find it relatively easy to adopt from outside Oman, for example from Asia or the Far East. Once you have successfully met all the requirements in your adopted child's home country, you should have little trouble bringing your child back to Oman and applying for a residence visa. Check the regulations involved in securing your citizenship for your adopted child; your embassy will be able to help with this matter.

Babysitting & Childcare

Childcare – the dilemma facing all working parents. Options are limited and there is no network of childminders like you might find in your home country. If you have a live-in maid, and you trust her with your children, then you have a round-the-clock babysitter. Alternatively you could pay your part-time maid an extra hourly rate (around RO.1.5) to babysit for you when you need her. Word of mouth is a great way to find a babysitter, whether it's a friend's maid or a responsible teenager needing pocket money. Domestic help agencies may offer babysitting services, although there is no guarantee you will be able to get the same person each time (which means leaving your child with a stranger). You could also try asking at nursery schools – often teaching assistants will baby sit in the evenings to make some extra money.

in Salalah and Sohar. Protestants should contact the pastor at the office in Ruwi for an appointment (24 799 475). Both partners should be resident in Oman and must provide proof of their marital status, which can take the form of a letter from their sponsor or embassy. Partners from different countries must provide evidence from their respective embassies that they are free to marry. Widowed or divorced people must produce appropriate original documents indicating they are free to marry. Four witnesses, two from the bride's side and two from the groom's, must attend the wedding ceremony. Copies of the passport information page and visa of each partner must be provided. The church requires at least one month's notice to perform the ceremony and premarital counselling is recommended. The marriage certificate must be attested by both the Ministry of Foreign Affairs (consular section) Attestation Office and by the couple's respective embassies. There is no fee for the ceremony but a donation is welcomed. To marry in the Salalah or Sohar protestant churches, contact the pastors (23 235 677) in Salalah or in Sohar (26 840 606).

Catholics should contact the priest at the Catholic Church of Saints Peter & Paul in Ruwi (24 701 893) or at Holy Spirit Catholic Church in Ghala (24 590 373). The couple is expected to take instruction before the wedding ceremony takes place. You will need your original baptism certificates and a No objection certificate (NOC) from your priest stating that you have not previously been married in a church. A declaration of your intent to marry is posted on the public noticeboard of the church for a period, after which, if there are no objections, the priest will fix a date for the ceremony. The parish priest will advise you of his fee accordingly.

Civil Weddings
Couples wanting a non-religious ceremony should contact their local embassy or consulate, as they may have regulations and referrals to arrange for a local civil marriage, which can then be registered at their embassy. Many people opt to hold their wedding receptions in Oman's plush hotels. Several hotels offer facilities for hosting weddings.

The Paperwork
All marriages should be registered at the Department of Notary Public in Al Khuwair within 30 days. To register your marriage, you will need a completed application form, and the marriage notification (from the Ministry of Justice) or a marriage certificate authenticated by the Oman diplomatic mission in the country where the marriage took place (if not in Oman). If one of the newly-weds is an Omani, they should produce their resident card or passport and ID card, as well as an approval letter from the Ministry of Interior. A marriage can be registered by the husband or the wife, or by their fathers. Although the Department of Notary Public is part of the Ministry of Justice, it is not located in the same building in Al Khuwair. The Ministry of Justice is located on Ministry Street, but the Department of Notary Public is located in Dohat Al Adab Street, one street down from the Radisson Blu Hotel. The phone number is 24 485 795, although not many employees speak English, so it might be better to go down there in person. The opening hours are 7.30am to 2.30pm.

Wedding Accessories
When it comes to finding the perfect dress, there are literally hundreds of tailor shops dotted around Muscat. The best way to find a good one is to ask around, and it's always a good idea to try them out with a smaller job before you hand over your priceless fabric.

Muslims
Two Muslims wishing to marry should apply at the marriage section of the Shariah Court in Wattayah. You will need two witnesses, both of whom should be Muslims. The woman does not need the permission of her father or brother to marry, unlike in some other Middle East countries. Passports and passport photocopies are required and you may marry immediately. The Shariah Court is located just off the Wattayah Roundabout, next to the Royal Oman Police (ROP) football stadium.

Hindus
Hindus can be married through the Shiva Temple (24 737 311), the Darsait Temple (24 798 548) and the Indian Embassy (24 684 500). Contact the Indian Embassy for further details.

Divorce
Unless you are married to an Omani, you may find it simpler to get divorced in your home country. Whether you choose to carry out the divorce in Oman or back home, you should contact your embassy first for guidance on the procedures and laws that apply to separation of assets, custody of children and legal status. While they may be able to provide some guidance, you should also contact a good lawyer in your home country, to advise on all aspects.

All divorces occurring in the Sultanate need to be reported within 30 days from the date of the event. You will need a completed application form, divorce notification from the Ministry of Justice or divorce certificate authenticated by the Oman Diplomatic mission in the country where the divorce took place. If one of the married couple is an Omani citizen, their resident card or passport and their ID card should be produced, along with an approval letter from the Ministry of Interior. Divorces are finalised at the Department of Notary Public (24 485 795).

Death Certificate & Registration

In the unhappy event of the death of a friend or relative, the Royal Oman Police (ROP) must be informed immediately. The ROP will make a report and you must also inform the deceased's sponsor, who is responsible for registering the death with the authorities. Death registration must be done within two weeks. To register the death, the sponsor should produce a completed application form (which you get from the ROP), a notification from the Ministry of Health, the ID of the deceased, the resident card or passport, and a letter from an official authority notifying that the burial has been carried out or that the body has been sent out of the country. Remember that in Muslim societies, bodies must be buried as soon as possible (in some cases, before sunset on the day of the death), so things can happen very fast. If there are any suspicious circumstances, the ROP will take photographs of the body. Post mortems, which are carried out at the ROP hospital in Wattayah, are only performed in the event of a suspicious or accidental death. In the case of an accident, doctors in the hospital will release the death certificate unless there is a post mortem pending, in which case the ROP will do so. The certificate is usually released to the sponsor. There is no charge for the death certificate, although it will not be released until all hospital bills are settled. Ensure that the cause of death is stated on the death certificate. From hospital, the deceased is taken to the mortuary.

In order to release the body, you or your sponsor must obtain a letter from the relevant embassy authorising the removal of the deceased from the hospital. This letter should be taken to the ROP, who will issue a letter for the hospital. You or your sponsor must arrange transport for the body, so you will need to buy a coffin and hire an ambulance. If you can't afford an ambulance, the deceased can be transported in your car. If desired, you can transport the deceased to their home country. To do this you should talk to the relevant airline to enquire about their procedures. You will need a release letter from your embassy, and the body will need to be embalmed. The ROP hospital charges RO.120 for embalming, and Khoula Hospital charges RO.100.

If you wish to perform a burial in Oman, you should get a letter to that effect from your embassy. Give this to the ROP, who will supply you with a letter for the hospital to release the body. Contact the church of your choice to perform the funeral service. Your embassy will contact the municipality. For non-Muslims, there is a cemetery at PDO.

On a precautionary note, if you intend to stay in Oman for some time you should seriously consider making a will under Shariah law, particularly if you are married. If one partner dies, it is so much easier for the remaining partner to sort out legalities quickly. Otherwise, it can take a long time to resolve questions of inheritance of items that are in your partner's name – and you can't leave the country until it's done.

Making A Will

Just like having savings, getting household insurance and contributing towards some kind of pension scheme, having a valid will in place is one of those essential things that everybody should do. As an expat, it is strongly advisable to make your will in your country of residence so that local laws do not adversely affect it.

If you become a property owner in Oman, you must make sure that you have changed your will accordingly as Shariah law has a very different view on who inherits your possessions in the event of your death. A good Oman-based law firm will be able to assist you with a locally viable will.

Pets

There is a mixed attitude towards pets in Oman, so if you are an animal lover and have a pet, it is advisable to keep them under strict control at all times. There are cases of animal abuse, mainly caused by a lack of education in the proper care of animals.

There are many volunteers in Oman who are working quietly behind the scenes helping to rehome stray dogs and cats from the streets. For general information on how to donate money or your time call 95 504 302. Alternatively, you can check out the Facebook page of Oman Animal Adoption & Fostering.

Cats & Dogs

It is a commonly held misconception that Muslims dislike dogs, but the Quran forbids the maltreatment of animals, including dogs, so the problem does not have a religious foundation. In the Arab culture in general, however, dogs are not held in high regard and are not usually seen as fluffy, lovable members of the family. On the other hand, there are many dog owners in Oman.

All dogs must be registered with the municipality and inoculations must be kept up to date. Puppies should be vaccinated at six weeks old and then annually. It is recommended that cats and dogs are sterilised to stop them from roaming (and adding to the stray population), although this is not compulsory.

Stray cats are a huge problem in Oman – they are often called 'string' cats because they are as thin as a piece of string. Every now and then the municipality has a crackdown where they round up and shoot or gas strays and it doesn't warn when this will happen so best to make sure your pet wears a collar at all times.

If you do adopt a stray, make sure it is vaccinated, dewormed, and sprayed for fleas. Oman is not a rabies-free country, so be very careful. If you are bitten by a stray animal (cats can carry rabies as well as dogs), go to Accident and Emergency at Khoula Hospital in Wattayah for an anti-rabies shot (only government hospitals have stocks of the vaccine).

Petshops

There is now quite a good selection of petshops in Muscat. Conditions in which the animals are kept vary from shop to shop with Animal World in the Al Araimi Complex arguably the best. The reputable shops provide papers for the 'pedigree' animals.

You can pay up to RO.400 for a dog and RO.200 for a 'pedigree' cat (sort of Persian or Siamese without papers). These cats are locally bred – genuine pedigree animals, with papers, come from Eastern Europe and will cost you twice as much. You can have your cat or dog vaccinated at the petshop and the first set of jabs is free, but they don't give all the vaccinations your pet will need. It's better to pay a visit to a reputable vet who can provide the essential rabies vaccination and give your new pet a check-up. Grooming is available at most of the petshops.

Vets & Kennels

Although there are not a huge number of vets practising in Muscat, you can still find good quality healthcare for your pet. Most clinics offer grooming and pet boarding as well as assisting you in arranging the paperwork involved in bringing a pet to Oman and having it registered, or taking it home again.

PetCare veterinary clinic is based in Al Azaiba and it offers a range of services including vaccinations, animal registration and import/export. Canadian Jebel K9 Training and Services offers boarding for dogs, in-house training and behaviour modification classes.

Bringing Your Pet To Oman

There are a number of regulations regarding the importing of your pet, which involves its fair share of paperwork and time. Before you leave your home country, you need to make sure that all vaccinations are up to date and stamped in its veterinary record booklet (which should be in English). The rabies vaccination, in particular, should be up to date. You will also need two health certificates from the vet in your home country: one should be dated no more than six months before your departure, and one should be obtained 10 days before your pet is due to travel. Check which airlines will carry pets, and book a space for yours.

With the help of your sponsor, you need to get a pet import certificate (RO.5) from the Ministry of Agriculture and Fisheries Animal Health Department (24 696 300). This certificate, along with a copy of the vaccination records and health certificates, should accompany your pet on arrival into Oman. Certificates must be produced at the airport on arrival of the animal to the quarantine office. If the authorities are not satisfied with the certificates, they can quarantine your pet for six months (so check with your local vet and the Oman embassy in your home country about the exact requirements). Clearing your pet at Seeb International Airport will take two to three hours. Although there are no special facilities for animals, they are placed in a special ventilated area where they won't suffer from the high temperatures.

Requirements For Importing Cats & Dogs

- Dogs and cats must be fully vaccinated, including for rabies, at least one month and no more than 12 months before arrival in Oman.
- Dogs and cats must be at least four months old when imported.
- The rabies vaccination sticker must be applied to the vaccination card.
- An import permit must be obtained from the Ministry of Agriculture before arrival.
- The original vaccination card and health certificate must travel with the animal, and they must be in English or have an English translation.

Pet Services

Animal World Al Araimi Complex, 968 24 561 211
Canadian Jebel K-9 Training & Services
968 99 419 595, *canadianjebelk9.com*
Creatures Petshop SABCO Commercial Centre, 968 24 563 721
Creatures Trading Ground floor SABCO Commercial Center, Shop 39, 968 24 563 721, *creaturestrading.com*
Pet Planet Markaza Al Bahja, 968 24 533 487, *petplanet-oman.com*

Veterinary Clinics

Al Hossan Pet Surgery Way 1822, Mina Al Fahal Rd, House 1494, 968 24 562 263
Al Marai Al Omaniya Nr Sohar Roundabout, 968 26 840 660
Al Qurum Veterinary Clinic Way 1822, Bldg 1467, 968 24 562 263, *muscatvets.com*
Capital Veterinary Centre SABCO Commercial Centre, 968 24 567 736, *vetoman.com*
Muscat Veterinary Clinic 968 99 100 056, *mvc-oman.com*
Private Veterinary Clinic 968 24 560 459
Royal Vet Royal Stables 968 24 420 322
Samha For Veterinary Services Nr Roundabout, Barka, 320 Al Batinah, 968 26 882 927
Tafani Veterinary Clinic Way 4863, Shop 3983A, 968 24 491 971, *tafanivets.com*

Taking Your Pet Home

When you leave Oman you need to start the procedure for taking your pet home a few weeks before your departure. Check with your airline about their policy on pets – if your pet is small enough you may be allowed to take it as carry-on luggage, rather than as cargo.

The regulations for exporting your pet depend on the country you are taking them to, so check beforehand. The basic requirements are usually the same though. You will need a valid vaccination card which should have been issued not more than one year and not less than 30 days ago. You need to get a pet health certificate from the municipality or the Ministry of Agriculture and Fisheries (normally issued one week before departure). Contact your airline to find out the best place to get a travel box that meets their regulations (normally it is made of wood or fibre glass).

For more information, a vet or kennels in your destination country, or the airline you are using, can give you more specific regulations such as quarantine rules.

Education

Oman, and Muscat in particular, is home to several international schools catering to children of various nationalities. Government schools are for Omani citizens only, so if you are living in Oman as an expat you will have to send your child to a private school. While it is advisable to visit as many schools as you can to get an idea of the academic standards and extra-mural facilities, remember that it makes sense to stick to a national curriculum that fits in with your future plans. For example, if you will probably end up living back in the UK during some stage of your child's education, it is sensible to enrol your child in a school that teaches the English National Curriculum.

A Little Bit Of Brit

Teaching co-ed students from 3 to 18 according to the National Curriculum for England (from primary to GCSEs and A Levels), the British School Muscat is highly thought of for its high standards and is regularly inspected by the UK's strict OFSTED framework. As well as traditional classes, the school offers several additional language options, as well as being active in sports and the arts. However, BSM is more than one of the country's leading schools, and forms something of a social hub for the local expat community.

If possible, have a chat to other expats to ask for their advice on schools. Try to visit schools during the school day and ask if you can see a class in progress.

You will sometimes find that there are waiting lists for certain schools or nurseries, so register your child as early as you possibly can. To enrol your child in a school, you will need to submit the following:
- School application form
- Passport photos of your child
- Copies of your child's birth certificate
- Up-to-date immunisation record
- Reports from your child's previous school (if applicable)

The school will inform you of any other documents they need, as well as any registration fees.

Nurseries & Pre-Schools

If you have a child of nursery age, you will find quite a lot of choice in Muscat. Facilities and standards vary enormously, as do the fees, so it is worth checking out a few different nurseries before you make your decision. Some nurseries accept children as young as six months, but this is the exception rather than the rule. There are often waiting lists for the more popular nurseries, so put your child's name down early if there is one you have your heart set on.

Nurseries are usually open in the mornings only. Some offer flexibility in terms of how many days per week your child will attend, so if you don't want your child to go to school for a full five days a week, you may be able to choose four, three or even two days a week. Different nurseries have different teaching styles – some encourage learning through play and some have a more structured curriculum. It is up to you to decide what system will be more beneficial to your child. Other factors to consider are child to teacher ratio, staff qualifications, and provision of extra services such as meals and transport.

Nurseries & Pre-Schools

Abu Abnan Nursery Villa 1679, Way 1932, Road 17, 968 24 605 704
American British Academy (ABA) Al Khuwair Heights District, 968 24 955 800, *abaoman.edu.om*
Art Of Living Nursery Villa 3701, Way 4032, 968 24 613 130
Bright Beginnings Nursery Way1737, Villa 61, Al Nadhayer St, Nr British School, 968 24 699 387, *bbnursery.com*
Kids World Nursery House 9411A, Way 897, Mawaleh North, Nr The Wave Muscat, 968 99 254 455, *kidsworldoman.com*
Little Flowers Nursery Way 3032, Villa 169, 968 24 703 317, *nurseriesofoman.com*
Little Gems Al Azaiba, 968 24 498 464, *littlegemsoman.com*
National Nursery Montessori Villa 1045, Way 2414, Qurum Heights, 968 24 560 096, *montessorioman.com*

EDUCATING A NEW GENERATION OF CULTURAL HERITAGE PROFESSIONALS

UCL is London's Global University. At UCL Qatar we offer a world-leading selection of postgraduate degree programmes, focusing on archaeology, conservation and museum studies. Through outstanding teaching and innovative research, we are creating the leaders of tomorrow.

Discover more and apply online at **www.ucl.ac.uk/qatar**

UCL Qatar, PO Box 23689, Georgetown Building,
Hamad bin Khalifa University, Doha, Qatar

T: +974 4457 8680
E: admissions.qatar@ucl.ac.uk UCLQatar  UCL_Qatar

Oasis Kindergarten 968 24 691 348, *ok-oman.com*
Small Steps Nursery Way 4848, Villa 2979,
968 24 495 802, *ssnursery.com*
Tender Buds Nursery Way 2472, Villa 4472,
968 24 691 055, *nurseriesofoman.com*
The American Intl School Nr Ghala Church, Ghala St,
968 24 595 180, *taism.com*

Primary & Secondary Schools

Standards of teaching in Oman's schools are usually high and schools tend to have excellent facilities with extracurricular activities offered. International schools will often employ teachers who have been trained in, and have teaching experience from, the country relevant to the curriculum. The curriculum will probably be an important factor in choosing a school for your child – it makes sense to choose a curriculum that will make it easy for your child to slot back into a school in your home country (or in whatever country you might end up in one day). Be aware that waiting lists can be very long so prioritise this when you confirm the move to Oman. A relocation company like Sununu Muscat (sununumuscat.com) can help.

Primary & Secondary Schools
American British Academy (ABA) Al Khuwair Heights District, 968 24 955 800, *abaoman.edu.om*
Azzan Bin Qais International School Nr Dolphin Village Residential Complex, Bowshar St, 968 24 503 081, *azzanbinqais.com*

British School Muscat 19 Street, 968 24 600 842, *britishschoolmuscat.com*
École Française de Mascate Way 5914, Al Feteh, 968 24 596 600, *efmascate.voila.net*
Indian School Nr Ministry of Tourism, As Sultan Qaboos St, 968 24 491 587, *indianschool.com*
Indian School 968 24 707 567, *indianschoolmuscat.com*
Muscat International School Madinat Al Sultan Qaboos St, 968 24 565 550, *misoman.org*
Pakistan School Muscat 2519 Way, Off Ruwi St, 968 24 702 489, *pakistanschool.edu.om*
The American Intl School Nr Ghala Church, Ghala St, 968 24 595 180, *taism.com*
The International School Of Choueifat Muscat Al Hail South Seeb, Block 323, Way 2345, 968 24 534 000, *iscoman-sabis.net*
The Sultan's School A'Soroor St, 3117 Way, Al Hail South, 968 24 536 777, *sultansschool.org*

University & Higher Education

Over the past 10 years, there has been great investment in the expansion of higher education institutions (HEI) in Oman. Sultan Qaboos University (SQU) is still the largest government funded university and expatriate students are not permitted to apply. However, by 2011, there were 29 private institutions and colleges with an enrolment of some 35,000 students with expatriates making up a substantial percentage. The Omani Ministry of Higher Education encourages these private

Educational standards in Oman are high

BRITISH SCHOOL
MUSCAT

Providing high quality British education for children aged 3-18 for over 40 years.

BRITISH EDUCATION INTERNATIONAL FUTURE

PO Box 1907, Ruwi 112, Sultanate of Oman.
+968 2460 0842.
admin@britishschoolmuscat.com

britishschoolmuscat.com

HEI to choose highly reputable universities as partners in academic affiliation agreements for the purpose of monitoring and improving quality, diversifying programme offerings, and increasing the prestige of the diploma/degree awarded by the HEI.

Carnegie Mellon University Qatar

This institution is popular with international students and is one of the premier research universities in the world. It offers five undergraduate majors: Biological Sciences, Business Administration, Computational Biology, Computer Science and Information Systems.

Many students still choose to go abroad for their higher level education. However, by 2014, there were over 30 private institutions and colleges in Oman, with an enrolment of some 40,000 students, with expatriates making up a substantial percentage.

University & Higher Education

Bayan College Al Azaiba, 968 24 691 183, *bayancollege.edu.om*
Caledonian College Al Hail South, As Seeb St, 968 24 536 165, *cce.edu.om*
Gulf College Nr Centrepoint, 968 24 600 665, *gulfcollege.edu.om*
Gutech German University Of Technology In Oman Way 36, Building 331, North Ghubrah, 968 24 493 051, *gutech.edu.om*
Oman Medical College Nr Muscat Private Hospital, Bowshar St, 968 26 844 004, *omc.edu.om*

UCL Qatar

University College London (UCL) was the first British university to open a campus in Qatar, partnering with Qatar Foundation and Qatar Museums Authority. This institution offers three postgraduate study programmes: an MA in Museum and Gallery Practice, an MA in The Archaeology of the Arab and Islamic World and an MSc in Conservation Studies.

Overseas Study

Looking to attend university elsewhere in the Gulf? Dubai isn't the only regional education powerhouse. Abu Dhabi has a couple of higher education opportunities, such as a Paris-Sorbonne campus, while Qatar is hot on its heels with world-class offerings such as UCL Qatar, Carnegie Mellon University Qatar, Virginia Commonwealth University Qatar and Northwestern University in Qatar. Each institution boasts the latest facilities and top-notch faculties, and they are popular options for students who want to remain in the region for their higher education.

Special Needs Education

There are no dedicated schools in Oman for expatriate children with special needs. However, there are centres that accommodate both Omani and expatriate children as well as special support departments in some schools.

Special Needs Education

Association Of Early Intervention For Children With Disability 18th November Rd, Villa 3215, Al Azaiba, 968 24 496 960, *aei.org.om*
Centre For Special Education Indian School Muscat 968 24 702 567, *ismoman.com*
Creative Center For Rehabilitation Way 1748, 968 95 303 700, *ccr-oman.com*

Learning Arabic

English is so widely used in Oman that you can get by without having to learn a single word of Arabic. However, some say that to enrich the cultural experience of your time in this part of the world, knowing some basic Arabic is helpful. It can even help you in the workplace, as locals are sure to appreciate your effort to communicate with them in their mother tongue. Plus, if you have children, there is a good chance they will be learning some Arabic at school, so it can be useful to know a bit yourself. You could join a school for group lessons or find a personal tutor. The following language academies offer courses for beginners to advanced students.

Language Schools

Berlitz Language Center Villa 1455, Way 2419, 968 24 566 293, *berlitz.ae*
British Council Nr Petrol Station, As Sultan Qaboos St Muscat, 968 24 681 000, *britishcouncil.org*
ELS Language Centers Al Khuwair, 968 24 613 440, *elsoman.com*
Goethe Institut Bldg 1954, Rd 3024, 968 24 603 841, *goethe.de/gulfregion*
Gulf Arabic Programme Al Jazeel Administrative Training Institute, Buraimi, 968 25 640 078, *gapschool.net*
Modern Gulf Institute Nr Markaz Al Bahja Shopping Centre, 968 24 542 737, *moderngulf.com*
New Horizons Computer Learning Centers NTI Building, Nr British Council, 968 24 486 600, *newhorizons.com*
Polyglot Institute Oman Tamimah Complex Wattayah Muscat, 968 24 666 666, *polyglot.org*
Salalah Language International 968 95 628 825, *salalahlanguageinternational.com*
The French-Omani Centre 207 Al Inshirah St, Muscat, 968 24 697 579, *ambafrance-om.org*

HEALTH

Expats and tourists are not entitled to use government hospitals but must instead register with one of the private hospitals or clinics, with the exception of expats requiring emergency treatment that is not available in private hospitals and expats working for the Omani government. If you are an expat and you do require treatment at a government hospital or clinic, you will be charged for their services. Muscat Private Hospital and KIMS Oman Hospital are clean and well-staffed with English speaking professionals. Most people who receive medical treatment in Oman can say their experience was a positive one. However, private medical care is costly, and visitors and non-residents are strongly advised to take out medical insurance. All babies, regardless of nationality, can receive free vaccinations at the government health centres throughout the country. The children must be registered at the health centre nearest to their homes.

Your employer may provide health insurance for you but it may be less than fully comprehensive. It is vital that you arrange insurance for yourself and your family as treatment here can be very costly. Dental and maternity cover are usually optional and not provided as standard; women may need to be with an insurer for at least one year to qualify for maternity cover.

Hospitals
Al Raffah Hospital Al Batinah, 968 26 704 639, *asterhospital.com*
Badr Al Samaa Hospital 968 24 799 760, *badralsamaahospitals.com*
Khoula Hospital Maydan Al Fath St, 968 24 560 455
Kims Oman Hospital Nr Muscat Municipality HQ, 968 24 760 100, *kimsoman.com*
Lifeline Hospital Falaj Al Qabail, 968 26 753 084, *lifelineoman.com*
Muscat Private Hospital Bowshar St, 968 24 583 600, *muscatprivatehospital.com*
Starcare Hospital 968 24 557 200, *starcarehospital.com*
The Royal Hospital Al Gubrah St, Off Al Azaiba R/A, 968 24 599 000, *royalhospital.med.om*

General Practice Clinics
Al Azaiba Health Centre 968 24 497 233
Al Ghubrah Health Centre 968 24 497 226
Al Wadi Al Kabeer Health Center 968 24 812 944
Baushar Polyclinic 968 24 593 311
Muttrah Health Center 968 24 711 296
Ruwi Health Center 968 24 786 088

Obstetrics & Gynaecology Clinics
Advanced Fertility & Genetics Centre 968 24 489 647
Al Massaraat Medical Centre Nr Al Qurum Complex, 968 24 566 435
Al Rimah Medical Centre Rex Road, 968 24 700 515
Apollo Medical Centre 968 24 787 766, *apollomuscat.com*
Atlas Star Medical Centre 968 24 504 000, *healthcare.atlasera.com*
Dr Maurice Al Asfour Specialised Medical Centre Nr Al Qurum Natural Park, 968 24 560 673
Hatat Polyclinic Hatat House Wadi Adai Street, 968 24 563 641
Medicare Centre 968 24 699 082
Muscat Private Hospital Bowshar St, 968 24 583 600, *muscatprivatehospital.com*

Specialist Clinics & Practitioners
Al Afaq Medical Diagnostic & Imaging Centre Al Rawabi Complex, Nr Royal Hospital, 968 24 501 162
Al Amal Medical & Health Care Centre Bldg 2765, Street 41, 968 24 485 052
Al Hayat Polyclinic Nr Friday Market & Al Jadeeda Supermarket, 968 26 845 104, *alhayatclinic.com*
Al Lamki Polyclinic Golden Furniture Bldg, 968 24 489 543
Al Masarrah Hospital 968 24 878 723
Al Rimah Medical Centre Rex Road, 968 24 700 515
Atlas Star Medical Centre Nr Sheraton Hotel, 968 24 811 743, *healthcare.atlasera.com*
Dr Maurice Al Asfour Specialised Medical Centre Nr Al Qurum Natural Park, 968 24 560 673
Elixir Health Centre 968 24 571 800, *elixir-oman.com*
Emirates Medical Center Nr Salallah Mall, North Owkad, 968 23 212 145, *emc-oman.com*
Lama Polyclinic Nr Al Qabil R/A, 968 24 799 077, *lamapolyclinicoman.com*
Medicare Centre 968 24 699 082
Medident Madinat Qaboos Medical Centre Way 2124, Road 3, 968 24 600 668, *medidentoman.com*
Muscat Eye Laser Center House 877, Way 3013, Sarooj St, 968 24 691 414, *muscateye.com*
Muscat Private Hospital Bowshar St, 968 24 583 600, *muscatprivatehospital.com*
Qurum Medical Centre 61 Al Ilam St, 968 24 692 898, *qurummedicalcentre.com*

Accidents & Emergencies

If you have a medical emergency while in Oman, you can just turn up at any government hospital's accident and emergency department to be seen by a doctor. You may then be transferred to any private hospital of your choosing for further specialist treatment if required. Charges depend upon what kind of treatment you receive, but are not cheap, regardless of which medical centre you choose. A consultation with a doctor will set you back around RO.20, even before any medication or treatment is dispensed. Medical insurance is a must.

The ambulance service in Oman is fairly new and the fleet of vehicles with trained staff is still relatively small. Response times are not published so it's difficult to say how reliable a service it actually is. This may be due in part to the fact that other road users do not automatically move out of the way to let an ambulance through the traffic, or are already blocking the emergency lane. Some of the hospitals and clinics have their own ambulance service but again, may take some time to reach you.

The golden rule is never to attempt to move an injured person, but in a place where ambulance response times are slow, you may have to weigh up the risks and decide whether it would be better to transport the victim to hospital in your own car.

Alternative Therapies

Muscat is a cultural crossroads and many of its residents come from countries where traditional therapies are practised. Consequently, there is a good balance of holistic treatments and orthodox western medicine available. Natural medicine can be very effective and, because the treatments are aimed at balancing the whole person, your therapist will need to know a lot about you. Be prepared to spend up to two hours on the first consultation so that your therapist can build up a picture of your background and medical history. Alternative treatments can cost as much as western medicine.

While they rarely offer the quick fix that one expects from orthodox practice, they work slowly and gently with the body's natural processes, so be prepared to stick with it to get a result. As always, word of mouth is the best way to find the most appropriate treatment. For general advice on a range of alternative medical treatments, contact the Al Kawakeb Complex Ayurvedic Clinic, Qurum (24 494 762) or the All Season Ayurveda Clinic, MSQ (24 475 280).

Alternative Therapies
1st Chiropractic Centre Way 3034, Villa 2715, 968 24 472 274
Acu-Magnetic Treatment Centre 968 24 487 828
Al Muthanna Ayurvedic Clinic 968 24 484 049
Al Nama Medical Centre 968 24 494 762, *alnamamedicalcenter.com*
Al Salsabeel Herbal Center 968 99 389 547
Ayurvedic Clinic 968 24 478 618
Chinese Massage Centre 968 99 890 804
Chinese Medical & Herbal Clinic 968 24 799 729

Noor Al Madeena Herbal Clinic Al Kaaf Bldg, Nr Sultan Qaboos Mosque, 968 24 780 519
Roots & Herbs 968 24 799 097
Taimour Ayurvedic Clinic 968 24 799 689

Acupressure & Acupuncture
One of the oldest healing methods in the world, acupressure involves the systematic placement of pressure with fingertips on established meridian points on the body. This therapy can be used to relieve pain, soothe the nerves and stimulate the body, as determined necessary by the therapist. Acupuncture is an ancient Chinese technique that uses needles to access the body's meridian points. The technique is surprisingly painless and is quickly becoming an alternative or complement to western medicine, as it aids ailments such as asthma, rheumatism, and even more serious diseases. It has also been known to work wonders on animals.

Back Treatment
Treatment for back problems is widely available with some excellent specialists.

Chiropractic and osteopathy treatments concentrate on manipulating the skeleton in a non-intrusive manner to improve the functioning of the nervous system or blood supply to the body. Chiropractic is based on the manipulative treatment of misalignments in the joints, especially those of the spinal column, while osteopathy involves the manipulation and massage of the skeleton and musculature.

Pilates is said to be the safest form of neuromuscular reconditioning and back strengthening available. Les Mills' Body Training System classes are also extremely effective, particularly BodyPump, BodyBalance and RPM. The Palm Beach Club at the InterContinental Hotel (24 680 000) has five Body Training System licences. A number of clinics offer therapeutic massage for back pain, and word of mouth is a good way to get a recommendation.

Cosmetic Treatment & Surgery
There are reputable options if you want a little 'touch-up' in the form of cosmetic surgery. Muscat Private Hospital (24 583 600) has resident plastic surgeons, and Emirates Medical Center (24 604 540) offers a huge range of treatments. They also have regular visits by specialists from around the world.

Homeopathy
This form of treatment has been practised in Europe for 200 years. It is a safe and effective treatment for jump starting the body's formidable self-healing powers. Working at both the physical and emotional levels, it treats the whole person rather than the

symptoms, using remedies derived from a variety of natural sources. Practitioners undergo rigorous training and many are also qualified western medical doctors. Homeopathic remedies are not available over the counter in Oman as they are in many countries, but there are several practising homeopaths and clinics including Whispers of Serenity in Al Azaiba.

Physiotherapy

If you're unfortunate enough to be on the end of a nasty injury or muscular skeletal illness and require physiotherapy, you'll find excellent and well-trained care at Muscat Private Hospital and the Physiotherapy and Rehabilitation Centre (24 605 115).

Reflexology & Massage Therapy

Reflexology is another scientifically detailed method of bringing the body and mind back into balance. Based on the premise that reflex points on the feet and hands correspond to the organs and body systems, and that massaging these points improves and maintains health, reflexology works by stimulating the body's natural self-healing process. When considering reflexology, remember the following safety guidelines: do not eat right before your massage; keep drinking water during the course of your massage; and get your doctor's permission if you suffer from asthma, diabetes, a heart condition, kidney problems, high blood pressure or epilepsy. While many spas and salons offer massage and reflexology, there are those which offer a more focused therapeutic approach to the holistic healing qualities of reflexology and massage.

Sports Injuries

Many expats lead active lives, working hard and then playing hard. But accidents and injuries do happen, so whether you get roughed up playing rugby, pull something in the gym, or simply trip over the cat, you'll be pleased to hear there are some excellent facilities to help you on the road to recovery.

Counselling & Therapy

In addition to the normal pressures of modern living, expat life can have its particular challenges. Moving to a different culture can be stressful, even for the most resilient personalities. Although people are generally friendly here, they have their own busy lives and it can be lonely until you settle in. If you need someone to talk to there are places you can go for support. The Al Harub Medical Center (24 600 750) in Shatti has both life coaches and psychotherapists available, while Muscat Private Hospital (MPH), University Hospital and Hatat Polyclinic can put you in touch with counsellors, psychologists and psychiatrists.

Dentists & Orthodontists

Private dentistry in Oman is, like most other private medical services, of a high standard. Various practitioners offer not only general check-ups and basic dental care, but also dental surgery and cosmetic dentistry. Prices tend to match the level of service (high), and unfortunately most standard health insurance packages will not cover dental costs (except for emergency treatment required as the result of an accident). Most policies offer the option of paying a higher premium to cover dentistry.

Dentists & Orthodontists

Al Amal Medical & Health Care Centre Bldg 2765, Street 41, 968 24 485 052
Al Essa Dental Clinic Gulf House, Nr Bank Al Markazi, CBD, 968 24 797 406
Al Ghubrah Dental Clinic & Orthodontic Nr Boat R/A, 968 24 597 708
American Dental Center Al Masa Mall, 968 24 695 422, *adcoman.com*
Amira Dental Clinic 968 24 565 477
Emirates Medical Center Al Sarooj Plaza, 968 24 604 540, *emc-oman.com*
Harub Dental Surgery Qurum Heights, 968 24 563 814, *harubdental.com*
Medident Madinat Qaboos Medical Centre Way 2124, Road 3, 968 24 600 668, *medidentoman.com*
Muscat Dental Specialists Villa 1301, Way 3017, 968 24 600 664, *muscatdental.com*
Precision Dental Clinic Al Hsoon Bldg, Nr Shatti Plaza, 968 24 696 247, *precisiondentalclinic.com*
Qurum Medical Centre 61 Al Ilam St, 968 24 692 898, *qurummedicalcentre.com*
Scientific Polyclinic 968 24 560 035
Sun Dental Centre Ghubrah R/A, Nr Al Raffah Hospital, 968 95 961 234, *sundentalmuscat.com*
Waneela Polyclinic Al Jadeeda Supermarket Bldg, 968 99 314 365
Wassan Specialty Dental Clinic 968 24 489 469, *wassandental.com*

Maternity Care

Oman labour law allows working mothers to continue to receive their basic salary, including allowances, for 50 days after the birth. If you have had a caesarean section, you may be granted extra leave depending on your doctor's recommendation. You are also allowed two hours a day for the rather hilariously titled 'milking time' for the next 12 to 24 weeks, so that you can go home and feed your baby. After that, you will be required to return to work as you did before the birth, unless your doctor has recommended that you take extra time.

Paternity leave is at the discretion of your employer, and not recognised as a father's right in Oman. Instead, it is common to take some of your annual leave if you want to spend time with your exhausted wife and new baby.

Maternity Care

Hatat Polyclinic Hatat House Wadi Adai Street, 968 24 563 641
Medident Madinat Qaboos Medical Centre Way 2124, Road #3, 968 24 600 668, *medidentoman.com*
Muscat Private Hospital Bowshar St, 968 24 583 600, *muscatprivatehospital.com*
Sultan Qaboos University Hospital 968 24 415 747, *squ.edu.om*

Opticians & Ophthalmologists

There are plenty of opticians in Oman, one of the most reputable eye clinics in the Sultanate being the Muscat Eye Laser Center. Additionally, the Finland Eye Center is also highly recommended. Most opticians offer free eye tests if you are ordering your glasses from them, as well as contact lenses.

Opticians & Ophthalmologists
Al Ghazal Opticians SABCO Commercial Centre, 968 24 563 546
Al Said Optics Al Qurum Complex, 968 24 566 272
Finland Eye Center Qurum Garden Blg, 968 24 564 488, *finlandeyecenter.com*
Grand Optics Muscat City Centre, 968 24 558 890, *grandoptics.com*
Magrabi Eye & Ear Center Al Rumaila Building 16, Al Nahda St, 968 24 568 870, *magrabihospitals.com*
Muscat Eye Laser Center House 877, Way 3013, Sarooj St, 968 24 691 414, *muscateye.com*
Oman Opticals 968 23 293 714
Yateem Optician Al Khamis Plaza, 968 24 563 716, *yateemgroup.com*

Paediatrics

Most hospitals and many private clinics have full-time paediatricians on staff. Check out groups like Muscat Mums (muscatmums.com) for a recommendation.

Paediatrics
Al Lamki Polyclinic Golden Furniture Bldg, 968 24 489 543
Apollo Medical Centre 968 24 787 766, *apollomuscat.com*
Atlas Star Medical Centre 968 24 504 000, *healthcare.atlasera.com*

Muscat Private Hospital Bowshar St, 968 24 583 600, *muscatprivatehospital.com*
The Royal Hospital Al Gubrah St, Off Al Azaiba R/A, 968 24 599 000, *royalhospital.med.om*

Pharmacies & Medications

Most pharmacies open from 10am to 1pm and 4pm to 10pm, Saturday to Thursday, though many now remain open all day. On Fridays, most open from 4pm to 10pm. There is always at least one open 24 hours a day – check the daily newspapers for details. Alternatively, call Muscat Pharmacy on 24 814 501.

Pharmacies & Medications
Abu Al Dahab Clinic & Pharmacy 23rd July St, New Salalah, 968 23 291 303
Hatat Polyclinic Hatat House Wadi Adai Street, 968 24 563 641
Medident Madinat Qaboos Medical Centre Way 2124, Road 3, 968 24 600 668, *medidentoman.com*
Muscat Pharmacy & Stores 968 24 814 501, *muscatpharmacy.net*
Muscat Private Hospital Bowshar St, 968 24 583 600, *muscatprivatehospital.com*
Scientific Pharmacy Villa 764, Street 2114, 968 24 605 060
Sultan Qaboos University Hospital 968 24 415 747, *squ.edu.om*

Support Groups

In 1992, Unicef, together with the Ministry of Health, set up CSG (Community Support Groups). With the help of the Omani Women's Association, CSG holds workshops and training to implement support networks throughout the region. Health centres, private clinics and hospitals are a good source of information for finding support groups.

Support Groups
Al Noor Association For The Blind Nr Holiday Inn, 968 24 483 118, *alnoor4blind.org.om*
Alcoholics Anonymous Top Medical Clinic, Nr Rawasco, 968 99 721 396, *e-aa.org*
Association Of Early Intervention For Children With Disability 18th November Rd, Villa 3215, Al Azaiba, 968 24 496 960, *aei.org.om*
Down Syndrome Support Group 968 95 621 200, *downsyndromeoman.com*
Muscat Mums *muscatmums.110mb.com*
Narcotics Anonymous Hatat Polyclinic, 968 95 223 881, *nainarabia.com*
The National Association For Cancer Awareness 968 24 498 716, *ocanceROrg.om*

Life's Better
when you See Better

Muscat Eye Laser Center introduces a whole new look.

At Muscat Eye Laser Center, we have been offering the highest level of comfort and after-care for over a decade.
It's been made possible through the hands of our experienced physicians and with the help of leading-edge technology.
To us, it's not just about advanced eyecare treatments; it's about helping you see life, the way it's meant to be.

مركز مسقط لعلاج العيون بالليزر
Muscat Eye Laser Center

Telephone +968 2469 1414
www.muscateye.com

WELL-BEING

For some, it takes little more than the soothing sound of the sea to relax mind and body. Even if that doesn't quite do the trick, mental and physical well-being is easily obtainable in Oman. Whether you choose to set the tone of your day with a morning yoga session, or you want to fix your weight, skin or hair, there are a number of centres that can help.

Beauty Salons

Beauty salons in Oman offer a wide variety of treatments and one of the more unique experiences is to have your hands and feet painted with henna. This is a traditional art, mainly done for weddings or special occasions. The intricate patterns fade after two to three weeks. You can easily identify which salons offer henna painting by the pictures of patterned hands and feet displayed in their shop windows.

You'll find that all the major hotels have their own in-house styling salons, which are open to both guests and the general public. Some of the more popular salons are listed below.

Beauty Salons
Angel Beauty Salon Nr Grand Hyatt Muscat, 968 24 698 511
Beauty Centre Jawharat A'Shati & Oasis By The Sea Commercial Complex, 968 24 602 074, *beautycenterllc.com*
Beauty Today Nr Al Qurum Complex, 968 24 568 991
Crowne Plaza Resort Salalah Al Khandaque St, 968 23 238 000, *crowneplaza.com*
Diva Hair & Beauty Salon House 284, Street 2333, 968 24 693 011
Hana's Hair & Skincare Centre Al Madina Plaza, 968 24 697 270
Hollywood Beauty Centre Nr Muscat International School, 968 24 568 292
Hyatt Spa Nr Grand Hyatt Hotel, 968 24 601 255
Lucy's Beauty Salon Al Asfoor Plaza, 968 24 571 757
Muscat Beauty Salon SABCO Commercial Centre, 968 24 562 541
Nails Jawharat A'Shati & Oasis By The Sea Commercial Complex, 968 24 699 440
Raz Hair & Beauty 968 24 692 219
Signature Hair & Beauty Way 4837, 18th November St, 968 24 490 282
The Spa Bar For Men Jawharat A'Shati & Oasis By The Sea Commercial Complex, 968 24 698 681

Hairdressers

Oman has a wide range of options for getting your hair done – at one end of the scale there are small barber shops where men can get a haircut and relaxing head massage for under RO.2 (and if you're feeling brave, opt for a cut-throat razor shave for a few hundred baisas more!). For ladies, there is a choice of basic cuts in a beauty salon (a standard cut without blow dry should cost around RO.5 or less), and top-of-the-range hair care in a swanky hairdressers, where you could spend RO.30 or more.

Hairdressers
Al Hana Saloon 968 24 561 668
Angel Beauty Salon Nr Grand Hyatt Muscat, 968 24 698 511
Beauty Centre Wadi Centre, Qurum Commercial Area, 968 24 563 321, *beautycenterllc.com*
Diva Hair & Beauty Salon House 284, Street 2333, 968 24 693 011
Raz Hair & Beauty 968 24 692 219
Signature Hair & Beauty Way 4837, 18th November St, 968 24 490 282

Health Clubs

Most health clubs offer workout facilities such as machines and weights, plus classes in anything from aerobics to yoga, while some also have swimming pools and tennis or squash courts. Many of the beach clubs also offer some sports and gym facilities so are worth considering if you want the added bonus of the beach. In addition to these, the Ras Al Hamra Club offers a wide variety of activities for PDO employees and members are sometimes allowed to sign guests in for specific occasions or events.

Remember that when using the changing rooms of your health club, some people may feel uncomfortable if you do not use the private cubicles to get changed. Respect the modesty that prevails in any Islamic country, and always remain as covered up as possible.

Health Clubs
Al Nahda Resort & Spa Nakhal St, Off Muscat Sohar Highway, 968 26 883 710, *alnahdaresort.com*
Al Nama Medical Centre 968 24 494 762, *alnamamedicalcenter.com*
Horizon Fitness 968 24 390 428, *horizonoman.com*
Mercure Al Falaj Health Club Al Falaj Hotel, 968 24 702 311, *omanhotels.com*
The Health Club The Chedi Muscat, 968 24 524 400, *chedimuscat.com*
The Platinum Healthclub The Platinum, Nr Oman Oil Petrol Pump, 968 24 392 500, *theplatinumoman.com*

Nutritionists & Slimming

Unfortunately there is no Weight Watchers or similar slimming group in Oman, so if you have a few pounds to shift, you're on your own. You might benefit from the various slimming treatments on offer at Ayana Spa in Shatti Al Qurum – depending on your needs they will recommend a combination of treatments such as ultrasonic treatment, lymphatic drainage, body sculpting massage and healthy eating programmes. Apollo Medical Centre in Ruwi has an obesity clinic aimed at helping you control your weight in a healthy way. While the clinic will focus on your eating habits and give you diet and exercise guidelines to follow, in severe cases of obesity they may prescribe certain medications. VLCC Wellness Centres offer dietary plans and slimming programmes from its locations in Shati Al Qurum (24 695 157) and Al Mawaleh (24 553 535) outside Muscat.

Most gyms have professionally trained staff who can advise you on a healthy eating plan along with an exercise regime. They will monitor your progress until you achieve the results you are after.

Spas

Ayana Spa
Al Sarooj Plaza 968 24 693 435
ayanaspa.com
Map **2 G2**

Looking and feeling good is taken to a whole new level here. The Balinese-inspired decor, with its water features and soft background music, puts you in the mood for some soothing pampering. You have a range of personalised spa treatments for body and hair to choose from (and they'll just happen to do wonders for your mind too), plus the usual manicures, pedicures and massages.

Treatments from the Institute of Biologique Recherché care for every skin type and condition, while the slimming programmes are executed by an expert team of professional aestheticians and therapists, using state of the art endermology, ultrasound and electrolypolisis machines.

CHI The Spa
Shangri-La's Barr Al Jissah Resort & Spa
968 24 776 828
shangri-la.com
Map **2 L4**

CHI creates a perfect world where your mind and body are surrounded in luxury and serenity, with smells and sounds all muted and mellow to ensure a totally restful experience. There are so many wonderful treatments on offer that it can be difficult to choose. The Aroma Vitality massage, however, comes highly recommended, leaving guests feeling both relaxed and rejuvenated after being tended on by professional therapists who fully embrace the serenity of the surroundings. The Spa is like a little hideaway where guests can enjoy privacy and luxuriate in the spacious relaxation areas and private garden patios. Dates, juices and water are available to complete the experience as you lounge and soak in the healthy energy.

CHI The Spa

Eram Spa

Al Nahda Resort & Spa 968 26 883 710
alnahdaresort.com
Map **1 F4**
This luxurious resort and spa in Barka is a haven of pampering for weary souls in need of some care. Whether you want to improve your fitness, lose some of those extra pounds, or just spend a few days of blissful relaxation away from the stresses of everyday life, Al Nahda's expert team of fitness and health specialists will be able to help. After you check into your beautiful villa or room, you can start your wellness programme and take the first step towards a better you. While at the resort, you can enjoy a healthy menu of spa cuisine, although a glass of wine or a big slice of chocolate cake is available too, in case you lose your resolve. A minimum stay of three days is recommended (but not compulsory).

Six Senses Spa

Six Senses Zighy Bay 968 26 735 555
sixsenses.com
Map **1 E2**
Six Senses Zighy Bay is renowned for its jaw-dropping luxury, and its spa is no exception. A holistic oasis nestled in the Zighy Bay mountainside with nine treatment rooms and two Arabian Hammams, the spa's wide-ranging menu of regional and Six Senses signature treatments focuses on holistic and pampering therapies using only natural products. administered by skilled therapists who combine eastern and western techniques with modern lifestyle programmes to balance the senses.

The Spa

The Chedi Muscat North Ghubra 32, Way 3215,
968 24 524 400
ghmhotels.com
Map **2 E3**
This fabulous space has the accolade of being the largest spa in Muscat, and is well equipped to invigorate your senses and sooth your soul. With 13 meditative spa suites (including double suites) and a spa lounge (where you can enjoy herbal tea while looking out on the ocean), this is the perfect place for an individual or a couple to relax. Embracing eastern philosophy, spa rituals here originate from the healing traditions of places such as Bali, India and Tibet. Enjoy the Chedi jade massage where two therapists work in synchronised movements, a bio-rhythm envelopment for jetlag which includes an energy body polish and a mud wrap or a bespoke facial for toning and moisturising.

Safana Spa

Sifawy Boutique Hotel, Jebel Sifah
968 24 749 111
sifawyhotel.com
Map **1 G4**
Visitors to the hugely popular Sifawy Boutique Hotel can finally enjoy some pampering. The newly opened Safana Spa is the most recent addition to the resort, and well worth the wait. The extensive menu includes a range of massages, body scrubs and facials designed to leave you feeling relaxed and pampered. Or, if it's just a quick treat you want, there are manicures, pedicures and waxing treatments too.

The Spa, The Chedi Muscat

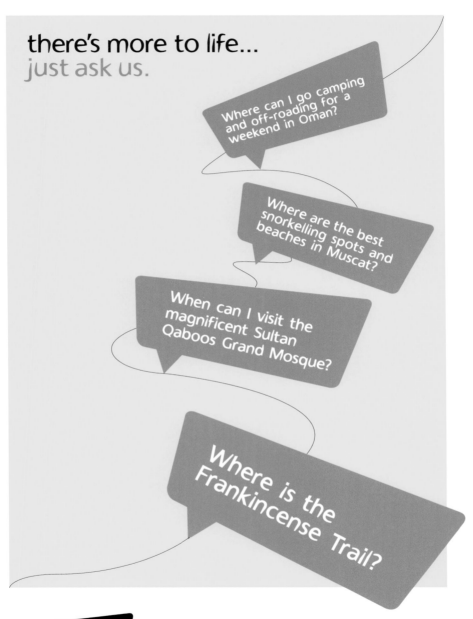

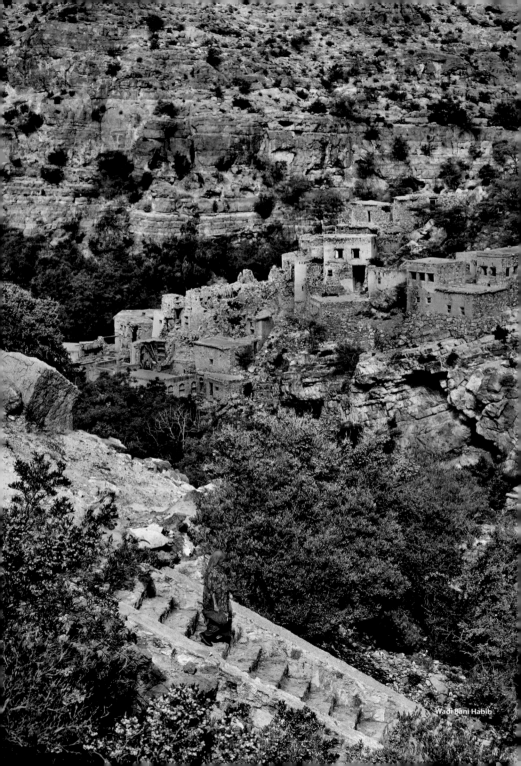

Wadi Bani Habib

DISCOVER OMAN

Mutrah Corniche

DISCOVER
MUSCAT

Between the rugged hills of this unique city lies a wealth of culture, leisure and adventure.

Although the pace of life may be slower and more relaxed in Oman, you'll still find plenty to do and see when you're in the mood for adventure. The fabled land of Sinbad the Sailor, Oman was on the must stop list of every explorer worth his weight in frankincense for centuries. Marco Polo is believed to have visited the area 50 years before famous Moroccan explorer Ibn Battuta, who started his pilgrimage to Mecca in 1325. Omanis passionately treasure their heritage, and rightly so, as its rich history makes this beautiful land that much more magical. Take full advantage and be sure to take time to explore the abundant remains of its ancient cities.

They don't call Muscat the 'pearl of Arabia' for nothing. Steeped in culture, with the city's diverse topography, its many museums, the famous souks and other commercial centres, a visit here allows you to discover a friendly and modern city of contrasting juxtapositions. There is no one place which you can visit to get a 'feel' for the capital. The areas are divided by low craggy hills and each part has its own distinctive character. The only way to do it is to get out and explore and take in all that it has to offer.

If you have a touch of the wild wanderer in you, there's many an adventure to be had, from desert driving, wadi bashing, turtle watching and mosque tours to discovering ancient forts and heritage sites. You can also try all manner of watersports and marine adventures on Muscat's stunning coastline – all within easy reach of the city.

Just call up one of the tour operators listed later in this chapter to make arrangements. If you can't find exactly what you're looking for, many will happily tailor a trip to suit.

PLACES OF INTEREST

Al Bustan & Sidab

The villages of Al Bustan and Sidab provide an interesting diversion from the main Muscat areas. Heading south along Al Bustan Street out of Ruwi, the spectacular mountain road takes you over the rise from Wadi Kabir, where you can see the village of Al Bustan nestled at the base of the hills with the sea in the background.

Just past the Sohar dhow landmark is the Al Bustan Palace Hotel, one of the most famous hotels in the Gulf. If you're not lucky enough to spend a night or two there, it's well worth making a reservation for a cocktail on the beach or dinner in the Beach Pavilion Restaurant and Bar.

From the Al Bustan roundabout, you can head up the coast towards the old town of Muscat. Along the way, you will find the scenic harbour area of Sidab. Fishing is the lifeblood of this area and traditions have been passed down through the generations. The Marine Science and Fisheries Centre is an academic institution that undertakes studies of different fish stocks, but it also has a small, interesting public aquarium and library where you can learn more about the area's aquaculture. On your way to Sidab you will pass Marina Bandar Al Rowdha and the Capital Area Yacht Club, both offering a chance to get closer to the ocean with all manner of marine activities for members and guests.

What About As Seeb?

Out near Muscat International Airport, As Seeb is where you'll find Sultan Qaboos University as well as the shopping centres, Muscat City Centre and Markaz Al Bahja. The Wave residential community is also in the area and it is home to a variety of eateries and the Al Mouj Golf Club.

Al Khuwair

In the heart of Muscat, Al Khuwair is home to many government ministries and embassies. There are some very impressive buildings to be seen in the area, most notably the head office of the HSBC Oman. The front doors are 10 metres high and are plated in 24 carat gold; the interior is just as impressive. If you pass by early enough in the morning, you'll see the doors being polished every day. The architecturally splendid Zawawi Mosque is also found in this area. Al Khuwair is home to Muscat's newest shopping centre, Muscat Grand Mall, and the popular City Seasons Hotel.

Al Qurum

The area known as Qurum (meaning 'mangrove' in English) lies in the centre of the greater Muscat area, stretching along the coast north of Madinat Al Sultan Qaboos and Ruwi. It is divided into two districts – Qurum and Shatti Al Qurum – each of which has quite different characteristics.

Qurum is one of Muscat's main shopping areas and you'll find four of the main shopping malls here: Al-Araimi Complex, SABCO Centre, Qurum Commercial Centre and Qurum City Centre. All are pleasant places to shop with a wide range of goods and services and plenty of free parking. The Jawharat A'Shati Centre in Shati Al Qurum is mainly a coffee-drinkers' hangout, thanks to the presence of Starbucks, Costa Coffee (across the road) and the very popular D'Arcy's Kitchen.

The largest park in Muscat – the Qurum National Park & Nature Reserve – is one of the main attractions in this area. During the cooler months, you'll find many people heading to the park in the early evening; some strolling, some striding, some reclining and some enjoying picnics. While it may be smaller than the Qurum National Park, Qurum Heights Park is another enjoyable, grassy, shaded respite from city life.

Several of Muscat's biggest hotels are in this area, including the Muscat InterContinental, the Crowne Plaza and the Grand Hyatt Muscat. All have great leisure facilities and, between them, they offer an excellent range of food and beverage outlets.

One of Qurum's main attractions is the Beach Promenade, although such is its appeal that it can become uncomfortably crowded during the last few hours before sunset and you'll have to look pretty hard to find yourself a spot in between all the informal football games and out of the way of passing joggers and walkers. However, it's a great place to witness an active slice of Muscat life.

Bandar Al Jissah & Qantab

Further down the coast from Al Bustan, the mountains increase in height and the landscape becomes notably more rugged. However, this rocky coastline hides a number of beautiful secluded coves. These bays, most of which are reachable by the road that winds over the mountain, are home to the beaches of Qantab and Jissah, the Oman Dive Center and the Shangri-La Barr Al Jissah Resort.

Many of the bays in this area have stretches of sandy beach sheltered by the rocky cliffs, and crystal clear waters that are perfect for snorkelling, diving and fishing. At Qantab Beach you'll find a number of friendly local fishermen offering to take you out fishing (for a price, of course).

A little further south is the Oman Dive Centre, regarded as one of the top dive centres in the world. It offers dive training in a customised dive pool, and organises dive trips for certified divers.

The Shangri-La Barr Al Jissah Resort has three distinct hotels: Al Bandar, the focal point of the resort; Al Waha, the largest of the hotels and the one that focuses on family fun and entertainment; and Al Husn, the ultimate luxury destination offering six-star service. The resort also offers some amazing food and beverage outlets in a beautiful setting.

Madinat Al Sultan Qaboos

This is predominantly a residential area and it is considered to be something of a traditional expat stronghold. The British School is located in this area while the American British Academy is in a neighbouring suburb. There are many small coffee shops and restaurants including Kargeen, D'Arcy's Kitchen, MacKenzie's Deli and Pavo Real.

Muscat (Old Town)

The old town of Muscat is situated on the coast at the eastern end of the Greater Muscat area between Mutrah and Sidab. It is a quiet and atmospheric place, based around its sheltered port which was historically important for trade.

The striking Alam Palace, home of Sultan Qaboos, was built on the waterfront in the 1970s and dominates the area. The palace is flanked by two forts overlooking the harbour: Jalali Fort and Mirani Fort. Both were built when Oman was under Portuguese control. The forts are rarely open to visitors due to their proximity to the palace and the fact that they are still in use by authorities. However, you are allowed to take photos of the exteriors.

The city wall of Muscat connects to mountain hills behind the old town of Muscat, along the natural bay. You can walk from the bay to the front side of the palace by passing the beautiful Al Khor Mosque, then turn left into Qasr Al Alam Street. Evidence of the city walls can still be seen – these walls used to completely surround the old town. You can also still see the three gates that were closed to protect the city from intruders.

At one of these gates you'll find the, which opened in 2001 and offers, among other attractions, a great view over the town from its roof. Within the old city walls you'll also find the Omani French Museum (Bait Fransa), and the Bait Al Zubair Museum is located just outside the walls on Al Saidiya Street. Bait Al Zubair is well worth a visit to find out how life was for Omanis centuries ago (it was a lot harder than it is now).

Mutrah

Mutrah rests between the sea and a protective circle of hills, and is neighboured by Qurum, Ruwi and the old town of Muscat. It has grown around its port, which today is far more vibrant than the port of the old town.

One of Muscat's most famous shopping experiences lies in Mutrah: the Mutrah Souk. The maze-like alleyways are always buzzing with activity and it is renowned as one of the best souks in the region. It has recently undergone a bit of a facelift and some might say that this has diminished its authenticity; however it is still well worth a visit for the sheer choice of goods on offer.

You'll find all the usual things like pashminas and tacky souvenirs, household goods and scented oils. But you'll also discover plenty of tiny shops stacked to the ceilings with dusty Omani silver (a good rummage through might result in a lucky find) and plenty of good quality frankincense. Look out for the place with barrels of silver and beads as you'll also find photos of supermodel Kate Moss taken in the shop trying on the wares. There are shops selling some rare Omani antiques too, such as pots, leatherwork, silver scrolls and khanjars (traditional daggers).

Mutrah Corniche shows how far Oman has come since the early 1970s. It runs for about 3km along the harbour, and is lined with pristine gardens, parks, waterfalls and statues. At the northern end, the quaint, old traders' houses and the Al Lawati Mosque showcase the traditional, whitewashed architecture that characterises the city, complete with windtowers designed to capture the slightest whisper of breeze in the days before air conditioning.

You'll also find the fish market on the edge of the dhow harbour, where you can witness the hustle and bustle of the local fishing industry. Small fishing boats start returning with their catches at around 6.30am, so get there early if you can. Right next to the fish market is an excellent fruit and vegetable market with a colourful range of exotic produce. With some good bargaining skills you should be able to save yourself some money compared with buying your produce in the supermarkets.

When the weather is not too hot, it is a pleasant walk from the souk area along the corniche to Mutrah Fort. Unfortunately, it is rarely open to visitors since it is still used by the authorities, although you are permitted

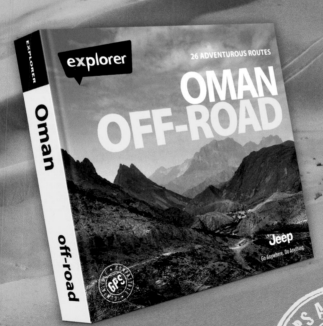

explorer

there's more to life...

FOR ADVENTURE SEEKERS

askexplorer.com/shop

   askexplorer

Aquarium and Marine Science & Fisheries Centre

Ministry of Fisheries, Nr Marina Bandar Al Rowdha
Muscat 968 24 736 449
omanet.om
Map 2 L3

This centre is located between the Al Bustan Palace hotel and the Capital Area Yacht Club. It showcases the rich and unique marine life that thrives in the Omani waters and along a coastline that measures nearly 3,165km. In cooperation with Sultan Qaboos University, the centre studies a range of marine species, with particular emphasis on the conservation of ecosystems and endangered species, including turtles. The centre is currently closed for renovation and is due to open mid 2014. It is advisable to call the centre before travelling to check new opening times.

Bait Adam

Nr Madinat Al Sultan Qaboos Bridge Turning,
Way 2 Muscat 968 24 605 033
omanet.om
Map 2 G3

Situated in Qurum, Bait Adam is in fact the creation of a single private collector, Lafif Al Bulushi. It boasts a rare and unique collection of artefacts from Oman's history, all laid out across five galleries. Open on request. Adults RO.5 and children RO.3.

Bait Al Baranda

Nr Fish R/A, Mutrah Corniche Muscat 968 24 714 262
omantourism.gov.om
Map 2 K2

This Mutrah museum recounts the history of Muscat, from its geological formation right up to the present day. It uses interactive technology that displays pictures of tectonic plate movements over the past 750 million years and showcases the activity that created the continents in the past and how they will change over the next 20 million years. The museum also includes documentation of the Sultanate of Oman's history since its inception. Open 9am to 1pm and 4pm to 6pm, Saturday to Thursday. Entry is RO.1 for adults and 500 baisas for children.

Bait Al Zubair

Al Saidiya St, Old Muscat Muscat 968 24 736 688
baitalzubairmuseum.com
Map 2 L2

A collection rather than a museum, Bait Al Zubair offers a fascinating insight into the Omani lifestyle and traditions, mixing ancient and modern. It is located in a beautiful restored house and each display is accompanied by excellent explanations and descriptions. The four major displays cover men's jewellery, khanjars and male attire; women's jewellery and female attire; household items including kitchenware, incense burners and rosewater sprinklers; and swords and firearms. There is a central photo gallery showing fascinating pictures from the 1920s up until the present day which are great for everyone from children to history enthusiasts.

Outside you'll find full-size recreations of stone-built Omani homes, a small souk, fishing boats and a flowing falaj. A gift shop sells a variety of items and paintings, custom-made miniatures of the pieces on display and other museum souvenirs. Opening hours are 9.30am to 6pm, Saturday to Thursday and entry costs RO.1.

Centre for Omani Dress

House 2414, Way 4731 Mawaleh South
968 24 552 585/99 463 697
centreforomanidress.com
Map 2 A3

This new centre is committed to the conversation, preservation and study of the dress identity of Oman. Located in Mawaleh South, this centre is home to the Museum of Omani Dress which has a wide selection of costumes and jewellery. Demonstrations and workshops are held on a regular basis and a range of items are for sale in the gift shop. Opening hours are Monday and Wednesday 9.30am to 12.30pm, but the centre hopes to expand on this so it is advisable to call before you plan your visit.

Children's Museum

Nr Qurum Natural Park Muscat 968 24 605 368
omantourism.gov.om
Map 2 H2

Kids of all ages will enjoy this interactive science museum. Solidly built displays clearly explain holography, lasers, the human body, energy, faxes, computers and many other fascinations of daily life. Plenty of button-pressing, handle-turning, pedalling, balancing, jumping and running space for kids to exhaust themselves before lunch. This museum is popular and can get crowded on Thursdays.

Entrance is free for children under 6, but costs 100 baisas for children aged 6 to 12, and 300 baisas for those aged 12 and over. The museum is open from 8am to 1.30pm, Saturday to Wednesday, and 9am to 1pm on Thursdays (closed on Fridays).

Currency Museum

Central Bank Of Oman Bldg, Nr HSBC Bank HQ
Muscat 968 24 796 102
omanet.om
Map 2 J3

Located in the head office of the Central Bank of Oman, in the CBD of Ruwi, the museum showcases modern and historic coinage, as well as a gallery of Oman's currency throughout the years. It is not limited to Omani currency. You can also see various colonial currencies that were in circulation in the early 20th century, as well as coins and notes of regional importance. It's opened from 8am to 3pm and costs 250 baisas to enter. Open Sunday to Thursday.

Ghalya's Museum of Modern Art
Near Mutrah Fort **968 24 711 640**
ghalyasmuseum.com
Map **2 K2**
Opened in 2011, this museum aims to showcase Omani life from 1950 to 1975 through historic artefacts from the homes of that period. It also houses a Clothes Museum and Art Gallery. It is open Saturday to Thursday, 9.30am to 6pm.

Muscat Gate Museum
Mutrah Corniche, Al Bahri Rd Muscat
omantourism.gov.om
Map **2 L2**
The Muscat Gate Museum, located on Mutrah Corniche, is housed in a fort-like building on the road leading out of Old Muscat. Opened in 2000, it illustrates the history of Muscat, Al Alam St and Oman from ancient times right up to the present day, with a special display on the city's springs, wells, underground waterways, souks, mosques, harbours and forts. The awe-inspiring view from the roof over the old town of Muscat is almost worth the visit alone. Open from 9.30am to 11.30am and 4.30pm to 7pm, Saturday to Thursday.

The National Museum
Old Muscat
omantourism.gov.om
Map **2 J3**
Formerly known as the Heritage and Culture Museum, the National Museum is scheduled to open in Old Muscat by the middle of 2014. It will have 13 permanent galleries and will feature more than 5,000 exhibits of various kinds.

Natural History Museum
Ministry Of National Heritage & Culture Complex,
Off Al Wazarat St **968 24 641 510**
omantourism.gov.om
Map **2 F3**
Housed within the Ministry of National Heritage & Culture, this is a fascinating and informative collection of exhibits on Oman's wildlife. You can see stuffed animals in their different natural habitats, many of which are unique to Oman and the Gulf region (such as the oryx and the Arabian leopard). The 'Oman Through Time' exhibition follows the history of Oman through fossils, and includes the development of oil and gas reserves.

The separate Whale Hall should not be missed – it is dominated by the suspended skeleton of a 25 year

Bait Al Zubair

old sperm whale. The quiet blue hall is filled with the sounds of whale and dolphin calls, and offers a wide range of information about the unique selection of whale species found off Oman's coast. The dolphin and whale skeletons that are displayed in the Whale Hall have all been recovered from Oman's beaches.

If you visit during the winter months, you can tour the botanical gardens next to the museum. These carefully tended gardens feature indigenous trees, shrubs and flora, including frankincense, desert rose, henna and aloe.

Entry costs 500 baisas for adults, 200 baisas for children between 6 and 12 and 100 baisas for children under 6. Opening times are Saturday to Wednesday, 8am to 1.30pm, and Thursday 9am to 1pm.

Oil & Gas Exhibition Centre & Museum
Nr PDO Gate 2, Sayh Al Malih St Muscat
968 24 677 834
pdo.co.om
Map **2 H2**
Given to the Omani people as a gift from Petroleum Development Oman (PDO), the largest oil and gas production company in the country, this is a well-designed interactive journey through the development, discovery, extraction and use of fossil fuels in Oman. Kids will love the interesting displays that include seismic computer games, nodding donkeys, and gigantic rotating drill bits.

It is open Sunday to Thursday 7.30am to 3.30pm and is free of charge. The Planetarium is situated beside the centre but prior booking is required to secure a seat at its shows. To make a booking at the Planetarium, call 968 24 676 117.

Islamic patterns

Omani French Museum

Nr Bayt Az Zubair Museum Al Saidiya St
968 24 736 613
omantourism.gov.om
Map **2 L2**

This museum is on the site of the first French Embassy, which is a carefully preserved example of 19th century Omani architecture. It celebrates the close ties between France and Oman over the past few centuries. Although the museum exhibits have French captions, there are usually brief English translations.

The ground floor of the museum features exhibitions on early French contacts, the history of Omani-Franco trade and on HM Sultan Qaboos' visit to France. Upstairs you'll find records, furniture, clothes and photographs of early French diplomats. One room holds not just regional Omani women's clothing, but also some antique French costumes. The museum is open from 9am to 1pm, Saturdays to Thursdays. Entrance costs 500 baisas for adults and 200 baisas for children aged six to 12. Children aged six or under enter free.

Omani Museum

Nr Ministry of Information, Al Ilam St Muscat
968 24 600 946
omantourism.gov.om
Map **2 G3**

The Omani Museum sits on top of Information Hill and is almost worth visiting for the view alone. It is run by the Ministry of Information and, although it is fairly small, it is very informative. It is the only museum in the capital city of Muscat that offers

detailed archaeological information and artefacts. The museum also has displays on agriculture, minerals, trade routes, architecture, dhows, arts and crafts, jewellery and weaponry.

The museum is open 8am to 1.30pm, Saturday to Wednesday, and 9am to 1pm on Thursday. Admission costs 500 baisas for adults (300 if with a family), 200 baisas for children aged between 6 and 12 and is free for children under 6 and school groups.

The Sultan's Armed Forces Museum

Bait Al Falaj Fort, Al Mujamma St Muscat
968 24 312 646
safmuseum.gov.om
Map **2 J2**

This showcase of Oman's military history is set in the main building and grounds of the beautiful Bait Al Falaj Fort, which was built in 1845 to be the garrison headquarters for Sultan Said bin Sultan's armed forces.

The museum features descriptions of the origins of Islam in Oman, tribal disputes and the many invasions of the coast by foreign powers. While these exhibits are a little on the dry side, the more recent military history is lavishly represented with uniforms, antique cannons, early machine guns, weapons confiscated from the rebels in Dhofar, models of military vehicles and planes, instruments, medals and even an ejector seat and parachute.

Outside you'll find exhibits of military hardware such as planes, helicopters, boats, rough terrain vehicles and the first car owned by HM Sultan Qaboos when he became Sultan – a Cadillac with inches-thick bulletproof glass.

You can also have a wander around wartime field headquarters and a military hospital. A representative of the army, navy or air force will guide you around the museum, which is a definite must-do for military enthusiasts.

The museum is open 8am to 1.30pm, Saturday to Wednesday, and 3pm to 6pm on Thursday and Friday. Admission is RO.1 for adults and 500 baisas for children.

Art Galleries

Art is highly valued throughout the Arab world, so galleries in the region tend to stock art of high quality and in various styles, from traditional Omani handicrafts to exhibitions from local painters. Although Oman has no art museums, its art galleries do offer peaceful surroundings where you can browse and sometimes buy. Most of the galleries also offer a framing service.

Al Madina Art Gallery

Al Inshirah St Muscat **968 24 691 380**
almadinaartgallery.com
Map **2 G2**

The Al Madina Art Gallery is a one-stop shop for many different forms of art in Oman. It has regular exhibitions of watercolours and oil paintings, and also hosts many special events throughout the year. If you have some time to kill, have a browse through the ample selection of prints – you could be rewarded with an attractive piece of art for a lot less than you would pay for an original.

Al Madina also stocks some interesting jewellery made from unconventional materials such as freshwater pearls or desert diamonds, making it a perfect stop if you're shopping for gifts to take home. And if a genuine Omani wooden chest is on your shopping list, this is the place to go if you want to make sure you are buying an original and not one that has been made in India.

Bait Al Zubair

Al Saidiya St, Old Muscat Muscat **968 24 736 688**
baitalzubairmuseum.com
Map **2 L2**

Although primarily a museum dedicated strictly to Omani culture and handicrafts, Bait Al Zubair does also hold a number of temporary art exhibitions during the year, featuring primarily works from local artists. Exhibitions explore aspects of Omani life and tradition throughout the country, and as far afield as Zanzibar, a former colony of Oman.

Owned by the Zubair family, Bait Al Zubair opened in a beautiful building in 1998 and is located near Al Alam Palace in Old Muscat.

Bait Muzna Gallery

House 234, Al Saidiya St Muscat **968 24 739 204**
baitmuznagallery.com
Map **2 L2**

Founded in 2000 in a three-storey traditional Omani house, Bait Muzna has been renovated into a modern, trendy space for exhibiting paintings, sculptures, photography, installation and concept art.

Workshops for artists are held regularly and there is a variety of gifts on sale including jewellery, fine art and prints. Opening hours are Saturday to Thursday, 9.30am to 7pm.

Ghalya's Museum of Modern Art

Near Mutrah Fort **968 247 116 40**
ghalyasmuseum.com
Map **2 K2**

Within this museum, there is a minimalist art gallery that showcases Omani and international modern artists. Exhibitions and workshops are also held here. Opening times for the gallery are Saturday to Thursday, 9.30am to 6pm.

MuscArt Gallery

18th November St, Al Ghubrah **968 24 493 912**
muscart.net
Map **2 E3**

This wonderfully named gallery and photography studio enables local artists and photographers to exhibit and market their work. It also offers regular workshops in order to help develop the art industry in Oman, and especially nurture young talent. Printing and framing services are also provided.

The Omani Society For Fine Arts

Nr Ramada Hotel Muscat **968 24 694 969**
osfa.gov.om
Map **2 G2**

The Omani Society For Fine Arts is a community where artists meet, share knowledge and display their work. The society holds regular exhibitions, meetings and events where people can learn more about a particular art form.

Stal Gallery

Madinat Al Sultan Qaboos **968 24 600 396**
stalgallery.com
Map **2 G2**

The latest addition to the Muscat art scene, Stal Gallery is a purpose-designed visual arts studio and exhibition space.

Its goal is to provide a venue and facilities for audiences and artists, primarily but not solely for the visual arts. This innovative gallery holds regular exhibitions as well as providing a dedicated residential artists' studio. It is open Sunday to Thursday, 10am to 6pm.

Oman, Naturally

Oman's landscapes are varied and unfailingly breathtaking, but there's also some impressive wildlife hidden amongst the dunes, mountains and coastal waters.

For many, Oman conjures up an image of dry, sandy and inhospitable deserts and, although the rolling dunes certainly play their role in the country's stunning landscape, the sultanate actually has incredible flora and fauna for visitors to discover.

Plants
Oman has around 1,200 native plant species. Of the indigenous flora, date palms provide oases of green covering about 49% of Oman's cultivated area. The deserts are fairly barren but after a bout of rain they are dotted with wild flowers. Coconut trees, banana trees and other tropical fruit trees thrive well in the subtropical climate of Salalah.

Oman is home to the frankincense tree (Boswelia sacra), which grows only in Dhofar, the Wadi Hadhramaut in Yemen, and Somalia. They are short trees with a gnarled trunk and silver-green leaves. Incisions are made on the bark to collect the aromatic resin. For hundreds of years, frankincense was more valuable than gold and Dhofar frankincense was said to be the finest and purest in the world. It was used not only as a fragrance, but also to embalm corpses and as a medicine. The frankincense trade brought immense wealth and importance to southern Arabia – even Alexander the Great had plans to invade the area in order to control the trade at its point of origin.

Mangroves
Mangrove trees (Avicennia marina) used to cover large stretches of Oman's coast but have been threatened with extinction in many areas. Some of the most beautiful and dense mangrove forests today are found in Qurum Natural Park in the heart of Muscat, and at Mahawt Island, 400km south of the capital. Qurum Natural Park contains an important site where prehistoric fishermen exploited mangrove resources, and a nursery that produces seedlings for replanting. Thanks to urgent conservation measures, mangrove forests now cover about 1,088 hectares of Oman's coastline.

Wildlife
Oman has a wide variety of indigenous wildlife which includes many endangered species such as the Arabian oryx, Arabian leopard, Arabian tahr (a mountain goat now found only in Oman), Nubian ibex and humpback whale. Realistically though the only large animals you are likely to see are camels, donkeys and goats, often roaming dangerously close to the road.

Birds
Some 460 species of birds (of which 80 are resident) are found at different times of the year – an impressive number considering that Oman has vast areas of desert and no real forests. Millions of birds wintering in East Africa pass over Oman on their spring or autumn migration to Central Asia.

Under The Sea
The waters off Oman are every bit as bountiful, making them extremely popular with divers. Around 150 species of commercial shell and non-shell fish, 21 species of whales and dolphins and other assorted marine creatures are found in Omani seas. The humpback whale feeds and breeds in the rich waters off central and southern Oman.

There are four breeds of sea turtle that come ashore to lay their eggs. The huge leatherback turtle is known to swim in the waters offshore but there are no records of it nesting in Oman.

The more popular nesting sites are Ras Al Jinz, Ras Al Hadd for green turtles, Masirah Island for the world's largest population of nesting loggerheads and the Daymaniyat Islands Nature Reserve – Oman's only marine reserve – for hawksbill turtles. Be aware that collecting live shells, turtle eggs and shellfish is forbidden in Oman. Several new varieties of seashells have been discovered on Oman's beaches.

Conservation
The Oman Whale & Dolphin Research Group is dedicated to learning more about the habits and needs of whales and dolphins in Oman, and the risks they face. If you see any whales or dolphins while you are in Oman, please report the sighting –there is a special form on the website of the research group that you can fill in. For more information on the project, head to the Environment Society of Oman's dedicated website, eso.org.om.

Oman Dive Centre

Finally, Oman Dive Centre is a popular destination, not just for learning to dive but also for a fun weekend away from the city as it is located in a beautiful bay just south of Muscat. It was recently taken over by Extra Divers, and there are two organised daily dives plus all the usual courses on offer for beginners and the more advanced.

A two-dive package, including all the equipment and transport to dive spots, costs around RO.35, although that figure will be a little higher still if you'd like to dive the Daymaniyat Islands. For RO.5 (less on weekdays), you can get a day pass to the Oman Dive Centre and make use of its facilities. The centre has a dive pool, which you can use when there are no lessons in progress, as well as a special kids' pool.

Both pools are shaded. You can also use the private beach. The dive centre has a beach bar, as well as an excellent in-house restaurant called Odyssey, and if it isn't too hot you can sit on the shaded terrace and enjoy lunch.

There are also a number of traditional-style barasti chalets on the beach that are available for hire if you want accommodation with a difference.

To get to Oman Dive Centre, when following the road from Ruwi and Wadi Kabir to Al Bustan, you will see the village of Qantab signposted to the right just past the top of the hill. Take this right turn and follow the road until you reach the roundabout, where you can turn left for Oman Dive Centre or go straight for the Shangri-La Barr Al Jissah Resort & Spa at the end of the road.

Oman Dive Centre

Boat Tours & Charters

Al Khayran
Marina Bandar Al Rowdha Haramil **24 737 288**
alkhayran.com
Map **2 L2**

Al Khayran is a semi-submersible boat to take you beneath the ocean without getting wet. Trips are available once a day on Fridays and Saturdays, from Marina Bandar Al Rowdha where a passenger boat zips you along the coastline past the Al Bustan and Shangri-La to the waiting vessel. Venture down the stairs and you'll find yourself in a submarine boasting windows onto the underwater world. Informative posters help you spot species of fish and even turtles. The two-hour trip includes soft drinks and costs RO.25 for adults, RO.5 for children over five years of age and children under five years of age are free. Omanis are charged RO.9 for adults, RO.5 for children over 5 years of age and children under five years of age are free.

Marina Bandar Al Rowdha
Haramil **24 737 288**
marinaoman.net
Map **2 L2**

This is one of the best launch spots for fishing, diving and sailing. It has 400 berths, and is fully equipped for launch, recovery, service and marine control. The marina can organise tours for whale watching, watersports, diving and fishing. For a more relaxing excursion, you can go on a traditional dhow cruise, or be transported to a secluded beach for an afternoon's sunbathing. There's a restaurant, Blue Marlin, which does a great alfresco breakfast.

Moon Light Dive Centre
Nr Grand Hyatt Muscat Hay As Saruj **99 317 700**
moonlightdive.com
Map **2 G2**

The Moon Light Dive Centre can deliver a customised cruise package to meet your requirements. It offers trips for groups (from four people to 10) in one of its three boats, which are based on the beach in Shatti Al Qurum, next to the Hyatt Regency Muscat. A typical cruise heads south along Muscat's spectacular coast, visiting rocky islands out at sea, secluded beaches or even marina cafes for breakfast or refreshments. Time can be allocated for other activities as per your requirements, such as fishing, snorkelling, sunbathing or watersports. For a three-hour trip, expect to pay around RO.25 per person with discounts for groups.

Jass Beach Sea Tourism
Marina Bandar Al Rowdha **95 599 660**
jassabeach.com
Map **2 L2**

This popular company offers a range of packages including dolphin watching, snorkeling and camping on the beaches.

Dhow Charters

Al Marsa Travel & Tourism
Musandam Dibba **968 26 836 550**
almarsamusandam.com
Map **1 E1**

Al Marsa has four purpose-built dhows that are suitable both for divers and tourists. You can relax on

Marina Bandar Al Rowdha

the sundeck for a day trip and discover fishing villages, or you can go on anything up to a seven-night voyage and explore Oman's incredibly haunting fjords.

The dhows are equipped for diving and other watersports with kayaks, snorkelling gear and even fishing equipment provided. Prices start at RO.38 for divers and RO.31.50 for non-divers. Based in Sharjah, they operate along the eastern coastline of the UAE and the Musandam Peninsula.

Ibn Qais & Partners

Marina Bandar Al Rowdha Muscat 968 24 692 074
Map 2 L3
Ibn Qais own the Lubna, a traditional dhow that's available for charter to any of the islands in Oman. The company provides everything you need while onboard, and even tailormake packages for special occasions. So, if you want a birthday or anniversary celebration with a difference, you can set sail on the Lubna for an evening of good food and entertainment. Sunset cruises set sail every Thursday and Sunday from 4pm to 6pm.

Khasab Travel & Tours

Nr Khasab Airport Khasab 968 26 730 464
khasabtours.com
Map 1 E1
Khasab Travel & Tours have a traditionally decorated Omani dhow on which to take you exploring in the fjords. The dhow is decked out with cushions and carpets for you to lounge on while enjoying the passing scenery.

The dhow will also stop and allow you to explore the villages of the Strait of Hormuz, and enjoy a session of swimming or snorkelling to explore the marine life around Telegraph Island. Refreshments and a buffet lunch are also included.

Musandam Sea Adventure Travel & Tourism

Musandam Khasab 968 26 730 424
msaoman.com
Map 1 E1
With its dramatic fjords, the Musandam area is often referred to as 'the Norway of the Middle East'. Take a dhow cruise and experience the area's rocky topography where mountains jut up out of pristine waters. Every now and then you can land and explore remote Omani villages, and then stop at Telegraph Island for a leisurely picnic and a spot of swimming and snorkelling.

Cruises vary in length from half-day to three-day options, and prices range from RO.15 to RO.150 per person, with children under three free and under-10s half price. Musandam Sea Adventure takes care of transportation, food, and lodging and creates comfortable, but adventurous, tours.

Dolphin & Whale Watching Tours

There are more than 20 species of whales and dolphins either living in or passing through the seas off the coast of Oman. Although no tour operator can guarantee a sighting of these beautiful sea creatures, the odds are definitely high that you will get to see a school of dolphins swimming alongside your boat and playing in its wake. Many tour operators will tentatively rate your chances of seeing dolphins at 85% to 90%. Whales are not so frequently seen – these gentle giants travel in smaller groups and stay under the surface for a lot longer, so you have to be a little bit more patient. Early mornings and evenings, when the seas are at their calmest, are the best times for whale sightings. It is possible to see them from the shore (usually in cliff areas, such as Musandam) but it is better to be out at sea in a boat, where the experience is closer and infinitely more exciting.

Working hard to monitor and protect these magnificent mammals is the Whale & Dolphin Research Group, part of the Environment Society of Oman (ESO). This is a group of volunteer scientists and other interested parties who work together to collect and disseminate knowledge about Oman's cetaceans (whales & dolphins). The group's activities include emergency rescue services for whales and dolphins, collection of cetacean bones, skulls and tissue samples, maintenance of a database of cetacean sightings and strandings, cooperation with local tour operators to promote responsible whale and dolphin watching activities, dissemination of information through articles in local and international publications to promote awareness of Oman's cetaceans and the need to protect their environment. For further information, see arabianwildlife.com or contact: Andy Wilson (95 920 461), Iain Benson (95 035 988), Louise Waters (99 473 140) or the main office (24 696 912).

Marina Bandar Al Rowdha

Muscat 968 24 737 288
marinaoman.net
Map 2 L3
The Marina Bandar Al Rowdha offers dolphin tours just a short distance off the coast of Muscat and is also the leaving point for the Al Khayran semi-submersible boat.

Muscat Diving & Adventure Center

Way 3323 Muscat 968 24 543 002
holiday-in-oman.com
Map 1 G4
This upbeat tour operator can take you out to sea to spot dolphins, and they estimate the chance of a

sighting at around 80%. The most common species seen are common, spinner and bottlenose. There are two boats which seat up to 15 and 20 people. Daily departures are at 7am and 10am. The cruises last for three to four hours, and the cost per person is RO.20 (which includes soft drinks).

Oman Dive Center

Nr Qantab R/A, Al Jissah St Muscat **968 24 824 240**
extradivers-worldwide.com
Map **1 G4**

Every morning, the Oman Dive Center organises a boat trip to go and spot dolphins off the coast of Muscat. Your chances of seeing dolphins (usually common, spinner, bottlenose or Indo-Pacific species) are high at any time of year and estimated at around 95%. Your chances of seeing whales are not as high, although they have been spotted from time to time (usually from October to May). The boat trip includes breakfast served onboard.

Safari Savvy

Off-road driving is exhilarating but extreme, and people who suffer from motion sickness may not enjoy the experience very much. You may rest assured that your driver is a skilled professional and knows exactly what he is doing, however, remember that you are the client and have the right to request him to slow down or tackle less challenging routes, if you feel the ride is too bumpy. Most drivers will take an easier route if you are with children, elderly people or people with special circumstances. Note that if you're pregnant, it may not be safe for you to go on an off-road tour.

Safari Tours

Dune Dinner

There are a range of dune dinners on offer, but on a typical tour you will be collected in the mid-afternoon, when you will be driven inland towards the Hajar Mountains and then off-road through the lush green scenery and freshwater pools of Wadi Abyad. Then you'll head for the undulating dunes of the nearby Abyad desert for some exciting dune driving, before stopping to watch the sun set over the sands. After a sumptuous barbecue, you'll head back to Muscat.

Full-Day Safari

This trip combines a visit to one of Oman's most spectacular wadis, Wadi Bani Khalid, with the breathtaking expanse of the Wahiba Desert. Different tour operators have different itineraries, but on the way from Muscat you will visit places such as the

ruined fort of Mudairib, Shab Village and the town of Sur. Some of the unforgettable sights you may see on the way are traditional mud-brick homes clinging to steep valley walls, clear streams carrying fresh water into deep pools, and man-made irrigation systems called 'falaj'. As you leave the mountains you'll head for the Wahiba Desert for an exhilarating ride over the dunes, some of which are 200 metres high.

Mountain Safari

The height and extent of Oman's mountain ranges surprise many visitors. Mountain safaris either head into the highest range, Jebel Akhdar, or up to Jebel Shams, which is Oman's highest peak at over 3,000m. On the way, you'll pass through towns (such as Nizwa) and remote villages set on terraces cut into the mountains. Ancient irrigation channels bring water to the villages to feed the crops. The top of Jebel Shams feels like the top of the world, with the entire mountain range and the awe-inspiring 'Grand Canyon' of Oman (a rocky canyon dropping thousands of metres from the plateau), way below.

Overnight Turtle Watching

Many tour operators offer trips to the famous Ras Al Jinz Turtle Sanctuary, where you can watch the rare sight of turtles coming onto the beach to lay their eggs. On your way to Ras Al Jinz you'll pass Quriyat, Wadi Shab, and the town of Sur, home to the most skilled dhow builders in Oman.

After arriving at the Turtle Sanctuary, you'll be served a beach barbecue before night falls and the turtles come lumbering onto the beach to lay their eggs and bury them in the sand. After a few hours sleep, you'll return to the beach and watch the mass of tiny hatchlings struggle out of their eggs and make their journey into the sea. On your return journey to Muscat you will get to see more of the countryside and historical settlements.

Wadi Drive

An off-road tour through the wadis can either be half-day, full-day or overnight, camping in the peaceful surroundings of the rocky wilderness. You'll get to see falaj irrigation channels, in place for centuries, bringing water from underground springs to irrigate palm plantations and vegetable terraces. Natural streams run all year round in several wadis, transforming the dry, rocky landscape into fertile areas of lush greenery and clear rock pools that are often home to fish, frogs and other wildlife. Hidden villages in the mountains, seemingly trapped in time, illustrate how people used to subsist in times gone by.

Wahiba Desert

The Wahiba Desert stretches all the way from the coast to the mountains. This tour travels into the middle of seemingly endless dunes of red and white sand. Dune driving is a must-do; a ride up and down the steep slopes, courtesy of a very skilled driver, is like a natural rollercoaster.

A visit to a traditional Bedouin homestead for Arabic coffee and dates usually follows the dune driving, as well as the chance to try riding a camel, the oldest form of desert transport.

Overnight Desert Safari

Leave the noise of the city behind you and experience the peace of the desert for a night. After an exhilarating drive through the dunes you will set up camp in a remote area of Wahiba, where Bedouin tribes have lived traditionally for thousands of years.

At sunset, you can enjoy a camel ride while a barbecue is prepared and then relax in comfortable surroundings under the starlit sky. In the morning, after a leisurely start, visit the flowing wadis to see the greenery and rugged mountain landscape, which form a complete contrast to the desert sights of the previous day.

Camel Rides

A visit to this part of the world is hardly complete unless you've been up close and personal with a 'ship of the desert'. A ride on a camel is hard to forget – you will generally mount the camel when it is lying down, and then you need to hang on for dear life while your humped steed unfolds its gangly legs to stand up. Once you're up though, it's fairly smooth riding and you can lose yourself in your 'Lawrence of Arabia' fantasies. Don't forget to take a photo!

Many tour operators incorporate a short camel ride on their desert safaris. Alternatively, for a unique adventure that's a lot more fun and memorable, you could try a camel ride into the spectacular sand dunes. Your guide will lead you to a Bedouin camp, where you can enjoy a well-deserved rest and some refreshments. Don't forget to take your camera, so you can remember this unique experience long after the aches subside.

Desert Nights Camp
Nr Sand Coloured Mosque, 11km from Al Wasil
Bidiyyah **92 818 388**
desertnightscamp.com
Map **1 G5**
Desert Nights Camp offers a variety of desert activities, including camel rides or desert cycles for kids. Based 220km from Muscat, you can augment your camel adventure with dune bashing, sand surfing and trips to nearby encampments at Wadi Bani Khalid and Ras Al Jinz on the coast, where you may even get to watch turtles coming ashore.

Muscat Diving & Adventure Centre
As Seeb **24 543 002**
holiday-in-oman.com
Map **1 G4**
The centre offers two main tours by camel, which are operated along eco-tourism lines. They work with Bedouin families of the Northern Region Sands (Wahiba) in Sharqiyya, and run expeditions in the Rub Al Khali in Dhofar. Camel trips or 'safaris' can vary in length from a short day ride to a 14 day trek across the sands. This is one of Oman's most authentic tours and it allows you the opportunity to see and engage in the Bedouin way of life with an overnight stop at a Bedu campsite.

Farm & Stable Tours

Ostrich Farm
Nr Al Nahda Resort Barka
Map **1 G4**
The Ostrich Breeding Farm in Barka started in 1993 when the eggs were imported from South Africa. They were the first ostriches to have been hatched in Oman since early last century when the birds became extinct in this region. The aim of the farm is to sustain a breeding group to meet the ever-increasing demands for healthy meat, fine leather and exquisite feathers. Ostrich meat is considered an excellent alternative to beef, since it is low in cholesterol, but has a very similar consistency and texture. The farm is also home to about 30 crocodiles. Entrance to the farm costs 500 baisas per adult and 300 baisas per child. It's open daily from 7am to 12pm and 3pm to 6pm. To get there, turn on to Nakhal Road from the Barka Roundabout, and after 4km you'll see the Majan Water Factory on the right. Turn right into the private road just before the factory, and the ostrich farm is the first farm on your left.

Places Of Worship Tours

Sultan Qaboos Grand Mosque
As Sultan Qaboos St Muscat
omantourism.gov.om
Map **2 E3**
This beautiful example of Islamic architecture provides a wonderful insight into the cultural heritage of Oman. It is also one of the few mosques that allow entry for non-Muslims. Apart from being a place of worship, this huge mosque is a centre for scholars and houses an Islamic reference library containing over 20,000 sources of information on Islamic sciences and culture. The mosque is lavishly decorated, and features a 263m

prayer carpet, 35 crystal chandeliers (the central one is 14 metres high and eight metres wide), and a floor entirely paved with marble.

There are strict rules – you have to take your shoes off before entering, and both men and women should wear conservative clothing (women should be covered up, including their hair), and children under 10 are not permitted. The hours for the tour are strictly between 8.30am and 11am from Saturday to Thursday.

Main Tour Operators

When booking a tour it is normal practice to do so three or four days in advance. You usually pay a 50% deposit when you make the booking, with the remainder payable when you are picked up at the start of the tour. Cancelling your tour without an appropriate notice period may result in the loss of your deposit. You will be picked up either from your hotel, residence or an agreed meeting point. At most times of year it is advisable to wear cool, comfortable clothing such as shorts and T-shirts. Hats and sunglasses are also recommended, as well as strong, flat-soled shoes as there is usually some walking involved. You might want to take sun protection, a camera and money (in case there's a chance to buy souvenirs).

Al Azure Tours Hay As Saruj, 99 856 888, *alazuretours.com*
Al Nimer Tourism Shatti Al Qurum, 24 713 270, *alnimertourism.com*
Bahwan Travel Agencies Ruwi, 24 704 455, *bahwantravels.com*
Desert Discovery Tours Al Azaiba, 24 493 232, *desertdiscovery.com*
Eihab Travels Various locations, 24 683 900, *ohigroup.com*
Empty Quarter Tours Madinat Al Sultan Qaboos, *emptyquartertours.com*
Golden Oryx Tours Ruwi, 24 489 853, *goldenoryx.com*
Grand Canyon Of Oman Tours Shatti Al Qurum, 92 605 102
Gulf Ventures Oman Al Ghubrah Al Janubiyyah, 24 490 733, *gulfventures.com*
Hormuz Line Tours & Cruises Khasab, 050 543 2717
Hud Hud Travels Madinat Al Sultan Qaboos, 92 920 670, *hudhudtravels.com*
Mark Tours Ruwi, 24 782 727, *marktoursoman.com*
Muscat Diving & Adventure Centre As Seeb, 24 543 002, *holiday-in-oman.com*
Sunny Day Tours, Travel & Adventures As Seeb, 24 490 055, *sunnydayoman.com*
Turtle Beach Resorts Sur, 25 540 068, *tbroman.com*

Tours Outside The City

East Salalah Tour
Leaving from Salalah and travelling east, this tour visits many historical sites and places of interest along the picturesque coast including the fishing village of Taqa with its watchtowers and castle. Further on is Khor Rouri, a freshwater creek now separated from the sea. It is the site of the ancient city of Samharam, known for its frankincense and for being the former capital of the Dhofar region. Also on the tour is Mohammed Bin Ali's Tomb, the Ayn Razat ornamental gardens, the Hamran Water Springs and the historical trading centre of Mirbat.

Nizwa Tour
Nizwa is the largest city in Oman's interior, and this full-day tour explores the fascinating sights and heritage of this historically significant place. After driving deep into the Hajar Mountains, you'll come to the oasis city of Nizwa, home to the Nizwa Fort (which dates back to the 17th century) and the magnificent Jabrin Fort, notable for its wall and ceiling decorations and secret passageways. Many ancient ruins, such as Bahla Fort (currently undergoing extensive renovation) and various mud-brick villages, can be seen among the date palm plantations and wadis.

Rustaq Tour
Batinah, the north-west region of Oman, has always been important for its abundant agriculture and strategic position as the trading centre between the mountains and coast. It is home to many forts including the oldest and largest in the country, Al Kersa Fort. En route you will visit ancient souks, hot springs and sandy beaches, all amid spectacular mountain scenery.

Ubar Tour
The discovery of the 'Lost City of Ubar' in the early 1990s caused great excitement in the archaeological world. This ancient city was at the crossroads of significant trade routes, making it a place of unrivalled wealth and splendour – when Marco Polo visited Ubar, he called it 'paradise'. However, at the height of its glory it sank into the desert sands, leaving no trace of its existence. Legend had it that to punish the residents of Ubar for their greed and lavish lifestyle, God caused the sand to swallow the city. When the lost city was uncovered, less than 20 years ago, it was discovered that a huge limestone cavern underneath Ubar had collapsed, causing the city to sink into the sand.

This full-day tour takes you through some stunning scenery as you drive through the Qara Mountains to the site of Ubar. After leaving Ubar you'll continue off-road as the tour ventures into the famous sands of Rub Al Khali (the Empty Quarter), for some dune driving.

Local Trips

If you are more into the idea of walking, then combining Wadi Shab with a dip in the sea at Fins would make for a great day out. It is important to stress that, in both cases, if you want to combine the two activities, you should set off fairly early in the morning or else camp the night before (or after) on the white sands in and around Fins Beach.

From Muscat there are many places worthy of visiting that are close at hand. If it is a day trip you are after, then consider visiting a wadi or a beach. For the best of both, take a trip to Wadi Tiwi where you could try a 4WD trip up the wadi – careful, it gets very narrow and steep in places – before having a picnic at the top of the wadi and heading back down to the white sand at Fins for a well-deserved dip in the sea.

A popular beach, frequented by expats and locals alike, is Yiti Beach and it makes for a good day trip, as well as a thrilling overnight adventure.

If the beach doesn't appeal, then the mountains are an attractive alternative for a day trip. If you set off early on a Friday morning, it is possible to drive to Nizwa in time to make the goat market, then take a drive up Jebel Akhdar. The numerous viewing points along the winding drive to the top make for great photo ops, or even good locations to stop and enjoy a spot of alfresco brunch. Like most of the other day trips around Muscat, this itinerary could easily be split into an overnight trip by going up to the top of Jebel Akhdar and spending the night camping at one of the convenient sites up top – or even at the Jebel Akhdar Hotel if you prefer a proper bed and running water. Then, in the morning, head back down and make an early stop at the atmospheric Nizwa market before returning to Muscat.

Jebel Shams can likewise be done as a day trip, if you're content with just doing 'the rim walk' which offers some incredible views; you can then drive to the top, get to the village and do the four-hour hike, before descending to Wadi Ghule for a picnic lunch. Better still is to do an overnight or weekend getaway, giving you time to do the challenging but rewarding hike to the top and back. Be under no illusions; this is a big day of hiking and it is best to start before sunrise as, even in the winter, temperatures can really climb.

For some water-based fun instead, you'll find plenty of diving and snorkelling adventures to be had within a 40 minute drive of the greater Muscat area. They're all easy day trips but the real spirit of adventure that Oman is famous for is best enjoyed by teaming one of these active trips with an overnight stay. Bander Khayran, which lies southeast of Muscat, is a great place for both snorkelling and diving, while you can also tackle a wide range of other marine sports, such as sailing, fishing and jet-skiing. It's just a 40 minute 4WD trip from the greater Muscat area. To make a good day great, take the boat to Bander Khayran – it leaves from Bandar Al Rowdha in Muscat and also takes around 40 minutes, with the added benefit of rugged cliffs, sugar cube villages and the Al Bustan Palace resort. If you're lucky, you may even get playful dolphins following the boat.

Offroad tracks await

OUT OF THE CITY

Wadi Bani Khalid

OUT OF THE CITY

Oman isn't all about Muscat. Outside the capital, there are mountains, deserts, islands and ancient cities to explore.

Beyond Muscat, Oman boasts stunning scenery, lost cities, towering forts and unexpected lush greenery. Travelling north will bring you to the cities of Barka, Nakhal and Sohar. If time allows, the Musandam peninsula to the north-west is highly recommended, with its main cities of Khasab and Bukha, and with scenery totally different from the rest of Oman. It features beautiful fjords and lagoons and is becoming an increasingly popular tourist destination particularly for scuba divers.

Travelling inland leads you to Rusayl, Rustaq, Nizwa, Bahla, Jabrin and also to the mountains of Jebel Shams, an experience not to be missed if you enjoy the surroundings of rocky mountains and total tranquillity. Going south via the interior route, you will pass the cities of Fanja, Sumail, Ibra, Al Mudayr, Al Mintrib, Sur and Ras Al Hadd. On the coastal route Tiwi

village is worth a stop, as is the ancient city of Qalhat, if only for the fact that this historical city, nowadays in ruins, was of such particular interest to Marco Polo and Ibn Battuta.

The southern province of Dhofar, with its capital Salalah, provides a welcome change in climate in the hot summer months. While the rest of Oman is paralysed by heat, the monsoon (khareef) blowing off the Indian Ocean ensures a high percentage of rainfall in this area, resulting in cool weather and beautiful greenery making it a perfect location to camp, hike and explore. Salalah continues to attract international as well as local visitors for its peace and tranquillity. It's also the stomping ground for new luxury hotels. Apart from the major regions to visit in Oman, this section also includes its largest island, Masirah, which is off the south-east coast.

BEYOND MUSCAT

Musandam

The Musandam peninsula is an Oman enclave to the north, which is divided from the rest of Oman by the United Arab Emirates. It is a beautiful, largely unspoiled area. The capital is Khasab, a quaint fishing port mostly unchanged by the modern world. The Strait of Hormuz lies to the north, with Iran just across the water, the Arabian Gulf is to the west and the Gulf of Oman lies to the east; hence the area is one of great strategic importance.

Musandam is dominated by the Hajar Mountains, which also run through the UAE and into the main part of Oman. It is sometimes referred to as the Norway of the Middle East, since the jagged mountain cliffs plunge directly into the sea, and the coastline features many inlets and fjords. The views along the coastal roads are stunning. Just a few metres off the coast you'll find beautiful and fertile coral beds, with an amazing variety of sea life including tropical fish, turtles, rays, eels, dolphins (a common sight) and, occasionally, whale sharks. It is some of the finest diving in the region and many residents from the UAE as well as those living further south in Oman travel to Musandam to scuba dive. Inland, the scenery is equally breathtaking, although you will need a 4WD and a good head for heights to explore it properly.

You can reach Musandam from Muscat by air, sea (via ferry) or by road. The flight takes around 90 minutes. Oman Air offers internal flights and holiday packages from Muscat to Musandam; a return flight costs around RO.50 and flights leave daily from Saturday to Wednesday. The National Ferries Company often offers deals too. Visitors travelling in Oman do not need an additional visa for Musandam.

To drive to Musandam from Oman you need to travel through the UAE. GCC nationals and Omanis are free to travel this route without needing any travel documents, but non-GCC residents of Oman need to apply for a road permit. Travelling from Muscat by road, you leave Oman by the border checkpoint at Khatmet Melaha. You then enter Fujairah (part of the UAE) and travel to the Al Dara border checkpoint in Ras Al Khaimah (also part of UAE). Here, you leave the United Arab Emirates and re-enter Omani territory at the border checkpoint. Khasab is 38km from this border. Visitors to Oman carrying a single-entry visa may not be allowed back into Oman once they have left. Check with your nearest Oman embassy for updated information.

Bukha

Bukha is located on the western side of the Musandam peninsula, with a coastline on the Arabian Gulf. The area borders the UAE emirate of Ras Al Khaimah and is 27km north of Khasab. This small town is overlooked by the ruin of an old fort, but there is little to see other than the remains of one watchtower. The Bukha Fort is more impressive, however, and is by the side of the main road just metres from the sea. It was built in the 17th century, restored in 1990, and it is certainly the town's biggest landmark. Traditionally, fishing and boat building have been the occupations of Bukha's residents, and the town has a harbour for a small number of vessels. There is also a pleasant strip of sandy beach with a number of shelters. The village of Al Jadi, about three kilometres north of Bukha, is picturesque and has a couple of fortifications, two of which are restored watchtowers.

Dibba

At the southern end of Musandam, straddling the border with the UAE, Dibba is a small town made up of three fishing villages. Unusually, each part comes under a different jurisdiction: Dibba Bayah is in Oman, Dibba Al Hisn belongs to Sharjah, and Dibba Muhallab is part of Fujairah. The three villages share an attractive bay, fishing communities, and excellent diving locations – from here you can arrange dhow trips to take you to unspoilt dive sites along the remote eastern coast of the Musandam peninsula. The Hajar Mountains provide a wonderful backdrop, rising in places to over 1,800m. There is a good public beach too, where seashell collectors may find a few treasures. Dibba is also a good starting point for some stunning off-road driving into the mountains, as well as hiking and climbing. Check out tour operator Absolute Adventure (adventure.ae) who provide a range of tailored excursions around the region.

The Omani part of Dibba is also home to Dibba Castle, a strongly fortified, double-walled castle built by the Al Shuhah tribe over 180 years ago. You can access the rooms, and provided you don't mind pigeons you can climb all the towers for some great views over the surrounding area and out to sea.

Khasab

Khasab, the capital of the Musandam region, is surrounded by imposing and dramatic mountains that dominate the entire area, with some peaks above 2,000m. The town of Khasab is relatively spread out and has numerous date palm plantations. There is a small souk and a beach, but the port is the main area of interest. The town relies on fishing, trade (mostly with ports in Iran) and agriculture for subsistence, and produces a range of fruit and vegetables. In fact 'khasab' is the Arabic word for 'fertile'. At one end of the bay is the restored Khasab Fort which is open to the public. There's not that much to see inside, but its setting against the mountainous background is spectacular. Kumzan Fort is just outside Khasab. It was built in about 1600AD by the Imam but little is left of it today, apart from the two watchtowers. About 10km west of Khasab is the village of Tawi where there are prehistoric rock carvings of warriors, boats and animals.

One of Khasab's biggest draws is the diving opportunities. These waters are not recommended for beginners, but experienced divers can enjoy spectacular underwater cliffs and an abundance of marine life at sites just a short boat ride away.

Activities In Musandam

Musandam is not a destination for a weekend of shopping or fine dining. Rather, the focus here is on escaping the daily grind of city life, immersing yourself in some of the region's most spectacular scenery and being adventurous enough to try the wide range of outdoor activities.

Boat Trips

An essential activity on any trip to Musandam, a dhow cruise around the fjords is a truly memorable experience. You can hire a dhow or a speedboat from the harbour at Khasab (remember to negotiate the rate before you leave, but expect to pay about RO.10 per hour for a speedboat and RO.25 per hour for dhows). Leisurely dhows are more stable and spacious – large enough for 20 to 25 people. Allow a minimum of three hours to explore the inlet closest to Khasab; tours usually include Telegraph Island and Hidden Cove. Alternatively, try the longer trip out to Kumzar – an ancient village set in an isolated inlet on the northernmost end of the peninsula.

On a full-day trip you'll see remote coastal villages, get a chance to swim and snorkel in the calm waters, and you are almost guaranteed to see dolphins. Khasab Travel & Tours (khasabtours.com) operates a number of dhows, or you can just turn up at the harbour and bargain hard with the independent boat owners to arrange your own private cruise. You can also just hire a small boat to take you out and drop you off on your own private beach, only 10 to 20 minutes from Khasab, then pick you up at an agreed time. It's common to pay only when you have returned to port, otherwise you might get left there for longer than you planned.

Off-Roading

To see the other side of Musandam, you can also drive up to the plateau beneath Jebel As Sayh (Jebel Harim), the highest peak in the area at 2,087m. This is an excellent area for camping, hiking, views across the mountain tops, and as a base for further exploration. Most of the year you can get to the top in a saloon car. If you have a 4WD, there are a number of tracks worth

exploring that head over the mountains to more secluded places such as Khor Najd, the only beach accessible by car in the fjords, or the acacia forest near Sal Al A'la. Check out Explorer's *UAE Off-road* guide for more information.

Hiking

This is a great area to get outside, stretch your legs and admire the scenery. There are hikes to suit all levels, including some challenging routes for the serious hiker, and the mountainous backdrop provides some fantastic views. If you like the idea of a hike without the hassle, try Khasab Travel & Tours in Khasab, or Absolute Adventure (adventure.ae) in Dibba, who will organise the hike, so all you have to do is turn up.

Diving & Snorkelling

Natural attractions abound underwater. Just below the ragged cliffs are coral beds with an amazing variety of sea life, including tropical fish, turtles, dolphins, sharks, and even whales. Some of the best dive sites in the Middle East are found here, and the area is becoming increasingly popular with divers as a result. At the weekends you'll find several diving companies out on the water exploring the deep blue. The lagoons offer a little more protection from the elements, and are great spots for snorkelling. There are more than 20 separate dive sites along the east coast for experienced divers including several cave dives. You can book dive trips from your hotel, or through companies such as Al Boom Diving (alboomdiving. com), Al Marsa Travel & Tourism (almarsamusandam. com), Sheesa Beach (sheesabeach.com) or Nomad Ocean Adventures (discovernomad.com).

Traquility on anchor

Al Dhahirah

With a name meaning 'the back', the Al Dhahirahh region lies in Oman's interior, to the west of the Hajar Mountains and bordering the UAE and Saudi Arabia. Due to the harsh environment, characterised by huge sandy plains, Al Dhahirahh is sparsely populated and there is not much in the way of modern-day comforts. Water is transported from the mountains to the towns using the age-old falaj system, which is deceptively sophisticated.

This is an area where you will get to see Omanis living their lives as they have done for centuries, and if you are fortunate you may get to see displays of traditional dances and crafts. It is also a great place for exploring old forts, ancient tombs and caves. In fact, it is home to the famous beehive tombs in Ibri (also called the Bat tombs), which have been listed as a UNESCO World Heritage site. While there is some debate as to whether these were actually used as tombs or whether they were rudimentary homes for small families, it is widely accepted that the tombs date back to early civilisations that lived in the region over 5,000 years ago. Ibri was historically a critical stopping point on the overland trading route.

Buraimi

The Buraimi governance is the part of the Buraimi Oasis that falls on the Oman side of the border; the part of the oasis that falls on the UAE side is called Al Ain. Although it spans what is in effect an international border, there are no checkpoints within the town itself and the official Oman-UAE border is located about 50km east of Buraimi. Non-GCC residents travelling from Oman will need a road permit. Like Ibri, Buraimi can trace its history back to its strategic position at the intersection of various caravan routes to and from Oman. There is an extensive falaj system that keeps the region fertile. Buraimi is an oasis and therefore is pleasantly green with plenty of date palm plantations. It also benefits from a cooler, less humid climate than coastal regions, making it a popular destination during the summer months.

It is home to a famous mud fort, Hisn Al Khandaq, which has been extensively restored and is open to visitors. There is also a must-see camel souk where the merchants will happily explain the differences between one camel and another, and may even make a serious attempt at convincing you to buy one! Watching the camels being loaded onto their new owners' pick-up trucks is a show in itself. You might find there is more to do in neighbouring Al Ain, although hotels are generally cheaper in Buraimi itself. A word of warning: UAE taxi drivers will cruise for passengers in Buraimi although they may refuse to use the meter, so it is up to you to negotiate a price before you get in the cab.

Ibri

Ibri lies 300km to the west of Muscat, between the foothills of the Hajar Mountains and the vast Rub Al Khali desert. With its central location, it was a historically important stopover for merchants travelling between the different regions of the Arabian Peninsula and trading remains active today. The bustling souk sells a range of merchandise including locally produced woven palm goods. The most fascinating sight though is the auction which takes place every morning, where residents, farmers and traders from the town and surrounding villages come together to haggle over dates, fruit and vegetables, livestock, camels and honey. The souk is situated near Ibri's impressive fort, which is notable for the large mosque set within its walls.

Batinah

With a coastline stretching north-west from Muscat to the UAE border, Batinah has a collection of beautiful coastal towns and villages that are well worth visiting. The most populated area after Muscat, Batinah has 12 wilayats: Awabi, Barka, Khabura, Liwa, Musanaah, Nakhal, Rustaq, Saham, Shinas, Sohar, Swaiq and Wadi Mawail. Inland, towards the Western Hajars, there are dramatic peaks and wadis, and numerous areas of historical interest.

Barka

Barka is a small coastal town west of Muscat. It makes for a rather interesting day trip or as a stop off on a visit to Sohar, further along the coast. Famous for its fortnightly bullfights and large central fort, Barka is located only a few hundred metres from the shore of the Gulf of Oman. The place is still home to craftsmen practising traditional trades including weaving. There are several attractions in the area that are certainly worth checking out when you're in the area including the historical fort, Bait Naa'man and the Ostrich Breeding Farm.

Nakhal

Only 30km inland from Barka and 100km from Muscat, with its restored fort set on a hill, Nakhal is definitely worth a quick trip. If you're feeling full of energy, you can climb up to the top of the watchtowers and be rewarded with truly magnificent views of the surrounding countryside and town. Inside the fort, visitors can see the prison, kitchen, living quarters of the Wali (leader) and the male and female majlis. The area is also well known for the Al Thowarah hot springs. The natural spring water is channelled into the falaj system to irrigate the surrounding date plantations, and you can dip your toe or have a paddle in the run-off water.

Rustaq

In the middle ages, Rustaq (or Rostaq) was the capital of Oman. However, today it is best known for its large and dramatic fort, which has been extended over the years. Rustaq is located in the Western Hajar Mountains about 170km south-west of Muscat. The fort has been restored and the main watchtower is believed to be of Sassanid origin. It was well placed to withstand long sieges since it has its own water supplies. Apparently, at one time there was a tunnel connecting this fort to the nearby fort in Al Hazm.

There is a small souk near the fort, selling a variety of items. Not far from there you'll find the hot springs that Rustaq is most famous for. The water in these springs is believed to have healing powers – it has a high sulphur content, which is supposed to provide relief for sufferers of arthritis and rheumatism.

About 20km north of Rustaq is the village of Al Hazm, which has an interesting fort. It was built in around 1700AD and the original falaj system is still in working order today. There is also an excellent view of the countryside from the watchtower.

Dakhiliya

Despite being isolated from the sea, Dakhiliya was historically important as many trade routes between the coast and the interior passed through the region. While you are in this part of the Sultanate, be sure to take your time and check out the various forts and ruins, namely Bahla Fort on Balhool Mountain and Jabrin Fort, where it is believed the Imam Bilarab (who built the place in the 1600s) is buried. Al Hoota Cave is nearby too; and seeing as you're here, you may as well nip across to check out the Batand Al Ayn tombs, which date back to the third millennium BC.

Bahla

The ancient walled city of Bahla is only two hours' drive away from Muscat, and just 40km from Nizwa. It has a small population of around 60,000, and contains 46 separate villages. While it is not yet on the mainstream tourist map (although efforts are being made to attract more tourists to the area), archaeology buffs and history enthusiasts will find that it is well worth a visit. It is believed to be one of the oldest inhabited regions in Oman, and archaeologists have found artefacts here dating back to the third century BC. It was historically a strategic stopover on the old trading route from Muscat to other parts of the Arabian Peninsula.

Apart from the historical buildings and the traditional way of life, Bahla also has a rich and diverse ecology – a balanced mixture of fertile land, mountains, wadis and desert. The productive soil, fed by a continuous supply of water from Jebel Akhdar,

has in the past yielded crops of wheat, barley, cotton and sugar cane, and today it is still home to many viable date plantations.

The town is characterised by its many winding roads, some so narrow that you have to pull over to let an oncoming car pass. Whether you explore the town of Bahla on foot or by car, you will find an eclectic balance of the new, functioning town, the ancient, fascinating ruins, and the many date plantations that are perfect picnic spots. Bahla is enclosed by a protective, fortified wall that stretches for 12km around the town. Although large sections of the wall are still standing, parts of it are in ruins and earmarked for eventual reconstruction.

Forts & Ruins

The Bahla Fort, situated on Balhool Mountain, is one of the main attractions in Bahla. It is included on UNESCO's list of World Heritage sites, and has undergone careful and extensive renovation under the organisation's sponsorship and supervision. The ruins of the fort tower 50 metres above the village, and although its famous windtowers have been almost totally destroyed over time, they were once thought to be the tallest structures in Oman. At the time of this guide going to print, Bahla Fort was still under renovation and not open to the public, but there were plans to re-open at some point. Contact the Ministry of Tourism hotline (800 777 99) to check if it is open before you travel. In the area around the fort you can wander through deserted mud-brick villages, the largest of which is Al Aqar. You can explore the ancient houses at your leisure, and in some houses you can even go up to higher storeys and look through the old window frames for a unique perspective.

Located about 12 kilometres south of Bahla is the fascinating three-storey Jabrin Fort, which has been extensively restored and redecorated. The Imam Bilarab originally built it in the 1600s as a grand country residence. His tomb is reportedly still located within the fort, to the left of the main entrance. It is believed that Jabrin Fort was home to one of the first schools in Oman, way back in the 17th century. Interesting for its wall and ceiling decorations and the water channels running through the kitchens, kids especially will love finding secret passageways and staircases, and climbing up the towers, which offer views out over the surrounding barren countryside. For more information on this and other forts in Oman, visit the website of the Ministry of Heritage and Culture (mhc.gov.om).

Bahla Souk

There is no better place to rub shoulders with the friendly people of Bahla than at the traditional market or 'souk'. Locals gather here to trade in livestock and socialise under the shade of a huge central tree.

Goats are tethered to this tree before being bought or sold. In the alleyways leading away from this central livestock trading area, you'll find many small shops that sell traditional crafts, Omani antiques (a particularly good spot to hunt for a genuine antique khanjar), rugs, spices and nuts. You can watch the local silversmith at work, repairing khanjars and jewellery in the same way it has been done for generations. The souk also has sections for fruit and vegetables, all of which are locally produced, and the locally grown dates are delicious. You can't visit the area without buying some distinctive Bahla pottery to take home with you. Bahla is a good source of high-quality clay, and there are many skilled potters in the area (all male – it is only in the southern regions of Oman that you'll find female potters). You can see them working at the traditional pottery site, which is just past the souk. There is also a pottery factory, built by the government in the late 1980s, and the Alladawi clay pots workshop that boasts four industrial kilns each able to produce around a hundred pots each month. While you will probably buy a piece of pottery for ornamental purposes (plant pots, vases, incense burners or candle holders), clay pots are still used for practical purposes in Bahla, such as carrying and cooling water, and storing food and dates.

Fanja

The picturesque village of Fanja is situated next to an extensive palm grove that runs alongside Wadi Fanja. It is around 70km from Muscat, and the approach is one of the most scenic views that Oman has to offer. The village has a dramatic tower perched on top of a hill offering spectacular views of the surrounding scenery and the wadi below. Fanja is renowned for its pottery and visitors can wander round the market bargaining for locally produced pots, local fruits and vegetables, honey and woven goods made from palm leaves.

Nizwa

About 140km from Muscat, Nizwa is a popular destination for tourists and residents. In the sixth and seventh centuries, Nizwa was the capital of Oman and the centre for trade between the coastal and interior regions. It is still the largest and most important town in this area of the interior. Historically, the town enjoyed a reputation as a haven for poets, writers, intellectuals, and religious leaders, and for centuries it was considered the cultural and political capital of the country. Positioned as it is alongside two wadis, Nizwa is a fertile sea of green with an oasis of date plantations stretching 8km from the town.

Its two notable attractions include Nizwa's 17th century fort and the magnificent Jabrin Fort, renowned for its wall and ceiling decorations and its secret passageways and staircases.

The 17th century Nizwa Fort is surprisingly large, and although not quite as visually impressive as some others, it is certainly one of the most interesting forts to visit. You can wander through the maze of passageways and up to the battlements, where the views out over Nizwa in all directions show the sheer size of the oasis, with palm trees extending as far as the eye can see. High-tech displays and areas with extensive exhibits are recent additions, transforming it into a top-class attraction where you could easily spend a few hours.

Ancient buildings survive in villages across the country

Nizwa Souk

In the centre of Nizwa, close to the fort and mosque, the souk lies hidden behind imposing sand-coloured walls. Enter through one of the enormous carved wooden doors and you'll find a small village of traditionally designed buildings, each labelled to indicate the products they sell – Silver Souk, Fish Souk and Meat Souk. Although these buildings are all clean, well lit and renovated, the place remains full of atmosphere and traders conduct business as they have done for centuries. The souks are well laid out and vibrant with local colour, especially in the early morning. The shop owners are an unobtrusive bunch and are happy to sit and drink coffee while you browse.

In the silver and craft souk, you'll find a mixture of old and new items made locally, such as Bahla pottery, old wooden chests, silverwork, antique rifles, and frankincense, as well as modern imports from India. You can watch silversmiths hammering intricate patterns into the hilts of khanjars (daggers) and join the many antique silver dealers who come here from Muscat in search of treasure for their stores. Although prices are rising as tourism increases, with hard bargaining you can sometimes get a better price than in Muscat.

The Goat Souk is the scene of a lively animal market early on Friday mornings from around 7am where cows, goats and sheep are auctioned. Sellers lead their cattle around in a circle hoping for a buyer. It's an open-air market located close to the entrance on the left, and worth visiting, especially just before the religious holidays when farmers sell their livestock for the festivities.

Sumail

The town of Sumail (or Samail) sits in the Sumail Gap, a natural valley that divides the Hajar Mountain chain into the Eastern and Western Hajars. As the most direct path between the coastal regions and the interior of the country, this route has always been an important artery. Irrigated by countless wadis and man-made falaj systems, the area is green and fertile, and the dates produced here are highly rated.

Dakhiliya Activities

Camping In Dakhiliya

The Western Hajars offer many places to set up camp in wadis or along hiking routes. Don't miss out on the magnificent views and photo opportunities to be had on Jebel Shams or the Sayq Plateau. You'll find that the higher areas are a lot cooler – temperatures average around 10 to 15°C cooler than down below, so it can therefore be more appealing than camping at lower altitudes. It is even possible to camp high up in the middle of summer.

On the Sayq Plateau, a popular place to camp is Diana's Viewpoint (named after Princess Diana, who visited in 1990). It is on the edge of a promontory with spectacular views, and there is plenty of space. As with camping anywhere in the wilderness, minimise your impact and leave no trace of your stay behind.

On Jebel Shams there is a good campsite at the start of the W4 hike, at around 1,950m. Also in the area, the off-road route to Qiyut off the Nizwa-Bahla road gets you quickly up high to masses of camping spots and great views.

On the northern side of the mountains you can camp in Wadi Al Abyad next to the pools, perfect for a dip to cool off in warmer weather, or try one of the campsites set spectacularly beneath the awesome north face of Jebel Shams in the 'treasure chest' of Oman, Wadi As Sahtan, which has almost endless possibilities for exploring.

Hiking In Dakhiliya

Oman has plenty to offer hikers, and the best area of all is the Western Hajar Mountains. There are many excellent routes to be enjoyed, ranging from short easy walks to spectacular viewpoints, to longer and more arduous treks up high peaks. Jebel Shams has numerous impressive hikes. One of the shorter ones is the four-hour Balcony Walk along Jebel Shams Plateau, which has incredible canyon views.

Be sure that on any hike, short or long, you consider the weather conditions. Always carry plenty of water and food, check your routes before setting out, notify someone as to your itinerary, and wear appropriate clothing. Be warned: no mountain rescue services exist, so anyone venturing out into mountains should be experienced, or be with someone who is.

Hikers can explore rocky canyons

Green areas provide a welcome change from the desert

Recently, the Ministry of Tourism has sponsored the installation of via ferrata routes in the Hajars, including on Jebal Shams. These are mountainous routes with fixed wire cables, metal rungs and ladders which allow adventurous walkers and climbers to ascend steep rocks and mountains in relative safety. Check out the Ministry of Tourism website (omantourism.gov.om) for a full list of routes.

Wadi Al Abyad

Just over an hour west of Muscat, the pools of Wadi Al Abyad are great to visit throughout the year. From the end of the track, a short stroll will get you to increasingly larger pools where you can easily spend the whole day. Alternatively, you can take the easy two-hour hike through the wadi to the town of Al Abyad.

Jebel Shams, Jebel Akhdar and Wadi An Nakhur are definite must-sees. Jebel Shams, the 'Mountain of the Sun', has a rugged terrain that is actually a fairly easy trek with several good camping locations. Below the summit, Wadi An Nakhur has some of the most stupendous views in the country, offering ample photo opportunities as you drive through the 'Grand Canyon of Oman'. The Sayq Plateau on top of Jebel Akhdar has spectacular scenery and beautiful little mountain villages.

Snake Canyon

Adventurers wishing to complete this spectacular, challenging hike should know that it involves some daring jumps into rock pools and a fair bit of swimming through ravines, although the addition of via ferrata routes makes some sections easier and faster, with several parts made even more thrilling

– there's an exciting series of traverses and zip line crossings some 100m above the canyon floor. It takes around three to four hours, and is something you'll remember forever. Keep a close eye on the weather, as rains from miles away could cause dangerous flash floods in a matter of minutes.

Misfat Al Abryyin

This ancient village, with terraced palm plantations built unusually on a steeply sloping hillside, is just a short distance from Al Hamra. Rich red soil, ancient houses and the ruins of a watchtower perched on the mountain add to the character of Misfat Al Abryyin. The falaj network is one of the most intricate in Oman and snakes its way around banana, lemon and date trees.

Dhofar

Dhofar is the southernmost region of Oman, bordering Saudi Arabia and the Republic of Yemen. Dhofar frankincense is regarded as the finest in the world and once made this area immensely wealthy and important. Visitors still flock to the coast to enjoy the lush greenery and cool weather.

Salalah

Salalah is the capital of Dhofar, the southernmost region of Oman, and is more than 1,000km from Muscat. It is possible to get there by road, but the drive is long and boring, with little of interest to see or do along the way. Therefore it's highly recommended that you fly, and Oman Air operates up to five flights a day from Muscat.

The lush landscape features plenty of greenery; you'll find an impressive grouping of trees in Wadi Qahshan that runs through the mountainous backdrop of the Mughsayl-Sarfait road which links Salalah with the Yemen border. This is also where frankincense trees grow and are farmed by local villagers. They cut into the trunks and allow the sap to seep out and harden into lumps, which are then scraped off and traded in bulk.

Salalah has a museum, and the souks are worthy of a visit. Al Husn Souk is the place to head if you're after silver jewellery or traditional souvenirs. It's also an excellent place to pick up some fine Dhofar frankincense. At Al Hafah Souk, south of Salalah, you'll find plenty of perfume and locally prepared food. Al Sinaw Souk is where Bedouin tribes used to conduct their business, and is famous for authentic Bedouin jewellery. If you are camping and need to get supplies, you'll find a branch of LuLu's Hypermarket in Salalah, which offers a wide range of goods.

In terms of restaurants and bars, the options in the town are really quite limited so the food and beverage outlets within Salalah's hotels are your best bet for an evening out. Both the Hilton and the Crowne Plaza have various outlets, which are popular with locals and tourists.

Souk Al Hafah

Set in the coconut groves of the Al Hafah area, three kilometres from Salalah, this is the best place in Oman to buy frankincense and incense powders. There are dozens of buckets sitting around with different qualities and compositions of perfumes and you can either ask a local to explain the differences to you, or just buy the one you like best. The scents are generally quite potent and a little goes a long way. Frankincense is poured into a bag and weighed, while incense comes in little silver or copper pots. Remember to buy some charcoal for burning the incense and some brightly painted clay Dhofari burners to put them in. At Souk Al Hafah, you can also buy textiles, as well as gold and silver, Indian and Arabic dresses and some traditional souvenirs for family and friends back home. Local coffee shops serve some tasty traditional snacks such as hummus and mishkak (Omani-style barbecued meat).

Beyond Salalah

Salalah is relatively small and, depending on the length of time you are there, you may decide that you want to explore further afield. Wadi Darbat is within easy driving distance from Salalah, and features some fantastic attractions. The Travertine Curtain, which looks like a huge pitted wall and is over 150m high, turns into a spectacular waterfall during the khareef (monsoon season) as the entire contents of Wadi Darbat flow over this escarpment – it's Arabia's answer to Niagara Falls. There are several paths taking you towards the base of the cliff, with the going getting easier as you move past the trees towards the open grassland. It's a fantastic spot to enjoy the spectacular views, just don't forget the camera. On a safety note, there are no guard rails, and the edge drops off steeply, so remain cautious at all time and keep children well back.

Wadi Darbat itself is misty, moody and muddy during the khareef, but in winter it is a verdant oasis. As you approach the wadi, just 2km from the Darbat turnoff, look out for the natural arch up to your right – this interesting feature can be reached with a short hike, and offers superb views over the surrounding valley, as well as a collection of small caves with stalactites and stalagmites. As inviting as it may seem, the water in Wadi Darbat is certainly not for swimming in, due to the risk of picking up a bilharzia infection, a nasty disease caused by parasitic worms.

Khor Ruwi, which is near the coastline in the Wadi Darbat area, used to be a bustling seaport, although it's hard to believe now. It is also home to an important archaeological site that was once the palace of the famed Queen of Sheba, and is where the waters of Wadi Darbat flow before finally reaching the ocean. The area is great for birdwatching, and flamingos are common from autumn to spring. From Khor Ruwi you can hike up to the headlands above the eastern entrance to the lagoon – a large, flat plateau eventually leads to an abrupt edge with a 30m drop to the ocean.

Ubar

At the crossroads of ancient trade routes, the Lost City of Ubar (referred to as Iram in the Quran) thrived as merchants came from far and wide to buy much sought-after incense. Traders converged to sell pottery, spices and fabric from India and China in return for the unique silver frankincense of Oman. The commerce made Ubar a city of unrivalled wealth and splendour and those who visited it referred to it as 'paradise'. According to the Quran, the wickedness of the inhabitants led Allah to destroy the city and all roads leading to it, causing it to sink into the sand. For a thousand years the city's location remained unknown, until British explorer Sir Ranulph Fiennes, during a 20 year search using modern satellite technology, discovered the city beneath the shifting sands of the Omani desert near Shisr, north of Salalah. Excavations have revealed the thick outer walls of a vast octagonal fortress with eight towers or pillars at its corners, and numerous pots and artefacts dating back thousands of years. Debate continues as to whether this is indeed Ubar, but the site is fascinating nonetheless and it was clearly an important desert settlement at one point. Tours of the city will take you through the stunning Qara Mountains.

Dhofar Must-Dos

There are some truly unique experiences to be had in Oman's southernmost region. Thousands of years of history as a major exporter of frankincense, some breathtaking scenery and a unique climate all add to the romanticism of the region. Here's some activities and attractions to check off your to-do list.

Frankincense Trail

Wadi Dawkah, with its resident frankincense trees, is a UNESCO World Heritage Site. After a short drive along a graded road, you will reach an outcrop overlooking several frankincense trees. The main areas of trees have been fenced off for protection, but if you want to get closer there are several trees just near the parking area.

Mountain Drive

Head off road and you'll be rewarded with spectacular views over Salalah and out to sea. A short drive takes you past a few great attractions such as a small lake in a stunning wadi, a large sinkhole as well as some massive baobab trees. In good weather, the viewpoints and campsites are unparalleled.

Salalah Museum

Get a feel for what life was really like for the small, yet growing, population of Salalah from as early as the 11th century. Check out ancient writings and manuscripts on display, as well as traditional equipment, old pottery and the earliest forms of currency. Contact the museum on 23 294 549 for current opening hours.

Blowholes

If you visit during khareef, drive along the coastline at Al Mughsayl to find one of the most spectacular natural sights in Oman – the Al Mughsayl blowholes. Thundering waves have eroded caverns underfoot and the only way out is up through small openings below the metal grates. Be sure to stand well back though; the force generated is quite astonishing.

Nabi Ayoub's Tomb

Nabi Ayoub (also known as the prophet Job) was a respected religious figure who is said to have used this area to conduct his daily prayers. He dedicated his life to God and was put to rest in the same spot – facing Jerusalem – where he chose to worship. Located only 40km from Salalah, this shrine remains a popular attraction for locals, tourists and residents.

Camping

Just 20km past the turnoff to the Tawi Atayr sinkhole, you'll find several sidetracks to the edge of the escarpment overlooking the east coast and the sleepy town of Mirbat. In winter the views are consistently spectacular and it is a highly recommended camping spot. In Khor Ruwi, you'll find some great campsites near the mouth of the lagoon, on the low, flat rocks just up from the beach. Just over 15km from the main road running along Jebel Al Qamar, there's a stunning birds'-eye view of the secluded beaches on Oman's south coast. There are also several spots perfect for camping here too just before and just after this viewpoint; however please remember not to disturb the locals, and if you camp here during the khareef (monsoon), be prepared for mud.

Al Wusta

In contrast to Oman's other regions, Al Wusta has few sites of historical interest, and is often only seen from a car window as people make the long drive between Muscat and Salalah. However, the region does boast areas of natural beauty, a mild summer climate and an abundance of wildlife. Al Wusta also has around 170km of coastline, which includes some amazing long stretches of white sandy beach.

The Jiddat Al Harasis region in Al Wusta is where Arabian oryx were last recorded in the wild, and a sanctuary for these magnificent desert creatures has been established there. The sanctuary has been supported by the World Wildlife Fund, and it has been remarkably successful – thanks to some careful breeding programmes, the first herd of Arabian oryx was released back into the wild in 1992.

Sharqiya

Sharqiya is a region of contrasts. The coastline features numerous fishing villages and ports, and the area's beaches are home to some of the most important turtle breeding grounds in the world. Inland, you'll find a combination of breathtaking wadis and dramatic expanses of sand dunes.

Masirah Island

Masirah Island lies 20km off the south-east coast of Oman and is the Sultanate's largest island. It is about 80km long and 18km wide, with hills in the centre and a circumference of picturesque isolated beaches. The island is off the coast of the Barr Al Hikman area, and can be accessed by taking a ferry from Shana'a – but only during high tide. The ferry leaves regularly but there are no set times and it seems to set off when full or when the ferry from the other side arrives. You can cross with your car, and the crossing takes around 90 minutes. There is a military base on the island, and the main town of Hilf, with its 8,000 residents, has some shops, and a couple of restaurants, but otherwise the island is relatively undeveloped.

There are, however, now four hotels on the island: the two-star Masirah Hotel (RO.21 for a double room); the two-star Serabis Hotel (RO.25 for a double room); the two-star Danat Al-Khaleej Hotel (RO.25 for a double room); and the four-star Masirah Island Resort (RO.75 for a double room).

The highest point of the island is Jebel Hamra at 275m, and a network of graded roads connects parts of the island. Masirah's beaches are internationally recognised for their importance as turtle breeding grounds. Four species of turtle come ashore to lay their eggs here – green turtles, hawksbill, olive ridley and loggerheads. Masirah is thought to be home to

the world's largest nesting population of loggerhead turtles, estimated at 30,000 females.

Over the past few years, Masirah has also become a hotspot for watersports enthusiasts: the beaches of the east coast offer some of the best surfing in the region, with waves of seven or eight feet on a good day. The summer months – far cooler here than in most of the rest of the Gulf – are also a good time for windsurfing, but the strong winds that lash the island during this time can be unpleasant and make camping on the beach quite uncomfortable.

Usually, however, the beaches are ideal for camping, and you'll find yourself sharing your habitat with the donkeys, camels, goats and gazelles that roam the island. Conchologists will be in their element here as the beaches are home to a vast range of shells, some of which are quite rare.

Ras Al Jinz

If you've come to see turtles, then you're in the right place. Some people think that winter is the best time to see the turtles, but you'll only see a few dozen per night. Summer is the peak season, with several hundred nesting every night. Summer is also a good time to visit Ras Al Jinz, because the ever-present winds and eastern exposure towards the Arabian Sea help keep the area a good 10-15°C cooler than Muscat. However, take note that this area is windy all year round, so pitching tents can be difficult, and you will constantly be seeking shelter from the wind.

Along with an interactive visitor centre and research station, new accommodation huts have been opened for those seeking a little style (rasaljinz-turtlereserve.com). For others, there are simple shelters and facilities to make use of (for a fee of RO.4) when camping in the area. A less windy (and more expensive) option is to stay at Al Naseem Tourist Camp (desertdiscovery.com), located shortly after you take the left turn towards Ras Al Jinz.

When you arrive at the turtle beach, check in and pay the small entrance fee. You might see some young turtle hatchlings on display. Information about the nature talks and turtle viewing sessions (which happen every night) can be obtained here. Thanks to the new visitor centre and facilities the nightly tours, which were once a little disorganised, are more structured, and the rush of tourists is better contained. On long weekends, Ras Al Jinz often sees more than a hundred visitors, all wanting to watch the turtles nesting at night.

Obey the directions given by the rangers (of which there are rarely more than two or three) and resist the urge to crowd forward when viewing the turtles. It should go without saying that you should not disturb nesting turtles, but observing the other visitors at Ras Al Jinz shows that a constant reminder is still necessary.

Turtle Power

Turtles are one of the ancient wonders of the seas and, evolutionarily speaking, have remained unchanged for approximately 90 million years. Of the seven recognised species of marine turtle, five are found in the seas of the Sultanate of Oman and are known to nest on its beaches. These are the green, hawksbill, olive ridley, leatherback, and loggerhead.

Most prevalent are the green turtle, with an estimated 20,000 females laying eggs from June to November on more than 275 beaches along Oman's coastline.

Once every two to four years, females typically lay two or three clutches (at two-week intervals), each of 100-120 eggs. The survival rate for turtles is abysmal: only two or three turtles per 10,000 reach adulthood. Like salmon, turtles return to lay eggs at the exact location of their birth. Although the eggs may hatch at different times, all baby turtles (5cm long on average) emerge from the sand at the same time and are guided by moonlight to the sea. Interestingly, the temperature of the sand determines the sex of turtles during their eight-week incubation. Temperatures in the range of 26 to 28°C are favourable for males while 30 to 34°C is ideal for females. Global warming provides further evidence that females are going to take over the world!

Adult turtles feed mainly on sea grass and sea weed and reach sexual maturity at around 20 years of age. Females travel as far as Somalia and India in search of food – a distance upwards of 3,000km. This is surprising given that a fully-grown turtle weighs 140 to 160kg and the shell is often greater than 1m in length.

If you visit any turtle beaches, stand back and don't disturb the nesting females. Avoid using any lights (including flash photography) – they disorient hatchlings and scare away adults. The best time for photos is at daybreak as the last of the females return to the sea.

The Great Outdoors

To really appreciate the splendour of Oman, head out and explore its magnificent, natural landscape and all its hidden wonders.

Desert

In the desert, there are various places to stay, all offering much the same experience. If you have a 4WD, then you'll be able to make your own way; if not, then the main desert camps all have a pick up point from where you'll be collected and transported to the camp. Most offer some kind of dune bashing experience, either in your own car or in a one of their cars with a driver provided, while some have extras such as swimming pools and quad bikes. The latter are perhaps the best option for families with children. All of the camps are booked on a dinner, bed and breakfast basis and some will even see Bedouin women come into the camp in the morning to sell their wares or offer camel rides.

The Al Areesh Camp can accommodate up to 150 guests in small huts and tents some with 'en-suite' bathrooms, while others digs have ablution facilities. The Al Raha Camp is further into the desert and definitely requires transport in (which comes at an extra cost) to get to the camp. Facilities here take a barasti beach hut or tent style.

The 1000 Nights Camp is deep into the Wahiba Sands and the campsite feels more genuine, although with a swimming pool, terrace and dining area, this is far from 'roughing it'. Accommodation is in Bedouin tents, Arabic tents and Sheikh tents, with roofless toilets and showers.

The Desert Nights Camp is at the most luxurious end of the scale. The camp offers 24 double tented 'suites', two deluxe family tents and four 'attached units'. There's an onsite restaurant and bar, as well as all manner of sports and excursions.

Mountains

There are two main mountains people tend to visit, namely Jebel Shams and Jebel Akhdar. Jebel Shams is the highest and the great thing about this mountain is the abundance of hiking trails. Jebel Akhdar is the green mountain and has an amazing scenic drive to get to the top, but a police road block at the bottom only allows 4WDs up as there have been many accidents (and deaths) due to brakes failing on the way down the mountain.

To get to the top of Jebel Akhdar, it is black top road all the way, with many twists and turns and a fairly steep gradient. To reach the top of Jebel Shams, the road is a little more difficult as it is black top only a part of the way and then changes to a dirt road.

Jebel Shams Resort offers various different chalets to choose from, as well as providing the full Bedouin tent experience too. There is a restaurant onsite, although this is a place you visit for the amazing views and experiences, rather than creature comforts. Jabel Shams Base Camp, offering 15 bungalows and 15 Bedouin tents is a stop for dedicated hikers as the rooms and services are basic but clean.

Al Jebel Al Akhdar Hotel is a simple but clean and not unpleasant hotel that has good but basic facilities including a restaurant and room service. For something truly special, Alila Jabal Akhdar is a new and luxurious hotel and resort that has great views out over the mountains.

Turtles

If you are looking for a unique and natural experience, then a night with the turtles is a must. When it comes to nature conservation, Oman still has much to learn and the turtle watching experience can be a bit over crowded at certain times of the year, but that is just testament to it being an amazing draw.

The leatherback turtles come up onto the beach to nest and lay their eggs, the greatest numbers doing so between June and October, but they can be seen all year round. It is a real treat to see the egg laying process in the late evening (around 11pm) but then, in the early hours of the morning (4am to 5am), you might be lucky enough to see the babies making their way back down to the ocean. The two main areas to see the turtles are Ras Al Jinz and Ras Al Hadd. Places to stay in both Ras Al Hadd and Ras Al Jinz are limited.

Turtle Beach Resort has been around for about 10 years. It is a traditional and basic venue, but offers 22 barasti-style huts. Ras Al Hadd Hotel is a nuts and bolts hotel offering clean rooms and a modest breakfast. Al Naseem Camp is a basic hutted camp with an ablution facility providing toilets and cold showers.

Along with an interactive visitors' centre, a research station, two restaurants, the Ras Al Jinz Turtle Reserve (rasaljinz-turtlereserve.com) recently opened some relatively luxurious accommodation; prices include bed, breakfast and a guided turtle viewing.

Unmissable scenery

Sur

Sur is an old fishing and trading port 300km south-east of Muscat. For centuries, the town was famed for its boat building and became quite prosperous as a result. Its fortunes did decline somewhat with the advent of more modern vessels and construction techniques, but Sur is enjoying something of a revival; with its pretty corniche and forts, the town is definitely worth a visit, as is the Sineslah Fort which overlooks Sur, offering breathtaking views of the area and its coastline. Sur is home to an interesting Marine Museum which is located on the premises of the Al-Aruba Sports Club near the main entrance to Sineslah Fort. It was established in 1987 to showcase Sur's maritime heritage and, inside, you can view equipment and tools of maritime navigation as well as photographs of Sur taken over a century ago.

The Arabic word Sur means a walled fortified area and there is evidence of the ancient defences throughout the town. As the first port of call in Arabia for traders from the Far East, it is believed that trading with the African coast dates back to as early as the 6th century AD.

The Khareef

The coastal region is subject to weather conditions quite different from the rest of the country, and as such the scenery is completely different to that in many areas further north. From June to September the monsoon rains (or khareef), active in the Indian Ocean clip, southern Dhofar and the countryside comes alive in an explosion of greenery, featuring lush green fields, swollen rivers and beautiful waterfalls. The foothills of the mountains, a few kilometres inland, are often covered with a thick blanket of fog during this time. The rain and fog cause a significant temperature drop, making Salalah a popular destination for residents of other Gulf countries trying to escape the summer heat.

From Muscat there are two roads to Sur. The Sur highway (Route 23) is the best option if you're looking for a smoother ride. The 300km single tarmac road, leading through the mountains and crossing some wadis, will take you to Sur in between three and four hours. Alternatively, you can take the coastal road (direction Quriyat-Sur). In terms of distance this route is much shorter (only about 150km), but it takes at least four hours to navigate. In Quriyat turn right to Sur at the roundabout, then follow the asphalt road and keep following the signposts to Sur (not Tiwi). Before long the tarmac changes to gravel.

There are a few highlights along this route: Bimmah Sinkhole is located 6km after Dibab Village, just 500m off the road on your right. Tiwi Beach (also known as White Sand Beach) makes a perfect stop

for some snorkelling or relaxing (just don't go on public holidays, especially if you don't like crowds). Wadi Shab, one of the most stunning wadis in Oman, is just past Tiwi Village. The end of the coastal road is marked by an oasis and the ancient city of Qalhat, which is famous for its dry stone walls, the remains of ancient water cisterns and the scattered headstones of a cemetery. There is also a shrine to a saintly woman known as Bibi Miriam, although it is in poor repair. From here you progress into the mountains, where you will encounter some steep slopes and hair-raising descents.

You will eventually reach the enormous LNG plant (liquefied natural gas). Head south for around 15km to get into Sur. If you came along the Muscat-Sur highway, you will first pass Sur Bilad, a suburb of Sur. Here you can visit the very impressive Bilad Fort.

Tiwi

Tiwi is a small fishing village up the coast from Sur, situated in a little cove between two of the most stunning wadis in the area – Wadi Tiwi and Wadi Shab. These verdant green oases are a must-see for anyone visiting the area, for their crystal clear pools and lush vegetation including palm and banana plantations. The residents of Tiwi are spread across nine small villages and there are endless opportunities for walking and exploring. In Wadi Shab you can start your tour with a trip across the water, courtesy of a small boat operated by locals. Further along the wadi you can swim through pools and access a cave that has a waterfall inside it. Tiwi Beach, also known as the White Sand Beach, is also a nice, tranquil spot to stop off at.

Lighthouse at Al Ayjah, Sur

UNITED ARAB EMIRATES

Abu Dhabi

Dubai may be the UAE's boldest, brashest member, but Abu Dhabi remains both the nation's capital and the richest of all the emirates, with a blossoming, burgeoning city to prove it. Recently, there has been a greater commitment to tourism, and projects such as Yas Island with its Grand Prix racetrack, Yas Waterworld, and Ferrari World theme park, and the development of the Desert Islands are proof of that. While there isn't much you can get in Abu Dhabi that you can't find in Dubai, its slightly slower pace makes for a refreshing change. The city lies on an island and is connected to the mainland by bridges. It is home to numerous internationally renowned hotels, a few shiny shopping malls, and of heritage sites and souks. Abu Dhabi is marketed as the cultural capital of the UAE and is home to an annual jazz festival, a film festival, and a music and arts festival; it also hosts numerous exhibitions throughout the year. Once complete, Saadiyat Island will become the focus for much of the cultural activity, and the home of the Louvre Abu Dhabi and the Guggenheim Abu Dhabi.

In the cooler months, the extended Corniche is a lovely spot for a stroll, and on weekend evenings the area comes alive with families meeting up to enjoy a barbecue and shisha. The many islands to the west of the city are popular with boating and watersports enthusiasts, and driving west past the city reveals gorgeous, untouched sea and a few open beaches. The emirate is also home to a large part of the Empty Quarter (Rub Al Khali), the largest sand desert in the world. The large Liwa Oasis crescent acts as a gateway to the endless dunes and is a popular weekend destination for adventure-hungry residents from Dubai.

Abu Dhabi Attractions

Abu Dhabi Corniche
Corniche St Abu Dhabi City
visitabudhabi.ae

Corniche Road has 6km of parks that include children's play areas, cycle and pedestrian paths, cafes and restaurants, and a beach park with lifeguard. There is plenty of parking on the city side of Corniche Road, and underpasses at the major intersections connect to the waterfront side. Bikes can be rented from outside the Hiltonia Beach Club for Dhs.30 per day.

Al Bateen
Nr Khaleej Al Arabi & Sultan bin Zayed Sts
Abu Dhabi City

This is one of Abu Dhabi's oldest districts and home to a dhow building yard, the Al Bateen Marina, a few historically accurate buildings and the future Al Bateen Wharf. It's a nice area to walk around, with plenty of open green spaces.

Ferrari World Abu Dhabi
Yas Island Drive Abu Dhabi City 971 2 496 8001
ferrariworldabudhabi.com

Billed as the world's largest indoor theme park, Ferrari World is part F1 amusement park and part museum dedicated to the Italian super car marque. There's plenty to keep little ones entertained and high-adrenaline rides (including the world's fastest rollercoaster) for teens and adults. The whole park sits under a giant, sweeping roof and the comfort of air conditioning makes it great for a family day out during those stifling summer months. General admission: Dhs.225 for adults and Dhs.185 for kids (under 1.3m).

Heritage Village
Nr Abu Dhabi Theatre 971 2 681 4455
torath.ae

Located near Marina Mall, this educational village offers a glimpse into the country's past. Traditional aspects of Bedouin life are explained and craftsmen demonstrate traditional skills.

Manarat Al Saadiyat
Saadiyat Cultural District Abu Dhabi City
971 2 657 5800
saadiyatculturaldistrict.ae

This visitors' centre is a taster of the cultural offerings to come on Saadiyat. Along with a presentation on the island's future development, there are exhibition spaces that have welcomed some impressive displays.

Qasr Al Hosn
Shk Zayed The First St Abu Dhabi City
abudhabi.ae

Also known as the Old or White Fort, this is the oldest building in Abu Dhabi and dates back to 1793. Located in central Abu Dhabi, the fort has undergone a series of renovations over the years and, at the time of writing, it was closed for a major renovation.

Sheikh Zayed Grand Mosque Center
Abu Dhabi City 971 2 441 6444
szgmc.ae
Map 1 C3

One of the largest mosques in the world, this architectural masterpiece can accommodate 40,000 worshippers. It features 82 domes and the world's largest hand-woven Persian carpet. It is open to non-

Muslims every day except Friday, and complimentary tours run at 10am from Sunday to Thursday.

Sir Bani Yas Island

Sir Bani Yas Island Abu Dhabi City 971 2 406 1400
desertislands.com
Half nature reserve, half luxury resort and spa, this is the centrepiece of Abu Dhabi's Desert Islands development. Home to the Arabian Wildlife Park, and Desert Islands Resort and Spa by Anantara, the island has thousands of free-roaming animals. Hiking, mountain biking and 4WD safaris, as well as snorkelling and kayaking trips, are available and you can reach the island by a private seaplane.

The Souk At Qaryat Al Beri

Qaryat Al Beri Complex Abu Dhabi City
971 2 558 1670
soukqaryatalberi.com
A recreation of a traditional Arabian souk, with small canals that weave their way between boutiques, cafes, restaurants and bars, many of which have spectacular views over the creek. The Shangri-La and Traders hotels make up part of the complex.

World Trade Center Souk

Abu Dhabi City 971 2 810 7814
wtcad.ae
The capital's latest shopping offering is rapidly becoming one of the city's major hubs, offering a mix of high fashion, traditional goods and great eating and drinking options. The Marriott Renaissance and Marriott Courtyard onsite offer further F&B options.

Yas Island

North-East of Abu Dhabi Abu Dhabi City
yasisland.ae
Yas Island has emerged as Abu Dhabi's latest tourism hotspot; in addition to hosting the annual Formula 1 Grand Prix at the Yas Marina Circuit, the island boasts several resorts with luxurious spas and restaurants, a world-class golf course, and Ferrari World, which houses the world's fastest rollercoaster. Located next to Ferrari World, Yas Waterworld boasts 43 rides, slides and attractions to keep young and old entertained. du Arena and Flash Forum stadiums stage concerts by internationally acclaimed musicians.

Abu Dhabi Hotels

Al Raha Beach Hotel

Nr Al Raha Mall Abu Dhabi City 971 2 508 0555
danathotels.com
Excellent service, a gorgeous spa and unsurpassed comfort in an idyllic boutique beach setting just outside Abu Dhabi city.

Aloft Abu Dhabi

Abu Dhabi National Exhibition Centre (ADNEC)
Abu Dhabi City 971 2 654 5000
aloftabudhabi.com
A real designer offering at the National Exhibition Centre, Aloft is a modern, trendy 408 bedroom affair.

Beach Rotana

Nr Abu Dhabi Mall Abu Dhabi City 971 2 697 9000
rotana.com
Offering loads of popular dining options, as well as a private beach, sports courts and the Zen spa.

Crowne Plaza Abu Dhabi Yas Island

Yas Plaza Abu Dhabi City 971 2 656 3000
ichotelsgroup.com
Sitting right next to Yas Links, this well-equipped hotel is just five minutes from Yas Marina and Ferrari World.

Danat Jebel Dhanna Resort

Western Region Abu Dhabi City 971 2 801 2222
jebeldhanna.danathotels.com
Located 220 kilometres west of Abu Dhabi city, close to Sir Bani Yas Island, this resort features plenty of watersports, a private beach and sand golf.

Emirates Palace Hotel

West Corniche Rd Abu Dhabi City 971 2 690 9000
kempinski.com
Emirates Palace is the ultimate in ostentatious luxury, with 14 bars and restaurants, 394 rooms and suites with butler service, an amazing collection of pools and a private beach. Large, open-air concerts are held in the 200 acre palace gardens in the cooler months. Guests can enjoy the 1.3km stretch of private beach, and the exclusive Anantara spa, not to mention several galleries, exhibits and boutiques.

Fairmont Bab Al Bahr

Khor Al Maqtaa Abu Dhabi City 971 2 654 3333
fairmont.com
This luxury hotel overlooks the creek between the mainland and the city's island, next door to the Qaryat Al Beri complex. The hotel's bars and restaurants have proven popular among locals, with Frankie's (named after owner and champion jockey Frankie Dettori), Marco Pierre White's Steakhouse and Grill and The Chocolate Gallery arguably the pick of the bunch.

Hilton Abu Dhabi

West Corniche Rd Abu Dhabi City 971 2 681 1900
hilton.com
This 10 storey luxury hotel on Corniche Road has three swimming pools and a private beach, plus a wide range of watersports. Each room boasts enviable views, and the hotel houses some of the best restaurants in the city, including Bocca.

. Emirates Palace

Sheikh Zayed Grand Mosque

Yas Viceroy Hotel

Hilton Capital Grand Abu Dhabi

Airport Rd Abu Dhabi City **971 2 617 0000**
hilton.com

The stunning wave-like glass building is home to
almost 300 rooms and suites that share state-of-the-
art facilities. The Sports City location (restaurants
look back out towards Sheikh Zayed Grand Mosque)
makes this predominantly a business hotel, but with
one of Abu Dhabi's largest spas and fitness centres, a
delightful pool area and several excellent outlets.

InterContinental Abu Dhabi

Abu Dhabi City **971 2 666 6888**
intercontinental.com/abudhabi

Adjacent to the marina, the hotel is surrounded by
lush parks and gardens. With five restaurants, four bars
and 330 deluxe rooms offering views of the city and
the Arabian Gulf, the hotel is popular with business
travellers. Following the hotel's recent renovation,
many of the restaurants and bars are worth a visit.

Jumeirah At Etihad Towers

Nr Emirates Palace Abu Dhabi City **971 2 811 5555**
jumeirah.com

Located in a soaring tower, almost 400 of the spacious
rooms in this hotel overlook Emirates Palace, the
breakwater and the Corniche; in fact, the views are so
good that a dedicated viewing platform is set to open
soon. The elegant, giant glass windowed lobby makes
quite an impression and it's a sense of luxury that
is reflected throughout the hotel, its rooms and the
excellent gym and spa.

Le Meridien Abu Dhabi

Nr Old Abu Dhabi Cooperative Society
Abu Dhabi City **971 2 644 6666**
lemeridienabudhabi.com

Famous for its health club and spa, private beach, and
Culinary Village, there is a children's swimming pool
and activities including tennis, squash and volleyball.

Liwa Hotel

Mezaira Abu Dhabi City **971 2 882 2000**
almarfapearlhotels.com/liwa

The majestic Liwa Hotel overlooks the Rub Al Khali
desert (also known as 'the Empty Quarter', one of the
most stunning panoramas in the world. The location
makes for dramatic photographs. Facilities include
a beautiful pool, a sauna, Jacuzzi and steam room,
tennis and volleyball courts.

One To One Hotel The Village

Abu Dhabi City **971 2 495 2000**
onetoonehotels.com

Resembling a boutique European hotel, this resort
offers a personal experience with stylish rooms and
some impressive F&B outlets.

Qasr Al Sarab Desert Resort By Anantara

No 1 Qasr Al Sarab Rd Abu Dhabi City **971 2 886 2088**
qasralsarab.anantara.com

This hotel has a stunning location amid the giant
dunes outside Liwa. Designed as an Arabic fort, guests
can enjoy a wide range of desert activities before
relaxing in oversized bathtubs, dining on gourmet
dishes and being pampered in the spa. You can also
book the 25 minute Rotana Jet service from Abu
Dhabi to Sir Bani Yas island for the ultimate escape.

Shangri-La Hotel Qaryat Al Beri

Qaryat Al Beri Complex Abu Dhabi City
971 2 509 8888
shangri-la.com

Overlooking the creek that separates Abu Dhabi island
from the mainland, the 214 rooms and suites all have
private terraces. The adjoining Souk Qaryat Al Beri
houses a variety of shops and restaurants connected
by waterways.

The St Regis Saadiyat Island Resort

Saadiyat Beach Abu Dhabi City **971 2 498 8888**
stregissaadiyatisland.com

The St Regis looks like a California beach retreat,
with the vastly proportioned public spaces and
stunning colonial style rooms all offering views over
the beautiful central pools, restaurant and private
windswept, sandy beach. With leisure facilities and
dining options (55 and 5th The Grill is particularly
recommended) worth travelling for, the St Regis feels
a million miles from the city.

Yas Island Rotana

Yas Plaza Hotels Abu Dhabi City **971 2 656 4000**
rotana.com

Another superb Yas Island hotel, with sports, fitness
and spa facilities that are modern and top notch in
terms of quality, as are the rooms and restaurants.

Yas Viceroy Abu Dhabi

Nr Yas Marina Circuit Abu Dhabi City **971 2 656 0000**
viceroyhotelsandresorts.com

Another of the UAE's iconic hotels, this architectural
wonder straddles the F1 circuit with a bridge that
offers the best views come race day. The hotel has
499 space-age rooms and some of the capital's best
restaurants.

Dubai

Cliches tend to trip off the tongue when describing
Abu Dhabi's little brother – the city of gold, sleepy
fishing village transformed into modern metropolis,
the Vegas of the Middle East, and so on. The truth is
that, while the emirate boasts an incredible number

attractions claiming to be the tallest, biggest or longest, it's not all bright lights – the atmospheric old town around the Creek, and the restored Al Fahidi Historical Neighbourhood area are musts for any visitor wanting to scratch Dubai's cultural surface, and the beautiful Jumeirah Mosque is one of the few mosques in the region open to non-Muslims, offering a rare chance to learn about the impact of Islam on the local people.

Dubai is also a great place for families and, from amusement parks and aquariums to child-friendly hotels and restaurants, you'll find plenty of ways to keep the kids busy while in town.

Beyond the city, the desert opens up further possibilities and many visitors choose to combine a city break with a couple of nights camping with a tour group, or relaxing at a luxury desert resort such as Al Maha or Bab Al Shams. That said, if it's bright lights you're after, Dubai outshines the rest of the region. The emirate has been successful in its quest for economic diversification, and its focus on tourism revenues has resulted in a fantastic array of superlative-laden attractions for tourists and residents alike. From skiing on real snow at Ski Dubai and plunging through shark-infested waters at Aquaventure, to shopping till you drop at Dubai Mall and surveying the entire city from the world's tallest building, Burj Khalifa, a weekend trip to Dubai promises an action-packed break. Its selection of five-star hotels, restaurants, bars and clubs will ensure a well fed and watered stay, and luxury spas and clean beaches provide ample opportunities to relax.

For more help on planning a trip to Dubai, log on to askexplorer.com where you can find listings of forthcoming events and further information about Dubai hotels and attractions, and where you can order a copy of *Dubai Visitors' Guide* or *Dubai Tourists' Map* – the essential guides for your weekend break.

Dubai Attractions

Adventure HQ
Times Square Dubai 971 4 346 6824
adventurehq.ae
In addition to stocking up on active wear and outdoors goods, adrenaline junkies will find plenty of indoor thrills, from the climbing wall to the skate park.

At The Top Burj Khalifa
Burj Khalifa Dubai 971 4 888 8124
atthetop.ae
In less than 60 seconds, a high-speed lift whisks visitors up to the 124th floor of the world's tallest tower. From the Burj Khalifa observation deck, you can survey a 360° view of the city. Advance bookings are Dhs.125 for adults and Dhs.95 for children; tickets bought on the day cost Dhs.400.

Dubai Aquarium & Underwater Zoo
The Dubai Mall Dubai 971 4 448 5200
thedubaiaquarium.com
Located, somewhat bizarrely, in the middle of The Dubai Mall, this aquarium displays over 33,000 tropical fish to passing shoppers free of charge. For a closer view of the main tank's inhabitants, however (which include fearsome looking but generally friendly sand tiger sharks) you can pay to walk through the 270° viewing tunnel. Also well worth a look is the Underwater Zoo, which includes residents such as penguins, piranhas and an octopus. If you're feeling really adventurous, you can even go for a scuba dive in the tank (call ahead to book), ride a glass-bottomed boat or feed the sharks.

Dubai Museum
Financial Centre Rd Dubai 971 4 353 1862
dubaiculture.ae
Located in Al Fahidi Fort, this museum is creative, well thought-out and interesting for all the family. The fort was originally built in 1787 as the residence of the ruler of Dubai and for sea defence, and then renovated in 1970 to house the museum. All aspects of Dubai's past are represented. You can walk through a souk from the 1950s, stroll through an oasis, see into a traditional house, get up close to local wildlife, learn about the archaeological finds or go 'underwater' to discover the pearl diving and fishing industries. There are some entertaining mannequins to pose with too. Entry costs Dhs.3 for adults and Dhs.1 for children under 6 years old.

Heritage & Diving Villages
Nr Shindagha Tunnel Dubai 971 4 393 9390
dubaiculture.ae
Located near the mouth of Dubai Creek, the Heritage & Diving Villages focus on Dubai's maritime past, pearl diving traditions and architecture. Visitors can observe traditional potters and weavers practising their craft the way it has been done for centuries. Local women serve traditionally cooked snacks – one of the rare opportunities you'll have to sample genuine Emirati cuisine. It is particularly lively during the Dubai Shopping Festival and Eid celebrations, with performances including traditional sword dancing. The village is very close to Sheikh Saeed Al Maktoum's House, the home of the much-loved former ruler of Dubai, which is a good example of a traditional home.

Jumeirah Mosque
Nr Palm Strip, Jumeira Rd Dubai 971 4 353 6666
cultures.ae
This is the most beautiful mosque in the city and perhaps the best known, as its image features on the Dhs.500 banknote. The Sheikh Mohammed Centre for Cultural Understanding (SMCCU, cultures.ae)

organises mosque tours for non-Muslims every day at 10am except Fridays. You must dress conservatively – no shorts and no sleeveless tops. Women must also cover their hair with a head scarf or shawl, and all visitors will be asked to remove their shoes. Cameras are allowed, pre-booking is essential and there is a registration fee of Dhs.10 per person.

KidZania

The Dubai Mall Dubai **971 4 448 5222**
kidzania.ae
This is fast becoming one of The Dubai Mall's main attractions, offering kids the opportunity to become adults for the day. Billed as a 'real-life city' for children, youngsters can dress up and act out more than 75 different roles, from policeman to pilot and doctor to designer. The KidZania city even has its own currency, which children can earn and spend. It's intended to be both fun and educational. Dhs.95 to 130 entry.

SEGA Republic

The Dubai Mall Dubai **971 4 448 8484**
segarepublic.com
Don't be fooled by the slightly retro decor - SEGA Republic is a brilliant indoor attraction perfect for a family day out. This theme park located in Dubai Mall offers a range of thrills and spills, courtesy of the nine main attractions and the 150 arcade games. A Power Pass (Dhs.150) gets you all-day access to the big attractions, which include stomach-flipping rides like the Sonic Hopper, the SpinGear and the Halfpipe Canyon. Unlike many other shopping mall amusement centres, SEGA Republic is for all ages, and features some truly unique thrills.

Ski slope, Mall of the Emirates, Dubai

Ski Dubai

Mall Of The Emirates Dubai **971 4 409 4090**
theplaymania.com
Ski Dubai is the Middle East's first indoor ski resort, with more than 22,500 square metres of real snow. The temperature hovers around -3°C even when it's closer to 50°C outside, making for a cool escape from the summer heat. Competent skiers and boarders can choose between five runs and a freestyle area; skiing and snowboarding lessons are available for beginners; and there is a huge snowpark for the little ones. You can roll down the Giant Ball run, turn down the tube slides, sightsee in the chairlift, or enjoy a mug of hot chocolate at -4°C. You can even get up close with a colony of snow penguins (skidubaipenguins.com). Slope pass and lesson prices include the hire charge for jackets, trousers, boots, socks, helmets – and either skis and poles or a snowboard – but it's worth bringing your own gloves as these are charged extra.

Souk Al Bahar

Nr Dubai Mall and The Palace Hotel Dubai **971 4 362 7011**
soukalbahar.ae
With atmospheric passageways, Souk Al Bahar is designed to resemble a traditional souk. It houses a host of designer boutiques and shops selling Arabian wares such as carpets, paintings, jewellery, clothes and perfumes, but its main attractions are the restaurants and bars, many of which have terraces with views of the Dubai Fountain and Burj Khalifa. Among the favourites include Mango Tree, BiCE Mare, Karma Kafe and Rivington Grill.

Souk Madinat Jumeirah

Nr Burj Al Arab Dubai **971 4 366 8888**
madinatjumeirah.com
This modern shopping mall is a recreation of a traditional souk with confusingly winding passageways, authentic architecture and interconnecting waterways traversed by motorised abras (traditional boats). It houses a collection of boutique shops, galleries, cafes and bars and the alfresco dining venues are always buzzing during the evenings of the cooler months.

The Dubai Mall

Nr Interchange 1 Dubai **971 4 362 7500**
thedubaimall.com
One of the world's largest shopping malls, The Dubai Mall is a shopper's paradise housing some 1,200 stores, including the famous New York department store, Bloomingdales. Even if you're not in town to shop, you should make a trip to the mall anyway to view the many attractions within. There is an Olympic-sized ice rink, an indoor waterfall, a 22 screen cinema, Sega World indoor theme park, KidZania edutainment

centre, the Dubai Aquarium and Underwater Zoo and some great alfresco dining venues with views of the spectacular musical displays of the Dubai Fountain.

The Lost Chambers Aquarium
Atlantis The Palm Dubai 971 4 426 1040
atlantisthepalm.com

The ruins of the mysterious lost city provide the theme for the aquarium at Atlantis. The maze of underwater halls and tunnels provide ample opportunity to get up close to the aquarium's 65,000 inhabitants, ranging from sharks and eels to rays and piranhas, as well as multitudes of exotic fish. The entrance fee is Dhs.100 for adults and Dhs.70 for 7 to 11 year olds. While you can see a lot from the windows in the hotel, it is worth splashing out for the views inside.

Dubai Hotels

Atlantis The Palm
Crescent Rd Dubai 971 4 426 0000
atlantisthepalm.com

With a staggering 1,539 rooms and suites, all with views of the sea or the Palm Jumeirah, Atlantis is certainly one of Dubai's grandest hotels. It has no less than four fancy restaurants featuring the cuisine of Michelin-starred chefs, including a branch of the world-famous chain Nobu. It is also home to Aquaventure, the biggest waterpark in the Middle East, and the Lost Chambers Aquarium. If you are looking to stay on the Palm Jumeirah, consider that a large number of new hotels have recently opened on the Palm, from chains such as Rixos, Sofitel, One & Only, Jumeirah Group, Fairmont and Kempinski.

Bonnington Jumeirah Lakes Towers
Cluster J Dubai 971 4 356 0000
bonningtontower.com

This British five-star institution made its Dubai debut in Jumeirah Lakes Towers. Containing both hotel suites and serviced apartments, as well as six restaurants and bars, and a leisure deck with infinity pool, it has great connections to Dubai Marina, as well as the rest of the city via the nearby Metro stop. The Irish bar, McGettigan's, is arguably one of the most popular watering holes in Dubai with a great outdoor area, buzzing vibe and live music.

Burj Al Arab
Nr Wild Wadi, Jumeira Dubai 971 4 301 7777
jumeirah.com

Standing on its own man-made island, this dramatic Dubai icon's unique architecture is recognised around the world. Suites have two floors and are serviced by a team of butlers. To make things even more luxurious, guests flying into Dubai area picked up from the airport in a Rolls Royce. To get into the hotel as a non-guest, you will need a restaurant reservation.

Desert Palm
Nr Dragon Mart Dubai 971 4 323 8888
desertpalm.peraquum.com

Located outside the bustle of the city, Desert Palm is so tranquil you'll never want to leave. Overlooking polo fields, guests can chose from suites, or private villas with a pool. The extensive spa menu features massage and holistic therapies including reiki. Signature restaurant Rare is a must for meat lovers, while Epicure is a lovely gourmet deli and a great breakfast venue.

Dubai Festival City
Dubai 971 4 800 332
dubaifestivalcity.com

DFC has two hotels. The InterContinental has extensive spa facilities and great views; next door is the Crowne Plaza, home of the Belgian Beer Cafe.

Hilton Dubai Creek
Nr Dubai Chamber of Commerce Dubai
971 4 227 1111
hilton.com

With very flash yet understated elegance, this ultra-minimalist hotel features interiors of wood, glass and chrome. Centrally located and overlooking the Dubai Creek, with splendid views of the Arabian dhow trading posts, the hotel has two renowned restaurants: Glasshouse Brasserie and the Dubai gastronomic darling, Table 9 by Nick and Scott.

Jumeirah Beach Hotel
Nr Wild Wadi Dubai 971 4 348 0000
jumeirah.com

Shaped like an ocean wave, with a fun and colourful interior, the hotel has 598 rooms and suites and 19 private villas, all with a sea view. It is also home to some excellent food and beverage outlets, including Uptown for happy hour cocktails and a great view of the Burj Al Arab. Kids and families will love Wild Wadi Water Park, which is located here.

Kempinski Hotel Mall Of The Emirates
Mall of the Emirates Dubai 971 4 341 0000
kempinski.com

Located in Mall Of The Emirates, this chic hotel's 400 deluxe rooms enjoy direct access to the shopping extravaganza of the iconic mall and Ski Dubai, the indoor ski slope. Check into one of the 15 exclusive ski chalet rooms, remove your boots, put your feet up to the (fake) fire and tuck into an apres-ski afternoon tea while watching the world slide by. Be sure to pay a visit to the gorgeous Softouch Spa, which specialises in Ayurvedic treatments.

Madinat Jumeirah

Nr Burj Al Arab Dubai **971 4 366 8888**
jumeirah.com

This extravagant resort has two hotels, Al Qasr and Mina A'Salam, with no fewer than 940 luxurious rooms and suites, and the exclusive Dar Al Masyaf summer houses, all linked by man-made waterways navigated by wooden abra boats which whisk guests around the resort. Nestled between the two hotels is the Souk Madinat, with over 95 shops and 44 bars and restaurants to choose from.

One&Only Royal Mirage

Nr Palm Jumeirah Dubai **971 4 399 9999**
oneandonlyresorts.com

This stunningly beautiful resort is home to three different properties: The Palace, Arabian Court and Residence & Spa. The service and dining (opt for the Beach, Bar & Grill for a romantic evening out; try delectable Moroccan cuisine in the opulent Tagine; or enjoy cocktails with a view in The Rooftop and Sports Lounge) are renowned, and a luxury spa treatment here is the ultimate indulgence. This hotel's sister resort, One&Only The Palm, is located directly across the water on the Palm Jumeirah and is just as spectacular if not more so. A ferry service connects the two properties.

Park Hyatt Dubai

Nr Dubai Creek Golf & Yacht Club Dubai
971 4 602 1234
dubai.park.hyatt.com

Enjoying a prime waterfront location within the grounds of Dubai Creek Golf & Yacht Club, the Park Hyatt is Mediterranean in style with low-rise buildings, natural colours and stylish decor. The hotel has 225 rooms and suites, all with beautiful views, as well as some great dining outlets and a luxurious spa, which features a luxury couple's massage option. Excellent restaurants inside the hotel include The Thai Kitchen and Traiteur.

Raffles Dubai

Nr Wafi Dubai **971 4 324 8888**
raffles.com

With 248 stunning suites, the renowned Raffles Amrita Spa and a unique Botanical Sky Garden, this is one of Dubai's most noteworthy city hotels. Nine food and beverage outlets offer a mix of international and far eastern cuisine.

The Address Downtown Dubai

Dubai **971 4 436 8888**
theaddress.com

Even at over 300 metres in height, The Address is dwarfed by its neighbour, the Burj Khalifa – but breathtaking views, beautiful, Arabian-themed interiors and eight dining outlets (including Neos, the panoramic bar on the 63rd floor) make this one of the most popular spots in town. There are also two more The Address hotels, both equally luxurious, located at Dubai Mall and Dubai Marina, while The Address brand runs the small boutique hotel at The Montgomerie golf course and The Palace – The Old Town in Downtown Dubai.

The Palace Downtown Dubai

Nr Dubai Mall Dubai **971 4 428 7888**
theaddress.com

Palatial indeed, The Palace faces the mighty Burj Khalifa and the spectacular Dubai Fountain. Styled with traditional Arabic architecture, this opulent hotel boasts 242 luxurious rooms and suites, a beautiful spa and some excellent restaurants, including Argentinean steakhouse Asado, and majlis-style shisha tents arranged around the stunning pool.

The Ritz-Carlton Dubai Hotel

Nr Meydan Beach Club & JBR Dubai **971 4 399 4000**
ritzcarlton.com

Even though it is the only low-rise building amid the sea of Marina towers behind it, all 138 rooms have beautiful views of the Gulf – The Ritz Carlton was, after all, here years before the rest of the marina was built. Afternoon tea in the Lobby Lounge is a must, and there are several other excellent restaurants and a very good spa onsite. The Ritz-Carlton has also added another property to its offerings, with a 341 room hotel in the DIFC area.

The Westin Dubai Mina Seyahi Beach Resort & Marina

Nr Dubai Media City Dubai **971 4 399 4141**
westinminaseyahi.com

Set on 1,200 metres of private beach, The Westin has 294 spacious rooms and suites with all the luxury amenities you would expect of a five-star hotel, including the aptly named Heavenly Spa. There are plenty of dining venues, including perennially popular Italian Bussola, Senyar for cocktails and tapas, and wine and cheese bar Oeno.

Al Ain

Al Ain is Abu Dhabi emirate's second city and possesses great historical significance for the UAE. Its location, on ancient trading routes between the country of Oman and the Arabian Gulf, rendered the oasis strategically important.

Commonly known as 'The Garden City', Al Ain features many oases and lovely patches and pockets of greenery for the public to enjoy. After a greening programme instigated by the late Sheikh Zayed,

Dubai's famous Burj Al Arab hotel

The Burj Khalifa visible in the distance

Atlantis The Palm, Dubai

the seven natural oases are now set amid tree-lined streets and beautiful urban parks. Its unique history means that Al Ain is home to several interesting sights and attractions, including the Hili Archaeological Garden, the family-friendly theme park Hili Fun City, and the Al Ain Museum.

Just on the outskirts of the city sits one of the largest mountains in the UAE, Jebel Hafeet. The rolling, grass-covered hills of Green Mubazzarah Park at the bottom of the mountain are great for picnics and mid afternoon naps. Al Ain's archaeological and historical legacy is of such significance that the city was recently placed onto the list of World Heritage Sites by UNESCO.

Al Ain Attractions

Al Ain Camel & Livestock Souk

Nr Bawadi Mall, Zayed Bin Sultan St Al Ain City
adach.ae

Conditions at the souk have improved dramatically with spacious pens for the animals and ample parking for visitors. A visit to the market is a fantastic way to mingle with locals and witness the lively event of camel and goat trading as it's taken place for centuries. Arrive early, preferably before 9am, to soak up the atmosphere.

Al Ain National Museum

Nr Sultan Fort, Zayed Bin Sultan St Al Ain City
971 3 764 1595
abudhabi.ae

Divided into three main sections – archaeology, ethnography and gifts – the presentations and displays include a selection of photographs, Bedouin jewellery, musical instruments, weapons and a traditional majlis.

Al Ain Oasis

Nr Al Ain Museum, Zayed Bin Sultan St Al Ain City
971 3 712 8429
visitabudhabi.ae

This impressive oasis in the heart of the city is filled with palm plantations, many of which are still working farms. The cool, shady walkways transport you from the heat and noise of the city to an otherworldly, tranquil haven. You are welcome to wander through the plantations, but it's best to stick to the paved areas. The farms have plenty of working examples of falaj, the traditional irrigation system which has been used for centuries to tap into underground wells. There are eight different entrances, some of which have arched gates, and there is no entry fee.

Al Ain Zoo

Nahyan Al Awwal St Al Ain City **971 3 799 2000**
alainzoo.ae

Stretching over 900 hectares, this is one of the largest and best zoos in the Gulf region. With ample greenery, a casual stroll through the paths that criss-cross the park makes for a wonderful family day out. As well as seeing large mammals, reptiles and big cats, you can get up close to some rare and common local species such as the Arabian oryx and sand gazelle, or pay a visit to the fantastic birdhouse. Since its founding, the zoo has been a centre for endangered species' conservation and visitors can look forward to spotting true rarities. Nearly 30% of the 180 species are endangered and the park is even home to a stunning pair of white tigers and white lions. A park train regularly departs from the central concourse, providing a whirlwind tour of the zoo. The park is open daily from 9am to 8pm in winter and from 4pm to 10pm during summer. In the warmer months, you can take part in a night safari (you can even hire night-vision goggles), Entrance is Dhs.15 for adults, Dhs.5 for children and it's free for under twos.

Al Jahili Fort

Nr Central Public Gardens Al Ain City
971 3 784 3996
abudhabi.ae

Celebrated as the birthplace of the late Sheikh Zayed bin Sultan Al Nahyan, the picturesque fort was erected in 1891 to defend Al Ain's precious palm groves. It is set in beautifully landscaped gardens and visitors are encouraged to explore the exterior. It's also the venue for concerts in the Abu Dhabi Classics series.

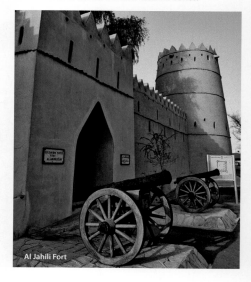
Al Jahili Fort

Hili Archaeological Park

Mohammed Bin Khalifa St Al Ain City 971 3 764 1595
abudhabi.ae

Located 10 kilometres outside Al Ain on the Dubai-Al Ain highway, the landscaped gardens are home to a Bronze Age settlement (2500-2000BC), which was excavated and restored in 1995. Many of the artefacts found during the excavation are displayed in the Al Ain National Museum. Other remains, including tombs and an Iron Age falaj, are largely located in a protected area outside the park. Entry is Dhs.1.

Hili Fun City

Mohd Bin Khalifa St Al Ain City 971 3 784 5542
hilifuncity.ae

This 22 hectare spacious, leafy park is perfect for family outings. There are plenty of beautifully landscaped spaces for picnics and barbecues, with arcade games and refreshment stands nearby. The park is being gradually updated and there are now more than 30 attractions – ranging from gentle toddler rides to white-knuckle thrillers for teens and adults – with more rides on the way. The park has an amphitheatre where various singing, dancing and circus shows are put on throughout the day. The park is open 4pm to 10pm Monday to Thursday, 12pm to 10pm Friday and Saturday, with Wednesdays reserved for ladies and children only.

The park is closed on Sundays and for Ramadan (when annual maintenance takes place). Special opening hours apply for the June-September period. Entrance costs Dhs.50 (Dhs.45 on Mondays and Tuesdays); admission is free for kids up to 89cm tall.

Wadi Adventure

Nr Green Mubazzarah, Off Al Ain Fayda Rd
Al Ain City 971 3 781 8422
wadiadventure.ae

Located at the bottom of Jebel Hafeet and beside Green Mubazzarah, Wadi Adventure is a man-made water adventure park. The three whitewater rafting and kayaking runs – with a combined length of more than 1.1km – are among the major draws, but you'll also find a gigantic surf pool complete with a man-made beach and 3m waves. The other facilities include regular swimming pools for adults and kids, a rope course, zip line and climbing wall, as well as several food and beverage outlets.

Al Ain Hotels

Al Ain Rotana

Shk Zayed Rd Al Ain City 971 3 754 5111
rotana.com

Located in the centre of the city, the hotel's rooms, suites and chalets are extremely spacious and modern.

The other facilities include a beautiful garden pool and good fitness facilities. In addition, the hotel is also a nightlife hub with six dining venues, including the ever-popular Trader Vic's and a highly recommended Lebanese restaurant.

Al Massa Hotel

Nr Hamdan Bin Mohd & Al Baladiah Sts Al Ain City
971 3 763 9003
almasahotels.com

This city centre establishment has 50 rooms and 12 suites, along with a cafe and Lebanese-style restaurant. It is a little dated but clean and welcoming if you're simply looking for a place to stay in the centre of town.

Asfar Resort

Nr Safeer Mall, Baniyas St Al Ain City 971 3 762 8882
asfarhotels.com

Located near Safeer Mall, around 4km from the Omani border, this relaxed resort offers 53 well-equipped rooms ranging from studios to two-bedroom suites. In addition to a sunny swimming pool and a palm tree lined lounging area, the facilities include a gym, while the resort's onsite restaurant, Rendezvous, serves up a wide range of international dishes.

Ayla Hotel

Khalifa Bin Zayed Al Awwal St Al Ain City
971 3 761 0111
aylahotels.com

The rooms are practical and tasteful, while there's a modern gym, indoor pool, sauna, Jacuzzi and basic spa offerings. Dining options are simple but adequate, but Ayla is aimed mainly at an Arabic market and outlets are not licensed. Western tourists shouldn't be put off – the hotel has a welcoming atmosphere.

City Seasons Hotel Al Ain

Khalifa Bin Zayed St Al Ain City 971 3 755 0220
cityseasonsalain.com

This hotel has 89 lovely rooms and suites with excellent facilities. Executive suites have a separate living room and kitchen facilities. The hotel has a fitness centre, swimming pool and sun deck and there are three restaurants to choose from, including an all-day dining restaurant.

Danat Al Ain Resort

Nr Khalid Bin Sultan & Al Salam Sts Al Ain City
971 3 704 6000
danathotels.com

One of the most enjoyable inland resorts in the UAE, this hotel has landscaped gardens, swimming pools, luxurious guestrooms, deluxe villas and a Royal Villa with a private Jacuzzi. It also has great facilities for families and a delightful spa.

Hilton Al Ain
Nr Khalid Bin Sultan & Zayed Bin Sultan Sts
Al Ain City **971 3 768 6666**
hilton.com

Located near the heart of Al Ain, this ageing hotel is a key landmark and sits in lush, landscaped gardens that contain a nine-hole golf course, tennis and squash courts, a health club and a nice pool area. It is particularly convenient for visiting Al Ain Zoo. The Hiltonia Sports Bar and Paco's Bar are popular haunts.

Mercure Grand Jebel Hafeet Al Ain
Hafeet Mountain Al Ain City **971 3 783 8888**
mercure.com

Situated in a spectacular location near the top of Jebel Hafeet, the Mercure offers incredible views of Al Ain from all of its simply decorated rooms and terraced restaurants. There are also three swimming pools, and a water slide. There is a pub, buffet restaurant and poolside cafe serving excellent evening barbecues.

Sharjah

Despite being eclipsed by Dubai in the international spotlight, Sharjah has substantially more culture and heritage to offer. So much so, that it was named the cultural capital of the Arab world by UNESCO in 1998, thanks to its eclectic mix of museums, heritage sites and traditional souks. The border between Dubai and Sharjah cities is barely noticeable when driving from one to the other. This means it's easy to explore Sharjah without having to check into a hotel.

Sharjah is built around Khalid Lagoon, also known as the creek, and the surrounding Buheirah Corniche is a popular spot for an evening stroll. From various points around the lagoon, small dhows can be hired to take you out on the water to see the city lights. Joining Khalid Lagoon to Al Khan Lagoon, Al Qasba (opposite) is home to a variety of cultural events, exhibitions, theatre and music – all held on the canal-side walkways or at dedicated venues. The city's main cultural centres, The Heritage Area and the Arts Area, are two of the most impressive collections of museums and heritage sites in the region. The ruling Al Qassimi family are renowned collectors of historical artefacts and art and, in an emirate known for its conservatism, many of the works held within the Arts Area are surprising in their modernity. Sharjah's cultural worth is so great that visitors should avoid trying to absorb it all in one trip.

Shoppers will have a blast too, searching for gifts in Sharjah's souks. There's also high-street shopping at Sharjah Mega Mall (megamall.ae).

Sharjah Attractions

Sharjah Aquarium
Nr Sharjah Maritime Museum Sharjah City
971 6 528 5288
sharjahaquarium.ae

Although eclipsed by the two aquariums that opened in Dubai in 2008, Sharjah Aquarium still draws big crowds, especially at the weekends. Situated next door to Sharjah Maritime Museum at the mouth of Al Khan Lagoon, its location allows visitors to view the Gulf's

Sharjah

natural underwater life. There are over 250 species in the aquarium, as well as many interactive displays for kids and adults to check out. Open 8am to 8pm Monday to Thursday, 4pm to 9pm on Fridays and 8am to 9pm on Saturdays. Admission is Dhs.20 for adults, Dhs.10 for children, and Dhs.50 for families.

Sharjah Art Museum
Nr Sharjah Arts Area Sharjah City **971 6 568 8222** sharjahmuseums.ae

One of the highlights of any visit to Sharjah is a trip to the Arts Area, and its centrepiece is the Sharjah Art Museum. This stunning museum was originally built to house the personal collection of over 300 paintings and maps belonging to the ruler, HH Dr Sheikh Sultan bin Mohammed Al Qassimi. Permanent displays include the work of 18th century artists, with oil paintings and watercolours depicting life in the Arab world, while other exhibits change frequently. There's an art reference library, bookshop and coffee shop, and the museum hosts various cultural activities. The museum is closed on Friday mornings, while Wednesday afternoons are for ladies only.

Sharjah Desert Park
Interchange 9, Al Dhaid Rd Sharjah City **971 6 531 1501** epaashj.com

Located 25 kilometres outside the city, the Sharjah Desert Park complex comprises the Natural History Museum, the Arabian Wildlife Centre, the Children's Farm and the recently opened Sharjah Botanical Museum. The Natural History and Botanical Museums feature interactive displays on the relationships between man and the natural world in the UAE and beyond, while at the Arabian Wildlife Centre you get the chance to see many reptiles, birds and mammals, including the rare Arabian leopard. The facilities are excellent and the animals are treated well. There is also a Children's Farm with animals that can be fed and petted. Picnic areas are available, plus cafes and shops. Closed on Tuesdays, entry costs Dhs.5 for children, Dhs.15 for adults.

Sharjah Discovery Centre
Al Dhaid Rd Sharjah City **971 6 558 6577** sharjahmuseums.ae

The Discovery Centre makes for a great family day out and children of all ages, including toddlers, can explore the many themed areas and interact with the exhibits. Explore the dynamics of water, the five senses and the mechanisms of building, or become a star on TV, climb a wall, and 'shop till you drop' in the children's supermarket. The aim is to teach youngsters in a practical, fun and interesting way. There is good pushchair access, an in-house cafe, and ample parking available.

Entrance is Dhs.5 for children and Dhs.10 for adults. The centre is open from 8am to 2pm Sunday to Thursday, and 4pm to 8pm Friday and Saturday.

Sharjah Maritime Museum
Nr Sharjah Aquarium Sharjah City **971 6 522 2002** sharjahmuseums.ae

With the goal of documenting the development of seafaring in the Middle East, the museum's displays feature fishing, trading, pearl diving and boat construction methods native to the UAE. Each room in the museum informs visitors about a different aspect of the marine industry. The museum also houses several real examples of traditional seafaring boats. Open 8am to 8pm, Saturday to Thursday, and 4pm to 8pm on Fridays.

Sharjah Museum Of Islamic Civilization
Corniche St, Nr Sharjah Creek Sharjah City **971 6 565 5455** sharjahmuseums.ae

With vaulted rooms, and impressive galleries and halls, the architecture of this recently-opened museum alone makes a visit worthwhile, but with over 5,000 Islamic artefacts, this is one of the best places to learn about Islam and Islamic culture. The museum is organised according to five themes: the Islamic religion, Islamic art, artefacts, craftsmen and weaponry, each in its own gallery. The Temporary Exhibition Gallery hosts a programme of visiting exhibitions. Entry for adults is Dhs.5; children are free.

Sharjah Science Museum
Nr Cultural Square Sharjah City **971 6 566 8777** sharjahmuseums.ae

This is the first interactive Science and Technology Centre in the UAE. The interactive museum's exhibits and demonstrations cover subjects such as aerodynamics, cryogenics, electricity and colour. There's also a planetarium and children's area where the under fives and their parents can learn together. The Learning Centre offers more in-depth programmes on many of the subjects covered in the museum. Entry costs Dhs.5 for children aged three to 17 years and Dhs.10 for adults.

Sharjah Hotels

Corniche Al Buhaira Hotel
Corniche Rd Sharjah **971 6 519 2222**

This is a beautiful new resort which is located right on the Corniche and boasts some of the best facilities in the emirate. It's located fairly close to Sharjah City Centre and Al Noor Mosque, making it a great base for exploring these two attractions. There are two restaurants, two cafes and a poolside bar.

Lou' Lou'a Beach Resort
Al Meena St Sharjah **971 6 528 5000**
loulouabeach.com
Beach resort situated on the Sharjah coast. Offers watersports and spa facilities.

Radisson Blu Resort Sharjah
Corniche Rd Sharjah **971 6 565 7777**
radissonblu.com
Located on the Sharjah Corniche, close to the city's main cultural attractions, the hotel has its own beach.

Sharjah Rotana
Nr Rolla Square Sharjah City **971 6 563 7777**
rotana.com
Well-located in the centre of the city, the Rotana caters mostly to business travellers.

Ajman

The smallest of the emirates, Ajman's centre is just 10 kilometres from Sharjah city centre, and the two cities pretty much merge along the coast. Ajman has a nice stretch of beach and a pleasant corniche to walk along, while the Kempinksi Hotel Ajman is a grand offering for those wanting a luxurious stay. If you're on a tighter budget, there are several cheaper options along the beach.

Ajman Museum houses a variety of interesting displays in a restored fort that is well worth visiting, as much for the building as for its contents. There are plans to develop a heritage city between the museum and the corniche to include a roofed market and cultural quarter; the museum quarter, gold market quarter and craft workshops will also be restored.

The tiny emirate is known for being one of the largest boat building centres in the region. While mainly modern boats emerge from the yards these days, you may still catch a glimpse of a traditionally built wooden dhow sailing out to sea. The emirate's main souk is a reminder of a slower pace of life and of days gone by, while the modern Ajman City Centre is home to shops, foodcourts and a cinema.

Ajman Attractions

Ajman Museum
Al Bustan Ajman **971 6 742 3824**
Map **1 D2**
Ajman Museum's interesting and well arranged displays have descriptions in both English and Arabic. The museum has a variety of exhibits, including a collection of Ajman-issued passports and dioramas of ancient life, but it's the building itself that will most impress visitors. Housed in a fortress dating back to

around 1775, the museum is a fascinating example of traditional architecture, with imposing watchtowers and traditional windtowers. Entry is Dhs.5 for adults. Morning opening times are 9am to 1pm then 4pm to 7pm in the evening. Closed on Fridays.

Ajman Hotels

Kempinski Hotel Ajman
Shk Humaid Bin Rashid Al Nuaimi St Ajman
971 6 714 5555
kempinski.com
Visitors to Ajman can relax on half a kilometre of the Kempinski's private beach or around its superb pool facilities. If you're feeling energetic, the hotel also offers watersports. It boasts 185 seaview rooms and a diverse range of international restaurants, cafes and bars, as well as a grand ballroom. The Softouch Spa offers a comprehensive spa menu, including an Ayurvedic massages and other treatments.

Fujairah

A trip to the east coast is a must – made up of the emirate of Fujairah and several enclaves belonging to Sharjah, the villages along the east coast sit between the rugged Hajar Mountains and the gorgeous Gulf of Oman. Fujairah city has seen little development compared to cities on the west coast, but the real draw here is the landscape. The mountains and wadis that stretch west of the coast contain some of the country's best and most accessible camping spots and the beaches, reefs and villages that line the coast attract visitors from Dubai throughout the year.

Previously, the journey to the east coast involved a two-hour drive that took in some of the country's most scenic mountain passes. If you're happy to sacrifice some of those views for time, however, the new Sheikh Khalifa Highway cuts the journey time between Dubai and Fujairah to just 30 minutes.

Bidiyah
The site of the oldest mosque in the UAE, Bidiyah, is one of the oldest settlements on the east coast and is believed to have been inhabited since 3000BC. The mosque is made from gypsum, stone and mud bricks finished off with plaster, and its original design of four domes supported by a central pillar was considered unique, but the shape was changed to stepped domes during renovations. It is believed to date back to the middle of the 15th century. The mosque is still used for daily prayer, so non-Muslim visitors can't enter. Built next to a low hillside with several watchtowers on the ridge behind, the area is now colourfully lit up at night.

Dibba

Located at the northern-most point of the east coast, on the border with Musandam, Dibba is made up of three fishing villages. Unusually, each part comes under a different jurisdiction: Dibba Al Hisn is part of Sharjah, Dibba Muhallab is Fujairah and Dibba Bayah is Oman. The three Dibbas share an attractive bay, fishing communities, and excellent diving locations – from here you can arrange dhow trips to take you to unspoilt dive locations in Musandam.

The Hajar Mountains, which run parallel to the east coast, provide a wonderful backdrop, rising in places to over 1,800 metres. There are some good public beaches too, where your only company will be crabs and seagulls, and where seashell collectors may find a few treasures.

Fujairah City

Fujairah town is a mix of old and new. Its hillsides are dotted with ancient forts and watchtowers, which add an air of mystery and charm; most are undergoing restoration work. Off the coast, the seas and coral reefs are great for fishing, diving and watersports. It is a good place for birdwatching during the spring and autumn migrations as it is on the route from Africa to Central Asia. Since Fujairah is close to the mountains and many areas of natural beauty, it makes an excellent base from which to explore the countryside and discover stunning wadis, forts, waterfalls and even natural hot springs.

Kalba

Just to the south of Fujairah you'll find Kalba, which is renowned for its mangrove forest and golden beaches. It's a pretty fishing village that still manages to retain much of its historical charm. The road through the mountains linking Kalba to Hatta makes for an interesting alternative for returning to Dubai.

Khor Kalba

Set in a beautiful tidal estuary (khor is the Arabic word for creek), Khor Kalba is one of the oldest mangrove forests in Arabia and is home to a variety of plant, marine and birdlife not found anywhere else in the UAE. The mangroves in the estuary flourish thanks to a mix of seawater and freshwater from the mountains, but they are now receding due to the excessive use of water from inland wells.

For birdwatchers, the area is especially good during the spring and autumn migrations when special species of bird include Sykes's warbler. It is also home to a rare subspecies of white collared kingfisher, which breeds here and in Oman, and nowhere else in the world. A canoe tour by Desert Rangers is ideal for reaching the heart of the reserve. There is also the distinct possibility that you'll catch a glimpse of the region's endangered turtles.

Al Hisn Kalba

Nr Bait Shk Saeed Bin Hamed Al Qassimi Kalba
971 9 512 3333
sdci.gov.ae

This complex consists of the restored residence of Sheikh Sayed Al Qassimi and Al Hisn Fort. It houses the town's museum and contains a limited display of weapons. It doesn't take long to get round but there's also a collection of rides for children. Entrance is Dhs.3 for individuals and Dhs.6 for families.

Fujairah Attractions

Dibba Castle

Al Gurfa Dibba

Hidden away in the Omani part of Dibba (aka Daba), next to vast farms and plantations, Dibba Castle is an interesting place to have a walk around. Built over 180 years ago, it has been restored and, while there aren't a lot of artefacts on show, you can access all the rooms and climb up the towers, where you'll get views over the castle and its surroundings. It is signposted off the road past the UAE border check post.

Fujairah Fort

Nr Fujairah Heritage Village, Al Shariya Fujairah
fujairahtourism.ae

Fujairah Fort has recently undergone a major renovation programme. Although you cannot enter the fort itself, the surrounding heritage buildings are open for viewing (and make for great photographs). Carbon dating estimates the main part of the fort to be over 500 years old.

Fujairah Heritage Village

Nr Fujairah Fort, Al Shariya Fujairah **971 9 222 1166**
fujmun.gov.ae

Situated just outside Fujairah city, this collection of fishing boats, simple dhows and tools depicts life in the UAE before oil was discovered. There are two spring-fed swimming pools for men and women and chalets can be hired by the day.

Fujairah Museum

Nr Fujairah Fort, Al Shariya Fujairah **971 9 222 9085**
fnrd.gov.ae

This interesting museum offers permanent exhibitions on traditional ways of life including the not-so-distant nomadic Bedouin culture. There are also several artefacts on display that were found during archaeological excavations throughout the emirate. Some of the items include weapons from the bronze and iron ages, finely painted pottery, carved soapstone vessels and silver coins. The museum is open from 7.30am to 6pm from Saturday to Thursday and from 2pm to 6pm on Friday. Entry fee is Dhs.5.

Fujairah Hotels

Fujairah Rotana Resort & Spa Al Aqah Beach

Dibba Rd Fujairah **971 9 244 9888**
rotana.com

Each of the 250 guest rooms and suites has its own
balcony and view over the sea. The hotel offers some
of the best dining options on the east coast, as well
as an indulgent spa, a private beach and a huge pool
with pool bar.

Golden Tulip Resort Dibba

Mina Rd Dibba **968 26 836 654**
goldentulipdibba.com

This a good option for an affordable getaway. From
the nearby Dibba Port you can take a dhow cruise,
and the hotel is also in a great location for some
impressive snorkelling.

Hilton Fujairah Resort

Al Faseel St, Al Faseel Fujairah **971 9 222 2411**
hilton.com

Set at the north end of Fujairah's corniche, just a
stone's throw from the foothills of the Hajars, this
relaxing resort has all facilities needed for a wonderful
weekend away. If you get tired of lounging by the
swimming pool, or activities like tennis, snooker,
basketball or even watersports on the private beach,
you could always explore the rugged splendour of the
surrounding mountains.

Iberotel Miramar Al Aqah Beach Resort

Dibba Rd Fujairah **971 9 244 9994**
iberotel.com

A lovely low-rise Moroccan style resort with luxurious
rooms spread around a huge pool area, the hotel
has onsite shops, a spa, a gym and several good
restaurants. Also boasts a watersports centre.

Le Meridien Al Aqah Beach Resort

Dibba Rd Fujairah **971 9 244 9000**
lemeridien-alaqah.com

All of the rooms at Le Meridien Al Aqah have views
over the Indian Ocean, and the grounds are covered
by lush foliage. It is particularly geared up for
families, with a kids' pool and outdoor and indoor
play areas. There's an extensive spa, a dive centre,
and entertainment options include a cinema, bars
and restaurants serving a range of Thai, Indian and
European cuisine.

Radisson Blu Resort Fujairah

Al Faqeet, Dibba Fujairah **971 9 244 9700**
radissonblu.com

Its pastel exterior might be an acquired taste, but
the modern, business-like interior and wonderful
restaurants that lie within make this hotel a bit of a
treat for the senses. The whole place is reminiscent of
a spa, with clean lines and wholesome colours. There
is, in fact, a wonderful Japanese spa and plenty of
private beach.

Sandy Beach Hotel & Resort

Khorfakkan Rd, Dibba Fujairah **971 9 244 5555**
sandybm.com

Snoopy Island, one of the best diving spots in the
country, is right off the coast from the Sandy Beach
Hotel, making it a firm favourite with UAE residents.
Day trippers can purchase a day-pass to access the
temperature-controlled pool, watersports and beach
bar services. There is also a five-star PADI Dive Centre
within the hotel that rents diving and snorkelling
gear for exploring the reefs around Snoopy
Island. Open for all-day dining, there's a basic but
reasonable restaurant.

Ras Al Khaimah

With the Hajar Mountains rising just behind the city,
the Arabian Gulf stretching out from the shore and
the desert starting in the south near the farms and
ghaf forests of Digdagga, Ras Al Khaimah (RAK) has
possibly the best scenery of any emirate. The most
northerly emirate, a creek divides the main city into
the old town and the newer Al Nakheel district.

The past couple of years have witnessed RAK's
transformation into a prominent weekend destination,
especially with outdoor lovers and weekend
warriors, and several new resorts have opened for
the overworked residents of Dubai and Abu Dhabi.
The Tower Links Golf Course (towerlinks.com) is laid
out among the mangroves around the creek and is
popular at weekends, as is the Al Hamra Village Golf
And Beach Resort (casahotels.com).

Ras Al Khaimah contains several archaeological
sites, some dating back all the way to 3000BC. Take
the Al Ram road out of the Al Nakheel district and
towards the Hajar Mountains to discover some of
the area's history, including the Dhayah Fort, Shimal
Archaeological Site and Sheba's Palace. The bare ruins
of the Dhayah Fort can be spotted from the road, but
you might need a 4WD to access them. Further inland
are the Shimal archaeological site and Sheba's Palace.
Both are a little obscure, but worth the difficulty of
finding them. Shimal includes a tomb from the Umm
An Nar period, roughly 5,000 years ago. Built as a
communal burial place, the remains of more than 400
bodies have now been found there. Further down the
same road is another tomb dating back to the Wadi
Suq period (2000BC). Many of the artefacts discovered
in these locations are at the National Museum, while
the Pearl Excursion and Pearl Museum (rakpearls.com)
showcase more recent heritage and trade.

At the other end of the spectrum, Manar Mall (manarmall.com) is a large shopping and leisure facility, housing a cinema complex, family entertainment centre and dining options overlooking the creek and mangroves; Al Hamra Mall and Safeer Mall are also popular.

The town is a good starting point for exploring the surrounding mountains, visiting the ancient sites of Ghalilah and Shimal, the hot springs at Khatt and the camel race track at Digdagga. There are also several chances to get into the mountains north of the city, as well as south of RAK in places like Jebel Yibir – the tallest mountain in the country, where a new track takes you close to the top for spectacular views.

Ras Al Khaimah Attractions

Ice Land Water Park
Al Jazeera, Al Hamra Ras Al Khaimah 971 7 206 7888
icelandwaterpark.com
This impressive waterpark is the first major attraction to open in the giant WOW RAK tourist destination. The polar-themed Ice Land has more than 50 rides and attractions, including Penguin Falls, Snow River and Mount Cyclone. Open from 10am every day. Entry is Dhs.150 for adults, Dhs.100 for children under 1.2m.

National Museum Of Ras Al Khaimah
Nr Police HQ, Off Al Hisn Rd Ras Al Khaimah
971 7 233 3411
rasalkhaimahtourism.com
Housed in an impressive fort that was once the home of the present ruler of Ras Al Khaimah, this museum focuses on local natural history and archaeological displays, including a variety of paraphernalia from pre-oil, Bedouin life. Look out for fossils set in the rock strata of the walls of the fort – these date back 190 million years. The building has battlements, a working windtower and ornate, carved wooden doors. Entrance is only Dhs.2 for adults and Dhs.1 for children; directions can be found on the museum website. Open every day except on Tuesdays and public holidays.

Ras Al Khaimah Hotels

Al Hamra Fort Hotel & Beach Resort
Al Jazeerah St Ras Al Khaimah 971 7 244 6666
alhamrafort.com
With traditional Arabic architecture set among acres of lush gardens and along a strip of sandy beach, this hotel offers a peaceful getaway. A range of watersports and activities, including two floodlit golf courses and an onsite dive centre, will keep you entertained, and the eight themed eateries offer a wide variety of international cuisines and atmosphere.

Al Hamra Residence
Al Jazeerah St Ras Al Khaimah 971 7 206 7222
alhamraresorts.com
Located on a private beach in the Arabian Gulf, this resort offers luxurious suites with fully equipped kitchenettes. The Sea Breeze restaurant serves traditional Arabic food, while guests can have a refreshing swim in the outdoor pool. The resort is just a five-minute drive from Al Hamra Golf Club.

Banyan Tree Al Wadi, Ras Al Khaimah

Banyan Tree Al Wadi

Al Mazraa Ras Al Khaimah **971 7 206 7777**
banyantree.com

Banyan Tree Al Wadi combines superior luxury with exclusive spa facilities, desert activities and a wildlife conservation area. Set within Wadi Khadeja, the villas are designed for optimum relaxation with private pools and views of the desert.

Golden Tulip Khatt Springs Resort & Spa

Nr Hajar Mountains, Khatt Ras Al Khaimah
971 7 244 8777
goldentulipkhattsprings.com

Simple and subdued, Golden Tulip Khatt Springs Resort & Spa relies on mountain views, uninterrupted tranquillity and incredible spa packages to attract weekend visitors. Next to the hotel, you can take a dip in the public Khatt Hot Springs – piping hot water which, it is claimed, has curative powers. Men and women have separate pools and a variety of massages is also available.

Hilton Ras Al Khaimah Resort & Spa

Al Maareedh St Ras Al Khaimah **971 7 228 8844**
hilton.com

Tucked away on an exclusive bay, out of sight of the city, the resort's many guest rooms and villas are perfect for a beach break. The pool bar, spa and laid-back dining options make this one of the most relaxing destinations in the region. Guests of the older Hilton Ras Al Khaimah (hilton.com), located in the city, can use the facilities.

The Cove Rotana Resort

Arcoob Ras Al Khaimah **971 7 206 6000**
rotana.com

Built into the hills overlooking the Arabian Gulf, The Cove's sprawling layout of 204 rooms, 72 private villas and winding pathways is reminiscent of an old Mediterranean hill town. The resort revolves around an immaculate lagoon, protected from the sea by 600 metres of pristine beach. A Bodylines spa and several impressive restaurants round out the package.

Umm Al Quwain

Nestled between Ajman and Ras Al Khaimah, not much has changed in Umm Al Quwain over the years. The emirate has six forts, and a few old watchtowers. With its mangroves and birdlife, the lagoon is a popular weekend spot for boat trips and watersports. Another popular family activity is crab hunting at Flamingo Beach Resort. At nightfall, hunters set off into the shallow waters with a guide, where they spear crabs which are barbecued and served for dinner. The area north of the lagoon is a regional activity centre. Emirates Motorplex (motorplex.ae) hosts motorsport events, including the Emirates Motocross Championship, and Dreamland Aqua Park is one of the emirate's most popular attractions. Barracuda Beach Resort is a favoured destination for Dubai residents thanks to its well-stocked duty-free liquor store.

Umm Al Quwain Attractions

Dreamland Aqua Park

**Nr Barracuda Beach Resort, RAK Highway,
Al Rafaah** Umm Al Quwain **971 6 768 1888**
dreamlanduae.com

With over 25 water rides, including four 'twisting dragons', Dreamland Aqua Park is massive. If extreme slides aren't your thing, there's the lazy river, a wave pool, an aqua play area, and a high-salinity floating pool. Overnight accommodation in tents or wooden cabins is also available, with BBQ packages as well. Admission is Dhs.135 for adults and Dhs.85 for children under 1.2m, while children under two go free. The park is open all-year-round; Fridays, Saturdays and holidays are for families only.

Umm Al Quwain Hotels

Barracuda Beach Resort

Nr Dreamland Aqua Park, Khor Al Baida
Umm Al Quwain **971 6 768 1555**
barracuda.ae

Known throughout the UAE for its popular tax-free booze emporium, Barracuda is also a pleasant resort for quick weekend getaways. Aside from the main hotel, the resort offers several lagoon-side one-bedroom chalets.

Flamingo Beach Resort

Nr Horsehead R/A Umm Al Quwain **971 6 765 0000**
flamingoresort.ae

Cheap and cheerful, this family-friendly resort is a popular destination for weekend breaks. The building is surrounded by a shallow lagoon interspersed with green islands that attract a rich array of birdlife including migrating flamingos. Guided crab hunts take place in the evenings and are available for guests and non-guests, followed by a barbecue. Other activities include a flamingo tour by boat and deep sea fishing.

Imar Spa

Nr Palma Beach Hotel, Al Khor Umm Al Quwain
971 6 766 4440
imarspa.com

This five-star ladies-only haven has a peaceful, seaside setting. There's a small private beach and terrace, and a fabulous temperature-controlled pool.

RELAX & REFRESH

Dune bashing

RELAX & REFRESH

From aerobics and art classes to volleyball and diving, there's something for everyone in Oman.

Oman is a land of opportunity when it comes to getting involved in sports and activities, or taking your pursuits to new levels. The rugged mountains, unspoilt wadis, the sea and the vast desert sands provide beautiful surroundings in which to try out a range of outdoor pastimes, particularly in winter when the weather is warm but not blistering. Typically, residents of Oman spend their winter weekends camping on the beach, swimming, or tackling the dunes of the Wahiba Sands in a 4WD – or even trying out sandskiing.

Even the heat of the summer doesn't stop some sports enthusiasts from spending their leisure hours sailing the Gulf or hitting the greens. Alternatively, if you stay in Oman during the summer, you can always retreat to the mountains or to Salalah for its refreshing rainy season, where you can enjoy cooler weather. In Muscat there is always the air-conditioned gym option, or the opportunity to take up a new hobby or complete a short course.

The Musandam peninsula shouldn't be overlooked either, the rocky northern Omani territory a popular place for UAE residents to explore. The impressive fjords are perfect places for diving and snorkelling, with fishing a major draw, and not just for the locals who make their living from it. Off-roading can also be accommodated with some fantastic trails and excellent camping spots, however it's the cities of Oman where you'll find the widest range of activities.

As in most places, word of mouth is one of the best ways to get details and information about your favourite pastime. An assortment of sports and activities are available in Oman, and the choice is growing all of the time, so you will be well rewarded if you hunt around. Good luck and enjoy!

ACTIVITIES & HOBBIES

Aerobics & Fitness Classes

Aerobics is an excellent way to keep fit throughout the year, no matter what the temperature is outside. Classes are available in most of the hotels and health clubs, and you can choose from different disciplines and timings to suit you. More adventurous options are appearing all of the time, so make sure to keep an eye out for fun new takes on these classes.

Aqua aerobics is an excellent way to combine aerobic activity with the chance to splash about in water. It's great for people of all ages, body shapes and with various medical conditions as the water provides protection for the joints, allowing for active movements without so much stress on weaker joints. Many of the local health clubs offer aqua aerobics.

Art Classes

Al Madina Art Gallery
145/6 Inshirah St, Madinat Al Sultan Qaboos
968 24 691 380
almadinaartgallery.com
Map **2 G2**

This is a one-stop shop for many different forms of art in Oman. It has regular exhibitions and also has art lessons for adults and children from time to time.

Bait Muzna Gallery
Old Muscat **968 24 739 204**
baitmuznagallery.com
Map **2 L2**

Bait Muzna Gallery is located in a traditional Omani house that has been renovated into a modern space for exhibiting works of art. It regularly offers art workshops for adults.

The Omani Society For Fine Arts
Nr Ramada Hotel, Muscat **968 24 694 969**
osfa.gov.om
Map **2 G2**

The Omani Society for Fine Arts was established in 1993 to encourage fine art and photography in the country. The group organises a number of activities and initiatives to support artists in Oman and participates in various international exhibitions and events. One of the group's aims is also to encourage and support youngsters and hobbyists.

Birdwatching

Due to its location at the junction of three bio-geographical areas, the keen observer can see Palaearctic and African bird species, as well as others from further east. It doesn't require much to take yourself on a birding expedition – as long as you follow the usual rules of not heading off-road without a guide and all the necessary equipment. To find out more about birding in Oman and what books are available, log on to birdsoman.com.

Some tour companies offer birdwatching trips, including the Muscat Diving & Adventure Centre, Gulf Leisure and African Sea Safaris. Birdwatchers in Oman can take advantage of the fact that it lies on the migration path for thousands of exotic birds doing the long haul flight between Asia and Africa. The beaches and lagoons along the coastline are good places to spot a rich variety of marine birdlife from storks and herons to flamingos and ducks. You can also contact the Oman Bird Group via the Natural History Museum, and the Muscat Diving & Adventure Center. Gulf Leisure also offers birdwatching trips, as does Arabian Sea Safaris (arabianseasafaris.com) who offer birding tours for RO.30 per person. You can also check out options for birdwatching tours in Oman at birdquest-tours.com/oman and birdingpal.org/oman.

Muscat Diving & Adventure Center
Way 3323, Muscat **968 24 543 002**
holiday-in-oman.com
Map **2 L3**

This company does birdwatching tours throughout the week (upon request). You'll be collected from your hotel and accompanied by an experienced birder who will help you to identify your sightings and fill you in on all the details about Oman's birdlife, from the little green bee-eater to the huge lappet faced vulture.

Bowling

Al Masa Bowling
Al Masa Mall, Shatti Al Qurum **968 24 693 991**
Map **2 G2**

This popular bowling alley is conveniently situated in Al Masa Mall. It's open every day from 10am to midnight and bowling costs RO.2 per person per game.

Oman Bowling Centre
Nr Holiday Inn, Muscat **968 24 480 747**
omanbowling.com
Map **2 F3**

This large bowling centre has 10 computerized lanes and a good set-up that includes a coffee shop. It is open from 10am to midnight every day and bowling costs RO.1.500 per person per game.

Star Bowling

Funzone, Beside Qurum Natural Park **968 97 103 568**
Map **2 H2**

This new bowling alley is located in the Funzone entertainment complex in Qurum. Opening times are 10am to midnight, Saturday to Thursday, and 2pm to midnight on Fridays. It costs RO.1.500 per person per game or RO.10 per hour per lane (up to eight people).

Bridge

The Dolphin Village

Bowshar **968 99 432 353**
dolphinvillagemuscat.com
Map **2 F4**

Bridge is played here usually on Sunday and Tuesday mornings. Refreshments are available in the restaurant.

Muscat Bridge League

PDO RAH Club, Muscat **968 99 354 467/99 318 328**
Map **2 H1**

Dedicated bridge players in Oman have been organising weekly bridge sessions every Saturday evening for over 20 years. Attendance ranges from five to seven tables and the game is played over 22 to 24 boards. There is a nominal table charge. Full day sessions are occasionally held here. The game is friendly, with varying degrees of competence, and visiting players are always welcome. In an effort to popularise the game further, Muscat Bridge League is planning to hold sessions to teach the game to those interested.

Camping

Typically, residents of Oman spend their winter weekends camping on the beach, swimming, or tackling the dunes of the Wahiba Sands in a 4WD and trying out sand skiing. Even the heat of the summer doesn't stop some hardy sports enthusiasts from spending their leisure hours sailing the Gulf or hitting the greens. Alternatively, if you stay in Oman during the summer, you can always retreat to the mountains, where the weather is cooler.

Canoeing & Kayaking

There may not be any rivers or lakes in Oman, but its coastline is fantastic for canoeing and kayaking. The coast is full of inlets and sheltered bays, many of which have isolated beaches that make for excellent picnic spots. Paddling allows you access to otherwise hidden places of natural beauty and it's a good way to appreciate the country's abundant bird and marine life. Adventurous canoeists with sea-going canoes can tour the stunning waterways of the Musandam peninsula, where they'll see spectacularly rocky coastlines with fjord-like inlets and towering cliffs – some of which reach heights of 1,000m.

Muscat Diving & Adventure Center

Way 3323 **968 24 543 002**
holiday-in-oman.com
Map **2 L3**

Muscat Diving & Adventure Center hires out single and double sea kayaks. Renting a kayak (with or without a guide) costs from RO.20 per person. You'll need to put down a credit card deposit – presumably to prevent you from sailing off into the sunset.

Canyoning

Oman's interesting topography makes canyoning a popular activity here. It's not for the timid though as it's often challenging and technical, and involves using various methods, such as abseiling, scrambling and swimming, to ascend or descend a canyon. There are some awesome treks in the country including Wadi Shab, Snake Canyon, Wadi Hajir, Wadi Haylayn and Wadi Qashah, each with its own individual challenge and beauty and each with opportunities for canyoning.

There are risks associated with scrambling or abseiling down uneven and slippery surfaces, so it's advisable that you go as part of a group and ensure that you have at least basic knowledge of first aid. Dress lightly, take sun protection along and always expect to get wet. Although canyoning is an activity more commonly enjoyed by experienced groups, some tour companies do offer adventurous treks: check out Absolute Adventure (adventure.ae).

Caving

Caving here ranges from the fairly safe to the extremely dangerous. Even with an experienced leader, it's not for the casual tourist or the poorly equipped; it is important that you understand the dangers. Make sure you take plenty of water and basic first aid equipment. Some of the cave exploration here is among the most hair-raising in the world and should only be attempted by experienced, fit cavers, preferably accompanied by someone who has traversed the caves here before. The caving network in the Hajar Mountains of Oman is extensive, and much of it has yet to be explored and mapped. The area includes what's believed to be the second largest cave system in the world. The most famous cave in Oman, and the most stunning in terms of size, is the Majlis Al Jinn. Entering it is not for the fainthearted as it starts with a 180m abseil from the entrance in the roof.

fourth, and at times it will feel very similar to driving on the road.

When the track becomes undulating or you head into the dunes, slow down, keep a steady pace and stay alert for obstacles. You should try to use the accelerator more than anything else, barely touching the brakes or clutch. If you do brake, do so lightly and smoothly to avoid sinking into the sand.

At first even small dunes can seem quite extreme, so take things cautiously. Plan your ascents to take the smoothest route and try to reduce your speed so that you coast over the top of a rise or a dune at close to walking pace so you will be in control for the descent. Go easy on the gas – it is far better to fail to make a climb because you were going too slow than to end up jumping over the top of a dune.

When you get over the top, brake gently and stop just on the downward slope. This will allow you to start going again easily. You will often not know what the slope is like until you are right on it; point your car straight down the dune and let your engine do most of the controlling of your speed.

Drivers of automatic cars can do the same using the accelerator; pressing down hard will change down gears, but you may need to use the gear stick to ensure the car doesn't change back up before you want it to, robbing you of the momentum and power you need to climb dunes. Descending, you will need to change into first or second so the car doesn't race away from you.

Don't worry too much about getting stuck, it happens to everyone. If you do, don't keep revving the engine – chances are it will just dig you in further. Get out of your car to assess the situation, and try to work out how it happened so you can learn for next time. Clearing a little sand from around the wheels and getting a few people to push will get most cars out of minor problems. If you are in deeper, you may need to dig the car free, lower the tyre pressures more or get someone to tow you out.

Essential Equipment

There are some basic technical requirements for anyone driving in the desert. A well-maintained and fully serviced vehicle, a spare tyre in good condition, a jack, a tool kit including everything to change a tyre, a sturdy plank or block of wood in case you need to change wheels in sand, a tow rope and shackles, a pressure gauge and a shovel are all essential. And as with any other time you venture out into the desert, you should always have at least one other car with you – even on the simplest routes you might get stuck deep enough to need towing out. Remember to make sure you have plenty of fuel in the tank too.

Other things that can help get you out of sticky situations include sand mats or trays (or your floor mats if you are not too attached to them), a compressor to re-inflate tyres, heavy duty gloves, jump leads, a fully charged mobile phone, and a GPS, which can help take the guesswork out of navigation. Also make sure everyone in your car has plenty of water, sun cream and a hat, and shoes rather than sandals, as the sand can still get very hot.

The Music Palace

House 2557, Way 1947, Muscat **968 24 602 445**
musicpalaceinoman.com
Map **2 G3**
This school offers a range of dance classes for children
including ballet and hip-hop. There are usually classes
during the week, weekends and even during holidays.

Desert Driving Courses

National Training Institute

Al Khuwair Service Rd, Muscat **968 24 472 121**
ntioman.com
Map **2 E4**
If you'd like to learn how to put your 4WD through its
paces off-road, or get some expert advice on desert,
wadi or mountain driving, sign up for one of NTI's
courses. You will learn the theoretical side of driving
off-road, followed by plenty of hands-on practice in
the vehicles. Instructors also offer advice on safety
precautions, emergency procedures and what to
do when things go wrong. There is also a two-day
defensive driving course to help you cope with the
roads (and other drivers) in Oman.

Occupational Training Institute

Bldg 1160, Way 1518, Muscat **968 24 604 741**
otitraining.com
Map **2 G2**
This institute offers a range of courses for drivers
of any ability and in all types of vehicles. Courses
provided include Off-road Desert Driving & Survival,
Safe Journey Management, Interior Driving Shills and
Tiredness & Fatigue.

Technical & Administrative
Training Institute

Villa 2545, Way 1947, Muscat **968 24 697 023**
tatioman.com
Map **2 G3**
This institute offers an array of driving courses that
are accredited by the UK-based Royal Society for the
Prevention of Accidents.

Diving

Almouj Marina

The Wave, Muscat **968 24 534 544**
almoujmarina.com
Map **2 B2**
Oman's premier berthing facility is home to Oman
Sail (omansail.com). They organise sailing and diving
adventures, including trips to the Daymaniyat Islands.
The islands are home to more than 100 species, such
as dolphins and hawksbill turtles.

Capital Area Yacht Club

Muscat **968 24 737 712**
caycoman.com
Map **2 L3**
CAYC Divers offer a variety of activities including
diving, snorkelling and wreck dives. They also run
PADI courses for those who want to learn how to dive,
and for divers who want to specialise or advance their
skills. CAYC is a members-only club but members are
welcome to bring guests along. Dive boats go out
every day of the week.

Extra Divers Al Sawadi

Al Sawadi Beach Resort & Spa Barka
968 26 795 545
alsawadibeach.com
Map **1 G3**
Extra Divers Al Sawadi offer good facilities for people
to take dive courses in, as well as trips to the famous
islands the company is named after. The dive centre
has new equipment for 15 divers and 50 snorkellers, a
classroom, and a library full of the latest PADI videos
and DVDs. They offer a range of PADI courses.

Extra Divers Musandam

Nr Golden Tulip Hotel Khasab **968 26 730 777**
goldentulipkhasab.com/diving
Map **1 E1**
Extra Divers Musandam has a dive centre in Khasab on
the Musandam peninsula. A relatively new operation,
the facilities include equipment hire, a compressor,
tanks, dive shop and a dry room. Staff offer instruction
for SSI (Scuba Schools International) and leads courses
in German, English and French. The company runs daily
two-tank dives for RO.47 from 9am to 3pm.

Global Scuba

Civil Aviation Club, Muscat **968 24 692 346**
global-scuba.com
Map **2 D2**
Global Scuba's dive centre is conveniently located just
30 minutes' drive from the Daymaniyat Islands by boat
and they also offer dive trips to Fahal Island. They run
a range of PADI courses, from beginner to advanced
and in a whole lot of specialities. They also do dolphin
watching and snorkelling trips for those who prefer to
keep their heads above water.

Khasab Travel & Tours

Nr Khasab Airport, Khasab **968 26 730 464**
khasabtours.com
Map **1 E1**
With the diving in the UAE and surrounding areas
being fairly limited, a dive trip off the Musandam
peninsula is a welcome addition to your log book.
Diving here has been described as being an
'experienced diver's dive' because of strong currents

The perfect home
for your boat

23°37'55"N 58°16'03"E

Located at The Wave, Muscat, Almouj Marina is a premier marina facility and flagship yachting and sailing destination in Oman. We deliver the highest level of personalised customer service to yacht owners, complemented by state-of-the-art eco-friendly facilities. Whether it's heading out to sea, or having a leisurely weekend with the family, Almouj Marina is perfect for your yacht – and for you.

For berthing enquiries or to find out more about our exclusive **3 month complimentary berthing** offer, please contact Almouj Marina on **+968 2453 4544** or at **info@almoujmarina.com**

www.almoujmarina.com

and some large fish. That said, the area offers a variety of sites, some more sheltered and shallow, which are perfect for beginners. Khasab Travel & Tours will take out groups with a minimum of two adults, to enjoy the good visibility and the excellent marine life.

Moon Light Dive Centre

Nr Grand Hyatt Muscat **968 99 317 700**
moonlightdive.com
Map **2 G2**

This is a five-star dive centre situated on the public beach next to the Grand Hyatt Muscat. The activities on the menu range from PADI dive courses, to dolphin watching, sunset cruising and fishing trips. If it's something more relaxing you're after, you have a choice of boat trips along the coast and its secluded bays, or superb snorkelling in some of the best waters in the Middle East. The centre also does equipment rental and repairs, and will even arrange hotel accommodation and land tours for you.

Muscat Diving & Adventure Center

Way 3323, Muscat **968 24 543 002**
holiday-in-oman.com
Map **1 G4**

Catering to all of your (water) sporting needs, the Muscat Diving & Adventure Center makes the most of the beauty and abundance of fascinating sea life that Oman has to offer. Experienced and proficient instructors are on hand to do Discover Scuba courses, or to organise trips for snorkellers and more experienced divers. A two-dive trip with full equipment costs from RO.55.

Nomad Ocean Adventures

Nr The Harbour, Al Biah, Dibba **968 26 836 069**
discovernomad.com
Map **1 E2**

Nomad Ocean Adventures can organise excursions according to your specifications. In addition to offering diving and snorkelling, they can also arrange for you to go on a dhow cruise, to go deep sea fishing, trekking or stay overnight in a traditional Arabian campsite. For qualified divers a single dive, with all equipment, starts at RO.20, while a weekend package costs around RO.70. For more details, call Christophe on his UAE mobile (+971 50 885 3238) or email him on chris@discovernomad.com.

Oman Dive Center

Nr Qantab R/A, Al Jissah St, Muscat **968 24 824 240**
extradivers-worldwide.com
Map **1 G4**

Popularly known as ODC, this centre is set in the picturesque and sheltered bay of Bandar Al Jissah. The bay is perfect for snorkellers and for novices to practise their new skills in before venturing out to the ocean. The training facilities here have been awarded five-star PADI status, and they run the full range of courses, including a first aid one. Activities include day and night diving, snorkelling, underwater photography and wreck diving. Day trips to the Daymaniyat Islands, the Quriyat wreck, and a new wreck dive at Al Munassir, can be arranged for divers and snorkellers, and ODC provide accommodation in their luxury barasti-style huts on the beach.

Marine life

Drama Groups

Ras Al Hamra Amateur Dramatics Society

PDO, Ras Al Hamra, Muscat **968 93 375 946**
rahads.pdorc.com
Map **2 H1**

This society produces a range of events throughout the year including plays, pantomimes, and comedy reviews. Performances are usually held in the theatre at the Ras Al Hamra Recreation Centre.

Environmental Groups

Oman is fortunate to have some beautiful natural assets together with a government that is interested and active in environmental issues, always making them a high priority. There are currently three nature reserves that have a facility for controlled tourism – the Daymaniyat Islands, the Ras Al Jinz turtle reserve and the Arabian Oryx Sanctuary. You may need a permit to visit these fascinating reserves and to find out more information about them; refer to their entries in the Out of the City chapter.

In addition to the government's efforts to promote protection of the environment, there are also several interest groups and environmental organisations in Oman. The Sultanate is a member of the International Whaling Commission, and although it is not yet a signatory to CITES (Convention on International Trade in Endangered Species), it follows the guidelines laid down by CITES, such as stopping the trade in endangered species. More locally, there are increasing numbers of recycling points around Muscat, sponsored by various local companies, and are mainly located near shopping centres.

ESO Whale & Dolphin Research Group

Muscat **968 24 790 945**
eso.org.om
Map **2 J2**

Part of the Environment Society of Oman (ESO), this is a group of volunteer scientists and other interested parties who collect and disseminate knowledge about Oman's dolphins and whales. They are independent researchers whose work is recognised and approved by local ministries. They work closely with the Oman Natural History Museum, the Ministry of Agriculture and Fisheries, and the Raysut Marine Laboratory. The group's primary activities include emergency rescue services for whales and dolphins, maintenance of a database of sightings and strandings, and co-operation with local tour operators to promote responsible whale and dolphin-watching activities. If you are interested in volunteering or just want to find out more about local whales and dolphins, check out the website or call Howard Gray on 92 497 536.

PDO Planetarium

Nr Oil & Gas Exhibition Centre, Seeh Al Maleh St, Muscat **968 24 675 542**
pdo.co.om
Map **2 H2**

Astronomers of all ages can gaze up at the twinkly dome of the PDO Planetarium, which opened in 2000. On Wednesdays at 7pm and Thursdays at 10am, shows are held in English, and on Wednesdays at 4pm and Thursdays at 11.30am, shows are held in Arabic. All last about an hour and are free of charge. The planetarium also hosts guest lecturers, conferences and workshops and can arrange special social gatherings when astronomical events occur. Advance booking is required.

The Historical Association Of Oman

Muscat **968 24 563 074**
hao.org.om
Various locations

The Historical Association of Oman (HAO) is a non profit-making organisation, established in 1972, with the aims of documenting and distributing information about Oman's history, whether natural, national, linguistic or cultural, and to encourage research. In addition to the usual activities including lectures, trips and publishing, the HAO conducts research and assists researchers from within the country as well as internationally. The most recent projects embarked upon are two documentation projects of old settlements in Bowshar and Manah funded by the US Ambassadors Fund for Cultural Preservation. Meetings are held twice a month on Monday evenings from 8pm, with venues varying so call for more details.

First Aid

Institute of HSE Management

Al Azaiba, Muscat **968 24 492 464**
ihsem.com
Map **2 D3**

The Institute of HSE Management is licensed by the National Examination Board of Occupational Safety and Health (NEBOSH) and the Institute of Safety and Health (IOSH) to conduct courses. Subsequently, first aid courses are run here on a regular basis and are a good investment for any explorer.

National Training Institute

Al Khuwair Service Rd, Muscat **968 24 472 121**
ntioman.com
Map **2 E4**

The first aid courses held here are accredited by the Institute of Occupational Safety and Health (IOSH) so they are of a high standard. This institute also has branches in Muscat and Sohar.

Oman Dive Center

Nr Qantab R/A, Al Jissah St, Muscat **968 24 824 240**
extradivers-worldwide.com
Map **1 G4**

While first aid will be covered briefly in some of the dive training it does, the Oman Dive Centre also offers a general introductory first aid course aptly named the Emergency First Responder. This course is suitable for everyone, not just divers, and can be taught either at the dive centre, or at a location of your choice.

Fishing

Coastal Fishing

The Sultanate of Oman boasts some of the best surf fishing in the world. The coastline from Al Khaluf down to Salalah is home to a variety of species belonging to the warm waters of the Indian Ocean. Depending on where you choose to cast your line, the species you're likely to catch include blue fish, trevally, shark, black bream, rays, grouper and spotted grunter. Blue fish will range from five pounds upwards, and ray and shark anywhere between 10 and 200.

Light and heavy tackle combos are a must for fishing these waters. All the various species tend to take turns in feeding during the day and night. Ensure your secondary tackle supplies are plentiful as you will often experience toothy beasts taking your bait. Fishing along these coastal coves is seasonal due to the severe weather conditions caused by the monsoon that can make things far too tricky.

The coastline of Oman beyond Al Khaluf can be taxing on both vehicles and supplies. This is not the place for a jaunt down to the beach with rod in hand and, in fact, most people choose not to travel the roads with their boats in tow, but rather to sail from one harbour to the next. The villagers along the coastline of Oman are very friendly and always happy to help, but do remember that you're in a Muslim country and have respect for their traditions and religious beliefs. Maps of the Oman coastline are available and it would be very helpful to have one on your first few trips at least.

Big Game Fishing

The season from October to April is best for big game fishing. The rest of the year tends to be slow, as the fish move further south to avoid the higher waters in summer. The true Indian Ocean meets the Gulf of Oman off Ras Al Hadd and you'll clearly see the difference between the colours and surface textures of these two bodies of water. The most common big game fish during the high season is yellowfin tuna. A tricky fish to hook by nature, successful fishermen sometimes land them in weights exceeding 100

pounds. Although much larger specimens are available to offshore anglers, these are usually only caught south of Muscat or much further out than the average angler cares to venture. On rare occasions, yellowfin tuna close to the 250lb mark have been caught within 10km of Muscat's coast.

Sailfish dominate the waters off Muscat during September and October; it's thought that they migrate through the region on their way to the Arabian Gulf for breeding. They're often caught close to shore and vary in weight from 60 to 110 pounds. Mai mai or dolphin fish are found in abundance from the end of July to September. Travelling in schools, these fish make for some fast, light-tackle action. They average about 15lbs, but you might occasionally land something in the 35-45lbs range. Black marlin sometimes travel into the coastal waters off Muscat but there's only been one confirmed capture to date – and that one weighed in at a whopping 400lb. Reports that marlin can be found in greater abundance off the coastal area of Ras Al Hadd have been confirmed by the local commercial fisheries who estimate that an average of 10 marlin a day are brought in by their boats. The season is typically from November to April. The length of the Oman coastline is met by underwater mountain ranges and drop-offs that go down to 300m and more in some areas. Due to the deep water ridges rising up into the warm coastal shallows, an abundance of game species are found feeding on the bait fish, that in turn thrive on the nutrients brought up from the depths – an excellent example of the natural food chain.

Gulf Leisure

Muscat **968 43 463 415**
gulfleisure.com

This company will arrange game fishing charter boats that are fully equipped, and which are led by Omani captains with a good knowledge of Muscat waters. For four hours of fishing with a maximum of four people, you can expect to pay around RO.170.

Sidab Sea Tours

Nr Marina Bander Al Rowdha, Muscat **968 99 461 834**
sidabseatours.com
Map **2 L3**

While there will always be tales of the one that got away, and some days when all of them do, you're almost guaranteed an end to the tall stories when you've got a local skipper who knows the waters like the back of his hand. Sidab Sea Tours organise four-hour professional game fishing excursions for RO.180 per boat (maximum six people), with barracuda, tuna, marlin and sailfish as the intended targets. For a more relaxed experience you can try traditional handline fishing 'Omani style'. Whatever you choose as your bait, all tackle and equipment is provided and soft drinks are available on board. A longer all day excursion can be arranged, which included a beach lunch, for around RO.300.

Water World Marine

Muscat **968 24 737 438**
waterworldoman.com
Map **2 L3**

Water World Marine established their presence in Oman in 1997 by stocking premium angling gear and the top brands in all the gadgets a fisherman needs. If you want to benefit from their expertise, you can charter one of their specialist sports fishing boats for the day and go looking for tuna with the best gear available (boats sail from the outlet in Marina Bandar). The less predatory can simply go on a leisure cruise around Muscat's bays and beaches. A full day charter costs around RO.400. All their charters are fully catered – just bring yourself, a hat and a towel. The operating hours are Saturday to Thursday, from 10am to 6pm. The Marina Bandar outlet is open Monday to Saturday, from 7am to 1pm and then from 4pm to 6pm.

Football

As in most places in the world, you don't have to travel far to see a game of football in Oman. Rural villages usually have a group knocking a ball around on the local sand and rock pitch – and you could probably join in if you wanted. There are also often teams having a kick-about on the beaches, particularly at the InterContinental beach strip. There's a semi-professional football league in Oman, which teams such as the Oman Club, Sidab and Quriyat participate in. A maximum of two expatriate players are allowed to join each of these clubs, so the majority of expat football fans play in the weekly social soccer games at the grounds of the Oman Club. The main teams include Loan Service, Deutsch PDO, Aerworks, British PDO, Royal Flight and the Sultan Qaboos University Squad. Unfortunately, all of the above teams only accept players from within their own organisations, making it difficult for newcomers to get into the game. So you could always start a team of your own, either via your company or group of friends.

Oman Football Association (OFA) is considered the biggest sports association in the sultanate with 43 clubs representing various states of the provinces of the country. 2012 saw the opening of the OFA Performance Centre while in 2013, the new 14 national team played its first game. For more information visit ofa.om. Established in 2013, Muscat Celtic football Club has players from many countries and welcomes new members. The players train on a weekly basis with UEFA qualified coaches. Check it out on facebook.com/muscat.celtic. For children, there

are coaching sessions with Muscat Football Academy (muscarfootballacademy.com) and the Arsenal Soccer School (playthearsenalway.com/oman). If it's Gaelic football you like, you'll be happy to learn that Clann na hOman Gaelic Football Club has been operational in Oman since 2003. There are training sessions and games on a regular basis and a kids Gaelic football club runs from September to April. For more details, see facebook.com/clann.homan.

Golf

Golf in Oman is a growing sport, both in popularity and the number of courses. Traditional 'brown' courses are gradually being replaced with a range of green courses, such as the 18-hole Muscat Hills Golf and Country Club (designed by top golf course designer David Thomas) in the hills behind the Golden Tulip Hotel in As Seeb. The completion of Oman's first green golf course is hoped to boost the country's tourism sector, and put the Sultanate on the golfing world map. Another 18 hole links course, designed by Greg Norman, was formally opened at The Wave in 2011.

Beach Clubs

Beach clubs offer a similar range of facilities to health clubs but with the added bonus of beach access. They are popular with families on weekends, and offer a peaceful environment in which you can swim, play sports or just lounge in the sun. Most include some excellent food and beverage outlets, so people tend to stay for the day.

There are several golf tournaments on Oman's annual calendar, such as the Oman Ladies' Open Championship, the Men's Oman National Championship and the Ras al Ghala Trophy.

Those who have never played golf in the Middle East should be warned that the game here can be more physically demanding – even acclimatised golfers avoid playing in the heat of the day during the summer months.

Almouj Golf

The Wave Muscat Muscat **968 22 005 990**
almoujgolf.com
Map **2 B2**

Following the natural lines of Muscat's coastline, Almouj Golf at The Wave is a links course. International golfing legend Greg Norman is responsible for the design of this 18 hole, par 72 championship golf course. It is also home to a golf academy with a swing studio, driving range and private golf lesson area. Dining is available in the Academy Restaurant.

Ghala Valley Golf Club, Ghala

Muscat **968 98 831 558**
ghalavalley.com
Map **2 E4**

Built into a natural wadi (dried river bed), the golf course lies within a beautiful mountain setting. Originally created as a sand course in 1971, it's now a grass course. The refurbishment of the clubhouse and restaurant is due to be completed by mid 2014. Full membership fees are RO.850 per year.

Marco Polo Golf Course

Crowne Plaza Resort Salalah Salalah
968 23 235 333
crowneplaza.com
Map **4 K8**

A relative newcomer on the Oman golfing scene, this is a grass course that includes a driving range, putting green and training area. The course itself is an unusual nine-hole, par three that's set in a coconut grove. You can hire golf clubs if you wish, and even benefit from the assistance of a professional golf instructor on request.

Muscat Hills Golf & Country Club

Nr Muscat International Airport, Muscat
968 24 514 080
muscathills.com
Map **2 C4**

The Muscat Hills Golf & Country Club has been carved into the jebels (mountains), with great care taken to maintain the natural beauty of the surrounding landscape. It opened in March 2009 and was the first

18 hole par 72 championship grass course in the Sultanate of Oman. The course is large with steep hills so it is advisable to hire a buggy. The restaurant is licensed and also serves light meals.

Ras Al Hamra Golf Club

PDO Camp, Muscat **968 95 784 945**
golfclub.pdorc.com
Map **2 H2**

The Ras Al Hamra Golf Course is currently being redeveloped into a green nine-hole floodlit course. There will also be a floodlit driving range as well as new clubhouse facilities and a pro-shop. The expected opening time for the course is mid 2014.

Hashing

Sometimes described as drinking clubs with a running problem, the Hash House Harriers form a worldwide family of social running clubs. The aim of running in this setup is not to win, but to merely be there and take part. The first hash club was formed in Kuala Lumpur in 1938, and it's now the largest running organisation in the world, with members in over 1,600 chapters in 180 countries.

Hashing consists of running, jogging or walking around varied courses, often cross-country, laid out by a couple of hares (people who run ahead and are effectively 'chased' by the rest of the group). It's a fun way to keep fit and meet new people, as clubs are very sociable and the running is generally not overly competitive and often the secondary reason for going.

Almouj Golf

Jebel Hash House Harriers
968 99 456 765
jebelhashoman.com
Various locations

Founded in 1985, the Jebel Hash is a social, non-competitive running club that forms part of the worldwide Hash House Harriers family. There are always two trails to follow – one for those who prefer to walk, and a longer one for the more energetic. A social gathering follows each run, so be prepared; running fit may not be all the fitness you need. The Jebel Hash runs take place anywhere within Muscat and its surroundings. Apart from meeting new people, it's a great way of seeing some places you might have otherwise missed.

Muscat Hash House Harriers
Muscat 968 99 322 680
muscath3.org
Various locations

More commonly known as the Muscat Hash, this group meets every Saturday evening at various locations around Muscat, depending on where the hare has set the run. Meeting times also vary in accordance with the changing times of dusk and there's a RO.1 fee for each meeting you attend. Celebrations of various international holidays are always lively.

Hiking

There are many documented treks in Oman, which are rated according to difficulty. But, whatever your hiking skills or fitness level, Muscat is full of easily accessible local walks that you can do on your own or as part of a group. If you prefer to venture further afield, Jebel Shams has numerous hikes.

The land's ancient geological history has created inspiring gorges, wadis, peaks, ridges and plateaus. The terrain is heavily eroded and shattered due to the harsh climate, but there are many excellent routes to be enjoyed. These range from short easy walks leading to spectacular viewpoints, to longer, more arduous treks up high peaks. Many of the paths follow ancient Bedouin and Shihuh trails through the mountains. Some of these are still used today as the only means of access to remote settlements.

The main mountain area, shared in part with the United Arab Emirates, is the Al Hajar Range, which splits into the Northern, Eastern and Western Hajars. The highest peak in this range, at just over 3,000m, is Jebel Shams in the west (in Arabic 'jebel' means mountain and 'shams' means sun). The spectacular 'Grand Canyon of Oman' is also in this area. One of the shorter, less rigorous hikes, at four hours, is the Balcony Walk (or Rim Walk) along the Jebel Shams

Plateau. Incredible canyon views and a trek through an abandoned village will delight everyone who sums up the energy to try it out. Adventure trekkers looking for a more challenging experience will be inspired by the Al Hawb to Jebel Shams summit route. This hike requires good climbing abilities and an overnight camp. It may take up to 12 hours to reach the summit and the trek can be a 20 hour round trip, depending on the descent path you choose, but the views at the top are the ultimate reward for all that hard work.

In the south, near Salalah, are the Dhofar Mountains, whose highest point is Jebel Samhan. Many of the mountains here are over 2,000m, providing excellent walking and fabulous views.

Be sure that on any hike, short or long, you consider the weather conditions. Always carry plenty of water and snacks, check your routes before setting out, notify a friend as to your whereabouts and your itinerary, and wear light boots and appropriate clothing. Take a compass or GPS and check the customs and conditions of the area before taking on any long trips.

Be warned: no mountain rescue services exist, and anyone venturing out into mountains should be reasonably experienced, or be with someone who knows the area. As long as you are properly prepared, your trek will be an outstanding experience leaving you with nothing but fond memories… and possibly sore feet!

Sports & Leisure Facilities

Muscat's health and beach clubs are one-stop fitness and leisure shops. They are mainly located in hotels and include access to the beach facilities, the hotel health club and various activities. You can expect to find specialised instructors for everything from aerobics to salsa, and swimming to tennis. Many health clubs have separate facilities for men and women, as well as 'ladies only' times. Shop around to see which clubs offers timings and facilities that are best suited to you.

Khasab Travel & Tours
Nr Khasab Airport 968 26 730 464
khasabtours.com

One of the most peaceful ways to visit the mountains of Musandam is to trek through them. Khasab Travels & Tours offers a number of routes, their favourite being one that takes you on a crossing from Sham Fjord to Kumzar. Your trail winds past an abandoned village with old pottery and derelict houses, and includes an overnight stop in the mountains. The views over the Gulf of Arabia and Gulf of Oman are amazing and they are well worth the travel. Groups must consist of at least 10 adults.

Muscat Diving & Adventure Center

Way 3323 **968 24 543 002**
holiday-in-oman.com
Map **2 L3**

Thanks to Oman's varied terrain, your trekking adventure can be as easy or as difficult as you want it to be. Whether you decide on little more than a brisk walk through a pleasant wadi, or a challenging hike through harsh rocky desert, the Muscat Diving & Adventure Center has a number of different routes for you. Each tour has a minimum group size of four.

Horse Riding

Arabia Stable

Qurum Natural Park **968 99 386 378**
Map **2 H2**

Arabia Stable (previously Al Fursan Stable) caters for riders of all ages and levels; from beginners through to competent riders. In addition to riding and show-jumping lessons given by their qualified trainers, it also offers pleasure trips to Qurum Garden, Qurum Nature Reserve, the Creek, and the breathtaking beach in Shatti Al Qurum, all accompanied by a guide for RO.15 per hour. It is open every day from 4pm to 7pm and it charges RO.80 for 8 lessons

Qurum Equestrian School

Qurum Natural Park **968 99 339 222**
Map **2 H2**

Located in the beautiful Qurum Natural Park, the Qurum Equestrian school is open Saturday to Thursday from 5pm to 9pm and teaches everyone from beginners to advanced riders. The school offers beach rides, carriage rides and carriage rental for weddings or special events. There are instructors who provide one-hour lessons in riding and show jumping, for those who just want to ride for enjoyment or those who want to ride competitively. The school has donkeys for small children to ride, and it has introduced a Pony Club for kids. Call the number above, or call Astrid on 99 422 401 for more details.

Ice Hockey

Oman Ice Hockey

Al Khuwair Al Janubiyyah
omanicehockey.com

The Omani National Ice Hockey team currently consists of 20 players, a coach, a team coordinator and a team manager, and that team was invited by the Kuwait Committee of Ice Hockey to compete in the first GCC Hockey Cup, which was held in Kuwait in May 2010. There are currently efforts to register Oman Ice Hockey as an Omani Association and, if that happens,

it will become the governing body for ice hockey in Oman, organising teams and competitions for both junior and senior level ice hockey. Check out the website for upcoming fixtures and tournaments.

Ice Skating

Fun Zone

Qurum Natural Park **968 24 662 951**
funzoneoman.com
Map **2 H2**

Opened in December 2011, the Fun Zone ice rink is open all day from 9am right through to midnight. Skate sessions cost RO.3 per person, including skate hire, and sessions are 90 minutes long – visit the website for accurate session times. Mondays are ladies-only between 9am and 6pm.

Jetskiing

Much of Oman's coastline is open and accessible, and jet-skiing is becoming a more popular pastime here, especially along the coast of Muscat. Be wary of fishermen and swimmers – it's a good idea to remain at least 500m from the shore. In the past, jet-skiers have been prosecuted for accidents involving jet skis. Most hotels and resorts hire out jet skis for about RO.10 for half an hour. Make sure you get a life jacket and a helmet with the jet ski.

Kids' Activities

There is a wide range of activities for children from tennis and football to horse riding and music lessons. Avid skateboarders who have PDO membership can go to the PDO skate park. Kids here are usually aged from 5 to 14, and they meet a few times during the week to skate together, show off new tricks and swap tips. The park has a specially constructed half-pipe, ramps and rails. Unfortunately, skaters without membership to PDO have to stick to street skating.

The British School Muscat also runs a few kids activities and is the venue for meets for the 1st Cubs and Beavers and the 4th Muscat Brownies. You can call the school on 24 600 842 to find out more details. Al Sawadi Beach Resort has some excellent facilities for children throughout the year, including a kids' pool and a huge playground. During the summer the resort has a special kids' festival, where children can take part in arts and crafts, sports and games, while you relax around the pool. If you fancy bringing your little ones to an indoor activity centre, check out Little Town in the Bareeq Al Shatti shopping mall and Busy Bees in the Al Noor Plaza in Madinat Al Sultan Qaboos.

Kids Rest

Al Qurum Complex Muscat **968 24 561 161**
Map **2 H2**

Kids Rest is a children's play area situated on the first floor of Al Qurum Complex. It is very popular as it has a large range of colourful toys as well as a soft-play area for tiny tots. Opening times are 10am to 1pm, Saturday to Thursday, and 4.30pm to 10pm on Fridays. Charges are RO.2.500 per child for an unlimited time. Children must be accompanied by an adult.

Little Town

Bareeq Al Shatti Muscat **968 99 421 645**
littletownoman.com
Map **2 G2**

This play area in the Bareeq Al Shatti mall offers an indoor play area for kids up to the age of seven. It is open Saturday to Wednesday 10am to 9pm, Thursdays from 10am to 10pm and Fridays from 4pm to 10pm. Children must be accompanied by an adult and the charge is RO.3 for a maximum stay of four hours.

Kitesurfing

Kitesurfing is one of the fastest growing extreme watersports. With plenty of uncrowded beaches and superb wind conditions, kitesurfing is definitely on the rise in Oman. You'll find a small group of kitesurf enthusiasts who gather on Thursday and Friday afternoons at Azaiba Beach. This is a relatively quiet and sandy spot that offers perfect kitesurfing conditions when winds exceed 10 knots. Be careful of the occasional car or group of people wandering across the beach, especially in the early evenings – you wouldn't want to become entangled with them.

During summer, hardcore kitesurfers escape the relatively light conditions of Muscat and head for the east coast, where the winds often reach 15 to 30 knots. In fact, Masirah Island is becoming one of the region's must-visit spots; in summer, kiters from all over the GCC flock there for the high winds and low temperatures. At present there is no kitesurf school or kitesurf shop in Oman, but chat with any one of the regulars and they'll offer advice about where to buy equipment and how to get started.

Kiteboarding Oman, Al Sawadi Beach & Masirah Island

Al Sawadi Beach Masirah Island **968 96 323 524**
kiteboarding-oman.com
Map **1 G7**

Opened in 2007, this kiteboarding school has branches on increasingly popular Masirah Island and at Al Sawadi Beach. Various lesson packages are available, some of which can lead to gaining personal kiteboarding licences.

Kitesurfing Oman

Azaiba Beach Muscat **968 94 006 007**
kitesurfing-lessons.com
Map **2 D3**

This kitesurfing school is located in Muscat with lessons taught on Azaiba Beach. A range of courses are available from beginner to refresher courses, so can cater for every budding or expert kiteboarder's needs more than ably.

Libraries

Biblioteque Francaise

The French-Omani Centre Muscat **968 24 697 579**
ambafrance-om.org
Map **2 G3**

This is a lending and information resource for French books, DVDs and CDs. It has an excellent and wide selection of fiction and non-fiction literature by French authors, as well as magazines, DVDs and children's books. To join the library, you pay a subscription of RO.10 for six months. This entitles you to borrow up to a maximum of eight books and books can be kept for a maximum of three weeks.

British Council Young Learner's Zone

Nr Petrol Station, As Sultan Qaboos St Muscat
968 24 681 000
britishcouncil.org
Map **2 G3**

The British Council has a special area in the centre to stimulate young minds with a range of books, magazines, comics and games. DVDs and CDs can also be borrowed.

Information Resource Centre (IRC)

American Embassy, Muscat **968 24 643 400**
oman.usembassy.gov
Map **2 F3**

This highly informative reference library specialises in US policy, legislation, trade data and social and cultural issues. In addition, the IRC offers students and researchers access to the internet and computer databases. There is also a reading section – the IRC carries around 20 periodicals in hard copy, including *Time*, *Newsweek*, Business Week, *National Geographic*, *Fortune* and the *Harvard Business Review* so you can keep updated without paying the high cover prices of imported titles to the region.

Full text versions of more than 200 online journals and magazines are also available. There are many books on American states, literature, art, social history and science as well as information on Oman. Note that the library is open by appointment only, so contact the embassy before you visit otherwise you may end up disappointed with your trip.

My Book and Me
Way 37 Muscat **968 24 121 327**
Map **2 D3**
The thirst for a public lending service has seen independent libraries cropping up such as My Book and Me. This library has a wide range of children's books as well as a coffee shop and a children's play area. It's worth a visit for the fun knick-knacks that are laid around the place and the inspirational wall almost as much for its range of reading material. It is open Monday to Wednesday from 10am to 1pm and from 4pm to 9pm. On Thursdays and Saturdays, opening times are 10am to 7pm.

Oman Chamber Of Commerce & Industry
CBD Area Muscat **968 24 707 674**
chamberoman.com
Map **2 J3**
This small but well-stocked library has a range of reference books, periodicals, newspapers, trade and industrial catalogues and directories. Most are in Arabic, but there is a small collection of English books on business or trade-related subjects, such as economics, accounting, management and finance. An internet facility is available at a nominal charge and there are a number of CD-ROMS and business related videos. You may borrow books from the library but you must pay a bond of value of the book plus 100% of the value, plus 500 baisa per book. The library is open Sunday to Thursday from 8am to 2pm.

Public Knowledge Library
Nr PDO main gates Muscat **968 24 673 111**
publiclibrary.gov.om
Map **2 H2**
This library contains over 14,500 volumes, with a balanced split between Arabic and English. The subjects covered are mainly in the areas of science and technology, but there are also materials covering topics in the humanities and social sciences, such as environmental issues and Omani history. You'll also find general encyclopaedias, language resources, dictionaries and atlases here, and a video collection has been added to the library's resources. The library is open Sunday to Thursday from 8am to 2pm, and from 4pm to 9pm.

The Lazy Bookworm
109 Block A, Bahwan Twin Buildings Muscat
968 94 353 903
Map **2 F3**
This independent lending library offers a wide selection of reading material with more than 6,000 books available and bills itself as an exclusive reading community for kids. Opening hours are Sunday to Thursday from 5.30pm to 8pm, and then Saturday from 4pm to 6pm.

Martial Arts
Black Stallion Martial Arts
Al Falaj Hotel **968 24 702 311/ 99 743 557**
Map **2 H2**
Black Stallion offers a variety of martial arts classes for children and adults. Options include karate, taekwondo kicks, aikido, judo, nun-chacko, kick-boxing, Philippine arnis and gymnastics. Classes range in cost from RO.22 for children and RO.27 for adults per month (three lessons per week). Classes are given on Sundays, Tuesdays and Thursdays.

Fit & Tough
Hammer Gym Al Khuwair 33 **968 94 216 608**
Map **2 F3**
Fit & Tough holds classes at the Hammer Gym. They teach students of all levels and provide one-on-one coaching with street combat expert Jess Beltran. The classes will help you to gain confidence, develop strength (of the mental and physical sort) and improve your physique.

Harmony Music, Art and Karate Training
Dohat Al Adab Street Muscat **968 24 704 303**
Map **2 K2**
This training centre runs a number of karate courses for different levels and age groups.

Muscat Mixed Martial Arts Club
Al Maneef Sports Center Muscat **968 99 216 092**
Map **2 F3**
Mixed martial arts is one of the fastest growing sports on the planet and this popular club offers a range of classes for everyone to get involved in the phenomenon, catering for beginners and right up to advanced students. Some students go on to compete internationally too. Classes are usually held Sunday to Thursday from 8pm to 10pm.

Motocross
Oman Automobile Club
Nr Golden Tulip Hotel **968 24 510 239**
omanauto.org
Map **2 C3**
The Oman Automobile Club offers many activities, one of which is motocross. The OAC has an excellent 1km sandy motocross track complete with hills, jumps, twists and turns. It's terrific for learning on or sharpening your skills. Club membership is required and you need to provide your own bikes and equipment, although there is an area where you can store your bike for a fee. The OAC hosts a number of local and international rallies throughout the year with off-road rallies held once a month.

Motorcycling

Harley Owners' Group – Muscat Chapter
Nr Zakher Mall **968 24 489 428**
hog-muscat.com
Map **2 G3**
When the Harley Davidson showroom opened in 1998, the Muscat chapter of the Harley Owners' Group began. The Harley Owners' Group (HOG), which includes expats and Omanis, meets at the 'HOG Pen' (a coffee shop) in the Harley Davidson showroom regularly and arranges activities, rides and events for Harley Davidson enthusiasts and their families. Rides are usually held on Tuesday evenings and Friday mornings and an overnight ride is organised at least once a month (during the cooler months). For more information visit the Harley Davidson showroom or visit the hogmuscat website (hog-muscat.com).

Oman Riders Club
sjsoman.com **968 24 510 276**
Various locations
The mission of this club is to unite all motorcycle riders under one umbrella in order to promote local and international safety rules and regulations. It also supports local charity events.

Mountain Biking

Muscat has some great mountain biking routes – due to its location amid the rocky mountains along the coast, the city offers rides virtually from your door. There are many off-road tracks winding their way through the quiet areas, wadis and along the coast that provide a wide range of challenges for all levels of biker. The Bowshar dunes are close to the city and offer some great rides, as do Sayh Ad Dhabi or the route from the InterContinental to the desalination plant.

Riding in the mountains is adventurous and generally rocky, technical and challenging. There are many tracks to follow and the terrain is on a par with the classic trail areas of Utah and Arizona in the USA. Those who are just getting into mountain biking should start on the tracks in the gentler hilly areas. For hardcore mountain bikers there is a good range of topography, from highly technical rocky trails to mountain routes that can take hours to climb and minutes to descend. Be prepared and sensible – the sun is strong, you'll need far more water than you think. It's also very easy to get lost or have an accident so every precaution should be taken before embarking on a mountain biking adventure.

Muscat Diving & Adventure Center now offer mountain biking trips. For more information on biking in Oman, or to get together with other mountain bikers contact Muscat Cycling Club or Bike Oman.

Bike and Hike Oman
The View Hotel Muscat **968 24 400 873**
bikeandhikeoman.com
Various locations
Bike and Hike Oman was established in 2012 and offers guided tours with full suspension mountain bikes. There is a wide range of trips to choose from, including Culture Bike Tours, Nature Bike Tours, Canyon Bike Tours, High Altitude Bike Tours, Heritage Hiking Tours and Mountain Oasis Hiking Tours.

Bike Oman
Muscat
bikeoman.com
Various locations
This groups meet for weekly mountain rides using around 15 different trails which can vary in distance between 15km and 40km. There is also an annual mountain bike race on a prepared, marked-out route with an average of 5km to 10km. During the heat of the summer, the group organises night rides.

Music Lessons

Classic Music & Arts Institute
Nr Qurum Natural Park Muscat **968 24 560 025**
Map **2 H2**
The institute's team of fully trained musicians offers a wide range of lessons in piano, vocals, cello, Arabic violin and beginner oud, and classical and acoustic guitar. They often have other visiting musicians and they are happy to connect musicians with teachers in the area. Costs are kept reasonable and children are encouraged to use their skills in ensemble work. Lessons are available for children aged seven and older. Each child receives a report from their teacher and regular concerts are arranged for the institute's aspiring musicians.

Harmony Music, Art and Karate Training
Dohat Al Adab Street Muscat **968 24 704 303**
Map **2 K2**
This centre caters for all ages and abilities, and has a variety of lessons in different musical instruments.

Melody Music Centre
Way 1952 Muscat **968 2 470 3130**
Map **2 J3**
Since the Melody Music Centre opened in the mid 90s, it has obtained recognition from the UK's Associated Board of the Royal Schools of Music to teach both a theoretical and practical syllabus. Examinations take place for different grades, ranging from Preparatory Grade One to Grade Eight levels. The centre also offers classes in piano, keyboard, guitar, drums, conga drums, violin, arnatic vocal and classical dance

(Bharatanatyam). There are branches in Al Khuwair (24 486 647) and in Wadi Kabir (24 811 482).

The Music Palace
House 2557, Way 1947 Muscat **968 24 602 445**
musicpalaceoman.com
Map **2 G3**
This school is centrally located in Muscat and offers a wide range of lessons in piano, violin and guitar.

Pilates

Horizon Fitness
Various locations
horizonoman.com
Various locations
These popular gyms offer 60 minute Pilates classes that help you build flexibility, strength and endurance. Gym locations include Madinat Al Sultan Qaboos, Al Khoud, Al Azaiba and Mawalah South.

Quad Bikes

The rough terrain and dunes of Oman's remote areas attract all kinds of motor sports enthusiasts. If you're into motorbikes, quads or dune buggies, and you have your own, it's easy to take yourself and a few friends for a fun day out – you don't run the risk of bumping into anyone else and you can explore at will. The Bowshar Sands, just outside Muscat, are very popular and it is a great place to fly your bike or quad off a dune. If you don't have your own quad, you can rent one at many of the hotels and beach resorts. Unlike dune buggies, quad bikes have no roll cages and therefore extra care should be taken. Where possible get training and wear protective gear to make the most of your thrills-and-spills adventure.

Off-Roading
With vast areas of virtually untouched wilderness in Oman, wadi and dune bashing are popular activities Most off-road journeys are on existing tracks to protect the environment from any damage – the dunes and wadis support a surprising variety of flora and fauna that exist in a delicate balance.

Dune bashing, or desert driving, is one of the toughest challenges for both car and driver – it's also a great deal of fun once you've mastered it. The golden rule is never to go alone. If you're new to this activity it's essential to go with an experienced off-roader. Driving on sand requires very different skills to road driving. Useful equipment to take with you includes shovels, strong tow ropes, a pressure gauge, foot pump or compressor, matting or planks of wood, a full tool kit for the car, a spare tyre in good condition, a car jack (with an extra piece of wood to prevent it from sinking in the sand), extra petrol and plenty of water for both cars and passengers.

If you don't think your driving skills are up to scratch, you could try dune bashing through any of the major tour companies. Alternatively, some places offer driving tuition for these conditions, which is an excellent way to build your confidence in a relatively safe environment before doing it for real.

Safety First
It is always advisable to go off-road with at least two vehicles. If anything goes wrong, you'll be glad of an extra pair of hands and a tow. Although it requires marginally less skill than in the desert, when you drive in the mountains and wadis you still need to use your common sense and forward planning (you need to think ahead about choice of gears for the hills and river crossings, for example).

Driving in the wadis is more straightforward. Wadis are (usually dry) gullies, carved through the rock by rushing floodwaters, following the course of seasonal rivers. The main safety precaution to take when wadi bashing is to keep your eyes open for developing thunder storms – the wadis can fill up quickly and you will need to make your way to higher ground smartly to avoid flash floods.

Close to Muscat are the Bowshar dunes. Although this is a small area, it has numerous criss-cross tracks through the sand that provide you with an easy introduction to this challenging sport. When you're ready for more serious stuff, head for the Wahiba Sands, just over two hours from Muscat, for endless stretches of undulating desert. Or try The Empty Quarter (Rub Al Khali), which is spectacular in its seclusion, remoteness and the impressive size of the dunes. Alternatively, the Hajar Mountains offer amazing drives through rugged mountain scenery. You'll pass remote mountain villages and freshwater rock pools as the rough tracks take you to incredible views up to 3,000m above sea level.

The better-known wadis are often over-visited, especially by tour companies, not necessarily because they're the best but because they are the easiest to get to. If you're more adventurous, you can find some amazing, almost untouched places.

For further information and tips for driving off road, check out Explorer's *Oman Off-Road* guide. This fabulous book features detailed routes, stunning satellite imagery, information on outdoor activities, striking photos and a useful off-road directory. Look out for the GPS enabled app for mobile phones and tablets, which offers many of the book's features but allows for accurate location pin-pointing on the maps.

Dirt biking

Mountain biking

Desert camping

Reiki

Reiki (pronounced ray-key) is a hands-on healing art developed in the early 1900s by Mikao Usui in Japan. The word Reiki comes from the Japanese words Rei and Ki, meaning universal life energy, and is used to describe both the energy and the Usui system of using it. The technique is based on the belief that energy can be channelled into a patient by means of touch and converted into 'universal life force energy', which has a healing effect. Like meditation, Reiki can emotionally cleanse, physically invigorate and leave you more focused. You can learn the art of Reiki to practise on yourself or others, directly or remotely. Contact Whispers of Serenity Clinic in Al Azaiba (whispers-of-serenity.com) on 24 614 268 for individual appointments, classes and group sessions.

Running

Muscat Road Runners

muscatroadrunners.com
Various locations
Muscat Road Runners is a multinational group that gets together several times a week to run. Founded in 1983, it now has around 80 members with regular participation of up to 45 people of all abilities. It costs nothing to join but 500 baisas is charged for the Wednesday run. For more information, email chairman@muscatroadrunners.com.

Oman Athletics Association

omanathletic.org
Various locations
The OAA's main role is to train the national Omani team in track and field events, preparing them for national and international competitions. The organisation also arranges local competitions – from short runs to marathons – which are open to everyone. There are categories for adults and children and medals are awarded for first, second and third positions. The OAA maintains a list of contacts for all sporting activities, so if you would like details about a particular event or interest, email oma@mf.iaaf.org.

Sailing

Sailing off the coast of Muscat is a wonderful experience, both in winter when temperatures are perfect for watersports, and in the summer when it offers a great escape from the scorching heat inland. Unfortunately, much of the club sailing in and around Muscat is closed to outsiders and the facilities are limited to employees of particular companies. That said, sailing regattas are held regularly and the people

at Marina Bander Al Rowdha (24 737 288), Capital Area Yacht Club (24 737 712) and Almouj Marina (24 534 400) can give you more information on these. There is also the Oman Laser Association; this is definitely a sport where word of mouth is the best way to get information and it pays to be patient.

Many companies will take you out for a pleasure or fishing cruise, either for a couple of hours or for a full day. Muscat Diving and Adventure Centre (24 543 002) offer a wide range of activities so call them and find out what they can offer you. There are also companies, like Oman Charter, from whom you can charter your own boat – whether you take it for a single day or several weeks is up to you, but it is one way to experience the ultimate freedom out on the stunning turquoise seas.

Oman Sail

The Wave Muscat Sales Centre Muscat
968 24 181 400
omansail.com
Map **2 B2**
This centre has grown out of the successful national programme to reinvigorate the skills of sailing that served in times gone by. Very popular with the schools and other associations, the lessons are taught by professional instructors and even sometimes the superstar sailors themselves, who take a very hands-on method of education. Sailing packages consisting of theory and practical aspects starts from around RO.40 and are available from a number of locations around Oman.

Sailing vessel

Ras Al Hamra Sailing Club

Muscat **968 24 672 710/96 766 472**
rahbc.pdorc.com
Various locations

The Laser is a one-man sailing boat and in Oman Laser sailing is represented by this club. It has been promoting the interests of laser sailing and small boat sailing in general here for over 20 years. They organise around 10 competitions annually. The races are competitive yet friendly affairs, and more experienced sailors readily share tips and techniques. Most races are held at the RAH Recreation Club, with occasional events in Sawadi Resort or the Marina Bandar Al-Rowdha. There are some co-organised events aimed at expanding the Omani Laser fleet, which includes instruction for beginners and organised races. Races are organised at places like Al Sawadi Beach Resort, Civil Aviation Beach Club, Capital Area Yacht Club and Marina Bandar Al Rowdha. Find out more on rahbc.pdorc.com/Sailing/laser/laser-home.htm.

Sandboarding & Skiing

Head out to any stretch of desert in the interior of Oman, find yourself some big dunes and feel the rush of the wind as you take a fast ride down the sandy slopes. It's an easy sport to learn, it doesn't hurt when you fall, and you'll feel a real sense of achievement when you master it and glide to the bottom. Most people tend to use old snowboards, but you'll even find the odd skier taking to the sandy slopes. Standard snowboards or skis can be used. The best places for sandboarding and skiing are where you'll find the biggest dunes – the Wahiba Sands area or the massive dunes of the Empty Quarter in the south-west of the country. Many tour companies and camps provide equipment and direction. One of these is the Desert Camp at Wahiba Sands, which offers sandskiing or surfing from their permanent campsite. Visit 1000nightscamp.com for more details.

Scouts & Guides

1st Muscat Guides

Muscat
bgifc.org.uk
Various locations

British Guides in Foreign Countries is a division of the United Kingdom Guide Association, which caters for girls wishing to continue their Guiding while living overseas. The groups are open to all nationalities, but there is sometimes a waiting list and priority is given to girls who have been members in their own country. All of the packs base their programme on the British system to provide continuity.

1st Oman Scout Group

Muscat **968 99 242 078**
omanbga.org
Map **2 G3**

The Scout Association started in Oman in 1975 and acts under the auspices of the United Kingdom British Groups Abroad. There are different groups for different ages, Beavers (ages 6 to 8), Cubs (ages 8 to 10), Scouts (ages 10 to 14) and Explorers (ages 14 to 18). The association focuses on outdoor activities such as camping, map reading, astronomy, cycling, first aid and conservation, and members can earn a variety of challenge badges. For more information, contact Sonia on 99 242 078.

Singing

Muscat Singers

The Bosch Center for Performing Arts, The American International School (TAIS), Ghala, Muscat
muscatsingers.org
Map **2 G3**

One of the longest established choirs in Muscat, this group welcomes new singers from all backgrounds and nationalities. The choir covers a broad spectrum of music ranging from classical and light opera through to folk and jazz. Much of the singing is in parts and there is always a need for new members of all singing styles. The ability to read music is not essential but previous experience of choral singing is useful. The minimum age is 15 years, but there is no upper limit. The choir meets on Sunday nights at 7.30pm at TAIS.

Snorkelling

If you don't have your PADI certification for diving, don't despair – a mask and snorkel are all you really need for a fabulous view of Oman's awesome marine life. The number and variety of underwater sea creatures are incredible, the seas are pristine and the temperatures are pleasantly warm throughout the year. This activity does not require much equipment: a mask, snorkel, a pair of fins to motor you along and plenty of sun protection (a rash vest is also a very good investment). Most hotels or dive centres will rent out equipment, and you can buy good gear at dive shops. Costs vary greatly so shop around.

Social Groups

When living in a new country, it can be reassuring to meet up with people from home or with similar interests. Fortunately, Oman has many such groups.

American Women's Group Oman
Muscat
awgoman.com
Various locations
AWG is an international women's social organisation that's been serving the women of Muscat for over 30 years. It boasts almost 1,000 members representing more than 45 nationalities. Meetings are held in hotels and each features a short programme, announcements, sign-up sheets for the various activities, and the opportunity to meet and talk with other women. See awgoman.com for the latest meeting times and further information.

Australians and New Zealanders in Oman
Various locations
anzoman.com
Various locations
This group was formed to facilitate social interaction with a particular focus on celebrating events unique to both countries such as ANZAC remembrance, the Melbourne Cup and the national day festivities associated with Australia Day and Waitangi Day. Membership is open to anyone living in Oman hailing from Australia, New Zealand and the South Pacific Islands. Email anzinoman@gmail.com for more details.

Caledonian Society Of Oman
968 95 807 758
caledoniansocietyofoman.com
Various locations
One of the oldest expatriate societies in Oman, the Caledonian Society of Oman welcomes everyone of Scottish descent as well as those who appreciate all things Scottish. Every year it holds the St. Andrew's Day Ball and the Burns' Supper, which raise money for both Omani and Scottish charities. Kilts are optional, but a love of Scotland is not.

Oman Irish Society
Various locations
omanirishsociety.com
Various locations
This voluntary organisation offers fun, friendship and a hearty 'cead mile failte' to all. Each year, it organises many social events including the St. Patrick's Day Ball, a golf classic, and a fun beach day. Everyone is welcome to join. For more information email irishinoman@hotmail.com.

Royal Omani Amateur Radio Society
Muscat
a47rs.org
Map **2 H2**
ROARS was founded in 1972 and its membership currently stands at around 180 people. The Society offers courses, limited to Omanis, who want to obtain amateur radio licences, and classes are held on Sunday and Tuesday evenings. Anyone of any nationality may join, if they have a current amateur radio licence from their home country. Membership costs RO.15 per year and the society holds seminars, expeditions, trips and social gatherings several times a year.

The National Association For Cancer Awareness
Muscat **968 24 498 716**
ocancer.org.om
Map **2 D3**
Cancer survivor Ms Yuthar Al-Rawahy promised herself while she was under active treatment, that if she were to survive her third bout of cancer, she would develop a patient advocacy group in Oman. The association's aim is to create awareness about cancer, teaching self-examination in order that early diagnosis can be made, and to help people to accept their diagnosis and work towards successful treatment. The association has met with much support from cancer patients, their friends and relatives and it is the first patient advocacy group in the country.

Women's Guild In Oman
Muscat
womensguildoman.com
Various locations
This group has a great reputation in Oman for distributing funds to charities here. While fundraising is an important part of the guild, it also sets out to provide an opportunity for women to enjoy a varied programme of speakers and events (including coffee mornings and popular Crystal Ball annual fundraiser) and to offer its members fellowship. Membership is open to women of all ages and nationalities and it currently boasts over 1,000 members. The regular newsletter is an invaluable resource for events around Muscat, news and classified adverts.

Squash

Palm Beach Club
InterContinental Muscat **968 24 680 000**
ihg.com
Map **2 G2**
There are indoor squash facilities at the Palm Beach Club. They cannot be rented by the hour but for RO.10 you can use the facilities at the club for a full day.

Surfing

The idea of surfing in Oman may not inspire images of Hawaii style waves, but you'd be surprised by how popular the sport is here. Although it might not be one of the world's greatest surf spots, Oman is certainly one of the better places to catch a wave in the Gulf because part of its coast lies on the Indian Ocean. Surfers in other Gulf countries, like the UAE, often make regular trips to Oman to get their fix. While there are currently no major surf clubs in Oman, the Dubai surfers' group has an excellent website that gives information on surfing in the UAE, the Arabian Gulf and in Oman (check out surfersofdubai.com).

The eastern side of Masirah Island is one of the better surfing spots. It's easily reached by ferry from Sana on the mainland, followed by a short drive to the other side of the island. Waves here average four to six feet, depending on the season.

Swimming

Most hotels have swimming pools that are open for public use. Day charges range from RO.2.5 (at Al Falaj) to RO.10 (at the five-star hotels); expect to pay more at the weekend. You can also swim off the beaches. Remember to be modest in your choice of swimwear and wear it only on the beach. The tides and currents here can be surprisingly strong, so do not underestimate them. For your own safety it's better to choose somewhere with a few people around.

In summer jellyfish can be a problem, both in the water and washed up on the beach. All varieties are poisonous but one particular variety, the box jellyfish, can be lethal. Stone fish and sea snakes are also not creatures you want to tangle with, but they tend to keep well away from the more populated areas.

Snorkelling

Tennis

You'll find courts at hotels, or courts belonging to private organisations that are only open to members. Many hotels have floodlit courts for evening games. Prices for hiring courts vary between about RO.3 and RO.6. The Oman Tennis Association oversees the national Omani team in tournaments at home and abroad. The association also organises a variety of annual local tournaments, mainly held at hotels and open to players of various abilities, although some are for professionals only. Coaching is available at the hotels and again prices vary, up to RO.20 per hour.

Cliff Club
Crowne Plaza Muscat 968 24 660 660
ichotelsgroup.com
Map **2 H2**
Resident tennis professional Mr Vasu (92 352 204) offers tennis coaching. For non-members, a one-hour lesson will cost RO.15 or you can buy a package of five lessons for RO.70. Group lessons are available.

Triathlon

Triathlon enthusiasts enjoy a good challenge and Oman's rugged terrain certainly provides one. Check out the Oman Triathlon page on Facebook for information on training, as well as the numerous annual events. Hash House Harriers clubs (jebelhashoman.com) are also good sources of information regarding triathlon schedules.

Volleyball

The Bowshar Club is great for sport-loving women in Oman. They were the first Omani Club to start a woman's football team and now have a women's volleyball tournament, in conjunction with the Oman Women Sports Development Committee (OWSDC). It covers football, volleyball and basketball and is open to girls between 12 and 19. Call the Oman Volleyball Association for more information (24 121 140).

Yoga

Yoga is a form of exercise that benefits body and mind. A class usually consists of a series of postures and ends with a meditation session. Sign up for classes at hotel health clubs. At the Palm Beach Club (24 680 660) at the InterContinental Muscat, you can attend classes on Sundays and Tuesday at 8.15am and 6.45pm or on Thursdays at 9.30am. Members pay RO.3 and non-members are charged RO.5.

Souks full of life and colour

SHOPPING

Traditional jewellery

SHOPPING IN OMAN

From traditional garb to the latest high street stores and global brands, you'll find them all in Muscat's malls and markets.

Muscat is the shopping capital of Oman and offers a cosmopolitan range of shops and goods. From expensive boutiques to handicraft stalls and everything in between, shoppers are never far away from finding what they want. The fact that goods are tax-free means items like carpets, textiles and gold are often cheaper than they are in other countries, while many imported goods fetch prices similar to what they do elsewhere. The key to shopping like a pro in Muscat is to bargain where possible, or wait for the sales - prices can be cut up by up to 70%.

Oman has some of the liveliest, most authentic and colourful traditional markets (souks) in the region. Distinguished old men wearing dishdashas sit behind the counters in the small trinket shops around town, while bejewelled women in abayas haggle with authority. Modern shopping centres, replete with global brands and ample parking, are pivotal social hubs too. These provide ample air-conditioned entertainment for a plethora of nationalities that are there either to be see and be seen, shop or just pass the time.

Thursday, Friday and Saturday nights are definitely the busiest shopping times and it can often get a little too crowded around town, even for the hardcore shopping enthusiast. During Ramadan, some of the stores are open until midnight, supermarkets are packed to the brim with unbelievable amounts of food, and the queues are very long, especially in the evenings. Most of the shops have sales during the annual Muscat Festival that takes place in January and in the months around the two Eid holidays, and there are invariably numerous promotions and raffles up for grabs.

SHOPPING

Refunds, Exchanges & Consumer Rights

In general, you'll have no problem in trying to exchange goods that are faulty or that you've changed your mind about as long as they are unworn and you have the receipt. However, most retailers will only either exchange the item or give store credit; very few will refund you. Shop assistants are always willing to help and exchanging goods is generally easy enough. However, if you insist on a refund it's best to ask to see the manager or to leave your number and ask the assistant to call you once they've discussed your case with their supervisor.

Consumer Rights

Taking a retailer to court in Oman is likely to be a very lengthy and costly procedure and will probably cause you a great deal more stress than the original problem did. Instead, try to sort things out with a compromise. Perhaps you can have an item exchanged, or a service upgraded? The key is to remain calm and, if you're not getting anywhere, you could try to involve an Omani friend in your negotiations. If the problem cannot be resolved, contact the Oman Association for Consumer Protection (omanconsumer.org) on 24 567 981. You might struggle to get through, but once you do they may be able to help you sort out your problem.

Refund Policies

Some of the larger shops display their refund policies clearly (for example, underwear is non-returnable) and only allow exchanges for a limited period (usually seven days from the date of purchase). Many international department stores are more proactive with their customer service policies, so it may be best to stick with the big name shops when you're looking to buy larger, more expensive items.

How To Pay

International credit cards like Visa, MasterCard, Diner's Club and American Express are widely accepted by established retailers in Muscat and Salalah. Small traders in the souks and local convenience stores only take cash, but some jewellery shops in the Mutrah Souk will accept credit cards. You might be able to pay with post-dated local cheques when buying expensive items like cars, but this depends on your credentials and the vendor's reputation. There seems to be a fairly relaxed attitude to accepting foreign currency and in many places you can pay with dollars, sterling or one of the GCC currencies (the UAE dirham is accepted almost everywhere). However, it's always good to carry some local currency with you, and there are plenty of money exchanges.

Bargaining

Although bargaining can feel alien and uncomfortable for many visitors, it's a time-honoured tradition in this part of the world, one that both parties invariably get enjoyment from. Outside of the souks or the stores in Ruwi, bargaining is less common and involves more subtle hinting than overt haggling.

You can politely enquire if the price is 'before discount', or mention that you're paying cash. Sometimes even if you don't ask for a discount, the assistant will pass it on to you anyway, which can be a welcome surprise. In the souk though you're expected to haggle and if you're paying cash you'll find vendors will often drop the price substantially. In contrast to other countries in the region where you may be badgered into buying something after accepting a glass of mint tea, bargaining in Oman is less stressful and it can be fun if you relax and take your time. The key is to decide on how much you want to pay for the item (scout out other shops to get an idea) and to be prepared to walk away if you don't get it for that.

Be A Discount Diva

It seems like something is always on sale in Oman: if it's not slashed prices during the Muscat Festival or discounts over Eid, it's buy-two-get-one-free banded packs in Carrefour or 25% off everything in Marks & Spencer for one day only.

Shipping

Sending purchases abroad can be a tedious business but there are many shipping and cargo agencies that make it easier. Items can be sent by sea freight (the least expensive option), air freight or courier. You'll find companies that offer this service under 'Courier Services', 'Cargo Services' or 'Shipping Companies' in the Omantel telephone directory or in the newspapers' classified ads. Most airlines also have a cargo service division, but your chosen destination may not necessarily be on their list of routes. When buying carpets or furniture, some shops may arrange shipping for you. You should always ask what this will cost first – that antique wooden chest may not seem like such a bargain after adding in the shipping costs.

Where To Go For…

Looking for a special something with a bit of local flavour? Try one of these goods – they all make for great gifts.

Silver

The bling factor of the country is massively heightened by its reputation and popularity for high-quality silverware. Not just used for jewellery, silver is popular in decorating weapons as well as making everyday objects like coffee pots and pipes. As you explore the country, you'll notice that each region in the Sultanate has its own distinctive design. Don't be put off by the blackened and dusty bits of beauty; there is nothing that a little bit of polish can't fix. As the old adage goes: Seek and ye shall find some real treasures. For a good starting point, spend some time browsing Mutrah Souk.

Textiles

Oman is a haven for textile lovers with a wide variety of fabric, textures, prices, colours and prints for you to choose from. Even the smallest towns in Oman will have fabric stores so shop to your heart's (and wallet's) desire. Surprisingly, cotton isn't very big in the Arab world but silk and linen are extremely popular and plentiful. Look out for beautiful Indian printed cushion covers and bed spreads which can all be found in the souks or small stores around town. These will definitely bring a touch of the exotic to your new home or act as the perfect gift for family and friends back home.

Perfume

Strong heady smells tend to dominate much of Oman and pure frankincense, jasmine and musk actually originated from this very region. The souks are a fabulous place to find the perfect scent with hundreds of fragrances vying for your attention. Be careful; some of the purer stuff is super strong and a drop or two on your scarf can last for a few days.

Oud is highly valued in the Middle East and can fetch astonishing prices. Made from the resin of Aloeswood trees and imported from India, Cambodia and Malaysia, Oud is worn on clothes and skin and usually only on important occasions. Amouage is said to be 'the world's most valuable perfume' and is made here in Oman. You can visit the Amouage factory in Rusayl, past As Seeb, to see just how all the perfume is made (Sunday to Thursday, 8.30am to 4.30pm, amouage.com).

Carpets

Camel or goat hair, sheep wool or cotton, dyed, patterned or still in their natural states, weaving is considered one of Oman's major handicrafts and the skill has continued to be passed down through the generations.

Carpet shopping can be an absolute minefield but also an incredible pleasure with so much to look through and choose from. The best thing to do is have a set budget and know how big or small you want it to be. The origin, intricacy of design, material and whether it is machine-made or hand-woven will all dictate a carpet's value.

Hand-woven products tend to have more imperfections but this actually increases their value. Shop around and you are bound to find something to please your sensibilities and your pocket. And don't forget to haggle!

Souvenirs

From typical holiday trinkets to tasteful keepsakes there is a good range of souvenirs in Oman. In fact shopping for presents in Oman is really hard because it's so good you'll want one of everything for yourself! You'll find a good selection of traditional gifts like antique wooden wedding chests or pashminas, and the typical holiday buys like fridge magnets, T-shirts and soft toys. Traditional Arabic gear makes for the best presents though and a lot of the souks sell all the Arabic goodies you can imagine, although knick-knacks can usually be found in supermarkets and malls too.

Shop & Ship

If you want to get goods shipped from overseas to Oman, check out the 'Shop & Ship' service offered by Aramex (aramex.com). It gives you a UK or US mailbox, and then ships the contents of your mailbox to you at competitive rate. Be warned though; shops will sometimes issue a certificate stating that the item is worth less than it is to save you money on import duty. This is highly illegal, of course, but they seem to have no qualms about doing it.

Perfume

Colourful jewellery

Textiles

WHAT & WHERE TO BUY

You can get most of the things you need in Muscat although the shopping areas are rather scattered across the city and you'll need a car or taxi to move from one to another. The following pages cover the main categories of items, and where you can find them.

Alcohol

Anyone over 21 can buy alcohol at licensed bars, restaurants and some clubs, for consumption on the premises. However, to buy alcohol for home consumption you need a liquor licence. You have to have your employer request a licence, which looks like a mini passport, on your behalf, and not all companies will assist with this – it depends what kind of business it is and their attitudes towards alcohol. Muslims are not allowed to apply for a liquor licence. For more information on how to get your licence, see the Living in Oman chapter.

Alcohol is not sold in supermarkets but there are a number of bottle stores in Muscat. These are usually hidden away and there's no indication on the outside that these shops sell alcohol. Look for names like Onas, African + Eastern LLC, Gulf Supply Services, and Oman United Agency, or ask around. You can buy alcohol on the black market but it's a dodgy move and not recommended and besides, the cheaper the tipple, the worse the hangover. It's illegal to transport alcohol unless you're taking it from the shop or the airport duty free to your house (even then you should make sure you have a receipt in case you are stopped by the police).

African + Eastern Nr Pizza Hut, Al Bashair St, 968 24 602 121, *africaneastern.com*
Gulf Supply Services Al Wadi Centre, 6505 Way, 968 24 810 709, *gulfsupplyoman.com*
Oman United Agencies Nr Horizon Fitness, Madinat Qaboos St, 968 24 643 333, *ouaoman.com*

Art

Muscat has a reasonable selection of galleries. These sell paintings, mainly, and a selection of sculpture, jewellery and pottery, often created by local or expatriate artists. Foreign artists and photographers with an interest in Omani culture and landscapes often hold exhibitions in museums and galleries;

check the local papers or The Week for details of upcoming events. The Mutrah Souk, Qurum City Centre and Al Harthy Complex, the Omani Fine Arts Society, and the Bait Muzna Gallery are treasure troves of local and Arabian art.

Al Madina Art Gallery Al Inshirah St, 968 24 691 380, *almadinaartgallery.com*
Bait Muzna Gallery House 234, Al Saidiya St, 968 24 739 204, *baitmuznagallery.com*
Ghalyas Museum Of Modern Art 968 24 711 640, *ghalyasmuseum.com*
MuscArt Gallery 968 24 493 912, *muscart.net*
Stal Gallery Al Inshirah St, 968 24 600 396, *stalgallery.com*
The Omani Society For Fine Arts Nr Ramada Hotel, 968 24 694 969, *osfa.gov.om*

Art & Craft Supplies

Shah Nagardas Manji carries basic art supplies like oil paints, acrylics, pastels, brushes and drawing paper, and you'll find stores in Qurum, Madinat Al Sultan Qaboos and Ruwi. Serious artists are better off bringing their materials from home or ordering on the internet as specialised supplies are hard to come by. When you're ready to display your work, the many framing shops in Ruwi High Street provide quick, professional and inexpensive service.

Office Supplies Co 968 24 829 400, *officesuppliesllc.com*
Shah Nagardas Manji & Co 968 24 562 655, *shahnagardas.com*
The Omani Society For Fine Arts Nr Ramada Hotel, 968 24 694 969, *osfa.gov.om*

Bicycles

It's probably not wise to pedal down the Sultan Qaboos Highway, but there are plenty of quieter roads that are safe for cyclists. Mountain biking is popular and a ride around the steep hills of the Qantab area will certainly give your legs a workout.

Al Muianee Trading Al Amrat Rd, Wadi Hattat, 968 24 878 887
Babyshop Centrepoint, 968 96 473 101, *babyshopstores.com*
Oman Bicycle Shop Nr Radisson Hotel, 968 96 773 824, *omanbicycle.com*
Sun & Sand Sports Muscat City Centre, 968 24 558 355, *sunandsandsports.com*
Toys 'R' Us Markaz Al Bahja, 968 24 540 360, *toysrus.com*

Books

Due to the laws of supply and demand, the range of imported books and magazines available in Muscat is relatively limited. To bring a title into the country, it must first be checked for its content. Books that are deemed to be against the religious, cultural, political or moral sensitivities of the country will be banned. Of course, books can be ordered from sites such as amazon.com but packages are often opened and examined first.

Foreign newspapers and magazines are flown in regularly but are expensive. Magazines that contain illicit material are censored with the aid of a black marker pen, as opposed to being banned completely. Subscription magazines may take longer to reach you, as someone has to go through all the pictures of scantily clad women and dress them up with black ink.

Latest releases aside, there are some beautiful coffee table books full of inspired photographs of Oman and its people. These are really good for taking home to show family and friends that there's more to where you live than sand dunes. The Family Bookshop, Al Manahil and Turtle's cater primarily for English speakers, but also stock Arabic titles, and they both have a good selection of children's books. Al Batra Bookshop stocks mostly reference books, hobby books, some children's books and older fiction titles. Most of the larger hotels have small bookshops that stock a limited range of fiction, travel books and books on Oman. Supermarkets like Carrefour, Al Fair and The Sultan Center also carry a reasonable selection. If you can't find what you're looking for, you can order books online, although make sure you take into account the extra fee – the cost of postage may double the price of the book.

One particularly interesting bookshop is House of Prose in Qurum. A second-hand bookshop that stocks mainly fiction, travel and biographical titles, they have a buy-back policy that refunds half the price you originally paid for any of their books if you return it in good condition and can show the receipt. Their 'look-out list' is useful if you have a request for a particular title. They stock about 20,000 books in Muscat and another 20,000 at their shops in Dubai, and books can be sold back to either store.

As part of its Let's Read Campaign, the Dar Al Ataa charity organisation holds monthly second-hand book sales in Al Qurum Complex. For details on book sales and volunteer work, contact Jane Jaffer on 99 314 230.

Al Batra Bookshop Al Wadi Commercial Centre, 968 24 563 662, *albatra.com*
Al Wadi Commercial Centre 968 24 564 782
Borders Qurum City Centre, 968 24 470 489, *bordersstores.com.*

Carrefour Muscat City Centre, 968 80 073 232, *carrefouroman.com*
LuLu Hypermarket 968 24 504 504, *luluhypermarket.com*
Montblanc Muscat City Centre, 968 24 558 079, *rivoligroup.com*
Office Supplies Co 968 24 829 400, *officesuppliesllc.com*
Qurum City Centre Nr Muscat International School, 968 24 470 700, *qurumcitycentre.com*
SABCO Commercial Centre 968 24 566 701, *sabcogroup.com*
Sultan Center Al Harthy Complex Building 826, Way 511, 968 24 567 666, *sultan-center.com*

Stationery

Whether you're looking for a pencil sharpener or professional standard plotting paper, there are stationery shops all over the city. Hypermarkets like Carrefour and LuLu carry all the basics, including huge ranges of back-to-school supplies. While they may be cheap, you might find that to get the best deals you have to buy a pack of 20 identical pencil sharpeners or banded packs of pencils. Of course if you're looking for quality not quantity, head for Mont Blanc where you can offload hundreds of rials on a single pen.

Camera Equipment

Those who enjoy photography, whether amateur or pro, will find a reasonable selection of cameras in Muscat. You may not find all of a brand's models in the range, but you'll have a fair bit of choice and prices are comparable to what you pay in duty free stores. For the average holiday snapper there are plenty of choices. Most electronics shops sell a variety of film and digital point-and-shoot cameras. Sales staff are generally helpful and patient with even the greatest of technophobes. There is never any harm in trying to haggle over the price a little – you never know, it might just work, and you could get a reduced price or an extra or two thrown in for good measure. Most department stores also usually have some kind of photography section, with cameras from the likes of Nikon, Pentax, Olympus and Samsung.

Professional photographers or serious hobbyists should check out Salam Stores in Qurum. They carry medium format cameras (Bronica and Sigma), lenses and camera accessories, like Manfrotto tripods. They will also help you set up your darkroom, supply you with a Durst enlarger and train you in its use. Foto Magic is a reliable outlet for buying and developing film and downloading images from digital cameras, and has a branch in most shopping areas. You can also ask them to print pictures on greeting cards, mugs or T-shirts if you're looking for a personalised gift for someone.

Capital Store Al Qurum Complex, 968 99 811 050,
csoman.om
Centrepoint Madinat As Sultan Qaboos St,
968 96 473 101, *centrepointstores.com*
Khimji's Megastore 968 24 560 419, *khimjiblog.kr.om*
Markaz Al Bahja Al Seeb St, 968 24 540 200,
albahja.com
OHI Electronics Al Araimi Complex, 968 24 565 490,
ohielec.com
Photocentre Nr Qurum Commercial Centre,
968 24 565 305, *photocent.com*
SABCO Commercial Centre 968 24 566 701,
sabcogroup.com
Shah Nagardas Manji & Co 968 24 702 772,
shahnagardas.com
Zakher Mall Nr Radisson Hotel, Muscat,
968 24 489 884, *zakhermall.com*

Car Accessories

Cars are definitely one of the best buys in Oman, with
prices usually much lower than in your home country.
This could be your only chance to drive a really
luxurious petrol guzzler, rather than something more
practical. It is almost de rigeur to own a four-wheel
drive, even if the closest you get to off-roading is
parking on the pavement.

Wherever there are cars, there will be accessories
for them. Hypermarkets like Carrefour sell ranges that
include steering wheel covers, rubber mats, sheep skin
seat covers and even little vacuum cleaners that you
can plug into the cigarette lighter. The other outlets
listed here are the places to go if you need tyres, spare
parts, or if you want to transform your car to look like
something from MTV's Pimp My Ride.

Car Care Centre 968 99 337 786
Carrefour Muscat City Centre, 968 80 073 232,
carrefouroman.com
Hisin Majees Trading 968 24 811 442
Opal Marketing & Industry Nr Holiday Inn Hotel,
Muscat, 968 24 478 568, *precisiontunegcc.com*
Sadween Trading Nr Friday Market, 968 24 837 570

Carpets

Weaving is one of Oman's major handicrafts and
the skills have been passed down through the
generations. Camel and goat hair, sheep wool and
cotton are all used in weaving, either in their natural
state or coloured with plant dyes or murex shells.
Designs are usually simple stripes and occasionally
geometric figures.

Carpet shopping can be a minefield for those who
know little about it, so it's a good idea to read up on

it first and shop around to get an idea of designs and
cost. The price reflects the quality of the carpet, with
silk being more expensive than wool or cotton. There's
also a significant price difference between hand-made
and machine-made carpets – hand-made carpets will
have some imperfections in the design and weaving, yet
are usually more expensive. The more knots per
square inch, the better the quality of the carpet and
the higher the price.

Carpets from Turkey, Iran, Pakistan, Central Asia
and China are relatively easy to find in Muscat. It
seems that all of the shopping centres in the capital
have at least one carpet shop, which is very good
news for those who like their retail therapy in an
air-conditioned environment, and many of them sell
authentic antique carpets from Iran or Afghanistan
and will provide you with a certificate stating its age
and value. Unfortunately, it's not that easy to find
good quality imported carpets in other areas of Oman,
although Salalah and Nizwa may have opened a few
more options.

You can find local carpets in the Omani National
Heritage Gallery in Shatti Al Qurum, or you can buy
them directly from the weavers on the long, winding
road to Jebel Shams. A 1.5m x 2.5m sheep's wool rug
will cost around RO.30. Bargaining is expected and
you'll disappoint the seller if you don't even try. The
seller will elaborately roll out countless carpets for
you to view, but don't let this make you feel obliged
to buy. Once you've reach an agreed price though,
you're committed. Some shops will let their regular
customers take a carpet home for a few days to 'try it
out' with your furniture.

Carpets

Carpet Bazaar Jawharat A'Shati & Oasis By The Sea Commercial Complex, 968 24 696 142
Gulf Shell Trading Al Araimi Complex, 968 24 571 630
Oriental Carpets & Handicrafts Al Wadi Commercial Centre, 968 24 564 786
Persian Carpets Al Wadi Commercial Centre, 968 24 562 139

Computers

You'll find plenty of computer shops with knowledgeable staff and stock up to the ceilings in Muscat. The best of these are in Al Wadi Centre in Qurum, Computer Street in Ruwi and Carrefour in Qurum City Centre. You'll also find Emax at Muscat City Centre, which is fairly cheap, and there are authorised dealers for Apple in Al Harthy Complex and Dell Computers on the Al Khuwair slip road.

Prices aren't bad, but you must bargain before agreeing on a price. You can also strike a deal where a vendor will get you a PC, printer, scanner, desk and chair (depending, of course, on what you want), bring it all round and install it for you. Getting computers fixed is easy and usually cheap, but you may get frustrated at deadlines that aren't met.

Outside of Muscat you won't find much in terms of technology and may have to wait a long time for anything you've ordered. The Omani government has been clamping down on the sale of pirated software since it became a member of the World Trade Organisation. However, you can still find copies of PC and Playstation games in small shops in Ruwi and Qurum for as little as RO.1 if you're happy to turn a blind eye.

Carrefour Muscat City Centre, 968 80 073 232, *carrefouroman.com*
Computer Xpress 968 24 835 631
Faisal Al Alawi Trading Computer St, 968 24 702 812
Modern Electronic House SABCO Commercial Centre, 968 24 565 848

Eyewear

Life in Oman is definitely easier with a pair of sunglasses. The strength of the sun, the days at the beach and the long drives mean you're going to want to protect your eyes. All kinds of sunglasses are available in the malls, in Ruwi and in the souk, from designer eyewear to rip-offs and everything in between. Prices range from a few rials to many hundreds but as competition is fierce you can often find a good bargain in designer shades. Make sure they offer 100% UVA and UVB protection and are large and dark enough to protect your eyes from the sun's glare.

Polarised lenses are particularly good if you spend a lot of time on the water. Shopping centres have opticians that will make prescription glasses, sunglasses and contact lenses (hard, soft, gas permeable and thoric). They usually offer free eye tests if you order from them. Disposable contact lenses and coloured contact lenses are readily available. You'll find lens cleaning solutions at opticians and pharmacies.

Al Ghazal Opticians SABCO Commercial Centre, 968 24 563 546
Al Said Optics Al Qurum Complex, 968 24 566 272
Finland Eye Center Qurum Garden Blg, 968 24 564 488, *finlandeyecenter.com*
Grand Optics Muscat City Centre, 968 24 558 890, *grandoptics.com*
Hassan Opticals Co Al Harthy Complex, 968 24 565 499
Muscat Eye Laser Center House 877, Way 3013, Sarooj St, 968 24 691 414, *muscateye.com*
Oman Opticals 968 23 293 714
Ridwan Al Qurum Complex, 968 24 564 027
Yateem Optician Al Khamis Plaza, 968 24 563 716, *yateemgroup.com*

Fashion

Your fashion options in Muscat have expanded substantially over the last few years. This is largely thanks to the new Qurum City Centre, home of H&M, Monsoon and Next, and Muscat City Centre. This sizeable mall is located quite far out of town past Seeb Airport, but with its array of shops that you may well recognise from home – Mango, Fat Face, Gap, Forever 21, and Zara, to name a few – it's worth the trip. Stores here receive new stock every four to six months.

Markaz Al Bahja, past City Centre, has a Marks & Spencer and a few smaller shops. Some places will do alterations if your items don't quite fit. The Sultan Center has a small range of sportswear, and hypermarkets like LuLu and Carrefour also have clothing sections where you can pick up some basics for a reasonable price.

The Qurum shopping area contains five shopping centres and numerous shops within walking distance of each other. The Centrepoint stocks fashions for all ages and sizes and has a reasonably-priced accessories department. The store also runs frequent sales, check inside for the latest promotions.

There isn't a wide range of designer boutiques for women although men have been able to shop at places like Tahani, Cerutti, and Moustache in SABCO for some time. Moustach sells a variety of designer gear including Armani Jeans and Dolce & Gabbana. Jazz now caters for ladies and stocks Miss Sixty, Cerutti and Indian Rose.

Textiles from the souk

Sana Stores and Ruwi High Street are good places to pick up textiles, saris and salwarkameez, but for something different call Taalali in Mutrah Souk for an appointment. Florence Rusconi, a French designer, reworks traditional Omani clothes into new items. Accessories are also available.

Shoes & Clothing Sizes

Figuring out your size isn't rocket science – it just helps to do a bit of pre-planning. Firstly, check the label in an item; you'll often find international sizes printed on them. Secondly, check with the store; it will usually have a conversion chart either on display or available to use. Otherwise, you can remember that a UK size is always two sizes higher than a US size (so a UK 10 is a US 6). To convert European sizes into US sizes, subtract 32 (so a European 38 is actually a US 6). Therefore, you obviously subtract 28 to convert roughly from European sizes to UK sizes.

Shoes can be trickier; for example, a woman's UK 6 is a European 39 and a US 8.5. A man's UK 10 is a European 44 and a US 10.5. If in doubt, ask an assistant for help, but you'll soon start remembering your vital numbers across the various international incarnations.

You could also enlist the services of a tailor. Workmanship can vary but generally the quality is very high for the amount you pay. If you take along your fabric and a photo, drawing or sample of what you want, a tailor will copy it. Good sales are generally held during Ramadan and the Eid holidays, but also in January and September/October when shops are clearing old stock. Discounts of 70% are not uncommon, but be prepared to sort through a rack of odd sizes and last season's styles.

Lingerie

Lingerie is big business in the Middle East and you might be surprised by what's lurking under some of those conservative clothes. A browse around a specialist lingerie shop, like Calvin Klein, La Senza and Nayomi (in City Centre) and High Lady in Al Wadi Centre, can be eye opening.

If you're looking for something a bit more everyday and functional, you can try old favourites Next, Marks & Spencer or Bhs, all of which have a good cotton range to suit the climate. Prices can be inflated compared to in the UK, but you could always wait for the sales and stock up then. Carrefour and LuLu Hypermarkets have good lingerie sections, as does Splash (in Muscat City Centre) and Sana Fashions in Wadi Kabir. You'll find plenty of affordable underwear and nightwear at the Mutrah Souk and Ruwi High Street, if you're not particular about colours or cotton content.

Bhs Nr SABCO Centre, 968 24 562 456, *alshaya.com*
Carrefour Muscat City Centre, 968 80 073 232, *carrefouroman.com*
Inner Lines Muscat City Centre, 968 24 558 228
Mango Muscat City Centre, 968 24 558 244
Marks & Spencer Muscat City Centre, 968 24 558 455, *marksandspencerme.com*
Next Muscat City Centre, 968 24 558 801
Sana Fashions Nr Indian School, 968 24 810 289
Splash Muscat City Centre, 968 96 473 114, *splashfashions.com*

Shoes

From knee-high boots to plastic flip-flops, you'll be able to find the shoes you need in Muscat, although the range is not quite as good in other parts of Oman. Most sizes are available; just be sure to specify to the sales assistant whether you mean the UK or US size. Sports stores are best for trainers and running shoes, as staff will be able to advise you on fit and support. Shoe City, which has branches in the Centrepoint and Muscat City Centre, has a wide range of shoes for the whole family. You'll find good quality leather shoes in various outlets in Muscat and Qurum City Centre and in World of Shoes in the Al Khamis Plaza.

The Athlete's Foot Al Araimi Complex, 968 24 567 438, *theathletesfoot.com*
Bench Muscat City Centre, 968 24 558 048, *benchtm.com*
Bhs Nr SABCO Centre, 968 24 562 456, *alshaya.com*
Centrepoint Madinat As Sultan Qaboos St, 968 96 473 101, *centrepointstores.com*

Charles & Keith Muscat City Centre, 968 24 558 011, *charleskeith.com*
Clarks Al Khamis Plaza, 968 24 560 990
Giordano Muscat City Centre, 968 24 558 139
Hang Ten Muscat City Centre, 968 24 558 870
Jazz Jawharat A' Shati Commercial Complex, 968 24 695 965
Khimji Ramdas 968 24 795 901, *khimjiblog.kr.om*
Mango Muscat City Centre, 968 24 558 244
Marks & Spencer Muscat City Centre, 968 24 558 455, *marksandspencerme.com*
Milano Muscat City Centre, 968 24 558 834, *alshaya.com*
Monsoon Muscat City Centre, 968 27 455 8902
Moustache Jawharat A' Shati Commercial Complex, 968 24 693 392
Next Muscat City Centre, 968 24 558 801
Nine West SABCO Commercial Centre, 968 24 561 872
Promod Muscat City Centre, 968 24 558 240
Sana Fashions Nr Indian School, 968 24 810 289
Shoe Mart Muscat City Centre, 968 96 473 115
Splash Centrepoint, 968 96 473 101, *splashfashions.com*
Spring Muscat City Centre, 968 24 558 049
World Shoes Al Khamis Plaza, 968 24 565 259

Food

Oman has a good range of supermarkets and grocery shops that cater to its multinational population. Although there are some speciality items that you won't find, most things are available somewhere if you look hard enough or ask your friends. Prices vary considerably, even among supermarkets. Imported items are sometimes double what they would cost in their country of origin, and locally made equivalents are much cheaper and just as good. Carrefour (Qurum City Centre and Muscat City Centre), the Sultan Center, LuLu Hypermarket and Al Fair are the biggest and most popular supermarkets. The smaller ones, like Pic n Save and Family Supermarket, might not be as well laid out, but they do carry a wide range of goods that are sometimes even cheaper than you'll find in the hypermarkets.

During Ramadan, mountains of food are on sale, seemingly aimed at feeding large families - products are bundled up in bulk with sticky tape and sold for a rial so it's a good time to stock up on non-perishables. Carrefour, the well-known French hypermarket, sells everything from laptops and French cheeses to shoes and stationery. It has an excellent selection of fresh fruits, vegetables, meats and seafood and a good bakery where croissants, baguettes, European-style bread, cakes, and Arabic and Indian sweets are made on the premises. It also stocks a small section of Filipino and Indian foods.

Al Fair supermarket, with branches in Qurum, Madinat Al Sultan Qaboos, and Al Sarooj, is favoured by expats for its British, European and Asian foods. It's the only supermarket that sells frozen pork and pork products like paté, prosciutto, salami and ham. Al Fair also has a 'Monday Market' when special items are on sale. The LuLu Hypermarket in Al Ghubrah has a good fresh produce section selling fresh Thai herbs and grated coconut.

There are plenty of local convenience stores in residential areas, some of which have a small produce section. Petrol stations have also entered the market with their own forecourt shops – these little shops sell necessities from quick, hot snacks to washing powder, and some are open 24 hours a day. Look out for Select shops at Shell stations, and Souk shops at Al Maha.

Fruit & Vegetables

A lot of fresh fruits, vegetables and herbs are used in Middle Eastern cuisine, and produce coming from this region can be amazingly cheap. A box of Jordanian oranges, for example, costs as little as one rial – a bonus for people who love freshly squeezed orange juice. Excluding imported fresh produce, fruits and vegetables are, in general, very affordable, especially if bought from places like the fruit and vegetable markets in Wadi Kabir in Ruwi, Mutrah and Al Mawaleh on the road to Nizwa.

Fish

If you get to the Mutrah fish souk early in the morning you'll find the freshest catches straight off the boat. A browse among the stalls reveals an amazing variety

Fresh fish at the fish souk

of fish and seafood, some still squirming or struggling to get out of the baskets. Fishermen in the Azaiba beach area may also sell their daily catch to you. The larger supermarkets carry fresh seafood and fish (whole, filleted or in steaks), in slightly less-smelly surroundings.

Vegetarians

While vegetarians are certainly not as well catered for as in western countries, you shouldn't have too much difficulty finding suitable products in Oman to live off. Fresh and imported fruits and vegetables are widely available and are cheap, especially in the open-air markets around the towns. Spices and nuts imported from all over the world are sold by the scoop in large supermarkets. Al Fair also carries some soya-based products, but the choice is certainly more limited than you'll be used to.

Carrefour Muscat City Centre, 968 80 073 232, *carrefouroman.com*
LuLu Hypermarket 968 24 504 504, *luluhypermarket.com*
Markaz Al Bahja Al Seeb St, 968 24 540 200, *albahja.com*
Safeer Supermarket 968 24 479 211
Al Fair Supermark Al Sarooj Plaza, 968 24 607 075, *spinneys.com*
Sultan Center Al Harthy Complex Building 826, Way 511, 968 24 567 666, *sultan-center.com*

Furniture

It is possible to furnish a house quite cheaply in Oman although you may have trouble finding what you want if your tastes run to the minimalist or modern. A great new addition is Gecko in Jawaharat A'Shati mall, where you'll find pieces imported from Bali, in addition to gorgeous fabrics from Designer's Guild and the ever-popular Fatboy beanbags in a range of sizes and styles.

On the Al Khuwair service road, parallel to Sultan Qaboos Street, you'll find vast stores selling what Europeans call 'Arabic style' furniture (confusingly, Arabs call it 'European style'). Think overwhelming statuesque horses, mirrors looming precariously over you from your headboard and bright sofas with silver lions' claw legs. You can try and dilute the gaudiness somewhat by ordering them in different colours or sizes to those on display in the showroom. These shops also stock curtains and orthopaedic mattresses. Home Centre, Centrepoint and IDdesign, a Danish shop in Markaz Al Bahja that sells Scandinavian furniture, are all popular. These large stores generally have good sales during Ramadan and around autumn time especially during September.

While Muscat doesn't have its own IKEA yet, there is a huge store in Dubai and you'll be amazed at how much flat-pack furniture you can fit into one carload. There are also some excellent shops selling wooden furniture but don't be taken in by the 'antiques' label; most of the items here are mass-produced in India and then artificially aged. They still look good though and do the trick in creating a nice home. There are a few furniture stores in Qurum around Al Araimi and SABCO. Marina in the Al Araimi complex in Qurum has a wide range of quality furniture and prices are fixed so you don't have to worry about haggling.

There are many excellent wood and metal working shops in Wadi Kabir in Ruwi that will make any piece of furniture you want for a reasonable price. Ruwi is also a good place to find ready-made furniture and home furnishing shops – try Al Baladiyah Street and Ruwi High Street up to the Al Hamriyah Roundabout. You can reduce prices by bargaining. Stock isn't always unlimited though and things can disappear if you don't buy it there and then, so if you see something you love, grab it while you can. Every area has shops that make curtains and blinds. You'll probably have to wade through books and books of fabric samples, but the end result – custom-made curtains that fit your windows perfectly – will be worth it. While these places will be able to offer some helpful advice, it will make it easier and quicker for you if you go with something specific in mind, and even a picture or photo to show them if possible.

Al Batna Commercial Centre (Antiques) Al Qurum Complex, 968 24 560 284
Furniture Village Markaz Al Bahja, 968 24 481 701, *furniturevillage.net*
Hayat Furniture Nr Oman Intl Bank HQ, 968 24 478 664
Home Centre Muscat City Centre, 968 24 558 063, *landmarkgroupme.com*
IDdesign Markaz Al Bahja, 968 24 545 658, *iddesignoman.com*
International Golden Furniture (IGF) 968 24 600 335, *igfoman.com*
Lifestyle Muscat City Centre, 968 96 473 113, *lifestylegulf.com*
Maathir Al Araimi Complex, 968 24 562 585
Marina Gulf Trading Co. Al Araimi Complex, 968 24 562 221, *marinagulf.com*
Najeeb Alla Baksh (Antiques) Al Qurum Complex, 968 24 564 415
Tahani Antiques Jawharat A'Shati & Oasis By The Sea Commercial Complex, 968 24 601 866
Teejan Furnishing 968 24 489 490
The Shuram Group Jawharat A'Shati & Oasis By The Sea Commercial Complex, 968 24 600 919, *shuramgroup.com*
United Furniture Co 968 99 379 472

Gifts

While there is no shortage of shops in which to buy gifts, there are very few selling good quality greeting cards though Carrefour, Sultan Centre and Al Fair carry a limited range. Birthdays and most holidays (Christmas, Easter, Mothers' Day) are catered for and you can surprise friends back home with special Eid cards. The offerings here may be a little soppy or sentimental so, if you're after a wider range or a humorous card, try Hallmark in Muscat Grand Mall. For some witty cards imported from New York, check out the stand outside Totemin Jawharat A'Shati Complex. Cards with Omani themes, created by local artists, can be found in museum gift shops and at Murtada AK Trading in Mutrah Souk. Apart from costing less, they are good quality and make original alternatives to standard greeting cards. While postcards can cost as little as 100 baisas, greeting cards and wrapping paper are more expensive.

Carrefour Muscat City Centre, 968 80 073 232, *carrefouroman.com*
Marks & Spencer Muscat City Centre, 968 24 558 455, *marksandspencerme.com*
Murtada AK Trading Mutrah Souk, 968 24 711 632
Sultan Center Al Harthy Complex Building 826, Way 511, 968 24 567 666, *sultan-center.com*

Home Appliances

Muscat's shops stock a reasonable selection of electronics and home appliances, from well-known brands to knock-offs. Prices are competitive and can be brought down even further by bargaining. Widescreen televisions and home theatres are bargains compared to back home, although it's still smart to shop around. The branches of Carrefour in Muscat City Centre and Qurum City Centre have a wide range of inexpensive items, which is great for people furnishing a house without a company allowance, but prices here are fixed. Larger appliances such as washing machines and fridges are delivered and installed free of charge and a 12 month warranty is given on most items. Ruwi High Street is good for browsing and comparing prices as all the showrooms are here. If you don't see what you're looking for, ask, as it may be hidden in the back room.

If you live in Salalah you can usually find good deals on appliances in town, so there's no need to go all the way to Muscat. Warranties, after-sales service, delivery and installation should all be discussed before you buy. If you're intending to take anything overseas with you, confirm its compatibility with the power supply. Check notice boards or classifieds for second-hand items. Expats who are leaving often sell things at

reasonable prices in order to clear them quickly. This is especially good if you're looking for large white goods and appliances or air conditioners. You can also check out the range of items for sale on muscatads.com and oman.dubizzle.com.

Capital Store SABCO Commercial Centre, 968 99 811 969, *csoman.com*
Carrefour Muscat City Centre, 968 80 073 232, *carrefouroman.com*
LuLu Hypermarket 968 24 504 504, *luluhypermarket.com*
Muscat Electronics Co 968 24 796 591, *muscatelectronics.com*
OHI Electronics Al Araimi Complex, 968 24 565 490, *ohielec.com*
Sony Al Araimi Complex, 968 24 564 485, *sony-mea.com*

Handbags

Local ladies love their accessories – the humble handbag has become a major status symbol, especially since it is often the only item visible when dressed in the long black abaya. As a result, you can get some amazing creations (both in terms of craftsmanship and price) at various exclusive boutiques around town, plus stores such as Zara, Forever 21 and Accessorize. For the less label conscious, handbags are sold in most fashion, luggage and accessories shops, and even in supermarkets like Carrefour – so keep your eyes peeled for fabulous bags next time you are doing your weekly grocery shopping. Capital Store also sells a range of Givenchy handbags.

Al Araimi Complex Al Nahdah St, 968 24 566 557, *alaraimicomplex.com*
Capital Store 968 23 297 910, *csoman.om*
Carrefour Muscat City Centre, 968 80 073 232, *carrefouroman.com*
Centrepoint Madinat As Sultan Qaboos St, 968 96 473 101, *centrepointstores.com*
Lifestyle Muscat City Centre, 968 96 473 113, *lifestylegulf.com*
Mango Muscat City Centre, 968 24 558 244
Markaz Al Bahja Al Seeb St, 968 24 540 200, *albahja.com*
Marks & Spencer Muscat City Centre, 968 24 558 455, *marksandspencerme.com*
Monsoon Muscat City Centre, 968 27 455 8902
Next Muscat City Centre, 968 24 558 801
Qurum City Centre Nr Muscat International School, 968 24 470 700, *qurumcitycentre.com*
SABCO Commercial Centre 968 24 566 701, *sabcogroup.com*

Hardware & DIY

Honda Street in Ruwi is a veritable paradise for DIY enthusiasts. It's one long street of nothing much else except hardware, tools, paints and construction materials, from washers to entire bathroom suites in marble, it's all here on one street. Parking is always a problem, however, so it's best to arrive early in the morning. Carrefour, Sultan Center, Safeer and LuLu Hypermarket also have some good DIY equipment, but the smaller shops are sometimes better because then you can negotiate the price. The shops often have counters directly inside at the door, so you have to ask for what you want rather than browse around for it yourself. If you are not inclined to put up your own shelves, enquire at the shops and someone will come round and do it for a couple of rials. It's also worth pointing out that DIY furniture bought in Home Centre is not DIY at all. It is assembled in your home for free to save you the bother.

Carrefour Muscat City Centre, 968 80 073 232, *carrefouroman.com*
LuLu Hypermarket 968 23 218 400, *luluhypermarket.com*
Safeer Hypermarket Nr Azaiba Hotel, As Sultan Qaboos St
Souk Al Khuwair 23rd July St
Sultan Center Al Harthy Complex Building 826, Way 511, 968 24 567 666, *sultan-center.com*

Health Food & Special Dietary Requirements

While you won't find quite the same range of organic, bio and health foods that you'll find in your home country, things are improving in Oman. Al Fair has some non-dairy, low fat, low calorie products but these are usually mixed in with the regular items. The Sultan Center also has a very limited range in its dietetic section. GNC in Muscat City Centre stocks a comprehensive range of nutritional supplements and alternative remedies. Muscat Pharmacy, and The Health Store in the Al Qurum Complex, also stock nutritional supplements, and gym enthusiasts who swear by protein and food supplements should check out Sport One for the whey fill. The supermarkets also have a rather limited selection of multivitamins for kids and adults, but it's a good idea to check the sell-by dates.

Al Fair Al Qurum Complex, 968 24 561 912
General Nutrition Centre (GNC) Muscat City Centre, 968 24 558 222, *gnc.com.sa*
Muscat Pharmacy & Stores 968 24 814 501, *muscatpharmacy.net*

Jewellery & Watches

Silver

Omani silverwork has historically been held in such high regard in Gulf countries that many 'antique' pieces of silver today are labelled Omani to enhance their value and reputation. Silver has been used not only to make necklaces, anklets, rings, bracelets and other forms of wedding jewellery, but also to decorate weapons and create everyday objects such as coffee pots, pipes, thorn-picks and ear-cleaners. Each region in Oman has its distinctive designs.

Silver Currency

Maria Theresa (1717-1780) was a Hapsburg by birth and the wife and Empress of the Holy Roman Emperor Francis I. The Maria Theresa thaler made its debut in 1751 at a time when Omani traders were desperately in need of an internationally acceptable and reliable currency. They liked the texture of the coin and its consistent silver content so they adopted it. Craftsmen used the thalers to make intricate pieces of silver jewellery. When Oman's own currency was introduced in 1970 the need for thalers died out.

A short walk around the souks of Muscat and the interior will reveal a variety of dusty, black looking silver that will shine up nicely with a bit of polish. There are small boxes used to hold kohl, and huge earrings which might terrify you on first sight, but which are actually hooked over the top of the ears and not for pierced ears. A lot of this is wedding jewellery and although it might look ancient, it's unlikely to be very old. Traditionally, a woman's wedding jewellery was melted down and sold or refashioned on her death, but inherited pieces are not uncommon. Bedouin women may also sell their silver jewellery as Eid approaches in order to have some cash for celebrations; the souk in Sinaw is a good source. You may also see Maria Theresa dollars (or thalers) which were the legal currency in Oman until the 1960s. Take your time to browse and you can dig up some real treasures.

Watches

As with all jewellery, watches are cheaper here than in Europe. Supermarkets stock cheap to medium-priced watches, while dedicated watch showrooms stock pieces with prices that range from average to outlandish.

Al Felaij Jewellers Muscat City Centre, 968 24 558 518
Al Qurum Jewellers SABCO Commercial Centre, 968 24 562 558

Alukkas Jewellery Muscat City Centre, 968 24 558 034, *alukkas.com*

Damas 968 24 788 946, *damasjewel.com*

Hamdam Hasan Swaid Al Jimi SABCO Commercial Centre, 968 24 565 167

Himat Jewellers Muscat City Centre, 968 24 558 088, *himatjewellers.com*

Jewellery Corner SABCO Commercial Centre, 968 24 563 946

Khimji's Watches Al Ufouq Bldg, Way 3036, Shatti Al Qurum, 968 24 699 173, *khimjiblog.kr.om*

Mouawad Opera Galleria, East Arcade, Ministry of Foreign Affairs St., 968 22 027 777, *mouawad.com*

Muscat Watch Centre SABCO Commercial Centre, 968 24 562 459

Ruwi Jewellers Al Khamis Plaza, 968 24 565 977

Tiffany & Co. Jawahir Oman, 968 24 563 239, *tiffany.com*

Watch This Space

Those who love the finer things in life will be delighted to find that Muscat is home to a very upmarket watch and jewellery emporium – Khimji's Watches (khimjiblog. kr.om) showroom in Shatti Al Qurum. The showroom's brands include Rolex, Cartier, Chopard, Piaget, Mikimoto, Girard-Perregaux, Bell & Ross, Frederique Constant, Oris, Caran d'Ache and Tudor, with dedicated zones for the likes of Rolex and Chopard, where even the decor matches the brands' identities. Opening hours are Saturday to Thursday, 9am to 1pm and 4.30pm to 9pm. Call 800 75 000 for more information.

Kids' Items

You won't have any trouble shopping for children's clothes in Muscat. From the moment your baby is born right up until they are too cool for kids' clothes, there is a huge range available. The presence of some popular stores from your home country will be comforting, such as Marks & Spencer, H&M, Pumpkin Patch and Next, and you'll be able to kit your kids out in exactly the same clothes their friends back home are wearing (although maybe with a slight time delay). However, clothes in these outlets are often quite pricey compared to what you'd pay at home. If you're looking for cheap, cheerful clothing that you don't mind getting muddy or covered in paint, you'll find some bargains at Carrefour, Sana Fashions or LuLu Hypermarket. While some of the stock may seem a bit garish at first glance, a good rummage often yields some great results and it is not unknown to make brand-name discoveries. If you are stocking up on clothes for a new baby, head for Mothercare, Adams and Babyshop, where you'll find most of the things you'll need.

Muscat is a child-friendly city, and you'll find plenty of shops selling toys for your little angels. There is something for everyone, from hi-tech baby learning laptops to cheap plastic tat (which your kids will probably prefer, despite your best intentions). Remember, though, that not all toys conform to the correct international safety standards. This means that you will need to make a judgement call and ensure your kids only play with the dodgy toys under constant supervision.

Modern shopping facilities

Toys 'R' Us and Babyshop in Muscat City Centre carry everything from dolls to Lego. The supermarkets also stock good ranges of toys and Ruwi High Street is excellent for lower priced items. Mothercare, Babyshop and Adams are where to head if you're looking for soft toys suitable for newborns and infants. If you're looking for second-hand items like prams, cots and large toys, keep an eye on supermarket notice boards. Some churches and societies lend out baby equipment too, so ask around or contact Muscat Mums (muscatmums.com).

Adams Muscat City Centre, 968 24 558 914, *adams.co.uk*
Babyshop Muscat City Centre, 968 96 473 113, *babyshopstores.com*
Bhs Nr SABCO Centre, 968 24 562 456, *alshaya.com*
Carrefour Muscat City Centre, 968 80 073 232, *carrefouroman.com*
Hang Ten Muscat City Centre, 968 24 558 870
LuLu Hypermarket 968 24 504 504, *luluhypermarket.com*
Marks & Spencer Muscat City Centre, 968 24 558 455, *marksandspencerme.com*
Monsoon Muscat City Centre, 968 27 455 8902
Mothercare Nr SABCO Centre, 968 24 562 456, *mothercare.com*
Next Muscat City Centre, 968 24 558 801
Pumpkin Patch Muscat City Centre, 968 24 558 085, *pumpkinpatch.co.uk*
Safeer Hypermarket Nr Azaiba Hotel, As Sultan Qaboos St
Sana Fashions Nr Indian School, 968 24 810 289

Luggage & Leather

There's nothing like a full range of Louis Vuitton luggage to show off in airports, and since you'll probably be travelling back home once or twice a year, you may as well do it in style. Head for Capital Stores, Salam Stores, Salman Stores or Khimji's Luxury & Lifestyle for a range of luxury luggage at luxury prices. If you'd rather spend your money on holidays than hand luggage, there's a lane off Ruwi High Street that specialises in budget suitcases and bags in every colour and size. Somehow word of what you're looking for travels as you walk along the street, so by the time you reach the end traders will be offering you a "small black air cabin bag, madam?" LuLu Hypermarket also sells some suitcases and laptop bags. Carrefour and the Sultan Center have functional bags and suitcases, similar to those you'd find in the souk. Copies of designer handbags can be found in some shops, and these make good presents, although some are of better quality than others. If you're looking for a leather jacket, try men's clothing stores in Al Qurum and City Centre.

Maternity Wear

Fashion conscious mums-to-be won't find a huge choice of maternity clothing in Oman, although a few of the big name stores do have a limited selection. And if Marks & Spencer, Max and H&M don't deliver the goods in terms of flair and individual style, you could always ask a tailor to whip up something for you.

Marks & Spencer Muscat City Centre, 968 24 558 455, *marksandspencerme.com*
Mothercare Nr SABCO Centre, 968 24 562 456, *mothercare.com*
Next Muscat City Centre, 968 24 558 801

Medicine

A shop sign with a green cross, or an image of what looks like a snake wrapped around a glass, indicates a pharmacy (or a chemist), and you'll find them all over Oman.

Many drugs that you need a prescription for in other parts of the world can be bought over the counter without a visit to the doctor. Pharmacists are willing to listen to your symptoms and suggest a remedy, but will not prescribe antibiotics. They can also recommend a cheaper alternative of the same drug.

On your first attempt to buy a medicine that you regularly use in your home country, try taking an empty packet or the package insert with you if possible. The medicine you use may not be available here, but the pharmacist will be able to tell you of a suitable alternative. Remember to check the expiry date of the medicine before buying it.

Pharmacies also carry beauty products, sunscreen, baby care items and perfumes, usually at a set discount. Opening hours are usually from 9am to 1pm and 4pm to 10pm. The following pharmacies are open 24 hours a day: Muscat Pharmacy in Ruwi (24 702 542) and Al Sarooj (24 695 536).

A list of the pharmacies that are on 24 hour duty can be found in daily newspapers, as well as on 90.4 FM radio and the English Evening News on Oman TV. If you need over the counter medication for fever, a sore throat or muscle pain, try the larger supermarkets like Sultan Center and Carrefour.

Mobile Phones

A mobile phone (often known as GSM in Oman) is considered an essential accessory and most shopping areas and malls have at least one outlet selling a range of models. There are also some specialist stores, while all of the major electronic stores such as Jumbo and Emax sell mobiles, as does Carrefour.

Music & Movies

There are no megastores that sell music or movies in Oman, but there are many smaller outlets within shopping centres that stock current releases on CD and DVD. Carrefour and Sultan Center also carry a limited selection. The latest offerings by international musicians are available on CDs and sometimes cassettes. You can also get a reasonable range of Arabic, Bollywood and classical music. New releases tend to sell out quickly. If you can't find what you are looking for, some shop owners might be able to order certain titles for you; or you can order on the internet if you're prepared to pay the postage (try amazon.com). Censorship is alive and well and there may be some films that you can't get in Oman; or films that you can get but that have been cut. If you order online your package will usually be held at the post office until you go there in person to oversee a search. If anything in it is deemed offensive, it will be confiscated or censored. Of course there are the usual pirated DVDs and CDs doing the rounds – just remember that the chances are high that you'll get a poor quality copy.

Musical Instruments

Musicians will find it hard to get what they want in Oman as the number of shops that sell instruments is limited. Musiq Souq (24 562 265) in the Al Wadi Centre, Qurum, has the widest range and they also offer music lessons. Sheet music is not widely available and you might want to order it online or buy some on your next trip abroad. You can also check out Tunes (2447 8775) in Al Khuwair for a range of items.

Outdoor Goods

Oman is a perfect location for outdoor activities, and weekend breaks in a wadi or in the desert are popular. Mild temperatures and low humidity make the winter months of November to March the best time for camping, picnics, diving, kite surfing, climbing and trekking, or just sitting on your porch with a sundowner. Even in the summer, outdoor activities can be pleasant if you go to the mountains or south to Salalah during the 'khareef', or spend an evening on the beach (although the humidity can be taxing), where Omanis enjoy a good evening of chilling out, singing and barbecuing fresh seafood. Most of the supermarkets carry basic outdoor gear such as cooler boxes, barbecue stands, folding chairs and tables, gas stoves, tents and even portable toilets and showers. You can kit yourself out cheaply at Carrefour and Sultan Center while Ruwi High Street and the Mutrah Souk are good for plastic mats. If your idea of enjoying the outdoor life is limited to your patio or garden, take a trip to Centrepoint (formerly City Plaza) or Ruwi High Street for plastic chairs and tables.

Carrefour Muscat City Centre, 968 80 073 232, *carrefouroman.com*
Home Centre Muscat City Centre, 968 24 558 063, *landmarkgroupme.com*
Khimji's Megastore 968 24 560 419, *khimjiblog.kr.om*
LuLu Hypermarket 968 24 504 504, *luluhypermarket.com*

Party Accessories

Large formal or themed parties aren't that common in Oman, where garden parties and casual barbecues are more popular. Supermarkets and stationery shops serve basic party needs and Toys 'R' Us has a good kids' party selection. There are now a number of independent party organisers in Oman who can help you create that special event. Gatherings (gatherings.oman.com or 96 053 280) and Tiara by Yours Truly Events (facebook.com/TIARA by Yours Truly or 97 400 040) can provide all your party supplies and even provide entertainment.

Fancy Dress & Costumes

If you're looking for a fancy dress costume, a good option is Magic Party Costume Hire (98 289 535) in the Bareeq Al Shatti Shopping Mall who can both hire out a range of costumes or custom make outfits to suit your specific requirements. You can also check out Muscat Rentals on facebook.com/muscatrentals or email muscatrentals@gmail.com for more information. Another option is Art Appreciation costume rentals (99 452 940).

Al Fair Nr Al Sarooj Plaza, 968 24 607 075
Carrefour Muscat City Centre, 968 80 073 232, *carrefouroman.com*
LuLu Hypermarket Khaboora, 968 26 805 544, *luluhypermarket.com*
Markaz Al Bahja Al Seeb St, 968 24 540 200, *albahja.com*
Zakher Mall Nr Radisson Hotel, Muscat, 968 24 489 884, *zakhermall.com*

Oud

Oud is highly valued in the Middle East and can fetch astonishing prices. The perfume, worn on the clothes and the skin, is made from the resin of Aloeswood trees and is imported from India, Cambodia and Malaysia. It's usually worn only on important occasions such as Eid, weddings, funerals or to celebrate the birth of a child.

Perfumes & Cosmetics

Ajmal Perfumes Al Araimi Complex, 968 24 562 359, *ajmalperfume.com*
Al Bustan Fragrances Al Harthy Complex, 968 24 798 241, *perfumesofoman.com*
Amouage 968 99 346 811, *amouage.com*
Areej Muscat Muscat City Centre, 968 24 558 752
Capital Store 968 23 297 910, *csoman.om*
MAC Muscat City Centre, 968 24 558 842

Frankincense

Oman is home to the world's finest frankincense. Luban (frankincense in resin form) is often considered a really good purchase as a gift of personal luxury and the fragrance lasts for a long time. Frankincense is one of the essential notes used by Amouage – the Omani perfume house that is often documented as producing some of the world's finest fragrances, not to mention some of its most expensive.

Plants & Flowers

Given Oman's climate, flowers are a real luxury, so they make a really nice present for a special occasion or for someone you love. There's a reasonable selection of florists in Qurum – worth mentioning are Caravan in the Al Harthy Complex and The Flower Shop in SABCO. Bella La Rose in Al Qurum Complex specialises in (you guessed it) roses, and a stunning arrangement of 10 roses sprinkled with gold dust is reasonably priced at around RO.9. Simple bouquets can also be bought at Sultan Center, Al Fair and Carrefour, and cost between RO.2 and RO.7, depending on the number and kind of flowers included. The contact information for all, is listed below. It's usually cheaper, easier and much quicker, however, to send flowers internationally using a popular international website florist than by using a local florist, unfortunately.

Angel Flowers Ramada Muscat, 968 24 605 158
Bella La Rose Al Qurum Complex, 968 24 566 766
Caravans Floral Al Asfoor Plaza, 968 24 566 795
Carrefour Muscat City Centre, 968 80 073 232, *carrefouroman.com*
Carrefour Market *carrefouruae.com*
Green Flowers and Plants Qurum, 968 24 566 462
La Bonita Markaz Al Bahja, 968 24 535 197
Little Shop Of Flowers Jawharat A'Shati & Oasis By The Sea Commercial Complex, 968 24 603 383
Sultan Center Al Harthy Complex Building 826, Way 511, 968 24 567 666, *sultan-center.com*
The Flower Shop SABCO Commercial Centre, 968 24 560 043, *flowers-oman.com*

Second-Hand Items

Churches and charity groups will happily take your unwanted clothes, toys and appliances off your hands as donations for people in need. The Catholic Church in Ruwi operates a charity shop, which is worth a visit for its abundant selection of nearly new clothing and home furnishings.

For second-hand baby equipment contact Muscat Mums (muscatmums.com), who host garage sales and send out a weekly email newsletter with goods advertised. If you want to make a few rials out of stuff you no longer need, you can put a notice on supermarket noticeboards or book a classified ad in one of the local newspapers.

There is a row of shops behind the Polyglot Institute at the Wadi Adai Roundabout that sell second-hand furniture. They offer a delivery and assembly service for large items. House of Prose at Al Wadi Commercial Centre buys and sells used books and if you buy one from them, you can sell it back for the half the original price, provided it's in good condition and you have the receipt. For great deals, you can also check out muscatads.com and oman.dubizzle.com.

Highest Bidder

If you fancy a bit of competition when it comes to shopping (or just like to bag a real bargain) then visit omanbay.com. This website allows sellers to post items as diverse as shoes and boats for buyers to bid on. There are also occasionally properties to rent listed too and it's a great place for picking up cheap books in the '1 Rial Shop' section.

Souvenirs

Shopping for presents in Oman can be tough - because you'll invariably want to buy one of everything you'll want for yourself too. And why not? Traditional Arabic items make great gifts and ornaments. Popular items include the traditional coffee pot and small decorated cups used for drinking kahwa (Arabic coffee), incense burners, wedding chests and traditional Omani khanjars (daggers). Khanjars are almost always sold encased in an elaborately wrought sheath, and are arguably the most recognisable symbol of Oman. If you do buy one though, make sure you pack it in your suitcase rather than your hand luggage.

Other souvenirs that should evoke memories of your time in Arabia are miniature dhows crafted from wood or silver, Quran holders, pottery camels, the traditional hat worn by Omani men (a 'kumah'), clay pots and jars from Bahla, woven milking baskets with leather bottoms, and even ancient rifles.

Heavy silver Omani wedding jewellery is another wonderful souvenir and occasionally you'll find a rare piece or collector's item. Many souvenir items are made in India but sold as the real thing and it's not always easy to spot the fakes. Although the souks generally offer the best buys, it may be difficult to tell how authentic articles are unless you're an expert in Omani crafts.

The Oman Heritage Gallery, near the InterContinental Hotel in Shatti Al Qurum, is a government-run shop that sells genuine craft items. It was established to keep traditional skills such as pottery and weaving alive and the staff will be able to tell you about the various items, where they come from and how long they took to make. The goods are more expensive than in other places, but they are genuine – and you're helping to keep these traditions alive and providing an income for the artisans. If you want a comprehensive reminder of Omani crafts, you can pick up the hefty, highly informative and beautifully illustrated The Craft Heritage of Oman, a two-volume coffee table book that covers everything on the subject.

If you love humorous 'kitsch', you'll have a field day in the souks where you'll find singing camels (choose from the Macarana or Habibi for a more authentic feel), T-shirts featuring the adventures of Tintin and Snowy in Oman, or the famous mosque alarm clock that wakes you up with the call to prayer. Don't leave Oman without one.

SABCO Souk SABCO Commercial Centre, 968 24 566 701
Silver World Mutrah Souk, 968 24 714 373

Traditional items make good souvenirs

Sports Goods

Most shopping centres have sports shops that stock a good range of sports apparel and equipment. You'll easily find racquets, balls and exercise equipment, although prices may be a little steeper than you would like. Diving equipment is easy to track down; there are shops at the Oman Dive Center near Qantab and at ScubaTec in the Al Wadi Centre.

Adidas Muscat City Centre, 968 24 558 900, *adidas.com*
Magic Cup Sports 968 24 786 688
Marina Bandar Al Rowdha 968 24 737 288, *marinaoman.net*
Markaz Al Bahja Al Seeb St, 968 24 540 200, *albahja.com*
Muscat Sports Al Araimi Complex, 968 24 564 364, *mctsports.com*
Oman Dive Center Nr Qantab R/A, Al Jissah St, 968 24 824 240, *extradivers-worldwide.com*
Sports For All SABCO Commercial Centre, 968 24 560 086
Sun & Sand Sports Muscat City Centre, 968 24 558 355, *sunandsandsports.com*
Supa Sportsman Nr German Embassy, 968 24 833 192, *supasportsman.com*

Textiles & Haberdashery

There's an excellent array of textiles shops in Oman; you can buy just about any fabric in just about any colour you can think of, although as we mentioned earlier in this chapter, pure cotton can be difficult to find as it's not that popular among Arab customers as silk is. Even the smallest towns in Oman have fabric shops selling different materials by the yard, and shop assistants are only to willing to advise you on how much fabric you will need for the garment that you have in mind. In Muscat, you'll find textile shops in all of the major malls and on Ruwi High Street. In Ruwi, you can buy cheap saris that can make for interesting and innovative curtains and tablecloths. The Al Khamis Plaza in Qurum has two stores, Reise Oman and InStyle, that stock an enormous range of silk and linen, and a basement store that sells printed Indian cushions and bedspreads at reasonable prices. Abu Hani sells a range of printed cotton for making bedding and quilts.

Ahmed Abdul Rahman Traders 968 24 787 756
InStyle Al Khamis Plaza, 968 24 563 242
Mehdi Store 968 24 814 200
Mutrah Tailoring House 968 24 701 960
Raymond Shop 968 24 561 142
Reise Oman Al Khamis Plaza, 968 24 571 609

Tailoring

In Europe, having an outfit made to order is a luxury few can afford, but in Oman it's cheap and easy. The numerous fabric shops sell a vibrant range of material and there are many tailors to choose from. Generally, the best way to find a good one is through word of mouth recommendations.

In Muscat, most of the tailors are located in little shops in the back streets of Ruwi, the Mutrah Souk, or in the Al Wadi Centre or Al Khuwair Souk. The process is an interesting one and may test your patience in the beginning. The best results come from bringing a picture or an original garment for the tailor to copy, or the shop might have a few magazines for you to browse through.

Sometimes the language barrier can be problematic, but that's where the power of pictures comes in useful. When trying a tailor for the first time, order just one garment so you can check the quality of the work. Confirm the price before you leave the shop, and make sure you're clear about what the price includes (such as lining, zips or buttons) – and feel free to negotiate.

It's essential that you always try the garment on when you pick it up and before you leave, so that you can have alterations made if necessary. In this case, alterations are usually free of charge.

Wedding Items

While it is not common for expats to get married in Oman, if you decide to do so you should be able to find whatever items you need to plan the perfect day. However to get a little more variety, it might be worth travelling to Dubai in the UAE for a better selection. For dresses, head to Jumeira Road in the older part of Dubai in the Jumeira neighbourhood where you'll find several bridal stores including The Bridal Room (04 344 6076) and Frost.

For the best range of designer gowns head to Saks Fifth Avenue's bridal department in the BurJuman centre of Dubai. This stocks the latest off-the-peg designer gowns by Vera Wang and Reem Acra. There are also several specialist bridal designers with workshops in Dubai, but Arushi (04 344 4103) is renowned as one of the best. You can select the fabric yourself or it can be selected during the first meeting with the designer. Gowns take around one month to make, but Arushi is so popular, there is often a waiting list. Bridal accessories and shoes are available at Saks Fifth Avenue.

For the groom, there are several shops, again in Dubai, where formal wear can be hired, including The Wedding Shop, Elegance, and Formal Wear on 2nd December Road. Bridesmaid's dresses are in the children's department of Saks Fifth Avenue.

As for other essential items such as the flowers, stationery, bridesmaid's gifts and photography for the big day, you shouldn't have too much trouble finding this within Oman itself.

Al Azad Flower Shop Nr Centrepoint, 968 24 611 689
Bella La Rose Al Qurum Complex, 968 24 566 766
Caesar Flower & Gifts 968 24 484 899
Caravans Floral Al Asfoor Plaza, 968 24 566 795
Gatherings Online, 968 96 053 280, *gatheringsoman.com*
Greens Flowers & Plants Nr Sultan Centre, 968 24 496 975, *qbgoman.com*
Hemanth BG 968 95 453 858, *omanfotos.com*
Little Shop Of Flowers Jawharat A'Shati & Oasis By The Sea Commercial Complex, 968 24 603 383
Marks & Spencer Muscat City Centre, 968 24 558 455, *marksandspencerme.com*
Maya Parfenova Green Leaf Photography 968 96 049 464, *mayaparfenova-photography.com*
Monsoon Muscat City Centre, 968 27 455 8902
Proshots 968 24 692 469, *proshots.org*
Rahwanji Cards Nr Sana Fashion, 968 24 811 465, *ir-cards.com*
Rose For You Al Khuwair 33, 968 97 333 7000
Rosie Gabrielle Photography 968 95 219 032
Salim Al Harthy Photography 968 92 091 119, *salimphoto.com*
The Flower Shop SABCO Commercial Centre, 968 24 560 043, *flowers-oman.com*
The Ruwi Centre For Wedding Cards 968 24 816 775
Therese Johnson Photography 968 95 167 417, *theresejohnson.com*

Malls house global stores

PLACES TO SHOP

Department Stores

Capital Store

Muscat **968 24 561 888**
csoman.com

Capital Store is the ultimate luxury shopping destination. This is where to head if you're looking for a Mont Blanc watch or pen, branded luggage, Dior sunglasses, or jewellery by Misaki and Nina Ricci. Capital also stocks a fantastic range of crystal and china, tableware, appliances and homeware, as well as one of Oman's widest ranges of perfumes and cosmetics. You'll also find Pentax and Samsung digital cameras, and a range of accessories. Capital offers a great shopping experience if you've got the cash to splash.

In total, there are nine Capital Store branches around Oman: SABCO Centre (99 811 969), Qurum (99 811 050), Markaz Al Bahja (99 811 303), Qurum Commercial Centre (99 860 933), Centrepoint (99 811 363), Al Bustan (92 805 488), Sohar (99 866 283), Centrepoint Salalah (92 805 488) and Salalah (23 297 910).

Khimji's Luxury & Lifestyle

Muscat **968 80 075 000**
khimjiblog.kr.om
Map **2 J3**

The word megastore doesn't so much refer to the size of the store as to the mega, utmost exclusivity of the brands you'll find in these beautiful stores. Khimji's Leisure & Lifestyle stores are a veritable who's who of upmarket brands, showcasing the likes of Chanel, Benetton, Moulinex, Samsonite, Sheaffer, Ray-Ban, Nikon and Swarovski.

Departments cover everything from fashion, footwear and sunglasses to household goods, electrical appliances, gadgets, luggage, pens and perfumes. Other brands you'll find in-store include Bvlgari, Cross, Noritake and Mora. There are branches of Khimji's in Ruwi (24 796 161), Qurum (24 560 419), Madinat Al Sultan Qaboos (24 696 678) and Salalah (23 295 736).

Marks & Spencer

Muscat City Centre Muscat **968 24 558 455**
marksandspencerme.com
Map **2 A3**

M&S (as it is fondly called by British expats) is one of Britain's best-known and most trusted department store brands. It sells a range of quality men's, women's and children's clothes and shoes, as well as

a teeny-tiny range of food items (mainly sweets and chocolates, but it's enough to remind you how brilliant the UK's M&S food halls are). One thing that you should definitely keep a look out for whenever you are passing by is their book section: it is very small but they often have some great children's classic titles at surprisingly reasonable prices.

Marks & Spencer is famous for its underwear – they have some lacy numbers, practical cotton whites and a lovely range of sleepwear. Ladies will be pleased to discover that not only do they have a petite range, but their regular clothes go up to size 20 and in some lines, even larger. You'll also be able to shop here for purses and handbags, home furnishings (they stock a small range of household items like candles, cushions, cookware and utensils), and a fantastic selection of makeup and toiletries.

Al Marsa Village

Although not yet quite a fully-fledged shopping district, the Al Marsa Village community on The Wave Muscat has a small retail area that is now open, providing residents and visitors with some of the basics (Kwik Kleen, Al Fair Supermarket) as well as a handful of dining offerings, such as Costa Coffee, Shang Thai and Pizza Express.

Salman Stores

Muscat **968 97 155 556**
salmancorporation.com
Map **2 K2**

Salman Stores was founded in 1953 as a retailer of quality kitchen and home products. Just over 50 years later, the group has grown into a leading importer, distributor and retailer in Oman and their range of products has expanded dramatically. This is the place to go if you're looking for tableware, glass and crystal items, porcelain and china, cutlery, and electrical appliances. Salman also stocks a range of luxurious linen and luggage.

Only well-known brand names are good enough for Salman Stores, so you can expect to find Tefal cookware, Luminarc crystal, Singer sewing machines, Helios flasks and Giordano watches, to name a few. Salman Stores has branches in Qurum Complex (24 560 135), Mutrah (24 796 925), Ruwi (24 792 343) and Salalah (23 293 146).

Markets & Souks

Souk is the Arabic word for a place where a variety of goods are bought, sold or exchanged. Traditionally, dhows from the Far East, Africa, Ceylon and India would discharge their cargo and the goods would be bargained over in the souks adjacent to the docks.

Over the years, the items on sale have changed from spices, silk and perfume, to include electronic goods and the latest consumer trends. However, the atmosphere of a bustling market with noisy bargaining and friendly rivalry for customers remains. Souks are lively, colourful and full of people from all walks of life – so they're well worth a visit, even if you're not buying.

Oman's souks are some of the most fascinating in the Arab world, having retained the traditional way of doing business that has been lost in many places elsewhere. Apart from the obvious commercial purpose they serve, they're also a focal point for social interaction. In the interior, Bedouins come in from the desert and villagers from the mountains to meet other tribes or catch up on the latest news.

Every important town in Oman has at least one souk. The biggest and most famous of these are in Mutrah, Nizwa, Sinaw and Salalah and there's a women-only souk in Ibra every Wednesday morning. In addition to the permanent souks, pre-Eid markets known as 'habta' souks spring up overnight in places like Fanja, Samayil, Suroor, Nafa'a and Nizwa.

Visiting the souk is a fascinating experience at any time, but it's best to go in the late afternoon or early morning when the temperatures are cooler. Business begins at 7am (except for Mutrah souk, which starts at 9.30am) with a break for midday prayers from 12.30pm or 1pm until 4.30pm. By 10pm, everything starts to close. On Fridays, the souks only open in the afternoon and Fridays and Saturdays are the busiest – the best time to see the market at full throttle and to take an active part in it.

Gold Souk

Salalah
Map **4 G8**

People unfamiliar with Arabic gold may think it as poor quality, but the reverse is usually true. Most of the gold sold in the region is 24 carat, and often softer and better quality than gold bought elsewhere in the world. However, it is very yellow and you may find that the designs are a bit gaudy, depending on your tastes. A visit to the Salalah Gold Souk may give you an opportunity to see young Dhofari girls choosing their wedding gold. You can shop around for a traditional Dhofari design, or design your own piece and have it made. This souk shouldn't be confused with the gold souk in Souk Al Haffa – the Salalah Gold Souk is situated in the Salalah Centre (after Pizza Hut, turn right 50 metres before the traffic lights).

Mutrah Fish & Vegetable Market

Nr Sultan Qaboos Port Muscat
Map **2 K2**

The old fish market, at the Mutrah end of the Corniche, was a real traditional gem – as smelly, muddy and bloody as it would have been for hundreds of years.

Unfortunately, however, that site has now been closed and is being renovated to create a huge, state-of-the-art fish market that will have more floor space, as well as cafes and seafood restaurants – although perhaps less of its old school charm. In the meantime, there's a temporary fish market here near Sultan Qaboos Port where you can still witness the true hustle and bustle of an Arabic market. It's also the best place to buy fresh seafood at low prices, but you'll have to get there early to score the catch of the day. From 6.30am, the small fishing boats are dragged up the beach next to the market to unload their trophies. There's practically everything the Indian Ocean has to offer: tuna, hammour, kingfish, bream, octopus and prawns. Once you've wandered round the stalls and selected your fish, you can have it cleaned and gutted. It's fascinating to watch and the service costs only a few baisas.

Mutrah Souk

Nr Mutrah Corniche Muscat
omantourism.gov.om
Map **2 K2**

Also known locally as Al Dhalam Market, this is one of the most interesting souks in the Gulf. The warren-like souk is still a source of many Omani families' daily household supplies, as well as a draw for souvenir-hunting tourists. The main entrance is on Mutrah Corniche but there are many small streets in the village behind the Corniche that lead into the souk. The main thoroughfare is primarily for household goods, shoes and ready-made garments. Further inside, you can enjoy the mixed scent of frankincense, perfume oils, fresh jasmine and spices. The real excitement lies in exploring the side streets. The layout is confusing, but keep walking and you'll invariably end up either at the Corniche or at the main thoroughfare. Wander down any of the side alleys and you'll discover tiny shops full of dusty Omani silver, stalls of gleaming white dishdashas and embroidered kumahs, vivid cloth, multi-coloured head scarves, Omani pots, paintings, hookah pipes, framed khanjars, leatherwork and incense. There are plenty of bargains and no price is fixed.

When you get tired, you can stop at the juice bar before tackling the next section. Most of the shops here open from 9.30am to 1pm and 4pm to 10pm daily, but are closed on Friday mornings and on Eid holiday weekends. There is paid parking all along both sides of Corniche Road from the Fish Roundabout, although it does get quite congested in the evenings.

Sinaw Souk

Nr Al Mudaybi, A'Sharqiyah Sinaw
Map **1 G5**

About two hours' drive from Muscat is Sinaw (at the crossroads of Route 33 and Route 27), a surprisingly busy outpost town set between the Wahiba Sands and

Trader showing his products

Goods are handmade

Souks are great for browsing

the edge of the Empty Quarter. Behind mud-coloured walls and through green metal doors in the middle of the town is the souk, which is where Bedouins gather to do business and to socialise. It's all go around the outside walls, where camels, goats and young cattle are auctioned off.

Loading the animals into trucks is a tricky business and the camels in particular can deliver knockout kicks and need at least six men to push them in. Despite the indignity of it all, they manage to maintain their haughty demeanour. Fruits and vegetables are sold in the central covered area. Bedouin women wearing metallic face masks ('burqa') happily trade next to men – which is quite unusual – and joke with you as you try on one of their masks.

Around the covered area you'll find a range of small shops selling jewellery, and there are even places where you can watch old silver being melted down to fashion new jewellery. Sinaw is a good place to find increasingly rare Bedouin silverwork, especially in the weeks approaching Eid when many people come to trade livestock or old silver for little luxuries. The souk is closed on Eid holidays.

Shopping Malls

Main Shopping Malls

Al Araimi Complex

Al Nahdah St Muscat **968 24 566 557**
alaraimicomplex.com
Map **2 H2**

This bright and spacious complex boasts over 70 shops with a wide array of consumer items. There are several opticians and jewellery stores as well as three banks. The first floor is devoted mainly to reasonably priced ladies' clothes shops (Nice Lady, Urban) and textile shops (Silk Island, Lakhoos). The ground floor shops include a few perfume shops (Ajmal, Maathir), a luxury home decor store (Marina), a photo processing store (Foto Magic) and a good children's toy store (Smart Kids Toys). The basement holds many electronic and homeware stores as well as a recently opened pet store (Animal World).

The big parking lot is nearly always full as it's one of the last free parking areas in the Qurum shopping area. If you can't find a space, the adjacent carparks offer pay parking at reasonable rates. This is one of three main malls in the vicinity, and therefore you can expect the area to get incredibly busy at peak shopping times. However, check your watch if you go there and the carpark is deserted – most shops inside Al Araimi close down for the lunchtime shift (usually from 1pm to 4pm).

Bareeq Al Shatti

As Sultan Qaboos St **968 24 643 898**
bareeqalshatti.com
Map **2 G2**

One of the newest shopping spots in Muscat, Bareeq Al Shatti is situated below a popular residential block opposite the Beach Hotel in Shatti. It offers some great one-off shops and restaurants in addition to essentials such as a dental clinic, mini supermarket, hair salons, optician and a pharmacy. It's also a good choice for a quick bite, with several coffee shops and a foodcourt.

Kids will be entertained at Little Town, an indoor play area, while adults can use some free time at the beauticians and even a specialised eye lash salon. Arabic fusion restaurant Ubhar (24 699 826) is particularly recommended with its stylish interior, extensive menu and tasty choices for lunch and dinner, or just a juice with friends. Meanwhile, hungry teenagers and families flock to B+F Roadside Diner (24 698 836) for its retro menu of burger and shakes served in a modern interior. Bareeq Al Shatti's shops are open 10am to 10pm from Saturday to Thursday and from 2pm to 10pm on Fridays.

Jawharat A'Shati & Oasis By The Sea Commercial Complex

Way 2817, Nr InterContinental Hotel, Al Kharijiyah St
968 24 692 113
jascomplex.com
Map **2 G2**

These lively beachfront locations attract visitors from all over the city. Shops are arranged on either side of a carpark that's a little too small to cope with the weekend crowds. Lunchtime and weekday evenings are more relaxed. You'll find some unusual items on sale here, like hand-rolled cigars, Turkish ice-cream and Omani handicrafts, to mention a few. Totem sells unique clothing and footwear and Gecko has delightful home decor. A browse around The Oman Heritage Gallery is like spending time in a museum, and you can buy some beautiful traditional crafts hand-made by local artists. Nails, Muscat's only salon devoted purely to pampering your hands and feet, is on the first floor, and a new addition is a Spa Bar for men.

The main attraction, though, is the food. The centre is home to several restaurants, nearly all of which have open areas where you can watch the sun set over the sea. D'Arcy's Kitchen is the most popular, where hearty international food is served from breakfast to dinner.

Markaz Al Bahja

Al Seeb St **968 24 540 200**
albahja.com
Map **2 A2**

This pleasant, medium-sized shopping mall is located just past Muscat City Centre as you drive to Sohar. It is fairly quiet, but the main attraction is Danish furniture store IDdesign. Cafes include Mood Cafe, Costa and The Coffee Bean & Tea Leaf. On the first floor, you will find a foodcourt and the Fantasia amusement centre for children. This includes a mini rollercoaster, bumper boats, electronic games, etc. As well as IDdesign on the ground floor, there is also the well-stocked Al Fair supermarket. The ground floor has a cinema.

Muscat City Centre
As Seeb St **968 24 558 888**
Map **2 A3**

This is one of the busiest, biggest and most modern malls in Oman. Not even its location past Seeb Airport deters people who come from far and wide to shop here. At weekends the huge parking area is heaving with cars and you'll be lucky to find an empty space.

The main shop in City Centre is the French hypermarket, Carrefour. It is a great first stop for people setting up home in Oman – here can buy all the things you need for a new house such as brooms, mops, ironing boards, towels, pots and cooking utensils. On the food side, you can buy delicious French breads and pastries as well as other European products. Carrefour is open from 9am until midnight and is busiest at weekends and during Ramadan, when there are in-store promotions. If a mega shopping trip around this gigantic mall leaves you feeling peckish, the L-shaped foodcourt has the usual fast food places, as well as Arabic, Indian, Italian and Chinese cuisine. Next to the foodcourt there is a Magic Planet amusement centre for children.

Other shops in the mall sell fashion, shoes, jewellery and special items such as Omani halwa,

chocolate covered dates and local handicrafts. The latest additions include Marks & Spencer, Toys 'R' Us, Victoria's Secrets and Gap. The mall is open from 10am to 10pm and none of the shops close for lunch.

Muscat Grand Mall
Dohat Al Adab St **968 22 000 000**
muscatgrandmall.com
Map **2 F3**

One of the newest addition to shopping malls in Muscat, the centre has particularly large selection of shoe stores including Shoe Studio, Sketchers, Aldo, Charles & Keith, Nine West and Birkenstock. Facilities include a cinema and play centre while food lovers will be happy with the introduction to Muscat of Paul.

Qurum City Centre
Nr Muscat International School **968 24 470 700**
qurumcitycentre.com
Map **2 H2**

Qurum City Centre is one of the newest malls in the capital, offering some of the same stores as its sister destination out near the airport. It is anchored by an enormous Carrefour, which is a welcome addition to the area and packed at weekends. Other shops include Jumbo Electronics, Monsoon, H&M, Next, Mango, L'Occitane, Early Learning Centre and Adidas. In addition to these, you will also find telecom provider outlets, a pharmacy, National Bank of Oman, Foto Magic and Magrabi Opticals. Qurum City Centre is open from 10am to 10pm Saturday to Thursday, 2pm to 10pm on Fridays and Carrefour is open 9am to midnight throughout the week.

Air-conditioned malls contain many attractions

SABCO Commercial Centre

968 24 566 701
sabcogroup.com
Map **2 H2**

This was one of the first true shopping malls in Oman and, while there are some who prefer the more modern, glitzier malls, SABCO retains a loyal following of shoppers who love it because it is tried, tested and trusted. It's usually fairly quiet, so it's perfect if you hate the more frantic atmosphere of the busier centres. However, it's quite difficult to find parking and it's one of the few areas in Muscat where you must pay for it.

You can buy yourself a bottle of the world-famous (and locally made) Amouage perfume in Amouage's shop, Oman Perfumery, which is near the entrance to the mall. The jewellery shop upstairs is excellent for repairing jewellery, as well as for manufacturing pieces according to your own designs. SABCO is also home to upmarket outlets like Godiva, Cerruti, Raymond Weil and Philippe Charriot.

The main attractions for most visitors include Nine West, The Body Shop and The Flower Shop and the authentically decorated souk in the corner of the SABCO centre is an Aladdin's cave of old Omani silver, local handicrafts, souvenirs and pashminas from India. You may also find some Pakistani leather. Bargaining is allowed, making the prices competitive with Mutrah Souk.

Other Shopping Centres

Al Harthy Complex

Nr Sultan Centre 968 24 564 481
Map **2 H2**

This stand-alone building beside the bustling Sultan Centre looks either like a giant space rocket or a futuristic mosque. Whatever your interpretation, the mall is an impressive landmark, especially at night when the lattice roof and the blue dome are lit up. One of the calmer malls in terms of shopping and parking, it's popular for its internet cafe and Muscat Pizza. The Oman Association for Consumer Protection has an office on one of the upper floors, and it's worth paying them a visit if you have a complaint you haven't been able to resolve. At The Gallery you'll find paintings by Omani artists, while Cards Store has a fair selection of humorous greeting cards, toys and souvenir T-shirts.

Fresh and dried flowers can be ordered from Caravans, and the Modern Technical Computer Centre sells Apple computers and accessories. The first floor is almost entirely made up of shops for women and young girls, including the biggest branch of Muscat Pharmacy Perfumes and Cosmetics.

Also within the mall is a shop run by the Association for the Welfare of Handicapped Children where you can buy cheap accessories, cosmetics and T-shirts

– and shop as much as you like because it's all in the name of charity! A small amusement park in the basement will keep the kids occupied.

Al Khamis Plaza

Al Nahdah St, Qurum 968 24 562 791
Map **2 H2**

The medium-sized Al Khamis Plaza in Qurum is spread over three floors and the top floor is a shoe shopper's heaven. There's a branch of Clarks, and a World of Shoes where you can buy brands like Sebago, Caterpillar and Dockers and Arabic-style sandals for men and women. Other big draws are the textile shops that have an amazing range of Indian silks, men's shops with suits from Pierre Cardin and Lanvin, and the elaborate and exclusive Mouawad Jewellery. Parking is free, but demand is high.

Al Masa Mall

Nr Ramada Hotel, As Saruj Sultan Qaboos St
968 24 693 341
Map **2 G2**

Al Masa Mall's location in Shatti Al Qurum makes it popular and easily accessible for most of the city's residents. Al Masa Mall offers a decent shopping variety, with stores selling everything from electronic goods and cosmetics to home decor and furnishings. Some of the newest stores to open their doors include Radio Shack, Red Earth, Sanrio and Supa Sport.

The mall's large foodcourt and entertainment areas are particularly busy at evenings and weekends; almost every type of food imaginable is available, while there are many indoor games and arcades, as well as a dedicated kids' play centre and a ten pin bowling centre.

Al Qurum Complex

968 24 563 672
Map **2 H2**

Looking like a sprawling Omani fort, complete with flags and enormous, carved wooden doors guarding the Al Fair supermarket, QCC is a gathering place for locals and expats. It is also popular with families who take the kids to Kids Rest, the play area upstairs. The opening of Canadian coffee shop chain, Second Cup, over the road has resulted in a definite surge in customer traffic. To the left of the main entrance of the shopping centre is a small souk where you can pick up a wide range of leather goods, trinkets and Omani handicrafts. The Al Fair Supermarket, which sells western food products (including pork) occupies one wing of QCC. Just outside Al Fair is an Oman International Bank ATM.

The other half of Qurum Commercial Centre is a shopping centre with a range of jewellery, phone, carpet and perfume shops under a beautiful stained glass ceiling. Health nuts will love this centre too, as the Health Shop carries everything from multivitamin protein drinks, to blood pressure monitors. Island Natural Herbs has a wall of dried bark and herbs guarded by two old Omani men who can presumably concoct a cure for what ails you. Sport One is full of huge plastic jars of food supplements for those looking to increase their muscle mass. Opening hours are 8.30am to 10pm but individual shop hours may vary.

Centrepoint

Madinat As Sultan Qaboos St **968 96 473 101**
centrepointstores.com
Map **2 G3**

More of a department store than a mall, this large two-storey building is a very popular destination and home to all manner of stores catering to every taste and budget, from baby clothes to homeware and everything in between. There are outlets for Home Centre, Babyshop, Shoe Mart, Splash, and Lifestyle. There is also a small play area for children and a prayer room for Muslim customers. On the first floor, there is a wide variety of household items, decorative items, artificial flowers and furniture.

Opera Galleria

Royal Opera House Muscat **968 24 403 440**
rohmuscat.org.om
Map **2 G2**

This upmarket mall is attached to the Royal Opera House in Shatti Al Qurum and includes a selection of jewellery and fashion outlets. It also boasts the Omani Artisan House which aims to promote and sell traditional products made by Omani craftspeople.

There are a number of places to eat including mOre Cafe, The Indus and Fauchan Cafe.

Souk Al Khuwair

23rd July St
Map **2 F3**

Also known as the Al Khuwair Commercial Centre, this is not a souk in the traditional sense, but rather a collection of small shops in one huge block in the middle of Al Khuwair. It offers a range of goods and services including tailors, furniture makers, second-hand electrical shops, hardware shops, one-rial shops, launderettes, a bakery, a pharmacy and a few coffee shops. Cheap household items and fabrics are without doubt two of the main draws, but you can also have film developed here (or have digital images printed), and there's a government-run fruit and vegetable market where you can get quality fresh produce at a fraction of the price you'll find in supermarkets.

Zakher Mall

Nr Radisson Hotel, Muscat **968 24 489 884**
zakhermall.com
Map **2 G3**

Zakher is a small centre with the usual selection of shops found in other malls and an internet coffee shop. The shops cater mostly to an Arabic clientele, so if you're looking for dishdasha, Arabic art, or even a few traditional souvenirs, it's a good destination. You can also buy high-end Bang & Olufsen and G Hanz audio and video equipment at Photocentre on the ground floor, and it boasts a CD and video store and a full colour copy centre.

Some malls take on a surreal feel

Infinity pool with sea view

GOING OUT

GOING OUT

Everything you need to know about making the most of Oman's great restaurants and nightlife.

Shahrazad, Shangri-La's Barr Al Jissah Resort & Spa

One of the most important aspects of expat life is the social life; when you live far from your friends and family back home, building a strong support network is crucial. It's important to get out, meet new people and participate in the community.

For many, this means exploring the nightlife scene, from sampling the best restaurant menus to finding the best bars for watching sports, participating in a good old fashioned pub quiz, or simply relaxing with sundowners and a group of friends. While Oman may not boast quite the glitzy party scene that you'll find in other parts of the region, there are definitely enough places where you can indulge in a slap up meal, socialise with friends until the early hours or even party the night away.

The launch of numerous new hotels in Oman over the last few years has seen the number of culinary

treats on offer skyrocket. At one end of the spectrum, there are picturesque cocktail lounges and well-appointed clubs competing for your hard-earned rials. At the other end, bargain eateries, bars offering cheap-as-chips drinks deals and restaurants boasting bang-for-your-buck brunches are there to help at the end of the month.

You'll find the majority of licensed restaurants are in hotels and clubs due to licensing laws (that were actually relaxed quite recently), but don't make the mistake of missing out on some of the culinary delights that can be found in non-licensed independent restaurants and cafes. Not only is there some delicious food on offer, you will also find that the bill is generally much more wallet-friendly; a decent bottle of wine in a licensed restaurant can often cost more than your whole meal.

GOING OUT

Are you moving to Oman or planning a visit? Then bring your appetite. The country is home to an ever evolving restaurant scene, from the gourmet offerings in its luxurious hotels (the Shangri-La alone boasts over 20 restaurants) to hidden gems and street food surprises. When dinner is done and the sun has gone down, there are plenty of nocturnal neighbourhoods to explore, with much of the action being concentrated in Muscat. Keep exploring and you're sure to find your favourite nightlife spot.

Brunch & Other Deals

Friday brunch is perfect for a lazy start or end to the weekend, especially once the really hot weather arrives. Popular with all sections of the community, it provides Thursday night revellers with a gentle awakening, while for families it's a very pleasant way to spend the day together. Many venues put on a variety of fun activities for kids, allowing parents to relax and concentrate on the fine food and drinks. Different brunches appeal to different crowds; some have fantastic buffets, others boast spectacular surroundings, and some simply offer amazing prices for all you can eat. A number of the four and five-star hotels offer an incredibly enticing spread as well as use of their pool, gardens or beach as part of the deal. Ask around and find out who does what, where and for how much, and make a day of it.

Vegetarian

Vegetarians will probably be pleasantly surprised by the range and variety of vegetarian cuisine offered in Muscat's restaurants. Arabic food, although dominated by meat in the main course, offers a staggering range of mostly vegetarian mezze, and the general affection for fresh vegetables provides enough variety to satisfy even the most ravenous veggie diner. Also, due to the large number of Indians who are vegetarian by religion, you'll find numerous Indian restaurants that offer vegetarian dishes in a range of cooking styles. A word of warning: if you are a strict vegetarian, confirm that your meal is completely meat-free when ordering. Some of the restaurants cook their 'vegetarian' selection with animal fat, or on the same grill as meat dishes. Also, in some places you may need to check the ingredients of seemingly vegetarian dishes.

Street Food

Sidewalk stands throughout the city sell shawarma, rolled pita bread filled with lamb or chicken carved from a rotating spit, and plenty of salad. Costing about 300 baisas each, these are inexpensive, well worth trying, and offer an excellent fast food alternative to the usual burger. The stands generally also sell other dishes, such as falafel, ta'amiya, (small savoury balls of deep-fried beans) or foul (a paste made from fava beans). While most shawarma vendors offer virtually the same thing, there are some that stand out from the rest; surprisingly, these are often the smallest, low-key places that you happen on by chance. You'll find that regulars are often adamant that their particular favourite serves the best falafel in town - and you'll find your favourite too.

Dining Out

Muscat is home to a wide variety of dining experiences. Aside from the usual hotel options, there are some interesting independent Arabic restaurants to be found if you take the time to explore. With tourism being actively promoted in Oman, the nightlife is constantly improving.

While Muscat isn't famous for its buzzing party scene, some hotel bars have extended their opening hours to as late as 3am. Be aware though, that drunk and disorderly behaviour in public is frowned upon. Also, If you want to buy alcohol for consumption at home, you need to apply for a liquor licence. Only non-Muslim residents with a labour card are allowed to apply.

EATING OUT

Oman's multicultural heritage and population is reflected in the variety of international cuisine on offer. From Arabic to Mediterranean to Polynesian and everything in between, you'll have a fine time exploring. Eating out is a time-honoured Arabic pastime; it's seen as an opportunity for friends and family to exchange news, gossip and argue the merits of anything from a foreign leader to the latest mobile phone. Most restaurants open early in the evening, around 7pm but generally don't get busy until about 9pm. Lunchtimes can vary between noon and 3pm, so check before you arrive. Many of the places we've covered here are very popular, so if you want to dine out at the weekend, it's best to book a table, particularly if you're a large group.

Many of Oman's restaurants are situated in hotels, especially in Muscat, but there are also numerous independent restaurants around town, some of which are licensed. While the licensed restaurants are popular for obvious reasons, there are some excellent independent restaurants around town that shouldn't be ignored just because they are 'dry'.

The more upmarket restaurants tend to specialise in one or two types of cuisine, while the smaller outlets will often entice you with a variety so it's not uncommon to find an Indian restaurant also offers Thai and Chinese dishes. Many also have theme nights featuring different types of cuisine, such as seafood, Italian or sushi. Some have weekly buffet nights when you can eat, and sometimes drink, as much as you like for a good value, all-inclusive price. Easy on the purse strings but hard on the waist band.

Delivery & Takeaways

Most fast food outlets, including Burger King and Pizza Hut, offer free home delivery, but you can also order dishes from your favourite local eatery and have them delivered too. So you can get shawarmas, sweet and sour noodles or butter chicken delivered to your doorstep and enjoy all the comfort of eating in – without the washing up that usually goes with it.

Special Deals & Theme Nights

Some hotels hold occasional promotions with various themes – the InterContinental and Al Bustan Palace are particularly recommended. These offers also run alongside special nights, such as ladies' nights. Check out the entertainment publications and the venue itself for the latest updates. Events like quiz nights tend to be hosted by a bar or pub and many attract quite a following, with Rock Bottom particularly popular. As a bonus, the (liquid) prizes are often quite good.

Caterers

A popular way to put on a party, special occasion or business lunch, in-house catering allows you to relax and enjoy yourself, without worrying about the cooking (or cleaning up). A number of companies offer this service, so decide on the type of food you want, be it Indian, Chinese, Lebanese or finger food, and ask your favourite restaurant or cafe whether they do outside catering. Most of the larger hotels have a catering department that's usually capable of servicing extravagant five-star functions. You're not confined to the house – how about throwing a party in the desert or on a dhow? Depending on requirements, companies will provide anything from the meal to crockery, waiters, furniture and even a clearing up service.

Hygiene

Don't be fooled by the appearance of some of the outlets you come across in Oman. Many are probably not as bad as they might look. Then again, some of them are, so use your judgment. The local authorities are clamping down on hygiene so many places have bucked up their ideas and started to follow procedures and guidelines as laid out by the municipality.

Tipping

Tipping is up to you. The service charge is not generally passed on to the waiting staff and it applies regardless of whether the service was excellent or lousy. So if you would like to reward the waiting staff directly, a 10% tip will be much appreciated. Try to hand it directly to the person you'd like to thank, as at some establishments tips go straight into the till. Most people tend to leave their change as a tip, particularly in cafes.

NIGHTLIFE

Life in Muscat is led at a relatively sedate pace. This is good for your stress levels, but does mean less chance of a wild night on the town, especially compared to other cities in the region like Dubai or Bahrain. Given its size, Muscat has a reasonable variety of restaurants and bars, but places tend to wind down quite early. The following section covers cafes, bars, pubs and nightclubs as well as cultural entertainment such as theatre and comedy. The social scene may appear a little exclusive to a newcomer, with cliques that seem to have limited memberships. However, once you're in, you're in, and the expat community is in fact very friendly and welcoming.

Many people socialise at home, particularly after the bars and nightclubs have closed and especially during Ramadan. In addition, much of the nightlife revolves around the hotels, which generally organise events throughout the year. Special nights are arranged about a month in advance, so have your name added to their mailing lists to receive information on what's happening.

If you're after a bar scene, check out some of the places listed in the Restaurants section. Thursdays and Fridays are the busiest nights out. Most bars and nightclubs close between midnight and 1am, especially those in hotels, while the occasional bar will stay open until 3am.

Capri Court, Shangri-La's Barr Al Jissah Resort & Spa

Drinks

While Oman is a Muslim country, it has a relatively liberal attitude towards the consumption of alcohol by non-Muslims. Alcohol is generally available in licensed hotel restaurants and bars. However, drinking alcohol in these establishments can be an expensive pastime – nearly double what you are probably used to paying. Non-Muslims can apply for an alcohol permit that allows them to purchase alcohol from a liquor store. You're not likely to find a huge selection in your local off-licence, and wine can cost three times more than you usually pay, but spirits are cheaper. Local bottled water is produced either in Oman or the UAE and is of a high quality, even compared to premium imported brands. So instead of paying for an international label, try the local water which should go down well at around 200 baisas for a 1.5 litre bottle.

Cinemas

Al Bahja Cinema Markaz Al Bahja, , *albahjacinema.net*
City Cinema Muscat Grand Mall, 968 24 567 668, *citycinemaoman.net*
City Cinema, Shatti Al Qurum Bldg 195, Way 3005, Block 228, 968 24 607 360, *citycinemaoman.net*
Ruwi Cinema Nr Mansoor Ali Centre, 968 24 780 380

DVD & Video Rental

Because most people have satellite TV, DVD and video rental shops are not as booming as they used to be. There is the easy access to cheap, poor quality, pirated DVDs – the fact that they are illegal doesn't seem to deter many people and the salesmen do a roaring trade. However, there are times when rental places still come in handy – especially when it is too hot to go outside and there is nothing good on TV. Video Club in Al Khuwair (near Home Centre) usually has a good selection of fairly recent releases (24 600 079).

Comedy Nights

The comedy scene is Muscat is unfortunately rather limited for now, with shows being held infrequently. For info on upcoming events, check out aliveoman.com.

Concerts & Live Music

Whatever your musical tastes, chances are you'll find something to suit in Oman. Classical music performances are held at the Royal Opera House, with the seasons changing every six months or so. Check the schedule at their website (rohmuscat.org.om) but be warned that the tickets are often sold out weeks in advance. Some of the hotels, particularly the Grand Hyatt Muscat and the Al Bustan Palace also arrange events where, for example, the Royal Oman Symphony Orchestra might perform. There is a fairly active live music scene, and you might be able to catch a few performances from big name stars: keep an eye (or ear) out for announcements in newspapers, email newsletters and on the radio.

Door Policy

Some of the cooler hang-outs implement a members only policy that allows them to control the clientele frequenting the place. At quieter times though, non-members may have no problem getting in; basically, the management uses the rule to disallow entry if they don't like the look of you or your group. Large groups of men are often refused entry, so breaking up your group by recruiting some ladies is a worthwhile tactic. Getting irate really won't get you anywhere, so if you're refused entry your best bet is to move on and find somewhere else that's more accommodating.

Theatre

Theatre in Muscat is limited but there are occasional opportunities to see a professional performances. There is an amateur theatre group – Ras Al Hamra Amateur Dramatics Society (RAHADS) which produces a range of events throughout the year. These include plays, pantomimes, comedy reviews and murder mystery dinners. For more info, contact 93 375 946.

RESTAURANTS & CAFES

Some of the country's best restaurant offerings can be found in its world-class restaurants, as well as the Royal Opera House. But don't neglect to go off the beaten track in search of some hidden culinary gems.

The Yellow Star

The yellow star highlights the Oman gems that merit extra praise. It might be the atmosphere, the food, the cocktails, the music or the crowd, but any review that you see with the star attached is sure to be for somewhere that's a bit special.

Al Aktham

Nr Muscat International Hotel Muscat
968 24 489 292
alaktham.com
Map **2 F3**
Behind a rather run-down exterior hides a surprisingly large restaurant with an even larger menu. At Al Aktham you can choose from Arabian, Indian, Chinese and Filipino dishes or, if none of that appeals, there's continental too. It's a good place for a private dinner party in one of the screened rooms and you're sure to have an excellent value meal, served by polite and friendly staff.

Al Bahar

Millennium Resort Mussanah Mussanah
968 26 871 555
millenniumhotels.com
Map **1 G3**
Give your taste buds a treat and feast on the mouthwatering dishes produced by Chef Reiner Thieding and his team, in a tranquil, romantic setting overlooking the marina. The food is nothing short of spectacular, magnificently presented and absolutely scrumptious. When it comes to the main course, the Lasooniachari Jhing (tiger prawns) are so lip-smackingly good you'll definitely want to go back for more. The 'swan in love' profiteroles are the perfect ending to great evening out.

Al Diwan Restaurant

Ramada Muscat Muscat **968 24 603 555**
ramadamuscat.com
Map **2 G2**
Hungry but not entirely sure what you want? Then head down to the Ramada Hotel's Al Diwan dining area where you'll find Indian, Arabic, Chinese and international cuisine. The diversity of the menu is impressive, but like so many other places that try to be everything, overall quality and taste leaves a little to be desired.

Al Khiran Terrace Restaurant

Al Bustan Palace, A Ritz-Carlton Hotel Muscat
968 24 799 666
ritzcarlton.com
Map **2 L4**
A bright, open space with fantastic views of the garden and the beautiful bay is only the beginning – this is perhaps one of the friendliest restaurants in Oman. In addition to alfresco breakfasts, it serves up some of the most mouthwatering themed buffets in Muscat, but there's also an Italian a la carte menu available every night for those who prefer more restrained dining. The staff are attentive and will ensure your evening is one to remember.

Al Mas

Bowshar Hotel Muscat **968 24 491 105**
bowsharhotel.com
Map **2 F3**
Al Mas is located in the Bowshar Hotel, just north of the Ghubrah/Bowshar roundabout. The sleek decor sets the pace for this fabulous little eatery. Open most hours, this is more of a restaurant than a quick coffee stop, and its menu is bursting with Indian, Chinese and Arabic dishes that will tempt you to stay longer. Those wanting just a quick stop can choose from the small menu of snacks and light bites. The staff are friendly and convivial and the prices are surprisingly reasonable.

Al Tanoor

Shangri-La's Barr Al Jissah Resort & Spa
Al Bandar Muscat **968 24 776 565**
shangri-la.com
Map **1 G4**
This vibrant restaurant offers an a la carte menu with something for everyone, including the kids. Available from noon to 11pm, there are several theme nights to dive into. Be sure to reserve a table on Thursdays as seafood night is the most popular; Tuesday's Indian themed night and Wednesday's Omani buffet are not to be missed. To end the meal, choose from the many mouthwatering desserts.

Alauddin Restaurant

Khalil Bldg Muscat **968 24 600 667**
You'll be hard pushed to find someone who lives in Muscat and hasn't enjoyed food from Alauddin; it is an enduring favourite, and deservedly so. Don't expect the decor to knock your socks off, and you're not here for the booze either, because this place is not licensed,

but do arrive with high expectations of a gastronomic good time. Excellent Indian, superb Arabic, mouthwatering Chinese and tasty international cuisine are all available and all served to deliciously high standards. A Muscat must.

Atrium Tea Lounge

Al Bustan Palace, A Ritz-Carlton Hotel Muscat
968 24 799 666
ritzcarlton.com
Map 2 L4

You'll be hard pressed to find a better way to take in the splendour of the palatial Al Bustan than with high tea at the Atrium. Relax under the magnificent dome and imposing crystal chandelier with a coffee or tea and one of the delicious cakes or pastries. The friendly service, plush surroundings and the gentle music issuing from the piano makes it terribly easy to linger in the lap of luxury.

Automatic Restaurant

Nr SABCO Muscat 968 24 561 500
Map 2 H2

Automatic has established itself as the benchmark for fast Arabic food, among locals and expats alike. It's all about fresh juices, mezze and large portions for very reasonable prices. The waiters are efficient and the food quick to your table. Those with large appetites will be well-pleased with the four daily specials, while the range of traditional starters, salads, grilled meats and locally caught seafood should keep everyone happy. Friday brunch here is also a must.

Bait Al Bahr

Shangri-La's Barr Al Jissah Resort & Spa
Al Waha Muscat 968 24 776 565
shangri-la.com
Map 1 G4

If you fancy sampling some local delights from the nearby sea, Bait Al Bahr is a perfect choice. Standing alone from the main hotels, a stop off the lazy river route running throughout the resort, you are made to feel as unique as the location you are sitting in. Bag a table on the veranda and cool off in the ocean breeze while you select from the enticing menu. Obviously the emphasis is on succulent seafood, but there are some vegetarian choices too. Your chosen dish is presented to you by elegantly dressed waiting staff. Portions are on the small side, but decadently rich.

Beach Pavilion Restaurant & Bar

Al Bustan Palace, A Ritz-Carlton Hotel Muscat
968 24 799 666
ritzcarlton.com
Map 2 L4

The seashore location of the Beach Pavilion makes this a delightful place to enjoy a light lunch, watching the waves crash onto the shore as you tuck into good food. Home-baked rolls supplement smallish portions and the staff are only too happy to adjust a dish to suit your needs. Service can be slow at weekends and holidays – in fact, it's so popular that you'll be lucky to get a table at all, so make sure you book in advance. Newly rebuilt, this restaurant now serves fresh seafood, and comforting dishes like risotto, year round.

Bellapais

Al Rusayl Centre Rusayl 968 24 521 100
Map 2 A3

This unpretentious gem of a restaurant is well worth the 40km drive from downtown Muscat. Don't be put off by the decor – the quality of the food surpasses all initial impressions. Known for the authentic moussaka, baked lamb, steaks and seafood, it also offers Chinese and Indian dishes. Try the mezze to start – it's an ideal introduction to your gastronomic journey, whichever route you choose to continue on. Bellapais comes alive at lunchtimes, is quieter in the evenings but no one has been known to leave hungry.

Bin Ateeq Restaurant

Nr Shell & McDonald's Muscat 968 24 478 225
binateeqoman.com
Map 2 F3

One of the friendliest and most welcoming restaurants in Muscat, Bin Ateeq serves Omani food at its best. The takeaway queue is testament to the popularity with the locals but dining in is worth the experience. The cane-clad walls are reminiscent of a jungle hut, but air-conditioned huts, with TVs in every private dining room. Simply spiced meat, chicken and fish, all still on the bone, and mountains of fried fluffy rice are brought to you as you recline on your majlis cushion. Prepare to get messy.

Blue Marlin

Marina Bandar Al Rowdha Muscat 968 24 740 038
marinaoman.net
Map 2 L3

A haven of tranquillity, intimacy and serenity, the Blue Marlin makes the most of its picturesque location. The alfresco breakfasts by the pool (including full English and buffet options) are incredibly popular at the weekend and booking is recommended, especially in the cooler months. Come evening, a sundowner watching the boats is also particularly enjoyable. The modern European fare is fantastically prepared and presented, surpassed only by the service. The menu offers a good selection of seafood with a bit of a twist (the fish pie is fantastic), as well some unusual variations on non-fish dishes. This is one of the few restaurants where as much care is taken with the presentation as with the food itself.

Bollywood Chaat

Al Qurum Complex Muscat **968 24 565 653**
Map **2 H2**

This vegetarian restaurant has a Bollywood-themed menu of light meals and snacks, in a bright fast food-style setting. The heart-shaped potato cutlets (kajol cutlet) and the sweet and sticky dumplings (moon moon gulab jamun) are two dishes not to be missed. The fact that everything's so reasonably priced makes a meal here that little bit more special. Service is prompt and cheery and the staff willing to explain the ingredients of the dishes on offer.

Candle Cafe

Shatti Al Qurum Beach Muscat
Map **2 G2**

This unassuming gem is located in front of the Grand Hyatt Hotel on Qurum Beach. While it is an exclusive neighbourhood, the cafe has an easy-going vibe. With its very reasonable prices, you can enjoy Arabic grills, hot snacks including falafel, halloumi and sandwiches, and an extensive range of teas, coffees and juices. Shisha is also available. This popular venue is open from 7am to 1am.

Capri Court

Shangri-La's Barr Al Jissah Resort & Spa Al Bandar Muscat **968 24 776 565**
shangri-la.com
Map **1 G4**

Guests will be charmed by the menu which is varied without being too busy. The dishes on offer are fresh and wholesome with a nice mix of pasta, meat and fish as well as quite an extensive selection of vegetarian options. If you choose to dine alfresco you can relax to the sounds of the waves gently lapping to the shore. Service is prompt and knowledgeable without being intrusive and the waiters have lots of friendly advice. For the sweet toothed, a treasure trove of treats are on offer with the traditional Italian tiramisu taking centre stage. A well-researched wine list could turn any quiet dinner into a party and there is also a fresh and fruity mocktail menu to lend some zest to the occasion.

Chili's

Muscat City Centre Muscat **968 24 558 815**
chilisoman.com
Map **2 A3**

A real family favourite, Chili's has a great menu, a fun atmosphere and helpful, amiable staff. The menu caters to all tastes – even those who are counting the calories, with 'guiltless' and 'low carb' options. Chili's burgers are famous and the lunchtime specials of soup and salad combos are popular, but to really get your taste buds going, try the steak and fish dishes. Shame there are no guilt-free versions of the sinful

molten chocolate cake. Children are well catered for with activities and they get colouring pencils and sheets to keep them occupied and a varied menu to fill them up. It is also a good spot for kids' parties.

China Mood

Al Bustan Palace, A Ritz-Carlton Hotel Muscat **968 24 799 666**
ritzcarlton.com
Map **2 L4**

Acknowledged locally as one of the finest Chinese restaurants in Muscat, China Mood excels on many levels. For a start, the atmosphere is decadent and the staff superbly attentive, ensuring that your plate is consistently filled with fabulous colours, tastes and textures. The meat dishes are tender and juicy and the vegetables perfectly cooked and refreshingly free from the usual greasy oil slick. A fantastic place to enjoy a Far Eastern meal, although an early reservation is essential if you want to bag a table.

China Town Restaurant

Al Qurum Complex Muscat **968 24 567 974**
goldenspoongroup.com
Map **2 H2**

From the decorated facade, it's easy to guess that the dinner that awaits you inside China Town is going to be nothing less than splendid Chinese cuisine. Much-loved and well-known dishes are served in a serene setting and expectations of fabulous fare are well met. A takeaway and delivery service is also available, but those dining in will enjoy excellent food presented in a 'no-fuss' manner by friendly and courteous staff.

China Mood

Chinese Garden

Nr Oman Ice Rink Muscat **968 24 489 414**
Map **2 F3**

Although a tad garish in design, the Chinese Garden serves tasty and satisfying food in a no-frills, no big bills manner. The atmosphere within the small restaurant is friendly and the service is quick – the epitome of cheap and cheerful Chinese cuisine. It's a great place for a laidback supper.

Cinnzeo

Muscat **968 24 699 660**
binmirza.com
Map **2 G2**

The smell of freshly baked cinnamon rolls will draw you into this bakery cafe. Not only does it have a lovely atmosphere, but you can watch the bakers at work in the open kitchen. Try the world-famous cinnamon rolls with different toppings, or splash out (calorie-wise) on one of the decadent chocolate twists. All of these naughty-but-nice delights come straight from the oven – you can choose fruity sauce instead of chocolate or caramel if you want to kid yourself that you are being healthy. It's perfect for a yummy sugar fix, a good cup of coffee and friendly service in comfortable surroundings.

Come Prima

Crowne Plaza Muscat Muscat **968 24 660 660**
crowneplaza.com
Map **2 H2**

Inside or out, this establishment has some of the best views in town. Top these with garlic bread like it should be – hot, fresh, and very, very moreish – a traditional Italian menu with home-made pasta, pizza, meat and seafood dishes and you have yourself the making of an excellent night out. Food is served at a relaxed pace, allowing time for plenty of chatting. Come Prima is not the hippest restaurant in town, so come here to enjoy the food and your friends – not to be seen.

Copper Chimney

Nr Central Bank of Oman Muscat **968 24 780 207**
Map **2 J3**

Behind the imposing copper door of this restaurant lies an impressive interior and a fabulous kitchen. Best of all, the fine Indian fare served perfectly meets the high expectations that the decor raises, but without hurting your wallet. A domed ceiling, complete with great copper lamps, means you eat your meal in an airy, spacious room. And once you've ordered from the mouthwatering selection of dishes, you can watch your meal being cooked in the vast clay oven in the kitchen. For excellent Indian food in a grand setting, with reasonable prices, look no further than the Copper Chimney.

Curry House

Way 317, Bldg 1360 Muscat **968 24 564 033**
Map **2 J3**

Food eaten with your fingers always seems to taste better. While you don't have to eat with your fingers, the Curry House near the Al Wattayah Roundabout, is a truly authentic North Indian dining experience. The service is some of the best you'll find in Oman, and the delicious and cheap buffet has a superb selection of Indian cuisine. Many of the curries are served in 'karahi', lovely copper bowls imported from India, and all are accompanied by beautifully fragrant vegetable pilau. This is a cheap and very cheerful spot.

D'Arcy's Kitchen

Jawharat A'Shati & Oasis By The Sea Commercial Complex Muscat **968 24 600 234**
Map **2 G2**

Overlooking the sea, this sunny cafe in the buzzing Shatti Al Qurum area is a welcome stop for a late breakfast, lunch or a light dinner. Step inside and you'll feel as though you've walked into a farmhouse – a theme that's matched by the size of the servings. The interesting menu includes special salads, soups and burgers served with a selection of delicious fruit smoothies by friendly staff. Whether you pop in for a light meal or just a coffee, D'Arcy's treats you well. There is also a new branch in Madinat Al Sultan Qaboos with some extra dishes and fairy-lit outdoor area.

Fish Village

Nr Automatic Restaurant Muscat **968 24 480 918**
Map **2 F3**

It's not quite a village, but it is a great little restaurant that is worth a visit for the view alone. It is located opposite the Radisson Blu, looking out over the Taimer Mosque and on towards 'White Mountain'. The outside seating area is large and merges with the other restaurants on either side. It's a bustling area, with lots of locals congregating over shisha and a shawarma. If your appetite permits, treat yourself to spicy squid or a sizzling tagine.

Four Seasons Restaurant

Haffa House Hotel Muscat Muscat **968 24 707 207**
shanfarihotels.com
Map **2 J3**

Four Seasons has an a la carte menu, but it's the favourably priced buffet that draws the diners in time and again. The choice of fare is international and simple but tasty. You'll be offered a soup starter, the choice of four or five salads, five main courses and a couple of desserts. It certainly makes for good value, but the ambience and setting is more business, less pleasure. Nevertheless, it's not a bad choice for a laidback meal with friends.

Golden Spoon Restaurant

Nr Zawabi Mosque Muscat **968 24 482 263**
goldenspoongroup.com
Map **2 F3**

This is a popular casual spot for good, inexpensive Chinese and Indian food. The decor is a bit dark, but the attentive and friendly staff more than make up for it. The menu is extensive and there are always excellent daily specials to be had. Servings are very generous and each dish is full of flavour. It's tempting to make a meal of the sweet and sour soup, but don't – save room for tasty dishes like the murj masala.

Green Cedar Restaurant

Nr Al Sarooj Centre Muscat **968 24 601 199**
Map **2 G2**

This may just be a drive-through, nestled between Al Fair Supermarket and the petrol station, but the food is good enough to savour. There are a few tables outside if you wish to linger a little longer to fully appreciate your snack. You'll find the usual shawarma stand favourites like chicken or mutton sandwiches wrapped up with spicy sauce, in local bread. The real jewel though is the falafels, which are particularly tasty with lots of tahina sauce and crunchy vegetables. If you're lucky you may even come across a French fry in your sandwich – a local delicacy!

Sweet Tooth

In addition to bread, Arabic bakeries offer a wonderful range of pastries, biscuits and Lebanese sweets. Look out for 'borek', which are flat pastries, baked or fried with spinach or cheese fillings, or the biscuits stuffed with ground dates. All are delicious, and must be tried at least once. Omani Halwa is a sticky concoction of sugar, ghee (clarified butter), rosewater and saffron. It's made in huge batches and served in little dishes with a spoon.

Grill House

Nr City Plaza Muscat **968 24 603 660**
Map **2 G3**

At the Grill House, just a stone's throw from the Al Khuwair Roundabout near Madinat Qaboos, the service comes faster than usual and with a smile. You'll feast on well-prepared dishes of the Indian, Chinese and Thai ilk and leave thrilled at the tiny total on your bill. An enjoyable experience from start to satisfying finish.

Jade Garden

Al Qurum Resort Muscat **968 24 605 945**
Map **2 G2**

Even though it's located at the Al Qurum Resort on Qurum Beach, the Far Eastern restaurant just misses out on a sea view. Fortunately, the food is well worth your full attention. Choose from a selection of Chinese,

Thai and teppanyaki dishes and all the takeaway classics, including lemon chicken and seafood noodles. The typical oriental puddings, from lychees to delicious ice-creams, are fabulously indulgent. Service is prompt between courses and the atmosphere is peaceful, however Thursdays are sushi nights and very popular.

Jean's Grill

Sultan Center Muscat **968 24 560 567**
sultan-center.com
Map **2 H3**

Located within the Sultan Centre supermarket, Jean's Grill may seem an unlikely destination for lunch or dinner. However it offers an exciting international spread that's well worth stopping by for. Your choices begin with soups and salads, and carry on through to pasta, curries, grilled meats, fish and even braised duck. Tuck into pastries from around the world, unlimited soft drinks, tea and coffee and enjoy it all for a very reasonable set price. All-in-all the perfect pit stop after a mammoth shopping excursion.

Karachi Darbar

Nr Zawabi Mosque Muscat **968 24 479 360**
goldenspoongroup.com
Map **2 F3**

This is a fantastic fast food joint and perfect if your lunch hour allows you just enough time to grab something quick and tasty. A good sign is its popularity with the local community, particularly later in the day and around dinner time. The menu is limited and consists of curries and grilled dishes, but everything is delicious and the tandoori chicken is exceptional. Karachi Darbar is great value for money and casual dining – definitely one to try.

Kargeen Caffe

Madinat Al Sultan Qaboos Centre Muscat
968 24 699 055
kargeencaffe.com
Map **2 G3**

This is a quaint, tented cafe, full of quirky ornaments and furniture, which could easily be part of someone's home. The menu comprises hearty soups, salads and Arabic appetisers, as well as burgers, pizza and steak for mains and a range of cakes, desserts and fruity drinks. This outdoor cafe is a delightfully unusual way to enjoy a leisurely coffee-and-cake session or a complete meal within a great setting.

Khyber

CBD Area Muscat **968 24 781 901**
Map **2 K3**

Khyber serves an extensive range of Indian food with some Chinese options, and boasts two licensed bars and separate dining areas. Its location, near the

Al Bahar

Mokha Cafe

The Chedi Pool Cabana

Central Bank of Oman in Ruwi's busy CBD, means it's well-placed to meet the demands of hungry business executives and it offers excellent specials that reflect this. Specialities include delicious Indian sweets and home-made frozen and fried ice-cream. The restaurant boasts a mobile tandoori oven for catering events.

La Mer

Shatti Al Qurum Beach Muscat **968 24 662 924**
lamermuscat.com
Map **2 G2**
With an enviable view over Qurum Beach, La Mer is a recent addition to Muscat. The Tuesday night seafood festival offers delicious fresh fish at reasonable prices though there are multiple cuisines on offer for those not keen on seafood.

Le Mermaid

Nr Grand Hyatt Hotel Muscat **968 24 602 327**
Map **2 G2**
In the shadow of the Grand Hyatt, you'll find one of the coolest cafes in Muscat. With a large outside seating area complete with majlis tents, shisha and great sea views, this popular cafe has people dropping by from all over town. Dishing up a wide range of seafood, grills and snacks, Le Mermaid is a hidden treasure. Indulge in a refreshing fruit cocktail or choose from the range of coffees and local hot drinks.

Majlis Al Shams

InterContinental Muscat Muscat **968 24 680 000**
ihg.com
Map **2 G2**
A relaxing light lunch or an indulgent coffee and cake session are on offer at this cafe in the InterContinental Muscat. Despite its grand surroundings, it's a surprisingly peaceful and intimate spot, and you could happily while away time here, musing over the range of delectable cakes and pastries. It also has freshly made sandwiches, fresh juices, and a selection of teas and coffees. The service is extremely friendly and this, coupled with the comfortable sofas and chairs, means an afternoon here slips away very easily.

Marjan

Grand Hyatt Muscat Muscat **968 24 641 234**
muscat.grand.hyatt.com
Map **2 G2**
A restaurant with a split personality. By day, it's an extremely relaxed, child-friendly restaurant overlooking the pool and the sea. Families with young children will appreciate the kid's menu/activity booklet, high chairs and half portions. For lunch, you can choose from classics such as grilled tuna nicoise and club sandwich or try something authentically Indonesian such as the melt-in-your-mouth cumi goring (fried squid in a surprisingly tangy lime

mayonnaise). By night, Marjan is a very grown up place. Start off your alfresco evening with a cocktail inspired by the colonial era while being serenaded by a duo of Indonesian musicians. Evening diners can discover a much wider range of Indonesian dishes representing all regions of this diverse country. The redang daging (dry beef curry in coconut milk) is a delight. Or, if sushi is your thing, Chef Yudi can offer you a large selection, freshly prepared.

Mokha Cafe

Grand Hyatt Muscat Muscat **968 24 641 234**
muscat.hyatt.com
Map **2 G2**
The a la carte menu here has something for everyone in the form of seafood, pasta, steak and vegetarian dishes all served in both international and Arabic styles. If you're in town on a Saturday evening, try out the Tandoori buffet. Other theme nights include the Arabic night on a Tuesday and the Seafood night on a Thursday. Prices, including taxes are RO.20 for the Tandoori and Arabic buffets and RO.25 for the seafood buffet.

mOre Cafe

Opera Galleria Muscat **968 22 022 555**
oman.morecafe.co
Map **2 G2**
This new addition to Muscat has proved extremely popular for its delicious food at reasonable prices. Recommended dishes include the pumpkin soup, Thai green curry and pannekoeken (large Dutch pancakes). There is also a wide selection of breads, jams, chutneys and dressings to purchase. It is open seven days a week, from 9am to 11pm.

Mumtaz Mahal

2601 Way Muscat **968 24 605 907**
mumtazmahal.net
Map **2 H2**
Mumtaz Mahal is one of the most interesting dining experiences to be had in Muscat. Costumed waiters will ply you with baskets of poppadoms and dips (the date chutney is a must try) while you're making your choice. Vegetarians will be very happy here – there are plenty of paneer and spicy vegetable dishes on the menu – while meat lovers will be equally impressed and satisfied.

Musandam Cafe & Terrace Restaurant

InterContinental Muscat Muscat **968 24 680 000**
ihg.com
Map **2 G2**
A real winner for breakfast or brunch, the Musandam Cafe & Terrace is less of a sure thing for dinner, particularly during the off-season when you can expect typical hotel buffet fare. However, for a Friday

family brunch, this is the spot. Fresh fish and salads, roast meats, an egg station and pancake making make this an ideal venue for a young and hungry family. On Fridays, children can have their faces painted and watch magic shows while you fill up at the buffet. And at this casual eatery, no one minds gaudily-daubed children running amok between the tables.

Mydan

Millennium Resort Mussanah Mussanah
968 26 871 555
millenniumhotels.com
Map **1 G3**

Overlooking the marina, this restaurant offers both indoor and terrace seating, and guests can choose from the buffet or the a la carte menu for breakfast, lunch and dinner. The international buffet is particularly good value and there is a wide range of mouthwatering dishes that change on a daily basis. Chefs at the cooking stations are happy to cook fish/meat to your liking; the coq au vin and beef tenderloin are firm favourites. Staff are friendly and helpful and the atmosphere is relaxed.

Nando's

Al Qurum Complex Muscat **968 24 561 818**
binmirza.com
Map **2 H2**

Put simply, Nando's is decent grub served quickly. From main meals you eat with your hands, to the legendary chicken espetada, your appetite will be nicely satisfied. Nando's speciality is marinated chicken, butterfly grilled on a naked flame and then spiced with the seasoning of your choice – from mild and lemony to hot-lips chilli. For a warm greeting at the door, rustic decor and value prices, you just can't go wrong. There is also a branch of Nando's at Muscat City Centre.

Naseem Lounge

Millennium Resort Mussanah Mussanah
968 26 871 555
millenniumhotels.com
Map **1 G3**

A delightful hideaway, where you can lap up the air-conditioned comfort of armchairs during the hot summer months, or enjoy the cane, cushioned outdoor seating that looks out over the marina. A wide selection of cakes and sandwiches delight taste buds and there's a fine selection of coffees and teas, including South African rooibos tea.

O Sole Mio

Jawharat A'Shati & Oasis By The Sea Commercial Complex Muscat **968 24 601 343**
Map **2 G2**

The award-winning O Sole Mio is ideal for a candlelit dinner for two or an informal dinner with friends, thanks to its lively atmosphere and delicious Italian food. The menu is extensive, with plenty of grilled options for the health-conscious, and servings are ample. The staff are attentive and offer quick, efficient service. O Sole Mio's popularity stems from its prime location and its ability to deliver good food at reasonable prices, making it advisable to book in advance.

Naseem Lounge

Olivos Restaurant & Terrace

Radisson Blu Hotel Muscat **968 24 487 777**
radissonblu.com
Map **2 F3**

This all-day dining restaurant overlooks the hotel's swimming pool and gardens. It provides a nice enough, shaded setting for dining alfresco with themed nights and buffet style catering (although a wide range of international dishes is available off the a la carte menu too). With great service in a relaxed atmosphere, Olivos is a good value for money restaurant and the ideal location for a relaxed dinner with friends.

Palayok Restaurant

Nr OCC Muscat **968 24 797 290**
Map **2 J3**

It's a bit of a challenge to find Palayok, which is tucked away in Ruwi, but once you do you'll agree that the hunt was worth the effort. It looks a little dull on the outside but opens up into a bright, cheery little place. Mr Marlon will make you feel at home and offer you some excellent suggestions regarding the menu. Fresh vegetables, fish and meat are perfectly seasoned and dressed in delicious sauces to create some of the finest Asian eating in Muscat. Whether you decide to eat-in or take advantage of the home-delivery option, Palayok should be on your must-try list.

Drink Up

A variety of fresh juices are widely available, either from shawarma stands, juice shops, coffee shops or cafes. They are uniformly delicious, healthy and cheap, and made on the spot from fresh fruits such as mango, banana, kiwi, strawberry, watermelon and pineapple (alternatively, the mixed fruit cocktail is a blessing for the indecisive). Fresh lemon mint juice is also very popular (ask for no sugar if you prefer), as is the local laban, a heavy, salty buttermilk that's best drunk on its own (but doesn't go well in tea or coffee). Arabic mint tea is available, but it's probably not drunk as widely here as it is in other parts of the Arab world; however, Arabic coffee (thick and strong) is extremely popular and will have you on a caffeine high for days.

Passage To India

Hattat House Compound, Wadi Adai Muscat
968 24 563 452
Map **2 J3**

Passage To India is one of Ruwi's finest. Located at the back of Hatat House, it's a truly special evening out. For most of the evening traditional Indian music plays quietly in the background while you eat excellent food, but every now and then, dancers in exquisite costumes come out and perform beautifully synchronised dances from all over India. More than just a meal out, the combination of the relaxing ambience, efficient service, superb food and good value makes this an exceptional experience.

Pavo Real

Madinat Al Sultan Qaboos Centre Muscat
968 24 602 603
Map **2 G3**

Muscat is perhaps the last place in the world you'd expect to find a slice of real Mexico, but that's exactly what you get when you walk through the doors of Pavo Real. Don't over indulge in the complementary taco chips and salsa because you'll need room for the fabulous food and must-have margaritas (which are also available in non-alcoholic form). Pavo Real offers you all the ingredients for a great night out – awesome ambience, friendly service, absolutely delicious food and live music.

Prince's Restaurant

Nr Zawabi Mosque Muscat **968 24 482 213**
Map **2 F3**

Despite the rather gloomy interior, Prince's Restaurant serves up a wide and appealing range of Mughlai, Tandoori, Chinese and continental dishes at an appealing price. The decor is eclectic but the interior is comfortable and the service quiet and efficient. The smells from the kitchen encourage you to concentrate on the Indian specialities, such as the tandoori from the clay oven, which is delicious and filling. For a low price you can have a banquet fit for a prince.

RBG Bar & Grill

Park Inn By Radisson Muscat Muscat
968 24 507 888
rbggrill.com
Map **2 F3**

This busy restaurant offers a tempting variety of international cuisine, local specialities and signature grill dishes as well as great light bites. The spacious and stylish venue caters for those who wish to catch a football match while enjoying a great meal, as well as couples looking for a quiet, intimate meal for two. The presentation and quality of the food is superb, and it is no wonder the open plan kitchen is located in the centre of the restaurant, showing off the chefs' culinary talents.

Safari Rooftop Grill House

Grand Hyatt Muscat Muscat **968 24 641 234**
muscat.grand.hyatt.com
Map **2 G2**

If you're a fan of relaxed, open-air dining, succulent steaks and a good atmosphere, then you will definitely enjoy this rooftop restaurant. Overlooking the Gulf of Oman, the safari themed restaurant offers both buffet and al a carte dining; for an all-inclusive price, you can select from a range of salads, soups and starters on the buffet, and then take your pick from an al la carte menu featuring a selection of succulent steaks, specialty game meats and freshly caught seafood. An added bonus is that the excellent selection of beverages such as beer, wine and spirits are included in the all-inclusive price. The steak and lobster combination is a highlight and is highly recommended. Oktoberfest (each October) at the Safari Rooftop and Grillhouse features traditional Bavarian music, German delicacies and, of course, plenty of great tasting beer.

Samba

Shangri-La's Barr Al Jissah Resort & Spa Al Waha Muscat **968 24 776 565**
shangri-la.com
Map **1 G4**

The South American theme has touched on all aspects of this restaurant, from the terracotta tiled floors, to the splashes of vibrant colour, and of course, the food. The adventurous can try the cactus and date salad on the buffet or spicy seafood from the a la carte menu. While you can expect to be seated among families at Samba, the alfresco seating option is spacious and the service is excellent. Combined with a tequila bar, this can make for a very enjoyable evening.

Samharam Cafe

Haffa House Hotel Muscat Muscat **968 24 707 207**
shanfarihotels.com
Map **2 J3**

Far enough away from Muscat's bustling CBD to be relatively peaceful, Samharam is still a convenient retreat for a lunch break from the office or a leisurely informal evening meal. The food is simple but tasty and quick to arrive. The grills, pasta, sandwiches and fruit juices all make for filling fare. After your meal indulge in a headily pungent shisha, or sniff at the one being smoked near you.

Second Cup

Al Qurum Complex Muscat **968 24 566 616**
binmirza.com
Map **2 H2**

Customers love the warm, friendly ambience and the contemporary coffee-shop setting in Second Cup. However, any fears that it is more about style than substance are quickly laid to rest when you sample the range of coffees, teas and fruit drinks, all of which are expertly prepared. To complement your drink, Second Cup offers a delectable variety of delicious desserts that are freshly made each day. It's a great place to meet friends for a sociable 'coffee and cake' date, and if you're alone, you can keep busy by reading through the latest newspapers and magazines provided.

Senor Pico

InterContinental Muscat Muscat **968 24 680 000**
ihg.com
Map **2 G2**

An expat favourite, Senor Pico is nestled in the back corner of the InterContinental Muscat and is always busy with hotel guests and Muscat's legion of Mexican food fans. At first glance it's quaint and conducive to conversation, but don't be fooled. Come 10pm and the arrival of the band, this is one of the most happening restaurants in the city. The decor is cool Aztec, the cuisine is hot Mexican – fajitas, enchiladas, and the most fantastic, must-try nachos. The hot, sweet and spicy tomato and saffron soup is an amazing way to start your meal. You will also find an excellent selection of succulent grills. The food is hearty, well presented and deserves to be complemented with the best margarita in Muscat.

Shahrazad

Shangri-La's Barr Al Jissah Resort & Spa Al Husn Muscat **968 24 776 565**
shangri-la.com
Map **1 G4**

The mix of traditional and contemporary decor exudes a sense of calm and tranquillity and you can almost imagine yourself under the stars in Marrakesh as you look up at the glittering ceiling. The Moroccan staff are only too happy to explain how the restaurant's authentic cuisine is prepared and cooked. The menu is delightful, with one of its signature dishes - Tajin Marrakesha (braised lamb shanks with Moroccan olive oil, preserved lemon, garlic, cumin and ginger) - particularly worth trying. Moroccan wines are rare, so this is the opportunity to savour a Toual Red Syrah or one of the many others on the wine list. For a sweet ending, try the halaweyat which is an assortment of Moroccan pastries made with almonds, gum arabica and rose water. As you'd expect from the Shangri-La, the setting is grand and the service is impeccable; this is definitely a restaurant for a special occasion.

Shiraz

Crowne Plaza Muscat Muscat **968 24 660 660**
ihg.com
Map **2 H2**

Shiraz offers a hearty menu of Iranian favourites. A tented ceiling and open bread preparation area add to the already-plush setting. It's definitely advisable to take along a huge appetite for the generous, and complimentary, portions of cheese, salad and Arabic bread you'll be given before your meal. Shiraz's starters and desserts are a particular treat, while the main courses, sadly, are a tad bland by comparison. During the cooler months, day and evening diners will enjoy eating on the terrace with its views of the coastline and the mountain backdrop.

Silk Route Restaurant

Al Noor Plaza, Nr SABCO Muscat **968 24 696 967**
silk-routeoman.com
Map **2 H2**

Silk Route is not inexpensive, but it is one of the better Chinese restaurants in Muscat. It draws fans from both the local and expat communities so you can expect it to get really busy in the evenings, particularly at the weekend. It's a great family restaurant too, so book in advance. Once there, the varied menu of Chinese, Cantonese and Szechwan cuisines, includes delicious dim sum and a particularly good crispy aromatic duck. There is also a Thai menu. Service is friendly and helpful and the atmosphere is warm and welcoming.

Sirj Tea Lounge

Grand Hyatt Muscat Muscat **968 24 641 234**
muscat.grand.hyatt.com
Map **2 G2**

The scones, jam and cream here are a must. If afternoon (or morning) tea isn't your style, there is a variety of light, delicious meals to choose from, as well as many different teas, coffees and fruit juices, served throughout the day. In the afternoon and early evening, gentle music comes from the piano, thanks to the musical talents of the various pianists who play the striking black grand. Sitting in the air-conditioned comfort of this impressive lounge you can still take pleasure in the picturesque scenery through the giant glass windows forming the main wall of the impressive Hyatt Hotel, Muscat.

Spicy Village

Rusayl Commercial Complex, Nr Ministry of Defense Rusayl **968 24 510 120**
manappat.com
Map **2 J3**

With three outlets in Muscat, the Spicy Village in Rusayl serves authentic Indian and Chinese cuisine. It may lack atmosphere and a licence to serve alcohol, but its no frills approach offers customers generous portions of Asian food at very reasonable prices. Unfortunately, 'no frills' extends to the decor, atmosphere and ambience, but for cheap fare, this is the place.

Sultanah

Shangri-La's Barr Al Jissah Resort & Spa Al Husn Muscat **968 24 776 565**
shangri-la.com
Map **1 G4**

Perched high above the Shangri-La's bay in Al Husn, Sultanah offers first-rate dining, fantastic views and impeccable service. Following the theme of a cruise ship visiting different ports every night, the international menu offers choices from locations such as New York, Singapore and Paris. Creative, contemporary international cuisine at its finest, the menu includes gamy choices such as rabbit, with fish and seafood. The dining room affords panoramic views of the bay from large windows, while the covered terrace and open patio overlook the resort from the edge of the cliff – a jazz trio also play here in the evenings. The stunning views get more romantic at night when the twinkling lights of the resort provide the perfect accompaniment to your meal. Sultanah has to be in the running for best restaurant in Oman.

Sumhuram

Salalah Marriott Resort Mirbat **968 23 275 500**
marriott.com
Map **1 C10**

This all-day dining restaurant keeps the quality high, in spite of the long opening hours. The food is truly international – you'll find everything from Italian classics to must-try Omani delicacies – while there are both buffet and a la carte options. Breakfast too is a relaxed and diverse affair.

Shisha

Relaxing with a juice or hot drink in a shisha cafe is an extremely popular pastime in Oman and there are several excellent places where you can enjoy the traditional delights of the hubbly bubbly.

Tapas & Sablah

Shangri-La's Barr Al Jissah Resort & Spa Al Bandar Muscat **968 24 776 565**
shangri-la.com
Map **1 G4**

Spread around the attractively lit and atmospheric 'Sablah' square outside Al Bandar Hotel, the alfresco Tapas & Sablah is the only chance to sample Spanish cuisine in Muscat. The range of dishes is pretty authentic, and for some international twists on the tapas theme, they are complemented by some Arabic mezze and Asian tapas-style dishes. There are also specials, such as paella on offer, and the house sangria is worth sampling. Portions are generous – order less than you might normally, and top them up if your appetite keeps going. For vegetarians, the selection of tapas is great, and the vegetable paella is one of the best you'll find anywhere.

The Beach Restaurant

The Chedi Muscat Muscat **968 24 524 343**
chedimuscat.com
Map **2 E3**

The path to this glamorous beachside spot follows a candlelit walkway through the grounds of The Chedi. You can choose from outdoor dining or a table beneath the high ceilings, Colonial-style fans, modern wooden screens and rich burgundy silks of the restaurant. The well-chosen wine list allows you to order by the bottle or glass (try the delicious gavi di gavi white) and the menu is exclusively seafood, boasting chilled and cooked dishes with an undeniably Asian feel; think mussels in a spicy coconut broth and yellowfin tuna with a chilli and garlic risotto. The exotic flavours continue through to dessert with chocolate and coconut cheesecake served with Malibu sorbet. At the more expensive end of the scale, you're bound to leave this stunning spot feeling sated, de-stressed and spoilt.

The Chedi Pool Cabana
The Chedi Muscat Muscat **968 24 524 343**
chedimuscat.com
Map **2 E3**

This is one of those places you're unlikely to find unless someone has told you to look for it – but that's what makes it special. And it's worth noting the tip. The Cabana at the glamorous Chedi hotel is a tranquil and intimate place to enjoy a cool evening breeze and a choice of set menus, making it a perfect choice of venue during the cool winter months. Plus, the small number of tables ensures that each customer receives efficient service, and you'll feel truly looked after. The flavour is Mediterranean with an emphasis on seafood, served with finesse. An evening isn't complete without one of its wickedly decadent puddings. It's not a cheap night out, but it's definitely worth splashing your cash. Save this one for a special date or a memorable occasion.

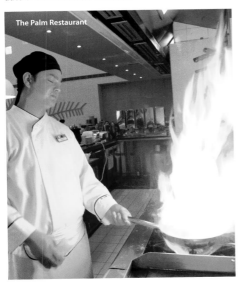
The Palm Restaurant

The Golden Oryx
Al Burj St, CBD Area Muscat **968 24 706 128**
thegoldenoryx.com
Map **2 J3**

The Golden Oryx is a bit of a drive, so the restaurant's popularity is a credit to the chefs. The decor is sumptuous and the service is impeccable, right down to the free water throughout your meal. The menu is Chinese, Thai and Mongolian, and the Chinese crispy duck in plum or barbecue sauce is a particular favourite. Make sure someone in your party orders the Thai chicken satay starters (and that you get a bite) – they're delicious, with loads of crunchy, decadently rich sauce. Not to be missed.

The Indus
Opera Galleria Muscat **968 22 022 888**
Map **2 G2**

Located at the Opera Galleria, this fine dining Indian restaurant boasts a variety of succulent meat and vegan kebabs made using traditional ingredients. The decor is a mixture of the modern and the traditional with Indian wall hangings and artefacts to add to the atmosphere. Their delicious curries include shrimps sauteed in spring onions, and Tandoori chicken.

The Lobby Lounge
The Chedi Muscat Muscat **968 24 524 343**
chedimuscat.com
Map **2 E3**

Another string to the bow of the tranquil haven that is The Chedi is the Lobby Lounge. Situated just beyond the majlis area at the entrance, the cafe is an intimate arrangement of comfy seating areas in a brightly sunlit room. What is a relatively laidback venue in the afternoon is transformed at night, when it makes the perfect spot for sundowners or after-dinner drinks. Guests spill outside to bag one of the sought-after tables around the giant gas fires in heavy black planters. You'll need to hover about to claim one – people don't give them up easily.

The Palm Restaurant
Park Inn By Radisson Muscat Muscat
968 24 507 888
parkinn.com
Map **2 F3**

A bright, friendly all-day buffet restaurant, breakfasts offer everything from fruit and Danish to a halal fry up or waffles. The daily (except for Thursdays) lunch buffet is served from noon to 3pm, with all manner of hot dishes, salads and soups up for grabs, while for dinner the buffet is complemented by an a la carte menu that offers a wide variety of dishes to satisfy even the most international of palates. If a quiet, unrushed meal is what you are after, this place will do.

The Restaurant

The Chedi Muscat Muscat 968 24 524 343
chedimuscat.com
Map 2 E3

The Restaurant boasts a fusion of contemporary Arabic and Far Eastern decor, aptly reflecting its menu. You can choose from sushi, tajin, fish or curries from one of the open kitchens, but leave room for the puddings, cakes and macaroons. You'll appreciate the warning as these are the best you'll ever taste in Muscat. Prices are high, especially for alcohol, but the wine list is extensive. After an excellent meal you can stroll around the tranquil garden or along the beach and enjoy your after-dinner coffee alfresco.

Tokyo Taro

Al Falaj Hotel Muscat 968 24 702 311
omanhotels.com
Map 2 J2

This place is vibrant with the smells and sounds of authentic Japanese food being prepared. Meat, vegetables and seafood sizzle at the teppanyaki bar and the green tea is on tap. If you're in a group you can book one of the private dining rooms and sit at a traditional banquet table to enjoy your meal. The setting is serene and convincing enough for you to imagine that you actually are in the land of the rising sun. Dining here affords you a tantalising – and delicious – glimpse of Japan.

Tomato

InterContinental Muscat Muscat 968 24 680 000
ihg.com
Map 2 G2

Deep in the beautiful gardens of the InterContinental Muscat, getting there requires a picturesque walk along the palm-tree-lined pathways near the swimming pool. All tables are located on a deck and there is no indoor option, making this a venue to be enjoyed when the weather is not too sticky. The food is the perfect combination of simple, wholesome classics and innovative flavours, and the funky cutlery and dazzling range of crockery wouldn't be out of place in any cutting-edge European eatery. Breakfasts are pleasant, and you can choose from three options – healthy, American or continental – while you enjoy another beautiful Muscat morning under the shade of a huge cream canopy. However, with ambient lighting and some delectable Mediterranean fare, dinners are also good.

Trader Vic's

InterContinental Muscat Muscat 968 24 680 080
tradervics.com
Map 2 G2

A popular venue, Trader Vic's is a dream for the indecisive diner. You'll find Caribbean cocktails, a Cuban band, an international menu and dishes prepared in a gigantic Chinese clay oven, all under one roof. It might sound like a bit of a mish mash but it's actually great and you would probably want to head here for the cocktail list alone. The tasty dishes and creative mixed drinks make it the perfect venue for after work drinks that end up turning out slightly more lively. The service is excellent and, if nothing else, this is one of the only places that does a really good Irish coffee. Dining here isn't cheap, but for a good night out, it's worth it.

Tropicana

Crowne Plaza Muscat Muscat 968 24 660 660
ihg.com
Map 2 H2

Located at the poolside of the Crowne Plaza hotel in Qurum, Tropicana has an international menu ranging from Oriental (with unlimited sushi and dim sum), Indian and Mediterranean classics to the good old American burger, and theme nights on Wednesdays and Thursdays. Lunchtimes see a loaded buffet and this tastefully decorated restaurant is well frequented in the afternoon hours. Appetising dishes arrive in generous proportions, accompanied by excellent service and a reasonable price tag. The poolside location offers a pleasant view, and outside seating is available.

Tuscany

Grand Hyatt Muscat Muscat 968 24 641 234
hyatt.com
Map 2 G2

Dining alfresco adds to the experience at this charming Italian restaurant; as you look out on the lush green gardens of the Grand Hyatt, you'll feel utterly spoiled. Service is very efficient, with waiters providing lots of good tips on the various dishes. The menu offers interesting choices of fresh and wholesome Italian food; all of the seafood is locally sourced and is complemented by wonderful presentation. The wine list is extensive and sourced from some of the best wine regions of Italy. Dine in true Italian style by bringing a big group of friends and taking your time over your delicious meal.

Woodlands

Nr Europcar Bldg, CBD Muscat 968 24 700 192
Map 2 J3

This is one restaurant that hits all the right spots: service with a genuine smile, fabulously large portions of delicious south Indian cuisine, and an easy on your wallet bill to top it all off. If you're having difficulty in deciding what to order, allow one of the friendly waiters to talk you through the menu, but if you're not a fire-eater beware those brutal south Indian chilies and spices. This is a good place for an easy night out that's sure to impress your friends.

BARS, PUBS & CLUBS

Chambers

Majan Continental Hotel Muscat **968 24 592 900**
majanhotel.com
Map **2 E4**

Chambers maybe small in size but it's big in stature. With a pool table, large screen TV and a few gaming machines, it draws a regular crowd of local and Eastern European men. You won't find any draft beer here, but the rest of the beverage selection is very reasonably priced.

Club Bar

Ruwi Hotel Muscat **968 24 704 244**
omanhotels.com
Map **2 J3**

Situated in the heart of the Ruwi business district, this is a small, no-frills hotel bar designed to serve the many businessmen in the area. It's friendly, low-lit and decked out in standard British pub paraphernalia. The service is quiet and efficient and while the menu is fairly standard, the food is good.

Copacabana

Grand Hyatt Muscat Muscat **968 24 641 234**
muscat.grand.hyatt.com
Map **2 G2**

On the ground floor of the Grand Hyatt hotel, this nightclub comes to life after midnight when people start to filter out of the pubs and restaurants. It is a spacious venue with a good dance floor but if you would like some privacy, you can hire the VIP room. On Monday and Wednesday nights, you can dance the night away to Arabic music. Light meals are available and there's an excellent beverages menu with champagne priced from RO.86 to RO.268. It's closed Saturdays and Sundays but is open Monday to Thursday from 10pm to 3am and from 10pm to 2am on Fridays.

Duke's Bar

Crowne Plaza Muscat Muscat **968 24 660 660**
ihg.com
Map **2 H2**

Given enough dark wood panelling, brass fittings and cosy leather seats, you can knock up an English theme pub almost anywhere. But only Duke's has the evocative rocky seascape view, framed by a giant picture window. The regulars here are a diverse bunch: locals and expats of many nationalities, kept busy with quiz nights, ladies' nights and various theme nights. The food is typical pub grub and can be enjoyed on the terrace outside if you can secure a sought-after table.

John Barry Bar

Grand Hyatt Muscat Muscat **968 24 641 234**
muscat.grand.hyatt.com
Map **2 G2**

Chefs from India, Italy and Oman work together at the John Barry Bar to create mouthwatering dishes offering guests plenty of choice from around the world. Servers buzz around dressed in naval attire and there is plenty of memorabilia on the walls from the original SS John Barry ship which was torpedoed off the coast of the Sultanate of Oman in 1944 by a German U Boat. The fish and chips, a simple but extremely satisfying dish, is cooked to perfection. No visit here would be complete without checking out the tantalizing cocktail and mocktail menu which fizzes with fresh concoctions to satisfy thirsty guests.

Left Bank

Nr Mumtaz Mahal Muscat **968 24 695 953**
emiratesleisureretail.com
Map **2 H2**

Perched above Qurum Natural Park is one of the hottest bar-restaurants in Muscat, with the slickest interior in town. Left Bank has a fantastic reputation for serving up high-quality fare and imaginative cocktails – and the applause is well deserved. The burgers, fish dishes and pastas are particularly recommended, as are the desserts which alone are worth the trip. While it's not a huge menu, each dish earns its place and everyone from gourmands to steak and veg fans are kept happy. The drinks list deserves special mention too. It gets busy at weekends so reservations are essential if you want one of those coveted booths.

O'Malleys

Radisson Blu Hotel Muscat **968 24 487 777**
radissonblu.com
Map **2 F3**

With its dark wooden bar furniture specially made in Ireland and authentic photographs and memorabilia, this is the place to go for a taste of the Emerald Isle. Sit at the bar and savour the lively atmosphere or enjoy a quieter moment by the fireplace in the lounge area. There is a nice selection of light meals with the Leenane leek & potato soup (served with delicious Irish soda bread) and the Irish stew being particularly tasty. There is an assortment of draft beers available including old country favourites Guinness and Kilkenny. As with most Irish bars, the atmosphere is friendly and relaxed and the courteous staff are very professional. And, of course, it's where all the festivities abound for St. Partrick's Day in March.

Piano Lounge

Shangri-La's Barr Al Jissah Resort & Spa Al Bandar
Muscat **968 24 776 565**
shangri-la.com
Map **1 G4**

Soft lighting, carpets, couches and cushions, the piano lounge makes an elegant addition to an evening out at the Shangri-La Barr Al Jissah Resort. The drinks menu has reasonably priced wine by the glass, beer and spirits, but this is definitely the place to treat yourself to a bottle of Moet or an aged malt whisky on the rocks.

Pub Al Ghazal

InterContinental Muscat Muscat **968 24 680 000**
ihg.com
Map **2 G2**

Set within the five-star InterContinental Muscat, this pub offers a traditional pub experience that's second to none. With a friendly atmosphere, a huge selection of beverages, delicious pub grub and regular quiz nights, what more could you want? Tables are screened so diners can enjoy a meal of steak or fish and chips, or just a light sandwich, in privacy. Good food, drinks, service and reasonable prices ensure this pub is nearly always crowded with regulars.

Safari Pub

Grand Hyatt Muscat Muscat **968 24 641 234**
muscat.grand.hyatt.com
Map **2 G2**

Set in a three-storey entertainment complex, the Safari Pub is located on the middle level of the venue. Standard pub grub is available (think chicken wings, potato skins, and steak & pepper pie) and is reasonably priced. There is a 40% discount on beverages and ladies can enjoy free margaritas every day from 6pm to 10pm.

Sama Terrazza

Park Inn By Radisson Muscat Muscat **968 24 507 888**
parkinn.com
Map **2 F3**

With panoramic views of the city, this stylish outdoor rooftop bar is the ideal venue to relax and unwind. Open during the cooler months (October to April) from 6pm to 1am, its laid back vibe is the perfect antidote to a long day in the city. While the food menu is limited to a small selection of tapas (the selection changed on a weekly basis), what is served is delicious and great value. A wide range of wines, beers and sophisticated cocktails is available. On Thursday and Friday nights, a DJ expertly mixes the music and provides a chill out atmosphere. This is the perfect place to kick off or end a night. During weekends, there's an entry fee of RO.5 for men inclusive of one beverage, while ladies get free entry.

The Deck

Millennium Resort Mussanah Mussanah
968 26 871 555
millenniumhotels.com
Map **1 G3**

This modern and relaxed lounge bar overlooks the 54 berth private marina. Guests have the option of sitting inside or outside but during the cooler months, the balcony is the place to be. There is a good selection of beers, spirits and cocktails and the menu features light meals and snacks including oysters, escargot and risotto balls. Guests also have the option of ordering from the more extensive menu from the Mydan restaurant in the resort.

The Lazy Lizard

Radisson Blu Hotel Muscat **968 24 487 777**
radissonblu.com
Map **2 F3**

After a long tiring day, this poolside venue is the perfect spot to chill out. Sit at the bar and choose from its wide selection of beers or relax at a candle-lit table under the palm trees and enjoy a cocktail. Light snacks are available with the Lebanese mixed grill a delicious option. Burgers, spring rolls and samosas are also popular and there is a good kids menu.

The Long Bar

Shangri-La's Barr Al Jissah Resort & Spa Al Bandar
Muscat **968 24 776 565**
shangri-la.com
Map **1 G4**

Long Bar has one of the best spots in Oman to enjoy a happy hour. Although it is a little out of the way, it is worth the drive to enjoy a beachfront sunset from the terrace as you work your way through the martini menu and tropical cocktails.

The Long Pool Cabana

The Chedi Muscat Muscat **968 24 524 343**
chedimuscat.com
Map **2 E3**

After a hard day's sun worshipping or sightseeing, this is the perfect place to unwind. Enjoy the view of the 103m long pool, the longest in the Middle East, while listening to chill out contemporary music. The menu consists of reasonably priced light meals of authentic Japanese and Malaysian cuisine.

The Pub

Al Falaj Hotel Muscat **968 24 702 311**
omanhotels.com
Map **2 J2**

The Pub is situated on the eighth floor of Muscat's second oldest hotel, which means spectacular views over Ruwi area, especially at night. The bar is quiet, frequented mainly by the hotel's guests.

John Barry Bar

Left Bank

Copacabana

INDEX

INDEX

NOTES

Explorer Products

Residents' Guides

Visitors' Guides

Photography Books & Calendars

Maps

Adventure & Lifestyle Guides

Apps & eBooks

+ Also available as applications. Visit askexplorer.com/apps.

* Now available in eBook format.

Visit askexplorer.com/shop.

Useful Numbers

Embassies & Consulates

Australian Embassy	
(Saudi Arabia)	00966 11250 0900
Bahrain Embassy	24 605 074
British Embassy	24 609 000
Canadian Consulate (Saudi Arabia)	0966 11488 2288
Chinese Embassy	24 696 698
Czech Embassy	
(Saudi Arabia)	00966 1450 3617
Danish Consulate	24 526 233
Egyptian Embassy	24 600 411
French Embassy	24 681 800
German Embassy	24 835 000
Indian Embassy	24 684 500
Iranian Embassy	24 696 944
Irish Consulate	24 701 282
Italian Embassy	24 695 131
Japanese Embassy	24 601 028
Jordanian Embassy	24 692 760
Kuwaiti Embassy	24 699 626
Lebanese Embassy	24 695 844
Malaysian Embassy	24 698 329
Netherlands Embassy	24 603 706
New Zealand Consulate	24 694 692
Norwegian Consulate	24 526 233
Pakistani Embassy	24 603 439
Philippine Embassy	24 605 140
Qatar Embassy	24 691 152/53/54
Russian Embassy	24 602 894
Saudi Arabian Embassy	24 698 780
Spanish Embassy	24 691 101
South African Embassy	24 647 300
Sri Lankan Embassy	24 697 841
Swedish Consulate	24 603 706
Swiss Consulate	24 568 202
Thai Embassy	24 602 684
UAE Embassy	24 600 302
US Embassy	24 698 989

Useful Numbers

Friendi Mobile	98 400 000
Nawras Customer Service:	
From Nawras mobile	1500
From any phone	9501 1500
Renna:	
From Renna mobile	1240
From any phone	9830 1240
Omantel Business Call Center	1235
Omantel Directory Enquiries	1318
Omantel Fixed & Internet Call Centre	1300
Omantel International Operator	
Connected Calls	1305
Omantel Marine & Coastal	
Radio Services	1302
Omantel Mobile Call Centre	1234
Omantel Payphone Faults & Complaints	1307
Omantel Telex Faults & Complaints	1301

Country & City Codes

Oman Country Code	968
Al Musanaah Area Code	26
Barka Area Code	26
Dabah Area Code	26
Jabal Al Akhdar Area Code	25
Jebel Sifah Area Code	24
Khasab Area Code	26
Mirbat Area Code	23
Muscat Area Code	24
Nizwa Area Code	25
Salalah Area Code	23
Sur Area Code	25

Emergency & Other Services

AAA Oman	24 797 700/24 605 555
CID Services	24 569 501
Electricity Emergency	24 698 818
Emergency: Police / Fire / Ambulance	9999/999

		Scientific Pharmacy	24 702 850
Municipality Emergency	800 772 222	Sultan Qaboos University	
Muscat Municipality	1111	Hospital	24 141 111

Oman National Transport	
Company (ONTC)	24 490 046

Airlines

Oman Power & Water		Air Arabia	24 700 828

Municipality Emergency	800 772 222
Muscat Municipality	1111
Oman National Transport	
Company (ONTC)	24 490 046
Oman Power & Water	
Procurement Company	24 508 400
Royal Oman Police	24 569 392
Traffic Services	24 510 227/228
Visa Services	24 512 961
Water Emergency	1442

Hospitals

Al Raffah Hospital (Sohar)	26 704 639
Badr Al Samaa Hospital (Ruwi)	24 799 760
Khoula Hospital	24 563 579
Kims Oman Hospital	24 760 100
Lifeline Hospital (Sohar)	26 651 111
Muscat Private Hospital	24 583 600
The Royal Hospital	24 599 000
Starcare Hospital	24 557 200

Health Centres & Clinics

Al Azaiba Health Centre	24 497 233
Al Ghubrah Health Centre	24 497 226
American Dental Center	24 695 422
Emirates Medical Center	24 604 540
Medident Madinat Qaboos	
Medical Centre	24 601 668
Muscat Dental Specialists	24 600 664
Muttrah Health Center	24 713 296
Precision Dental Clinic	24 696 247
Qurum Medical Centre	24 692 898
Ruwi Health Center	24 786 088
Wassan Specialty Dental Clinic	24 489 469

Pharmacies

Abu Al Dahab Clinic & Pharmacy	23 291 303
Hatat Polyclinic	24 563 641
Medident Madinat Qaboos	
Medical Centre	24 601 668
Muscat Pharmacy & Stores	24 814 501

Airlines

Air Arabia	24 700 828
Air Blue	24 704 318
Air France	24 784 545
Air India (Muscat)	24 818 666
Biman Bangladesh Airlines	24 701 128/24 702 060
British Airways	24 568 777
Egypt Air	24 794 113
Emirates	24 404 444
Etihad Airways	800 76423
fly Dubai (Muscat)	24 765 091 92
Gulf Air	24 482 777
Iran Air	24 787 423
Jet Airways	24 787 248/6
Kenya Airways	24 660 305
KLM Royal Dutch Airlines (Muscat)	24 701 166
Kuwait Airways	24 798 861/707 119/765 080/81
Lufthansa	24 796 692/780 230
Oman Air	24 531 111
Pakistan International Airlines	24 792 471
Qatar Airways	24 162 700
Royal Brunei Airlines	24 603 533
Royal Jordanian	24 796 693
Saudi Arabian Airlines	24 789 485
Singapore Airlines	24 791 233
Sri Lankan Airlines	24 784 545
Swiss Air	24 796 692
Thai Airways	24 705 934
Turkish Airlines	24 765 071/72
United Airways	24 660 310/11

Airport Information

Muscat International Airport:	
Flight Information	24 519 223/519 456
Baggage Services (Oman Air)	24 521 284
Passport & Residency Section	24 518 746
Salalah Airport:	
Flight Information	24 518 072

Oman Guide – 2nd Edition
Lead Editor Stacey Siebritz
Editor Mary Lynch
Proofread by Lidiya Baltova-Kalichuk
Data managed by Mimi Stankova
Designed by Ieyad Charaf, Jayde Fernandes
Maps by Zain Madathil
Photographs by Hardy Mendrofa, Henry Hilos, Pamela Grist, Pete Maloney, Victor Romero

Publishing
Chief Content Officer & Founder Alistair MacKenzie

Editorial
Managing Editor Carli Allan
Editors Lily Lawes, Kirsty Tuxford
Deputy Editor Stacey Siebritz
Research Manager Mimi Stankova
Researchers Amrit Raj, Roja P, Praseena, Shalu Sukumar, Maria Luisa Reyes, Lara Santizo, Jayleen Aguinaldo, Rabia Farooq, Jacqueline Reyes, Yuliya Molchanova
Production Controller / Account & Client Liaison Kinsi Grimen

Design & Photography
Art Director Ieyad Charaf
Layout Manager Jayde Fernandes
Junior Designer M. Shakkeer
Cartography Manager Zain Madathil
Cartographers Noushad Madathil, Dhanya Nellikkunnummal, Ramla Kambravan, Jithesh Kalathingal
GIS Analyst Aslam
Photographer & Image Editor Hardy Mendrofa

Sales & Marketing
Director of Sales Peter Saxby
Media Sales Area Managers Laura Zuffova, Sabrina Ahmed, Bryan Anes, Louise Burton, Simon Reddy
Digital Sales Manager Rola Touffaha
Business Development Manager Pouneh Hafizi
Corporate Sales Manager Zendi De Coning
Director of Retail Ivan Rodrigues
Retail Sales Coordinator Michelle Mascarenhas
Retail Sales Area Supervisors Ahmed Mainodin, Firos Khan
Retail Sales Merchandisers Johny Mathew, Shan Kumar, Mehmood Ullah
Retail Sales Drivers Shabsir Madathil, Nimicias Arachchige
Warehouse Assistant Mohamed Haji, Jithinraj M

Finance, HR & Administration
Accountant Cherry Enriquez
Accounts Assistants Sunil Suvarna, Jeanette Enecillo
Administrative Assistant Joy H. San Buenaventura
Reception Jayfee Manseguiao
Public Relations Officer Rafi Jamal
Office Assistant Shafeer Ahamed
Office Manager – India Jithesh Kalathingal

IT & Digital Solutions
Web Developer Mirza Ali Nasrullah, Waqas Razzaq
HTML/UI Developer Naveed Ahmed
IT Manager R. Ajay
Database Programmer Pradeep T.P.

Contact Us

General Enquiries
We'd love to hear your thoughts and answer any questions you have about this book or any other Explorer product. Contact us at **info@askexplorer.com**

Careers
If you fancy yourself as an Explorer, send your CV (stating the position you're interested in) to **jobs@askexplorer.com**

Contract Publishing
For enquiries about Explorer's Contract Publishing arm and design services contact **contracts@askexplorer.com**

Retail Sales
Our products are available in most good bookshops as well as online at askexplorer.com/shop. **retail@askexplorer.com**

PR & Marketing
For PR and marketing enquiries contact **marketing@askexplorer.com**

Corporate Sales & Licensing
For bulk sales and customisation options, as well as licensing of this book or any Explorer product, contact **leads@askexplorer.com**

Advertising & Sponsorship
For advertising and sponsorship, contact **sales@askexplorer.com**

Explorer Publishing & Distribution
PO Box 34275, Dubai, United Arab Emirates
askexplorer.com

Phone: +971 (0)4 340 8805
Fax: +971 (0)4 340 8806